THE INTERIOR BORDERLANDS

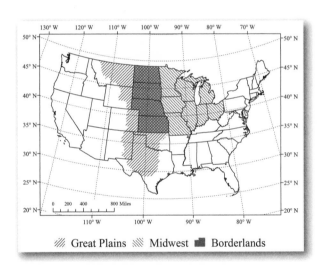

THE INTERIOR BORDERLANDS

REGIONAL IDENTITY IN THE MIDWEST AND GREAT PLAINS

Edited by Jon K. Lauck

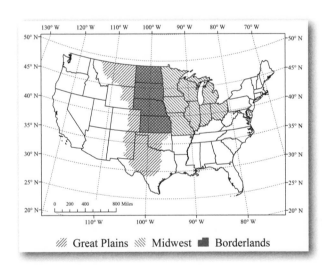

Great Plains   Midwest   Borderlands

THE CENTER FOR WESTERN STUDIES

Augustana University

2019

Publication made possible with funding from the Anne King Publications Endowment and Ronald R. Nelson Publications Endowment in the Center for Western Studies and from the National Endowment for the Humanities.

ISBN: 978-0-931170-12-6

Library of Congress Control Number: 2017930368

Number 2 in the Center for Western Studies Public Affairs Series

The Center for Western Studies (CWS) at Augustana University seeks to improve the quality of social and cultural life in the Northern Plains, achieve a better understanding of the region, its heritage, and its resources, and stimulate interest in the solution to regional problems. The Center promotes understanding of the region through its archives, library, museum and art exhibitions, publications, courses, internships, and public affairs programming. It is committed, ultimately, to defining the contribution of the Northern Plains to American civilization.

In 2019 and 2020, the Center celebrates 55 years since its founding in 1964 by writer and English professor Herbert Krause and 50 years since its establishment in 1970 by the Augustana University board of trustees.

Visit the Fantle Building for The Center for Western Studies
Augustana University, 2121 S. Summit Avenue, Sioux Falls, South Dakota
605-274-4007 • cws@augie.edu • www.augie.edu/cws • Facebook • Twitter

Half-title and title-page graphic courtesy of Christopher R. Laingen

Cover photo ©PaulHorsted.com farmland and Dogtooth Buttes west of Flasher, North Dakota

Printed in the United States of America by Anundsen Publishing Company

To

Brendtly Michael Lauck,
Son of the Interior Borderlands

Contents

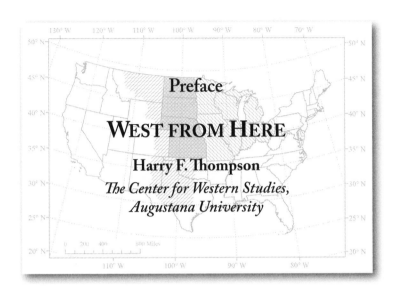

Preface

WEST FROM HERE

Harry F. Thompson

The Center for Western Studies,
Augustana University

T here is no generally accepted definition of the Midwest, or of the Great Plains, for that matter. Those who live in one or the other think they know where they are, but even they cannot agree on which states should be included. Is Ohio in the Midwest? Kentucky? Is Kansas in the Midwest or the Great Plains? The Dakotas—Midwest or Great Plains? Why should we be constrained by state borders, anyway? Perhaps the remedy is to deny the existence of the Midwest and Great Plains and agree that the United States is usefully understood regionally as East and West, with the Mississippi River running down the middle as the dividing line. Too simple? Such a solution would avoid academic debate—and then where would we be? There would be little reason for this book! Further, neither the South nor New England would permit such simplification.

I don't understand the term "Midwest." Does it mean "middle of the west" or "midway toward the west" or "in the middle of the west"? How about "mid-Atlantic"? It certainly doesn't mean "in the middle of the Atlantic." Well, not yet—but someday. In this preface, I will focus on the Great Plains, where I have lived most of my life. We all know that the Great Plains is in the West, if it is anywhere. Is it a region apart? I don't think so. I like to call it the "Great Plains/West." The Great Plains/West is not so much a place as a direction, maybe even an attitude. It is also a journey, perhaps a journey without end. It is a journey of hope, renewal, and second chances, one undertaken by the millions who ventured from other regions of the United States and from foreign lands, one that thousands continue to take to this day.

The impetus for this book on distinguishing between the Midwest and the Great Plains began in 2015 with a conference on the theme of "Where the West Begins?" (yes, with a question mark). The conference was itself an outgrowth of a college course I designed called "Finding the Great Plains," in which students search for recognizable characteristics of the region and consider some of the challenges facing the northern areas of the plains. We read and discuss such books as *The Horizontal World*, written by North Dakota native Debra Marquart, and *Great Plains*, written by an outsider, Ian Frazier, each seeking to understand the plains of the present by considering the plains of the past. We also read *Hollowing Out the Middle*, by Patrick J. Carr and Maria J. Kefalas, a study of small-town Iowa youth and what the future holds for the rural plains. In some ways, this 2001 study foretold of the despair experienced by rural residents of the Midwest and Great Plains, a sense of hopelessness that led them to support a presidential candidate whose rhetoric promised a return to what they thought were better days. Both the conference and the course titles intentionally invited discussion and debate. For the conference, which featured about sixty papers on some aspect of regional identity, Jon K. Lauck, the editor of this volume, assembled a panel on the topic "Where Does the Midwest End and the Great Plains Begin?" with presenters Lori Ann Lahlum, John E. Miller, Julie Courtwright, Joe Otto, and Jason Lee Brown.[1]

So where does the Midwest end and the Great Plains begin? In the classic novel of the immigrant experience in the plains, *Giants in the Earth* (1927), author O. E. Rölvaag, himself a traveler west, wrote about Per and Beret Hansa's coming by ox and wagon to Dakota Territory from Minnesota in the 1870s. They crossed the Rock River, Beaver Creek, and Split Rock Creek before arriving at Slip-Up Creek, named for the harrowing experience of attempting to get a wagon up the slippery creek bank. Geographically, they were about fifteen miles west of the Minnesota border. To these early settlers, they had come out onto the Great Plains and into the West. This was now their *vesterheim*, or "home in the west." Along the way, Per Hansa refers to his destination as "out there," "that country," and "Sunset Land." He sees himself and his young family as having "pushed on westward," journeying across "the prairie far and near," but "always westward." During Per's first night in the West, he feels the plain swell and rise, and, just before the morning light, he stands face-to-face with its darkness and expanse: "The vastness of the plain seemed to rise up on every hand— and suddenly the landscape had grown desolate; something bleak and cold had come into the silence, filling it with terror" (9). This is the Great Plains, not the Midwest.

Rölvaag, who journeyed from an island in Norway five miles below the Arctic Circle to Dakota Territory in 1896 to work as a farmhand with his uncle near Elk Point, ultimately abandoned farming and enrolled at Augustana Academy, graduating in 1901. Located twenty-three miles south of Sioux Falls, in Canton, the academy was a predecessor institution to Augustana University, the publisher of this book through its Center for Western Studies.[2] While a student, Rölvaag came to know one of the families that had settled along Slip-Up Creek, the Berdahls. He later married Jennie Berdahl, the daughter of Andrew and Karen Berdahl, in whose farmhouse he heard tales of the Norwegian settlement experience. These stories focused on the challenges and joys of the Norwegian (and Irish) settlers who arrived at Slip-Up Creek, between Renner and Garretson, now in South Dakota, in eleven covered wagons in 1873. Both the farmhouse, where he heard the tales, and the northwoods cabin, in which he wrote portions of *Giants in the Earth* in 1923, are located on the campus of Augustana University in Heritage Park, supported by the Nordland Heritage Foundation.[3]

A few words about the origins and mission of one of America's earliest western studies centers, located where the Midwest and Great Plains/ West meet, might assist in further distinguishing between the regions. The Center for Western Studies at Augustana University was founded in 1964 by Professor of English and Writer-in-Residence Herbert Krause, a novelist, essayist, and poet, originally from western Minnesota, who taught the Shakespeare seminar, along with courses in creative writing and regional literature. The president of Augustana had recruited Krause in 1939 from the writing program at the University of Iowa, where he was completing his doctorate, to establish a writing school where students would learn to appreciate and write about their own cultural heritage. In its early years, the "school," twenty-four years later a "center," focused on collecting books and documents about the region surrounding the university for the purpose of further research and publishing. In 1970 the university's board of trustees officially recognized the Center for Western Studies by expanding and integrating it into the university. This was a largely aspirational act because neither a funding mechanism nor a direct link to the academic program was established. It stumbled financially in its first years but today provides programs and funding for the university. Krause understood the region as a point of convergence of many ethnic identities, including Native American, French, Spanish, Yankee, Scandinavian, and German. He found that his desire to understand the region was shared by a group of Augustana faculty and community members. Among the center's purposes and goals, as stated in its constitution, first written in 1971, is to seek to improve the quality of social and cultural life in the region; achieve a better understanding of the region, its heritage, and its resources; and stimulate interest in the solution to regional problems. Today, the center's programs emphasize research and publishing, public affairs, and cultural diversity awareness—all funded by its own $10 million endowment.

The author of three novels set in Minnesota (covering the period from 1850 to 1920) and several essays on Western themes, Krause gave much thought to regional identity. In his own development as a writer, especially in his essays, he moved west to the Black Hills of South Dakota. In the essay "The Ornithology of the Great Plains" (he was an ornithologist of considerable accomplishment), Krause defined the region he sometimes called the Prairie Plains this way:

> Geographically, the Great Plains lie in a mighty belt extending from Texas to the Canadian border in the United States and beyond the Saskatchewan River in Canada. On their eastern side they include western sections of Oklahoma, Kansas, most of Nebraska, about half of South Dakota and a corner of North Dakota. On their western border they include eastern portions of New Mexico, Colorado, Wyoming and Montana. This is the area properly called the Great Plains. East of the Plains lie the Great Prairies which encompass eastern areas of Kansas, Nebraska and South Dakota, and nearly all of North Dakota.[4]

In his poems, Krause evokes the immigrant experience in the West, though always acknowledging Native Americans as the first inhabitants. In "Giant in the Wooded Earth," commissioned for the Minnesota Centennial of Statehood, in 1958, Krause reviews the historical highlights and contributions of Minnesota. At the poem's unveiling, actor Walter Abel spoke the lines accompanied by music by Aaron Copland, arranged and performed by the Minnesota Symphony Orchestra. In "The Builder and the Stone," a poem written on the occasion of a retiring Augustana president, Krause writes of Augustana moving "Westward to the going sun." In "The New Cathay," written as a salute to a new Augustana president, he re-envisions the immigrant quest as a search for knowledge: "We set our wagon trains and gunless sights / To find, not the lands beyond the wide Missouri . . . But . . . the country of the human mind."

In drawing up the center's constitution, Krause and friends intentionally referred not to the Midwest but to the Prairie Plains, the Great Plains, and the Trans-Mississippi West, specifically the states of North Dakota, Minnesota, Iowa, Nebraska, Wyoming, and Montana, with South Dakota at the center—Dakota Territory as organized in 1861.[5] Since the 1990s, the center has employed "Prairie Plains" as the designation of a series in the center's book publications program. As with the term "Midwest," it carries the advantage of useful ambiguity. Further emphasizing the region as part of the West, two of Krause's colleagues in the English Department who had been involved in the formation of the center, William Geyer and Arthur R. Huseboe, edited in 1978 a collection of essays in honor of Krause entitled *Where the West Begins* (without a question mark). The book was based on papers delivered at the previous year's annual meeting of the Western Literature Association, which had been hosted by Augustana.[6]

As the New Western History movement got underway in the 1980s, Notre Dame historian Walter Nugent conducted a survey among historians, journalists, and creative writers to answer the question, "Where is the American West?" In reporting the survey results, which I shared at the 2015 conference, he acknowledged, first, the centrality of the place-versus-process debate in Western studies: in other words, Frederick Jackson Turner and the traditionalists understand the West as process, whereas Patricia Nelson Limerick and the New West Historians see the West as a geographical place.[7] Nugent found that the majority of respondents believed that the West begins at the eastern borders of North Dakota, South Dakota, Nebraska, Missouri, Oklahoma, and Texas (approximating the Red-Missouri-Sabine Rivers, or the 98th meridian). Other respondents were split between those who thought the West begins either farther east, at the Mississippi River, or farther west, at the 100th meridian, near the Missouri River. Nugent thought historian Robert Utley's response germane because it allows for two Wests: "The chronological West is everything west of the north-south frontier line at any point in history. . . . My geographical West . . . is everything west of the eastern boundaries of the Dakotas, Nebraska, Kansas, and Oklahoma, with a line through Texas roughly represented by the Balcones Escarpment. This West extends all the way to the Pacific shore, with no exclusions" (23). For most of us, of course, the West is both process and place, but Nugent's survey results point to a majority opinion placing the Midwest-West border along the 98th meridian. By way of contrast, the recently formed Midwestern History Association includes the

Dakotas, Nebraska, and Kansas in the Midwest, along with Ohio, Indiana, Illinois, Michigan, Wisconsin, Iowa, Minnesota, and Missouri, though it allows for some sections of the Dakotas as not being "Midwestern." I think the inhabitants of the Dakotas, Nebraska, and Kansas would be shocked to learn they are *not* located in the Great Plains. Those of us who hold to the 98th meridian as the start of the Great Plains/West find of particular interest a recent article that argues that one of the effects of climate change is that the 100th meridian is approaching the 98th. In other words, the lack of rainfall in the eastern part of the Dakotas for the past several years approximates that of the western regions of the Dakotas, beginning near the Missouri River. In 2017, drought conditions were experienced throughout the Dakotas and Nebraska, persisting into the winter.[8]

A defining characteristic of America has been, and will continue to be, its waterways, in particular its rivers, writes Peter Zeihan in his recent study.[9] The Midwestern historians of the first half of the twentieth century had a sense of this, as evidenced by the specific geographical reference in their original name, Mississippi Valley Historical Association, but, as Jon Lauck details in his manifesto, *The Lost Region*, these historians abandoned their regional focus in the 1960s to become the Organization of American Historians. There is, in fact, an annual gathering of historians, based at the University of Nebraska–Omaha, that takes as its name the Missouri Valley History Conference, and the Organization of American Historians and the Western History Association have recently made room for sessions sponsored by the Midwestern History Association at their annual conferences.

In the opening plenary session of the "Where the West Begins?" conference, mentioned earlier, I suggested that the West begins with the Missouri River Basin, rather than the Missouri River itself. The eastern boundary of the basin in South Dakota is the Big Sioux River and its tributaries, including the Slip-Up Creek where Rölvaag began his immigrant trilogy, drawing on the experience of Norwegian settlers. As can be seen in the accompanying map, the basin extends along a north-south line running down the Dakotas into western Iowa and northwestern Missouri, west across northern Kansas, taking in the entirety of Nebraska, then north into Colorado, and including all but the mountain regions of Wyoming and Montana. The eastern extremity is marked by the Big Sioux River (flowing out of South Dakota), the James River (flowing out of North Dakota—both emptying into the Missouri), and the Missouri River, running along the Nebraska-Iowa and Kansas-Missouri borders and, ultimately, into the Mississippi River at St. Louis. Commensurate with majority opinion as

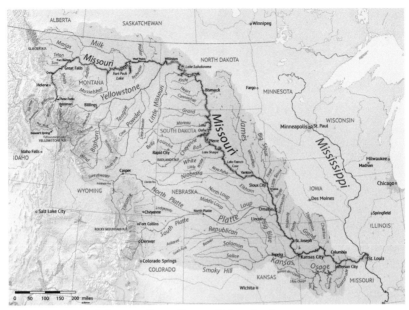

Missouri River Basin. *Wikipedia Commons.*
https://en.wikipedia.org/wiki/Missouri_River.

found in Nugent's survey, this "line," formed by rivers, is where the Midwest ends and the Great Plains/West begins![10]

Iowa-born novelist Fred Manfred has observed that no one from the area in which he set his farm novels—"the eastern half of South Dakota, the southwestern corner of Minnesota, the northwestern part of Iowa, and the northeastern section of Nebraska"—ever thinks to mention the individual states by name in conversation. Residents identify themselves more with the region, rather than with any single state, thereby evincing a disregard for the artificiality of state boundaries.[11] He began to follow this practice in 1946 while writing the novel *This Is the Year* (1947). Casting about for a name for this region, he settled on "Siouxland," derived from the Big Sioux River drainage, and drew a map demarking the four-state area, which appeared originally on the endpapers of *This Is the Year* (see below). To these residents, whom he called "Siouxlanders," he ascribed the following characteristics: they are culturally uniform; speak with a distinctive accent, "broad, full-toned, and very clear"; exhibit "a special kind of morality," valuing honesty, fair play, spirited competition, and individual freedom; follow "our own kind of justice," characterized by compassion for those less fortunate; and are intolerant of greed and arrogance. People not from this region Manfred called "outlanders."

Map of Siouxland from endpapers of *This Is the Year* (1947),
by Feika Feikema (Frederick Manfred).

In writing *Lord Grizzly* (1956), widely considered his best novel,
Manfred extended Siouxland west to accommodate mountain man Hugh
Glass's journey, which took place principally in South Dakota but included
eastern Montana and Wyoming. With that novel, he found a way to create
the historical and cultural context for his earlier farm novels and so con-

tinued with what he later called the Buckskin Man Series of five novels, which he based loosely on actual events and populated with historical figures.[12] The last book in the series, *King of Spades* (1966), is set in the Black Hills of western South Dakota. Here, John Clemens—the lawyer defending the main character, Earl Ransom—describes the Siouxlander in terms characteristic of Western figures:

> We're different out here....We not only tend to be more gloriously rebellious, but, as I think, more courteous.... Actually, rebellion and courtesy go together. Each one of us has his peculiar past and so we're not inclined to stick our noses into each other's affairs. The height of discourtesy out here is for a man to ask another where he came from. To ask that is to put oneself down as a fool....And, in turn, courtesy fosters the free man. We all know that when we are in the presence of courteous people we feel free to be ourselves....We are all different here in the West because we need each other more.[13]

Minnesotan Paul Gruchow, author of *The Necessity of Empty Places* and other works extolling the value of rural communities and environmental stewardship, acknowledges that without Manfred, Siouxland would be "almost definitionless." For Gruchow, Siouxland is largely synonymous with the Missouri River Basin:

> It is a parcel of the vast central grassland of our continent, roughly the drainage of the Missouri River; it lacks any great city, prominent peak, or mystic coast. It is beautiful but not scenic, sparsely populated but not roadless.... It is not East, but it is certainly not quite West either. It is a land of transitions, where the lush greenness of the old tallgrass prairie gives way to the shorter, sparer, brown shortgrass vegetation of the high plains, where farms yield to ranches, hills to buttes, loamy soil to sand.[14]

As Gruchow notes in this 1988 "Back Roads" column in *Minnesota Monthly* magazine (the source of this excerpt), Great Plains writer Hamlin Garland called this area the "middle border." Garland's realistic writings, such as *Main-Travelled Roads* (1891), focused on the details and travails of farm life in Wisconsin, Iowa, and the Dakotas—and the term "middle border" is certainly evocative of the region under discussion in this collection.

While acknowledging Manfred's broadening of the geographic sweep of Siouxland to fit his artistic vision of a vast region, extending from the

Mississippi to the Rockies and from Kansas to Canada, Arthur R. Huseboe, biographer of Herbert Krause and former director of the Center for Western Studies, sought an objective assessment of distinctive regional characteristics. This region Huseboe called Manfred's "greater Siouxland," or the northern plains.[15] Huseboe turned to a series of county-by-county maps created by Rodger Doyle, published between 1993 and 1998 in *U.S. News & World Report*, to illustrate the prevalence or absence of certain social characteristics in the various regions of the United States. Huseboe identifies the seven-state region of the Dakotas, Minnesota, Iowa, Nebraska, Kansas, and Montana as "a region of the northern plains [that] stands out above all others as a place of many virtues, a society that reveres law, religion, and education" (316).

Referencing Doyle's maps, Huseboe notes the following additional characteristics of the northern plains region: low incidence of gun violence leading to murder; highest percentages of enrolled students and graduates; and highest percentage of two-parent families. Huseboe argues that these and the following characteristics create "a distinct and integrated cultural region": high percentage of children and adults with health insurance, indicative of a caring culture; higher percentage of residents with Scandinavian heritage than in most of the nation; Lutherans as dominant religious group in the Dakotas and Minnesota, with a large percentage of Catholics; and a high level of contentment or "mellowness." Doyle's maps, then, in Huseboe's estimation, show that the inhabitants of the northern plains are "safer, better educated, and in their own estimation more content than in any other region of the country" (318). Huseboe does acknowledge two important points with regard to this assessment: the northern plains contain large, even dominant, German ethnic groups; and gun violence, often caused by drug addiction, especially methamphetamine use, has only increased, for example, on the nine Native American reservations in South Dakota.[16]

The Great Plains/West we find in the writings of Rölvaag, Krause, and Manfred, in Nugent's survey results, in the distinctive geographical region created by the Missouri River Basin, including the Big Sioux River Basin, and in the apparent cultural "uniformity" of the region argue for a "break" between the Midwest and the Great Plains along a line where the Big Sioux River flows into the Missouri River, or the 98th meridian.

Iowa-born-and-bred writer Bill Bryson finds that his experience in trying to get a meal on a Saturday night in Sundance, Wyoming, revealed to him the main difference between the Midwest and West, which for him includes South Dakota—and it seems to come down to basic manners.[17]

Notes

[1] The Dakota Conference on the Northern Plains, which observed its fiftieth anniversary in 2018, has been an annual program of the Center for Western Studies at Augustana University since 1990. The conference is supported in part by a challenge grant from the National Endowment for the Humanities, completed in 2013. From its founding in 1967 until 1989, the conference was a program of the business and history departments at Dakota State University, in Madison, South Dakota. A unique characteristic of the conference, one that particularly appealed to the NEH, is its blend of both academic and nonacademic, or "amateur," scholars.

[2] Augustana University, in Sioux Falls, South Dakota, does have a sister institution in the Midwest, Augustana College, Rock Island, Illinois. The two were once one, founded in 1860 in Chicago, but the Norwegians, being a bit more adventuresome, or cantankerous, than the Swedes, lit out for the territory, as Huckleberry Finn put it, and crossed not only the Mississippi River but the Big Sioux River, coming in 1918 to Sioux Falls, after settling for a time in Paxton, Illinois, Marshall, Wisconsin, Beloit, Iowa, and Canton, Dakota Territory. The sports teams at both colleges are known as The Vikings—and predate the Minnesota Vikings by decades.

[3] Clarence Berdahl, "The Slip-Up Settlement and Ole Rölvaag," in *A Common Land, a Diverse People: Ethnic Identity on the Prairie Plains*, ed. Harry F. Thompson, Arthur R. Huseboe, and Sandra Looney (Sioux Falls: Nordland Heritage Foundation, 1987), 41–49.

[4] Herbert Krause, *Poems and Essays of Herbert Krause*, ed. Arthur R. Huseboe (Sioux Falls: Center for Western Studies, 1990). All quotations of Krause's writings are from this edition. For a recent assessment of Krause as a regionalist, see Patrick Hicks, introduction to *The Thresher*, by Herbert Krause (Indianapolis: Bobbs-Merrill, 1946; repr., Sioux Falls: Center for Western Studies, 2017), v–xvi.

[5] For the past forty years, the center has chosen to refer to its region of focus as the northern plains. In her classic study of the demise of independent proprietorship in North Dakota and South Dakota, Catherine McNicol Stock places the Dakotas squarely in what she calls the northern plains; see her *Main Street in Crisis: The Great Depression and the Old Middle Class on the Northern Plains* (Chapel Hill: University of North Carolina Press, 1992).

[6] The first center project was the survey titled "Changing Social Patterns on the Lingering Frontier," which received a grant from the Rockefeller Foundation. The project was undertaken by Herbert Krause and William Wyatt, a member of the Augustana history department. Another was a compilation of the newspaper accounts of the 1874 Black Hills Expedition led by Lt. Col. George Custer, supported by a grant from the South Dakota Bicentennial Commission. Illustrated with numerous photographs, including those by expedition photographer William W. Illingworth, this volume was published by Brevet Press in 1978 as *Prelude to Glory*, edited by Herbert Krause and Gary D. Olson.

[7] Walter Nugent, "Where Is the American West?" *Montana: The Magazine of the Northern Plains* 42 (Summer 1992): 2–23.

[8] "Jon Lauck on the Midwestern History Association," interview with Jon Lauck by *Organization of American Historians Blog*, May 7, 2015, http://www.processhistory. org/jon-lauck-on-the-midwestern-history-association/. Harvey Leifert, "Dividing Line: The Past, Present and Future of the 100th Meridian," *Earth*, January 22, 2018,

https://www.earthmagazine.org/article/dividing-line-past-present-and-future-100th-meridian.

9 Peter Zeihan, *The Accidental Superpower: The Generation of American Preeminence and the Coming Global Disorder* (New York: Twelve, 2014).

10 For information about geomorphic history derived from topographic evidence relative to the Missouri River Drainage Basin and Big Sioux River–Rock River Drainage Basin, see www.geomorphologyresearch.com. See also Big Sioux River watershed map at www.eastdakota.org/files/Download/program_guidelines.pdf.

11 Frederick Manfred, "The Siouxlander," in *Duke's Mixture* (Sioux Falls: Center for Western Studies, 1994), 221–27.

12 For a consideration of Frederick Manfred as a historical novelist, see Harry F. Thompson, "History, Historicity, and the Western American Novel: Frederick Manfred's *Scarlet Plume* and the Dakota War of 1862," *Western American Literature* 37 (Spring 2002): 50–82.

13 Frederick Manfred, *King of Spades*. 1966. (Lincoln: University of Nebraska Press, 1983), 278.

14 Paul Gruchow, "The Art of the Whole Rose," *Minnesota Monthly* (May 1988): 22–25.

15 Arthur R. Huseboe, "From Feika Feikema to Manfred, from the Big Sioux Basin to the Northern Plains," *Great Plains Quarterly* 21 (Fall 2001): 309–19.

16 Bridget Bennett, "Reservation Crime Would Nearly Double South Dakota Stats," KSFY, March 20, 2017, http://www.ksfy.com/content/news/Reservation-crime-would-nearly-double-South-Dakota-stats-416659913.html.

17 "And there you have the difference between the Midwest and the West, ladies and gentlemen. People in the Midwest are nice. In the Midwest the hostess would have felt bad about my going hungry. She would have found me a table at the back of the room [the restaurant was closed for a private party of Shriners] or at least fixed me up with a couple of roast beef sandwiches and a slab of apple pie to take back to the motel." He thinks even the Shriners might have made room for him at one of their tables. "People in the Midwest are good and they are kind to strangers. But here in Sundance the milk of human kindness was exceeded in tininess only by the size of the Shriners' brains." See Bryson's *The Lost Continent: Travels in Small-Town America* (New York: Harper Perennial, 1990), 284.

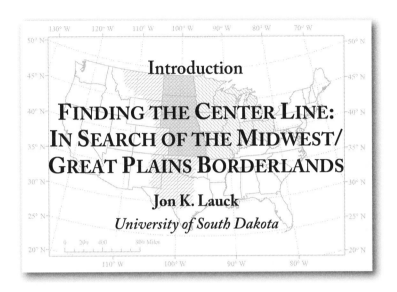

Introduction

FINDING THE CENTER LINE: IN SEARCH OF THE MIDWEST/ GREAT PLAINS BORDERLANDS

Jon K. Lauck
University of South Dakota

It happens when you drive west out of Fargo on Interstate 94 or west out of Sioux Falls on Interstate 90 or west out of Omaha on Interstate 80 or west out of Kansas City on Interstate 70. Or, if you prefer the "blue highways," the narrower roads of the American interior that the Kansan William Least Heat-Moon made famous, it happens when you drive west out of Grand Forks on Highway 2 or west out of Brookings on Highway 14 or west out of Sioux City on Highway 20 or west out of Fort Scott on Highway 54.[2] As you head west you will notice the changes starting just past Jamestown, North Dakota, or just past Mitchell, South Dakota, or just past Grand Island, Nebraska, or just past Salina, Kansas. You might even see some signs by the side of the road signaling that you are crossing the 100th meridian, the north/south line that roughly cuts the United States in half. We might call it the Center Line.

Within fifty miles or so of these 100th meridian signs as you are driving west, you pass from one American region to another, from the American Midwest to the Great Plains. "Beyond the Hundredth Meridian," in the phrase and demarcation line made emblematic by Wallace Stegner in his biography of the naturalist and Midwesterner John Wesley Powell, the world changes.[3] The borderline is not stark. It slowly develops. There is no bright line of separation. But soon you begin to notice fewer and fewer trees. The rolling land flattens in places. Midwestern green turns to shades of High Plains yellow and brown. There are more horses in the fields. More people wear cowboy hats and fewer people wear implement caps—Stetson begins to trump John Deere. More structures are abandoned. Corn and soybeans are replaced by wheat and range land. It is windier. Beyond the trees and rolling hills and riverine valleys of the Midwest, the sky is wider. The sun sets on a distant plains horizon, quite probably a wheat field or a pasture, and is rarely blocked by a forest or hill. As the historian and former director of the University of Nebraska's Center for Great Plains Studies Frederick Luebke observed, "if a person travels westward across Kansas or Nebraska, he knows, as the migrants on the Oregon Trail knew more than a century ago, that he is passing almost imperceptibly from one physiographic region to another."[4] Paul Sharp, a Missourian who knew his Midwest/Plains geographies—he was president of Midwestern colleges such as Drake University (Iowa) and Hiram College (Ohio) and the plains-based University of Oklahoma, and he taught at Iowa State University, the University of Wisconsin–Madison, and the University of Minnesota—explained that the eastern boundary of the Great Plains was an "indefinite zone of transition in which the ninety-eighth meridian has become the symbol of the changing characteristics that distinguish it from the prairies of the Middle West."[5]

The transition zone between the American Midwest and the Great Plains is a borderland, in the recent parlance of Western historians, who "now find borderlands everywhere."[6] To be more specific, it is an interior borderland, as it does not divide the United States from another nation as do the famous borderlands of the Southwest, the study of which give birth to the term.[7] The late eighteenth century, as Jeremy Adelman and Stephen Aron explain, was the "twilight for the Great Lakes borderland" for the old Midwest, once a site of clashing empires and rivalries over the fur trade and hence a zone of fluctuating and confusing lines of separation and "middle grounds."[8] This era ended in the early nineteenth century, however, and the Midwest began to emerge as an identifiable, unified, and self-conscious region within the new United States.[9] "Up and down the Mississippi and all along the Missouri River," Adelman and Aron note, "American sovereignty faced no colonial or national rival after the War of 1812."[10] After an earlier era of shifting boundaries and borderlands, this territory was solidly American. Our focus here is the American *interior* borderland between this Midwest and the plains farther west, a dividing line that could be seen and felt by those settlers who were moving west during the nineteenth century through the massive Mississippi and Missouri River watersheds.

The Midwest/Great Plains borderland is more porous than other interior borders, such as the Ohio River dividing the Old Northwest from the once-rebellious South.[11] It is not akin to the Appalachians, which tended to block off the backcountry for settlers until the American Revolution was over. It is not Hadrian's Wall or the Great Wall of China or a Berlin Wall of concrete, steel, rebar, barbed wire, and machine-gun towers. One can just drive across the Midwest/Great Plains borderlands and do so, perhaps like many people, without much noticing, which makes this space all the more complex and elusive. It remains woefully understudied, despite the recent boom in borderland histories, a condition that prompted the scholars assembled here to combine their energies and give some life to this neglected zone between oft-overlooked and oft-abused American regions.

To help lodge it more firmly in the public imagination, the borderland between the Midwest and the Great Plains would benefit from a memorable moniker.[12] The historian John D. Hicks smartly recognized the uniqueness of this area and settled on the simple name "Western Middle West," a mostly accurate description but not one that is very revealing to the uninitiated and one that shortchanges the plains side of the line. Frederick Manfred, who grew up in northwestern Iowa and spent most of his mature writing life on a charming hill in southwestern Minnesota, dubbed the area "Siouxland," as Harry Thompson notes in this volume. Manfred wanted his "literary territory"—Iowa, South Dakota, Minnesota, Nebraska—to have a designation and began to compare it to "Wessex and Hardy . . . and John Steinbeck's Salinas Valley."[13] But Siouxland lacks clarity to many, is too personal to Manfred, and probably gives offense to some. Hamlin Garland's "middle border" designation once made great sense, but this was meant to be a moving frontier line during a historic era of settlement and no longer applies.

Instead, I suggest the Center Line, which denotes a division, as on a road, but not a hard line or barrier or concrete median or wall, one easily crossed over without much thought. If one is not paying attention, crossing the line can even be quite dangerous, but infrequently so on a lightly traveled High Plains blue highway. Perhaps buzz strips—those little divots on the line separating lanes of traffic that make a loud whir when a distracted driver drifts toward the middle—in the form of this book and others with a regionalist orientation can alert us to crossing the line. The Center Line, roughly the area extending fifty miles or so on either side of the 100th meridian, also divides the country down the middle. Not too far off the line are towns in Kansas and South Dakota that claim to be the precise physical center of the country (one, Belle Fourche, South Dakota, factors in Alaska, while the other, Lebanon, Kansas, does not). These are towns that the *New York Times*, as if on cue, dismisses as lost in the "middle of nowhere," an impulse stemming from a coastal embrace of "flyover country" imagery.[14] The line passes straight through the country's central heartland, which we all pray holds, lest the republic face Yeatsian disintegration, and thus it is crucial to study.

To explore the undulating boundary between the Midwest and the Great Plains and to give it a name is to embrace the power of place and spatial differentiation. It is to give regions and sub-regions and localized niches their due and not allow them to be flattened and standardized into monotonous and forgettable dots on a map and marginalized from the main currents of American life. It is to heed the warning of David Pichaske about members of a younger generation of writers, too decoupled from place, who only see western Minnesota, like the *New York Times*, as "the middle of nowhere," and to honor his advice to remember older writers, like Bill Holm, who understood where they were from.[15] We need to, in short, avoid the "simplification of space."[16] We need deep and detailed maps of places, as Susan Naramore Maher explains, to "reestablish worlds that have been lost, to show us ways of honoring a diminished space, and to resist the larger culture's neglect of the rural center of America."[17] We need to understand our varied interior regions and the borderlands between them and the nation's understudied nooks and crannies if we seek a robust and multidimensional civic life and not one dominated by a few coastal population centers.[18] Less grandly, we might simply aim to transcend a time when prominent American writers, seeking to find "nothing," drove to the Dakotas, and instead embrace the idea that there is much to be found in places along the Center Line.[19] It isn't nothing in the middle of nowhere—it's the physical center of a great republic, a place of people with stories worth knowing.

As someone who grew up along the western edge of the Midwest, I take a particular interest in the Midwest/Plains borderlands. When I was born my family lived on a farm in Lake County, South Dakota, a slice of country that always felt fully Midwestern. Our farm was in the flyway between two lakes, Lake Madison and Lake Herman, and it had a good-sized pond and slough that made for fine duck hunting and gave the livestock a place to drink. We had lots of trees. We raised corn, Midwestern style, and fed it to calves bought farther west, out where there was more ranching, and brought them back to our feedlot. In terms of major metropolitan areas, we were oriented toward Minneapolis, home to the Minnesota Vikings and the reason many people wore purple and gold in the winter. In terms of a local city in which to find an airport or zoo, we traveled fifty miles to the southeast to Sioux Falls, which is nestled into a geographic corner where Iowa, Minnesota, and South Dakota converge. Our local town, five miles north, was Madison, so named by Wisconsin settlers who thought the area reminded them of Wisconsin's picturesque capital, perched on the banks of Lake Mendota.[20]

To the north of Madison sits an archipelago of glacial lakes, formed twenty thousand years ago, which left the area more closely approximating mid- to northern Minnesota and less akin to flattened grassy prairie. Some argue that this region is the true headwaters of the Mississippi River, not Minnesota's Lake Itasca.[21] When driving into this area from the north, the naturalist Jerry Wilson saw its landscape as a "lavish feast, compared to a fourth bowl of oatmeal" (his image for the region of North Dakota he had just departed was oatmeal), a land "dotted with sky blue glacial lakes and ponds."[22] The elongated diamond-shaped area surrounding this lush region and the town of Madison, our farm, Lake County, and on down to Sioux Falls was drained by the Big Sioux River watershed. This is the area that Frederick Manfred thought of designating the "Big Sioux River Country."[23] It is also where, as a young man, Paul Errington began fur trapping in the area's lakes and marshes on his way to becoming a famous naturalist and contemporary of Iowa-born and Wisconsin-based Aldo Leopold.[24] The Big Sioux gathers in Grant County, South Dakota, right next to the Minnesota border, and runs south, curving slightly east, and during its final leg forms the border between Iowa and South Dakota. The river bends northward for a few miles through Sioux Falls, gushing over some exposed pink quartzite rock, giving the city its name. On its last stretch the Big Sioux follows the Loess Hills and finally dumps into the Missouri River at Sioux City, Iowa, where the states of South Dakota, Iowa, and Nebraska converge, and its waters are carried on down to Omaha, Kansas City, and beyond by the Big Mo.

The Big Sioux River basin is complemented by other geographies lying on the Midwestern edge of the Midwest/Plains borderland such as the prosperous Red River Valley, which forms the border of Minnesota and North Dakota and drains the area to the north of the Big Sioux. The Red River basin lies just on the other side of the continental divide and carries its water into Canada and the Hudson Bay. To the south of the Big Sioux one finds the gleaming white cliffs of Nebraska on the south side of the

Missouri River, the beauties of the valley around Ponca, and, further south, the Flint Hills of Eastern Kansas, which William Least Heat-Moon pondered deeply.[25]

All these Midwesternish features and formations seem quite distinct from what comes farther west. Lake County and Madison, South Dakota, lie along the 97th meridian, which most observers place firmly in the Midwest. But when you drive west, life changes. When you get to Huron, eighty miles west, you will notice that the newspaper is named *The Plainsman*, which is surely a harbinger of what is to come. Fifty miles west of Huron is Miller, South Dakota, whose once well-traveled sale barn provided the calves for our corn-driven Midwestern feedlot back east. Fifty miles farther west along Highway 14, a route given life by the historian John E. Miller, is the town of Blunt, which sits along the famed 100th meridian.[26] Twenty miles west of Blunt is South Dakota's capital of Pierre and the Missouri River, which soon turns East and meets up with the Big Sioux River at Sioux City, Iowa. Across the wide Missouri from Pierre is Fort Pierre, or the "West River" country chronicled by the historian Paula Nelson.[27] For many Dakotans, the Missouri River is the informal border between the Midwest and the plains, or the beginning of the American West if one accepts the common organizational principle that the plains are a sub-region of the western United States broadly conceived.[28] In South Dakota, the regional distinctions are so ingrained and the usage of the terms so habitual that their pronunciations have morphed into "Eas-*triver*" and "Wes-*triver*."[29]

Comparing two South Dakota counties, one on either side of the Missouri River, gives a sense of the regional distinctions. Union County in southeastern South Dakota is where the Missouri River and Big Sioux River meet at the convergence of South Dakota, Iowa, and Nebraska. Harding County in northwestern South Dakota is where South Dakota, Wyoming, and Montana converge. Harding County is out on the High Plains where the counties are bigger, the population is smaller, the rainfall is sparser, cattle and sheep dominate the farm economy, and the limited cropping is focused on wheat, which needs less rain, in contrast to corn and soybeans, which fuel Midwestern hog production. And so Harding County is six times bigger than Union County, while Union County has ten times more people. Harding County produces 71,000 cattle and 30,000 sheep a year. Union County produces 24,000 cattle and 800 sheep a year. Harding County plants 28,000 acres of wheat a year and uses its remaining land for pasture and hay for livestock. Union County plants 125,000 acres of corn (to feed to 20,000 hogs), 112,000 acres of soybeans, and 400 acres of wheat.[30] Harding County is out where farmers experimented with dryland farming, where trees were sparse, and the practice of living in sod houses persisted decades after they were assumed to have been replaced by wood structures.[31] The agricultural historian Gilbert Fite, whose family had experienced how farmers could move from the Midwest to the more jarring and arid area of northwestern South Dakota, told this story well.[32] These distinctions also stand out in a dual reading of, say, *Country People* (1924), by Ruth Suckow, who grew up next to Union County in Iowa, and *Sheep* (1929), by Archie Gilfillan, who was a shepherd in western South Dakota while Suckow was writing her Midwestern farm novels.[33]

Similar to Fite, Suckow, and Gilfillan, other writers and scholars with sharp regionalist eyes have explored the distinctions between the Midwest and plains, including Maxine Allison Vande Vaarst, who recently explored these regional dividing points in the Dakotas. "At the ninety-seventh meridian," she explains, "where the Red River curls along their eastern border with Minnesota, the Dakotas are of a midwestern flavor. The grass is tall and verdant, and trees are plentiful. Corn is the primary agricultural crop. Sioux Falls and Fargo become far western extensions of the heartland ideal. At the 103rd meridian," or in the Harding County area, "the Dakotas are clearly western. The grass is short and rainfall is scarce. Livestock ranching supersedes farming, as the raising of crops with irrigation becomes more and more difficult with each mile west."[34] The editor of *South Dakota Magazine*, when visiting Witten, South Dakota, which sits directly on the 100th meridian, called it "a gateway town to the hard country."[35] Kent Blazer explained these regional divides for Nebraska and Craig Miner did so for Kansas.[36] More famously, in 1960, during his celebrated trip with his dog, John Steinbeck embraced the East versus West River divide and pinpointed Bismarck, North Dakota, on the Missouri River as the regional dividing line: "I came upon it with amazement. Here is where the map should fold. Here is the boundary between east and west."[37] Steinbeck's designation lives on across the river from Bismarck, in Mandan, where a sign announces "Where the West Begins."[38]

However much time Steinbeck spent in fancy hotels instead of actually in his camper seeing the contours of the country, as his later critics questioned, it was obvious to him that the world changed around the 100th meridian.[39] There is a good reason for Steinbeck's claim. Most prominently is the rain shadow cast by the Rocky Mountains. After climbing up the western slopes of the mountains the weather loses its moisture, and, when it comes down the eastern side, it has little rain to sprinkle on the land. The mountains would, as observers recognized throughout the nineteenth century, "rob the winds of their treasure."[40] Greeley, Colorado, gets fourteen inches of rain a year while, for the sake of comparison, the Gulf Coast gets fifty inches.[41] That means the region between the Rockies and the Missouri River has different soil and vegetation from the humid Midwest. As a result, there is wide variation in the nation's interior grasslands, from the shortgrass regions of the western Dakotas, Nebraska, and Kansas to the tallgrass prairie of the traditional Midwest to the "mixed tall grass–short grass prairie region in the gradient zone between" the two, or along the Center Line of the interior borderlands under discussion in this volume.[42] These variations are why geographers divide the country's vast central grasslands into the "steppes of the Great Plains and the Prairies of the mid-West."[43] Because this interior region is so far from the coasts and the moderating effects of the ocean, the temperature can vary, a lot. In Steele, North Dakota, the temperature has varied from 121° to -50°.[44] On the plains, which receive less moisture, hot and fast winds can quickly wilt a crop that might survive in the more humid Midwest. This is why the cost of crop insurance on wheat in Colorado is more than double the cost in Minnesota and, because of the extreme weather, why the High Plains has the nation's highest rates of hail insurance.[45] These distinct differences between the Midwest and plains are why, after analyzing fifty studies of the Great Plains, geographers can safely claim that the rain shadow zone making up the western Dakotas, Nebraska, and Kansas "comprises the core of the Great Plains region."[46]

In addition to the weather, history in various forms highlights interregional distinctions. Perhaps most foundational is the experience of Native American tribes, some of whom developed a woodland culture in the Midwest while others developed a horse- and buffalo-driven culture on the plains.[47] The history of women written in recent decades also highlights the difficulties of moving from the more populated and more fruitful Midwest to the more challenging plains, as the fictional experience of Ole Rölvaag's Beret and the actual experience of Hamlin Garland's mother make clear.[48] "There are no trees here," one Norwegian pioneer woman bluntly remarked upon arriving on the plains, where, another commented, "everything was changed and looked strange."[49] The drier and harsher conditions of the plains meant a lot more labor for farm women (especially hauling water, which was a simple matter in the humid Midwest).[50] The Populist movement was also stronger on the plains, where conditions were rougher and times were harder, than it was in the more prosperous Midwest.[51] The economic stress that preceded Populism on the plains "was not severe enough in the Midwest to convince farmers to cut the cultural ties that bound them to the traditional parties."[52]

The distinctions between the two regions have long been recognized, and previous observers have left a deeper history to explore and to serve as buzz strips on the Center Line. This history could be distorted, however, not least of which by observers' fears of crossing from the fertile shires of the Midwest to the Mordor-ish barrens of the Great Plains. Much of this distortion, it must be emphasized in an interregional study such as this, stems from the Midwesterners involved. The Midwest had been traversed and explored via the Great Lakes and a rich system of rivers that shaped its settlement patterns and the location of its cities.[53] Midwestern settlers had to drain swampy lowlands or clear massive stands of trees to open up spaces for farms, and it was "only with titanic labors that the early settler, single-handed, cleared the land of timber."[54] There was plenty of forest from which to hew their famed frontier log cabins.[55] When these Midwesterners and their progeny approached the Center Line, they knew how different the surrounding country was.[56] When reaching the central Dakotas, the Midwesterners "from Illinois, Wisconsin, and Minnesota cursed the wind and the often rainless sky."[57] North Dakota-born James Malin, a long-time historian at the University of Kansas who studied the American interior grasslands with great passion, rightly complained about the tendency to use a Midwestern vantage point—or "forest man's standards of western Europe and Eastern America"—when studying the Great Plains and thus the tendency to categorize the plains as a desert.[58]

In 1806, Ohio- and Illinois-raised Lieutenant Zebulon Montgomery Pike, on the way to the mountain that now bears his name, opined that the plains would "become in time as celebrated as the sandy deserts of Africa."[59] In response to Pike's infamous "Great American Desert" designation, in the 1850s Congress actually appropriated $30,000 for the purchase of two loads of camels to be used on the plains.[60] The botanist Edwin James, chronicler of Stephen Long's 1820 expedition, declared the plains a land of "hopeless and irreconcilable sterility."[61] He thought the region would remain the haunt of wandering bands of jackals.[62] As Long's expedition traveled west from Council Bluffs, Iowa, to the Rockies, it reported that the region "differed in no respect but its greater barrenness from that passed on the preceding day."[63] A book published in the 1860s highlighted regional distinctions in its discussion of the "Great Central Desert of the Continent, stretching from the far distant north to the Gulf of Mexico, and separating by four hundred miles of almost uninhabitable space the agriculturally rich prairies of the Mississippi Valley, from the minerally rich slopes and valleys of the Rocky Mountains."[64]

The pattern was set by Pike and other Midwesterners, who seemed to supply most of the early commentary on the plains and who were particularly unimpressed when they encountered the new region. In the famed Midwestern regionalist Timothy Flint's *The History and Geography of the Mississippi Valley* (1833), he relied on the Long expedition's conclusions that beyond the 98th meridian was country that "may be likened to the Great Sahara of the African deserts."[65] Consistent with Flint's view, most of the early settlers moving west from the Midwest skipped the plains in favor of Oregon, no small matter in terms of distance and cost.[66] General John Pope, who grew up in a prominent family in the Illinois country and also served as a surveyor in Minnesota, organized the Army's Department of the Missouri along regional lines, dividing a Midwestern section from a plains section and from a mountain section. In an 1866 report he lumped the Midwestern section, stretching from the Mississippi River to the 99th meridian, into one province and the 99th-meridian-to-the-Rockies plains ("high, arid plains, without timber" and "beyond the reach of agriculture") into another and the mountain region into yet another.[67] Beyond the 100th meridian, a reporter from the Midwestern-based *Cincinnati Commercial* pronounced, lay the "waste lands of the West . . . a region of varying mountain, desert, and rock; of prevailing drought or complete sterility, broken rarely by fertile valleys; or dead volcanoes and sandy wastes; of excessive chemicals, dust, gravel and other inorganic matter," all in need of "more abundant moisture."[68] An Ohio editor from the verdant Midwest, crossing to the Rockies, saw the plains as a "Dead Sea transfixed in solution by a fierce sun, and baked into sterility."[69]

After the Civil War ended, Union General William Tecumseh Sherman, famed for leaving a deep scar through another American region, took command of the Western military. As an Ohioan, he understood the fertile Midwest and could readily see where its agricultural bounty began to fade. "In general terms the settlements of Kansas, Dacotah and Iowa have nearly or quite reached the Western limit of land fit for cultivation, parallel 99° of West Longitude," Sherman wrote.[70] "Then begins the Great Plains 600 miles wide, fit only for Nomadic tribes of Indians, Tartars, or Buffaloes, then the Mountain regions useful chiefly for precious metals."[71] Sherman was blunt about Midwest/Great Plains distinctions. In a letter to the *St. Louis Republican*, he asked and answered his own question about the plains by making a comparison to the Midwest: "What are the uses to which the vast and desert regions of our country between the 100th parallel [*sic*] and the Pacific basin to be applied? We know they are useless for agriculture such as prevails in the fertile lands of the Mississippi basin."[72] After a trip into New Mexico, Sherman wrote his similarly famous brother John, a U.S. senator from Ohio, and made clear: "One county of Ohio will maintain a larger population than all New Mexico."[73] When he thought of the "naked plains of Nebraska, Kansas & Dakota," Sherman said, he thought he was right to advise emigrants to stick to the land of "water and firewood."[74] Why, he wondered, did settlers head for the plains "where water is scarce where fuel is dear if not absolutely beyond price—and where soil is often barren for want of the necessary rain fall. Yet the Allegheny Range with innumerable valleys abounding in rushing streams, boundless forests of timber and good soil remain in a state of nature."[75]

Another Civil War veteran, Major John Wesley Powell of the 20th Illinois Volunteers, also highlighted the regional distinctions in the postwar years and did so with the strongest of Midwestern bona fides. Powell grew up in a Methodist/abolitionist family that lived in Ohio, Wisconsin, and Illinois, and he thoroughly explored the Mississippi River Valley as a young man.[76] He rowed the Mississippi River from its great falls in Minneapolis down to the Gulf of Mexico, and he rowed down the Ohio River from Pittsburgh and also rowed the Des Moines River through Iowa and the Illinois River through the state he mostly considered home. He studied at Midwestern colleges—Illinois College, Illinois Institute (later Wheaton College), and Oberlin—and his fascination with natural history, sparked by his encounters with a curious Ohio farmer and collector, led him to positions with Illinois Wesleyan University, Illinois State Normal University, and the Museum of the Illinois State Natural History Society.[77] In his famous postwar explorations of the American West, Powell noted how the eastern portions of the country enjoyed "abundant rainfall for agricultural purposes," but as one went "westward the amount of aqueous precipitation diminishes in a general way until at last a region is reached where the climate is so arid that agriculture is not successful without irrigation."[78] The key dividing line was where average annual rainfall fell below twenty inches, a "meandering" line running north to south, but generally following the 100th meridian.[79] Another Midwesterner from Illinois and a founder of the Illinois Natural History Society, Cyrus Thomas, similarly saw the 100th meridian as the "dividing line between great agricultural, faunal, and floral areas."[80] From an "agricultural, climatological, and physical point of view," Thomas said, this was "the real dividing line between the eastern and western portions of the continent."[81]

After Powell, the greatest contributor to the characterization and branding of the plains came from the once-acclaimed historian Walter Prescott Webb, who gave the term "Great Plains" its currency. In his 1931 book *The Great Plains*, Webb argued for a hard distinction between the plains and points east and saw an "institutional fault line" separating the regions.[82] The book was widely hailed and recognized and even deemed the "most important book in the first half of the twentieth century by a living American historian" by the Mississippi Valley Historical Association.[83] While born in the Southern-oriented part of Texas on the state's eastern border, Webb mostly grew up west of Fort Worth in Stephens County, Texas, out in the vicinity of Abilene, Lubbock, and Midland, where the Great Plains began (or, like Mandan, "where the West begins," as the signs say).[84] Webb complained that the frontier that Frederick Jackson Turner was focused on "was east of the Mississippi," or in the traditional Midwest, a frequent complaint about the Wisconsin-oriented Turner.[85] The historians of the Midwest orbiting around Turner in the early twentieth century were not, for the most part, focused on Webb's plains.[86] Webb's sojourn into Turner's Midwest did not go well—he failed out of the University of Chicago Ph.D. program and "returned to Texas bitter and disillusioned."[87] But Webb's defeat at the University of Chicago was regionalism's gain. This was an era of regional studies, and, after landing at the University of Texas, Webb fell in with regionalists such as J. Frank Dobie, who gave shape to the identity of Texas and the desert Southwest.[88] This circle of intellectuals surely heightened Webb's regional consciousness and deepened his understanding of the plains.

Webb drew his lines too starkly, however, and made his claims too grand. He saw social life as determined by the particular environment of a place and not by the culture carried to that place by settlers. His analysis was mostly based on evidence from his native Texas, so he tended to focus on the "old-stock Americans of English and Scottish ancestry" and ignored the great ethnic diversity of the northern plains, which was full of German and Scandinavian immigrants.[89] Webb was also wrong that settlement on the northern and central plains stopped at the 98th meridian.[90] In a famous attack, the historian Fred Shannon called Webb to account.[91] Shannon grew up in Missouri and Indiana and taught at Iowa Wesleyan College on his way to earning his Ph.D. at the University of Iowa. He taught most of his career at Kansas State University and the University of Illinois with summer stints at Cornell College (in Iowa) and Ohio State University. Shannon could tell Webb's grand claims about a rigid regional divide were not adding up—he was an agricultural historian from the Midwest who had lived on the plains, after all, and knew what carried over from one region to the next. The ensuing spat "continued to be a part of the folklore of the profession for years afterward."[92] It was nice that the

Midwest could finally promote peace in the matter—"the two adversaries ended their feud at a dinner meeting of the Mississippi Valley Historical Association in Madison, Wisconsin, in 1954"—but revisiting the battle is always valuable for understanding some of the foundational criteria of regional boundary-setting and the debates over their merit.[93]

Webb's *The Great Plains* still has value, despite Shannon's reasonable if undiplomatic critique. The environmental historian Dan Flores views Webb's book as a "rank exercise in environmental determinism."[94] But Flores correctly sees Webb as taking an unyielding stance about the stark differences of the plains because of Webb's regionalist bearings. Texas is big, home to 254 counties, and Webb first lived in Panola County, on the Louisiana line, "deep in the heart of Southern culture, where thickly-timbered rolling hills screened the horizon and even the overhead sky was only partially visible through the soaring loblolly pines."[95] Later, Webb moved out to central Texas, along the Great Plains seam, where "King Cotton and backwoods truck-garden farms gave way to fenced spreads enclosing the Sacred Cow."[96] Flores finds great value in Webb's interregional awareness and, if "refined and more surgically applied," a fine example of how to explore the "particularism of distinctive *places*."[97] Flores condemns the profession of history for its "sniffing condescension" and hostility to place studies—except, of course, studies of New England or California, which manage to find favor in the profession—as "limiting, provincial, and probably antiquarian" and notes that regional historians "have routinely been dismissed as 'cow-chip historians.'"[98] Flores wants the profession to reconsider and revive interest in the work of Webb, James C. Malin, and Major Powell, whom he sees as the founders of American environmental history, and he wants historians, when studying places, to dig into the "reality of the specific," or the details of local culture, geography, and life.[99]

While Webb still deserves to be read, if we are to follow Flores's suggestions about finding the details and texture of particular places, few can match the analytical vision of Wallace Stegner. In his aptly named treatment, *American Places* (1981), among other works, Stegner takes a deep dive into various American regions and sub-regions and gives them meaning and texture. In his heartfelt defense of Grand Island, Nebraska, certainly a city of the Center Line, he explains the Midwest/Plains transition, where "you cross that imperceptible line beyond which the rainfall is less than twenty inches a year, and when you have crossed that you are moving into a different world, under another light, among another flora and fauna and through another variety of land forms."[100] This is where settlers "began to see prairie dogs and horned toads and antelope" and "where they reported the parching of lips and nostrils and were struck by a new dry clarity in the air" and "where they began wildly to underestimate distances."[101] Out west of Grand Island is a "country that strains the eyes and hazes the mind with its distances, a country of big weathers, big sky, exposure without hiding places."[102] All this is easy to see and convey for Stegner because he also knows the Midwest. He was born in Iowa (he received his Ph.D. at the University of Iowa too) and then moved out to the plains as a young man.[103] He recalls a boat trip down the Mississippi River, the spine of the Midwest, and explains its sundry waters and green and wooded shores and describes a river that "inherits the unfashionableness of the region it drains," a land of farms and small towns where people follow Ohio State football and read the *Chicago Tribune*.[104] Stegner tells the stories of Minnesota, Wisconsin, and Iowa river towns and muses on Lake Pepin, the wide spot in the Mississippi River overseen by Stockholm, Wisconsin, where water skiing was invented.[105]

Stegner's recounting of the beauties of Lake Pepin highlights how an understanding of the interior borderlands of the country can fail some authors. In her widely publicized (a front-page *New York Times Book Review* treatment by none other than Patricia Nelson Limerick) and widely praised (it won the National Book Critics Circle award and the Pulitzer Prize for biography) book about the life and times of Laura Ingalls Wilder, Caroline Fraser of course mentions Wilder's time at Lake Pepin.[106] But she fails to understand where the Midwest of places such as Lake Pepin ends and where the plains begins (not to mention her claims that pioneers received $143 a bushel for wheat, or about 143 times what they actually received).[107] Fraser claims that "boosterish marketing" of the Red River Valley misled farmers into settling the plains, but the Red River Valley is on the Midwestern side of the interior borderlands, half in Minnesota and near the 96th meridian.[108] Fraser argues that the Ingalls family was seduced onto the arid and "tornado-scarred, wind-whipped plains" close to the Rockies rain shadow, but in fact they settled near DeSmet, fifty miles from the Minnesota border and well within South Dakota's Midwestern-oriented East River region.[109] DeSmet receives twenty-six inches of rain a year, well above the magic number of twenty inches needed to overcome aridity set forth by John Wesley Powell, whom Fraser uses to make her argument. Oddly, she cites Gilbert Fite to prove her "huckster fantasy" thesis, but Fite was quite satisfied with the successes of farmers in South Dakota.[110]

The Fraser follies point up two fallacies that bedevil the literature of the interior borderlands caused in no small part by past Midwestern commentators. The first is the assumption that Midwestern yeoman farmers blindly tramped out of the humid woods of Wisconsin and were hoodwinked by speculators, railroads, bankers, and other evil forces into tilling a desert.[111] The aforementioned laundry list of nineteenth-century experts and explorers denouncing the plains as a wasteland is surely enough evidence to dispel the settlers-were-duped idea.[112] Given all the energy and money expended on schemes designed to coax some rain from the sky, these farmers were well aware that they were "on the wrong side of the dry line," or the 100th meridian, and had left the "well-watered, tree-filled" Midwest behind them.[113] It took a great deal of work by scientific "experts," mostly against the skepticism of farmers, to conjure evidence that agriculture might work out on the High Plains.[114] As Bradley Baltensperger explained, "potential settlers discounted many of the exaggerations of the promoters, relying instead on local newspapers and farm journals and information received from friends and relatives in the area."[115] A widely circulating folk song from the 1870s made the difficulties of plains farming quite clear:

> *Then come to [interchangeable plains] County, there a home*
> *for you all,*
> *Where the wind never ceases, and the rain*
> *never falls,*
> *Where the sun never sinks but always*
> *remains*
> *'Til it cooks you all up on your government claims.*
> *Hurrah for [interchangeable plains] County, where blizzards*
> *arise*
> *Where the wind's never cinched and the fall*
> *never dies*
> *Then come join its corps and tell of its fame,*
> *All you poor hungry men that stuck on a*
> *claim.[116]*

It is more accurate to say that Midwestern farmers, quite aware of the difficulties involved, made the decision to move to the plains. After being warned of the risks, as General Sherman explained in a laissez-faire statement capturing the mood of many officials, "each emigrant must choose for himself."[117] Many farmers did make the choice to move, a decision that Frederick Jackson Turner celebrated as frontier individualism, while others like Hamlin Garland derided it as perilous. In 1913, *Wallace's Farmer* observed that the "farmers of the United States have been playing leapfrog over each other for over a hundred years, in fact, ever since the Revolution."[118] There were more restless Pa Ingalls's than nervous Hamlin Garlands because the Midwest, settled a couple of generations earlier, was filling up and the sons and grandsons of Midwestern farmers wanted their own slice of the fee simple empire instead of farming another person's ground or moving to the city for factory work. The appeal of the agrarian ideal was intense for young and would-be yeomen.[119] Young Midwesterners, as David Wishart explains, "had been landless in their former states of Illinois, Missouri, Ohio, Wisconsin, and Michigan, and they were attracted by the free or cheap land" out on the plains.[120] The High Plains was a "poor man's country," or a place where those of modest means could acquire a farm, and make it "a land of promise to him who has the pioneering spirit."[121] Circa 1900, the tenancy rate in Iowa and Illinois was around 50 percent, while in the more lightly populated areas of the Midwest/Great Plains seam the tenancy rate was less than 20 percent.[122] While risky (Gilbert Fite's family's homestead out in West River was, not coincidentally, serviced by the post office in *Chance*, South Dakota), young farmers had a better shot at owning their own land, and, in the end, many of them succeeded.[123] A fifth of the farmers who moved out to the plains of eastern Montana, which had the nation's highest rates of loan foreclosure and farm abandonment, failed in their dryland farming venture.[124] But four out of five *did* make it.[125] The success of these farmers takes on added significance in light of recent scholarship overturning decades of received wisdom by finding that as many as 63 percent of homesteaders were successful (in dramatic contrast to the old claim that two-thirds of homesteaders failed).[126]

Despite the farmers-were-hoodwinked-by-experts narrative prominent in the history of the settlement of the plains—think of the focus on "rain follows the plow" ideas in the historiography—much of the scientific work from this era was valuable. While some theories may not have panned out, some crucial steps were taken, such as the U.S. Department of Agriculture searching out new plants and finding "hardy varieties from other countries where similar climatic conditions prevailed" and promoting plants that matured earlier and were more suitable to the shorter growing season of the plains.[127] Nils E. Hansen, for example, an Iowa State College graduate who became head of the Horticulture Department at South Dakota State College, went to Siberia, Turkestan, and China to find new varieties of alfalfa, millet, and sorghum that would grow on the plains.[128]

The farmers-were-bamboozled theory is linked to the fallacy that time stopped in 1870, right after the first Midwestern farmers who had moved to the plains saw their corn crop fail, and that these foolish interlopers made no adjustments to life in a new region. But this is also untrue. The new farmers of the plains readily adapted to the new situation. James Malin was particularly adept at describing how plains farmers made adjustments on their own based on their experiences and without the cajoling of experts.[129] Malin tracked, for example, the adaptations made in Kansas, such as the replacement of corn with winter wheat.[130] Malin explained how "soft winter wheat spread as kind of a folk movement" and how "farmers themselves adjusted and adapted to the soil and climate" and "were ahead of the agricultural colleges and the experiment stations."[131] In a related adjustment, western South Dakota farmers embraced sorghum.[132] These adaptations were similar to Webb's examples of using barbed wire for fencing where wood was limited, drilling wells where water did not flow in streams, and storing water in dugouts.[133] People also adjusted to the treelessness of the plains—the lack of wood that so concerned General Sherman—by planting trees. In Nebraska, civic leaders created Arbor Day in 1872.[134] This was not a new issue. A couple of decades earlier, settlers on the prairies of Iowa planted trees because they missed the forests of Ohio.[135] All these examples highlight Malin's theory of "possibilism," his inelegant word for the idea that any particular environment can be shaped or used in many different ways and that human agency leads to adjustments.[136]

The adaptation fallacy presumes a misunderstanding of nature and resulting damage to the lands of the Great Plains that gives rise to a fallacy of environmental despoliation, a theme that permeates Fraser's book and many like it. The claim, in short, is that the farmers who tilled the plains exposed too much dry land to high winds and, during the especially dry years of the 1930s, "caused the Dust Bowl," in Fraser's blunt phrasing.[137] But recent research rejects this view and demonstrates that dust bowls occurred long before plains farmers started planting crops.[138] From 1439 to 1468, long before one plow cut one row on the plains, Native Americans were forced to leave the area because of a bad drought.[139] Tree-ring data shows that there were fourteen droughts lasting five years or more since 1539 and that there were 160 years of drought out of 400.[140] The environmental disaster narrative is bolstered by references back to the earliest grim assessments of the plains and remains alive by way of the persistent power of 1930s photographic images and of recent apocalyptic assessments of the region, including calls to depopulate the plains and return it to a buffalo grazing zone, all in order to forestall a "Mad Max, total-desolation scenario."[141] Such images explain why, when he imagined where the end of the world might be and wanted to get there, the writer Charles Baxter made a dash for the Dakotas. Less doom-saying and less indulgence of old stereotypes and more focus on understanding the plains and how they are different from other regions such as the Midwest would be wise. It is the overall goal of this book.

To get a sense of the differences between the Midwest and Great Plains, the geographer Chris Laingen has assembled several maps that indicate how, for example, rainfall is different between the two regions, causing the Midwest to be wetter and more fertile and greener and the plains to be more dry and more hostile to farming. In his chapter for this volume, Laingen also points to glaciation, elevation, crops, population levels, light pollution, the use of business names (whether they have "Midwest" or some version of "Plains" in the title), and the bureaucratic divisions created by the Forest Service and the Environmental Protection Agency to demonstrate interregional variation. Laingen's geographic differences are depicted in the photographs of James and Susan Aber, who used aerial photography (by way of kites) to capture images from Kansas that highlight the divide between the two regions. These differences help to explain why counties in the Midwest and Great Plains, in Illinois and South Dakota for example, developed differently, as James Davis shows in his chapter. These counties were formed at different times, were different sizes, and had varying economic bases. The tendency of observers dating back to Coronado to see the green Midwest as "beautiful" and the Great Plains as "sublime," to borrow Edmund Burke's distinction, is explained by Gleaves Whitney in his chapter. Whitney also examines the complex ways in which people have thought about the lands where the tallgrass prairie parklands of the Midwest intersect with and merge into the shortgrass prairie of the Great Plains, and he traces how early modern borderlands on the prairie originated, grew, and declined.

The differences between the Midwest and Great Plains became evident quite quickly for some early settlers. Matthew Luckett notes how the grand expectations of some cattlemen crashed into the harsh conditions and aridity and general economic and environmental stresses of western Nebraska. The same fate befell the once-famous writer Hamlin Garland, who moved from Iowa into the Midwest/Great Plains borderland of Brown County, South Dakota. Garland met the difficult conditions of the western borderland and failed as a farmer and so, to our benefit, became a famous chronicler of the Middle Border, as Lance Nixon explains in his chapter. Regional variation, fights over water, and distrust among regions also proved to be the death knell of a unified governing authority for the Missouri River Basin stretching up along the Iowa and Nebraska borders and into the Dakotas and Montana, as Maria Howe explains in her chapter. Regional distinctions also permeate the chapter by Will Weaver, a writer closely attuned to the state-to-state differential between the wooded and green lake country of northern Minnesota and the land of agrarian struggle in the more arid confines of central South Dakota.

In the arena of culture, one can also find regional distinctions. In her review of women's literature in recent years, Rachael Hanel explores how writers have seen these regions differently. Women have tended to want to escape the privations of the plains, she notes, while Midwestern women have often wanted to return home to a place they see as a rooted refuge. Exploring a different form of literature—cookbooks—Debbie Hanson notes the differentiation between regional foodways. There are more Midwestern wild rice recipes up in Will Weaver's northern Minnesota lakes country, for example, and more beef-and-potato recipes on the cattle-oriented plains (and there really is a "Jell-O and casserole belt in the Dakotas").[142] When considering the vast changes in prairie literature more broadly, David Pichaske worries that the once-sharp voices of the Midwestern/Great Plains borderlands are now too dulled by the Internet and writing programs and deregionalization in general to be articulate voices of place. Newer literary voices are not, he argues, as adept at detecting the subtleties of life in the interior borderlands as was an earlier generation of writers.

The diminishment of these regional voices is linked to the condition of living in what has come to be viewed as an American "flyover" zone, as Nathalie Massip notes in her essay. This partially explains the minimal attention to the Center Line from historians. The surge of history that took the form of the "New Western History" largely elided the Midwest/ Great Plains borderland, for example, despite its birth in the region.[143] The burdens and clichés that accompany being in a flyover zone and how life there is represented in the broader culture is explored by Anna Hajdik, who links films such as *Fargo* and *Nebraska* to the shriveled cultural status of the middle of the country.

Despite receiving short shrift in recent years, these regions are critical to understanding American development. Brad Tennant explains how important these regions once were to the unfolding story of American history by reference to once-prominent voices such as Thomas Jefferson, Zebulon Pike, John O'Sullivan, and Frederick Jackson Turner. Joe Schiller explains how Indian tribes served different roles in the once-dominant American narrative, roles that reinforced regional divisions. Midwestern tribes were viewed as more peaceful and sedentary, while the plains Indians were considered more warlike and wild and the source of frontier difficulties. In her chapter, Mara Ioannides explains how regional differentiation affected the settlement of immigrant Jews in the late nineteenth century, with Midwestern Jews tending to join more settled urban communities linked to Midwestern identity and plains Jews in the Dakotas tending to become farmers in keeping with that area's predominant economic activity. Settlement streams also help to delineate regional divides, as Jay Price demonstrates in his chapter on Wichita, which was settled by Southern evangelicals, thus placing it outside the more typical migration patterns and the pale of settlement for the Midwest and Great Plains and orienting the city toward the South.

While much regional differentiation can be found between the Midwest and Great Plains, it is also important, following the criticisms of Webb, not to make the distinctions too sharp. Julie Courtwright argues that we cannot simply focus on differences in aridity and neglect the unities between these regions or the overlapping elements that can be found in both, including soils, grasses, wind, and prairie fires. Similarly, Paula Nelson asks us to focus on the details of the human stories in the borderlands. Some settlers made it; others failed. A great deal of human agency was involved and personal decision-making that transcended whatever region these settlers happened to live in at the time. Geography is not always destiny, Nelson argues, a point reinforced by a number of plains farmers who made it, against the odds.

This is all true, and it must be remembered. Geography is not destiny, and adaptation to new conditions is possible, as James Malin and others emphasized. The power of human transcendence that Nelson rightly pinpoints only underscores how regions—especially the hard regions—still influence our lives and constrain our choices and form our identities.[144] A region "has shaping power because of its unique geography," as the historian Anne Hyde, now editor of the *Western Historical Quarterly*, argues.[145] A survey of scholars in geography, history, and English who work in the Midwest or plains regions indicates they still recognize the unique geographies of their regions. The Midwest and the Great Plains were seen as distinct regions by 100 percent of the geographers, 87 percent of the historians, and 63 percent of the English professors surveyed by Michael Mullin in his chapter for this volume. Despite the recognition of these regional distinctions and the "shaping power" of place, however, much of the scholarly work on identity formation in recent years has tended to overlook region and place and to focus on other agendas. We hope, in this volume, to lend more attention to place and, in particular, to two regions that deserve more attention than they have received in recent decades. More generally, we hope these textured essays of place will help to transcend "middle of nowhere" and "flyover country" stereotypes and draw the coastal gaze to the Center Line.

Notes

1   The author thanks Virgil Dean, Frederick Errington, Richard Etulain, Sterling Evans, Don Hickey, Tom Isern, Mark Joy, Chris Laingen, Lori Lahlum, Frederick Luebke, Paula Nelson, Pamela Riney-Kehrberg, Joe Schiller, Will Weaver, Gleaves Whitney, and John Wunder for sharing sources and/or providing wonderful commentary on early drafts of this essay.

2   William Least Heat-Moon, *Blue Highways: A Journey into America* (New York: Little, Brown, 1982); Heat-Moon, *Writing Blue Highways: The Story of How a Book Happened* (Columbia: University of Missouri Press, 2014).

3   Stegner, *Beyond the Hundredth Meridian: John Wesley Powell and the Second Opening of the West* (New York: Houghton Mifflin, 1954).

4   Frederick C. Luebke, "Regionalism and the Great Plains: Problems of Concept and Method," *Western Historical Quarterly* 15, no. 1 (January 1984): 27.

5   Paul F. Sharp, "The Northern Great Plains: A Study in Canadian-American Regionalism," *Mississippi Valley Historical Review* 39, no. 1 (June 1952): 61.

6   Pekka Hamalainen and Samuel Truett, "On Borderlands," *Journal of American History* 98, no. 2 (September 2011): 339.

7   John Francis Bannon, *Herbert Eugene Bolton: The Historian and the Man* (Tucson: University of Arizona Press, 1978), 120–21. The term was coined in 1917 by the editor of Herbert Eugene Bolton, who wrote *The Spanish Borderlands: A Chronicle of Old Florida and the Southwest* (New Haven: Yale University Press, 1921).

8   Jeremy Adelman and Stephen Aron, "From Borderlands to Borders: Empires, Nation-States, and the Peoples in between in North American History," *American Historical Review* 104, no. 3 (June 1999): 822.

9   Jon K. Lauck, ed., *The Making of the Midwest: Essays on the Formation of Midwestern Identity, 1787–1900* (forthcoming from Hastings College Press, 2019).

10 Adelman and Aron, "From Borderlands to Borders," 829; Richard White, *The Middle Ground: Indians, Empires, and Republics in the Great Lakes Region, 1650–1815* (New York: Cambridge University Press, 1991).

11 On recent efforts to complicate the Ohio River divide, see Christopher Phillips, *The Rivers Ran Backward: The Civil War and the Remaking of the Middle Border* (New York: Oxford University Press, 2016).

12 When attempting to understand the American Southwest, Edward Spicer and Raymond Thompson commented that a "region ought to have a name, simple and suggestive of its distinctive qualities, because to lack a name is to invite fuzziness of treatment for any entity which one singles out for systematic study." James W. Byrkit, "Land, Sky, and People: The Southwest Defined," *Journal of the Southwest* 34, no. 3 (Autumn 1992): 257; quoting Edward Spicer and Raymond Thompson, eds., *Plural Society in the Southwest* (Albuquerque: University of New Mexico Press, 1975). On the complexity of the Southwest, see also David Yetman, "Musings on the Southwest as a Region by a Southwesterner," *Middle West Review* 4, no. 1 (Fall 2017): 101–9.

13 Arthur R. Huseboe, "From Feikema to Manfred, from the Big Sioux Basin to the Northern Plains," *Great Plains Quarterly* 21, no. 4 (Fall 2001): 309–10.

[14] Dan Barry, "In the Middle of Nowhere, a Nation's Center," *New York Times*, June 2, 2008; Anthony Harkins, "The Midwest and the Evolution of 'Flyover Country,'" *Middle West Review* 3, no. 1 (Fall 2016): 97–121.

[15] Pichaske, chapter 11 in this volume, referencing Forrest Peterson, *Buffalo Ridge: A Novel* (St. Cloud MN: North Star Press, 2012), 45. In his wildly successful travelogue, Robert Pirsig also characterized this area as "a kind of nowhere, famous for nothing at all." Pirsig, *Zen and the Art of Motorcycle Maintenance: An Inquiry into Values* (New York: William Morrow, 1974), 1.

[16] Hamalainen and Truett, "On Borderlands," 338; referencing James C. Scott, *Seeing like a State: How Certain Schemes to Improve the Human Condition Have Failed* (New Haven: Yale University Press, 1998).

[17] Susan Naramore Maher, "Deep Mapping the Great Plains: The Literary Cartography of Place," *Western American Literature* 36, no. 1 (Spring 2001): 7. See also Randall Roorda, "Deep Maps in Eco-Literature," *Michigan Quarterly Review* 40, no. 1 (Winter 2001): 257–72.

[18] See Jon K. Lauck, "Finding the Rural West," in *Bridging the Distance: Common Issues of the Rural West*, ed. David B. Danbom (Salt Lake City: University of Utah Press, 2015), 7–34.

[19] Jon K. Lauck, "Charles Baxter: An Interview," *Belt Magazine*, January 25, 2015: "My family lived on Minnesota Highway 7, and we always went east on Highway 7 into Minneapolis. West of us the highway went toward South Dakota. From time to time when I was growing up, I'd ask, 'What's in South Dakota?' and my mother always had one answer, which was, 'Nothing.' This intrigued me. When I finally had a car and had a driver's license, one of the first things I did was to drive around South Dakota for a few days just to see what nothing looked like. In those days, in the late '60s, if you were a young poet, there was a very common form of poetry that many of us were writing that was much in debt to European models and to people like [Robert] Bly and [James] Wright who were translating European, particularly Spanish and also South American writers. It was surrealist and imagistic. I took my cue from that. *The South Dakota Guidebook* was a joke title. Of course, it's not a guidebook to South Dakota. It has almost nothing to do with South Dakota. It's about a region of the mind, what was desolate in me and dark and empty. It's a guidebook to the way I was in those days."

[20] Jon K. Lauck, "Agriculture and Industry in Lake County," in *The History of Lake County* (Madison, SD: Lake County Historical Society, 1995), 252–80.

[21] Kim Ode, "Could the Mississippi River Actually Begin in South Dakota?" *Minneapolis Star Tribune*, July 25, 2016.

[22] Jerry Wilson, *American Artery: A Pan American Journey* (Sioux Falls, SD: Pine Hill Press, 2000), 36, 38.

[23] Huseboe, "From Feikema to Manfred," 310.

[24] A. W. Schorger, "Paul Lester Errington," *Auk* 83, no. 1 (January 1966): 53; James A. Pritchard, Diane M. Debinski, Brian Olechnowski, and Ron Vannimwegen, "The Landscape of Paul Errington's Work," *Wildlife Society Bulletin* 34, no. 5 (December 2006): 1411; Robert E. Kohler, "Paul Errington, Aldo Leopold, and Wildlife Ecology: Residential Science," *Historical Studies in the Natural Sciences* 41, no. 2 (2011): 222–26. For the role of Leopold in the life of Errington, see Errington, "In Appreciation of Aldo Leopold," *Journal of Wildlife Management* 12, no. 4 (October 1948): 341–50. On Errington's son's efforts to restore his father's Big Sioux River Valley farm to nature, see Deborah Gewertz and Frederick Errington, "From

Intensive Agriculture to Prairie Heritage: A Paradox of Land Repurposing in Eastern South Dakota, USA," *Journal of Peasant Studies* 44, no. 5 (2016): 1-23. On this area of the Big Sioux River Valley, see also Robert Amerson, *From the Hidewood: Memories of a Dakota Neighborhood* (St. Paul: Minnesota Historical Society Press, 1996). On the emergence of a regionalist environmental vision in the Midwest shaped by Midwesterners who had witnessed the changes to the wooded and watered region, see Christian Knoeller, *Reimagining Environmental History: Ecological Memory in the Wake of Landscape Change* (Reno: University of Nevada Press, 2017).

[25] William Least Heat-Moon, *PrairyErth: A Deep Map* (New York: Houghton Mifflin, 1991). For a recent analysis of deep mapping, including Heat-Moon's, see Susan Naramore Maher, *Deep Map Country: Literary Cartography of the Great Plains* (Lincoln: University of Nebraska Press, 2014). See also John Price, *Not Just Any Land: A Personal and Literary Journey in the American Grasslands* (Lincoln: University of Nebraska Press, 2004), 93–158.

[26] John E. Miller, *Looking for History on Highway 14* (Ames: Iowa State University Press, 1993).

[27] Paula M. Nelson, *After the West Was Won: Homesteaders and Town-Builders in Western South Dakota, 1900–1917* (Iowa City: University of Iowa Press, 1989); and *The Prairie Winnows Out Its Own: The West River Country of South Dakota in the Years of Depression and Dust* (Iowa City: University of Iowa Press, 1996). See also the account by the West River native and historian Dorothy Hubbard Schwieder, *Growing Up with the Town: Family and Community on the Great Plains* (Iowa City: University of Iowa Press, 2002).

[28] In his recent book, David J. Wishart stresses that the High Plains region west of the Missouri River "is very different country from relatively humid and verdant eastern Nebraska and Kansas" and the eastern Dakotas. Wishart, *The Last Days of the Rainbelt* (Lincoln: University of Nebraska Press, 2013), 29.

[29] Maxine Allison Vande Vaarst, "Here Folds the Map: Finding Where the West Begins," *South Dakota History* 46, no. 3 (Fall 2016): 263.

[30] Production statistics derived from 2012 data produced by the National Agricultural Statistics Service, U.S. Department of Agriculture. For another similar comparison of an East River South Dakota county (Sanborn) and a West River North Dakota county (Bowman), see John Hudson, "Two Dakota Homestead Frontiers," *Annals of the Association of American Geographers* 63, no. 4 (December 1973): 442–62.

[31] Mary Hargreaves, *Dry Farming in the Northern Plains* (Cambridge, MA: Harvard University Press, 1957); Molly Rozum, "It's Weathered Many a Storm: The Enduring Sod House in Northwest South Dakota," *South Dakota History* 47, no. 4 (Spring 2018): 295–368.

[32] Jon K. Lauck, "Gilbert Courtland Fite," *Western Historical Quarterly* 41, no. 4 (November 2010): 545–46; Lauck interview of Gilbert Fite, April 2007; Tom Lawrence, "'Legendary' Historian from Area Dies at 92," *Mitchell Daily Republic*, July 21, 2010.

[33] Ruth Suckow, *Country People* (New York: Knopf, 1924); Archer B. Gilfillan, *Sheep: Life on the South Dakota Range* (New York: Little, Brown, 1929).

[34] Vande Vaarst, "Here Folds the Map," 261. See also James D. McLaird, "From Bib Overalls to Cowboy Boots: East River/West River Differences in South Dakota," *South Dakota History* 19, no. 4 (Winter 1989): 454–91. For an exploration of the formative stage of East River South Dakota, see Jon K. Lauck, *Prairie Republic: The*

Political Culture of Dakota Territory, 1879–1889 (Norman: University of Oklahoma Press, 2010).

35 Bernie Hunhoff, "Witten: A Town on the 100th Meridian," *South Dakota Magazine*, January/February 2016.

36 Kent Blaser, "Where Is Nebraska Anyway?" *Nebraska History* 80 (1999): 3–14; H. Craig Miner, *West of Wichita: Settling the High Plains of Kansas, 1865–1890* (Lawrence: University Press of Kansas, 1986). See also Andrew Moore, *Dirt Meridian* (Bologna: Damiani, 2015).

37 John Steinbeck, *Travels with Charley: In Search of America* (New York: Viking, 1962), 135.

38 Mark Joy, professor of history at the University of Jamestown in North Dakota, first pointed out this sign. Joy to author, March 15, 2018. See also Tony Spilde, "Where the West Begins," *Bismarck Tribune*, June 25, 2003: "Mandan considers itself a western town, gateway to cowboys, Badlands and the setting sun."

39 Lewis Bazley, "'Loaded with Creative Fictions': Author Claims John Steinbeck Invented Much of His Road Trip Classic *Travels with Charley*," *London Daily Mail*, April 11, 2011; Charles McGrath, "A Reality Check for Steinbeck and Charley," *New York Times*, April 3, 2011.

40 G. K. Warren, "Exploration of the Country between the Missouri and Platte Rivers, &c. In a Topographical Survey," *North American Review* 87, no. 180 (July 1858): 67.

41 Norman J. Rosenberg, "Climate of the Great Plains Region of the United States," *Great Plains Quarterly* 7 (Winter 1986): 25.

42 John R. Borchert, "The Climate of the Central North American Grassland," *Annals of the Association of American Geographers* 40, no. 1 (March 1950): 2.

43 Borchert, "Climate of the Central North American Grassland," 1.

44 Rosenberg, "Climate of the Great Plains Region," 23.

45 Leslie Hewes, "Agricultural Risk in the Great Plains," in *The Great Plains: Environment and Culture*, ed. Brian W. Blouet and Frederick C. Luebke (Lincoln, University of Nebraska Press, 1977), 160; Rosenberg, "Climate of the Great Plains Region," 30.

46 Sonja Rossum and Stephen Lavin, "Where Are the Great Plains? A Cartographic Analysis," *Professional Geographer* 52, no. 3 (August 2000): 548.

47 See Joe Schiller, "Hiawatha and Leatherstocking, from Native Borderlands to Regional Border," chapter 15 in this volume.

48 See Cary W. DeWit, "Women's Sense of Place on the American High Plains," *Great Plains Quarterly* 21, no. 1 (Winter 2001): 29–44; and Julie Roy Jeffrey, *Frontier Women: The Trans-Mississippi West, 1840–1880* (New York: Hill and Wang, 1979). On how the "lives of prairie and plains women diverged markedly" and the "profoundly different rural experience for women" in the Midwest and plains, see Dorothy Schwieder and Deborah Fink, "U.S. Prairie and Plains Women in the 1920s: A Comparison of Women, Family, and Environment," *Agricultural History* 73, no. 2 (Spring 1999): 183. While the plains were more difficult than the Midwest for women, this is not to embrace the past exaggerated accounts of "agony and drudgery of pioneer women on the plains." Peg Wherry, "At Home on the Range: Reactions of Pioneer Women to the Kansas Plains Landscape," *Kansas Quarterly* 18 (Summer 1986): 71.

49 Lori Ann Lahlum, "'Everything Was Changed and Looked Strange': Norwegian Women in South Dakota," *South Dakota History* 35, no. 3 (Fall 2005): 194. See also Lahlum, "'There Are No Trees Here': Norwegian Women Encounter the Northern Prairies and Plains" (Ph.D. diss., University of Idaho, 2003); and Ronald Rees,

"Nostalgic Reaction and the Canadian Prairie Landscape," *Great Plains Quarterly* 2, no. 3 (Summer 1982): 157–58.

[50] Barbara Handy-Marchello, *Women of the Northern Plains: Gender and Settlement on the Homestead Frontier, 1870–1930* (St. Paul: Minnesota Historical Society Press, 2005), 58; Glenda Riley, *The Female Frontier: A Comparative View of Women on the Prairie and the Plains* (Lawrence: University Press of Kansas, 1988), 76–77; Nelson, *After the West Was Won*, 32–33. Midwestern women settlers in Minnesota, on the other hand, "expressed far more positive and complex responses" to moving to the farming frontier. Sara Brooks Sundberg, "'Picturing the Past': Farm Women on the Grasslands Frontier, 1850–1900," *Great Plains Quarterly* 30, no. 3 (Summer 2010): 204.

[51] David S. Trask, "Nebraska Populism as a Response to Environmental and Political Problems," in Blouet and Luebke, *Great Plains*, 61–80. On aridity causing Populism, see John D. Barnhart, "Rainfall and the Populist Party in Nebraska," *American Political Science Review* 19 (August 1925): 527–40. John D. Hicks also highlighted the importance of Populism to the *western* Middle West, or the plains borderlands, in "The Legacy of Populism in the Western Middle West," *Agricultural History* 23, no. 4 (October 1949): 225–36.

[52] Michael Pierce, "Farmers and the Failure of Populism in Ohio, 1890–1891," *Agricultural History* 74, no. 1 (Winter 2000): 60 (quotation); Jeffrey Ostler, *Prairie Populism: The Fate of Agrarian Radicalism in Kansas, Nebraska, and Iowa* (Lawrence: University Press of Kansas, 1993); R. Douglas Hurt, "The Farmers' Alliance and the People's Party in Ohio," *Old Northwest* 10, no. 4 (Winter 1984–1985): 439–62; William F. Holmes, "Why Populism Did Not Flourish in Iowa," *Reviews in American History* 22, no. 4 (December 1994): 608–13. Pierce and Ostler also highlight how state political systems in Midwestern states differed from those in plains states.

[53] James Davis, "How Nature and Culture Shaped Early Settlement in the Midwest," and Michael Allen, "The View from the River: Another Perspective on Midwestern History," both in *Toward a New Midwestern History*, ed. Jon K. Lauck, Gleaves Whitney, and Joseph Hogan (Lincoln: University of Nebraska Press, 2018).

[54] V. E. Shelford, "Deciduous Forest Man and the Grassland Fauna," *Science* 100, no. 2590 (August 1944): 138. On the arduous work of Midwestern tree clearing, see Martin L. Primack, "Land Clearing under Nineteenth-Century Techniques: Some Preliminary Calculations," *Journal of Economic History* 22, no. 4 (December 1962): 484–97. One plains settler noted how the "land is rich and there are no stones, stumps, bluffs, or marshes to hinder the use of any kind of Agricultural machinery." Wherry, "At Home on the Range," 76.

[55] C. A. Weslager, *The Log Cabin in America: From Pioneer Days to the Present* (New Brunswick, NJ: Rutgers University Press, 1969).

[56] David Wishart emphasizes how the settlers of the plains were mostly from the Midwest throughout *The Last Days of the Rainbelt*. See also John C. Hudson, "Who Was Forest Man? Sources of Migration to the Plains," *Great Plains Quarterly* 6, no. 2 (Spring 1986): 69–83; and Hudson, "North American Origins of Middlewestern Frontier Populations," *Annals of the Association of American Geographers* 78, no. 3 (1998): 395–413.

[57] Barbara Handy-Marchello, *Women of the Northern Plains: Gender and Settlement on the Homestead Frontier, 1870–1930* (St. Paul: Minnesota Historical Society Press, 2005), 25.

[58] James C. Malin, "Grassland, 'Treeless,' and 'Subhumid': A Discussion of Some Problems of the Terminology of Geography," *Geographical Review* 37, no. 2 (April 1947): 241 (quotation); James C. Malin, "The Agricultural Regionalism of the Trans-Mississippi West as Delineated by Cyrus Thomas," *Agricultural History* 21, no. 4 (October 1947): 209, 217. See also Rossum and Lavin, "Where Are the Great Plains?," 545; G. Malcom Lewis, "William Gilpin and the Concept of the Great Plains Region," *Annals of the Association of American Geographers* 56, no. 1 (March 1966): 44; Nancy Shoemaker, "Regions as Categories of Analysis," *Perspectives: Newsletter of the American Historical Association* 34 (November 1996): 10; Susan Rhoades Neel, "A Place of Extremes: Nature, History, and the American West," *Western Historical Quarterly* 25, no. 4 (Winter 1994): 496–97.

[59] Robert G. Athearn, "The Great Plains in Historical Perspective," *Montana: The Magazine of Western History* 8, no. 1 (Winter 1958): 13. See also Joni L. Kinsey, Rebecca Roberts, and Robert Sayre, "The Aesthetics of Plainness," *Prospects* 21 (1996): 262–63.

[60] E. Cotton Mather, "The American Great Plains," *Annals of the Association of American Geographers* 62, no. 2 (June 1972): 237.

[61] Athearn, "Great Plains in Historical Perspective," 13.

[62] Ralph C. Morris, "The Notion of a Great American Desert East of the Rockies," *Mississippi Valley Historical Review* 13, no. 2 (September 1926): 193.

[63] Richard H. Dillon, "Stephen Long's American Desert," *Montana: The Magazine of Western History* 18, no. 3 (Summer 1968): 65.

[64] Athearn, "Great Plains in Historical Perspective," 16.

[65] Morris, "Notion of a Great American Desert," 194; Terry A. Barnhart, "'A Common Feeling': Regional Identity and Historical Consciousness in the Old Northwest, 1820–1860," *Michigan Historical Review* 29, no. 1 (Spring 2003): 42.

[66] David Allen Johnson, *Founding the Far West: California, Oregon, and Nevada, 1840–1890* (Berkeley: University of California Press, 1992).

[67] Morris, "Notion of a Great American Desert," 197.

[68] Athearn, "Great Plains in Historical Perspective," 20.

[69] Dillon, "Stephen Long's American Desert," 73.

[70] Athearn, "Great Plains in Historical Perspective," 17.

[71] Athearn, "Great Plains in Historical Perspective," 17.

[72] Athearn, "Great Plains in Historical Perspective," 17.

[73] Athearn, "Great Plains in Historical Perspective," 19.

[74] Athearn, "Great Plains in Historical Perspective," 24.

[75] Athearn, "Great Plains in Historical Perspective," 24.

[76] Donald Worster, *A River Running West: The Life of John Wesley Powell* (New York: Oxford University Press, 2001), 21–60.

[77] Stegner, *Beyond the 100th Meridian*, 1–115.

[78] J. W. Powell, *A Report on the Lands of the Arid Region of the United States* (Washington D.C.: Government Printing Office, 1879), 1.

[79] Powell, *Report on the Lands*, 2–3.

[80] Cyrus Thomas, "Physical Geography and Agricultural Resources of Minnesota, Dakota, and Nebraska," in *Sixth Annual Report of the U.S. Geological and Geographical Survey of the Territories* (Washington, D.C.: Government Printing Office, 1873), 277.

[81] James C. Malin, "The Agricultural Regionalism of the Trans-Mississippi West as Delineated by Cyrus Thomas," *Agricultural History* 21, no. 4 (October 1947): 210.

[82] Walter Prescott Webb, *The Great Plains* (Boston: Ginn, 1931), 9.

[83] George O'Har, "Where the Buffalo Roam: Walter Prescott Webb's *The Great Plains*," *Technology and Culture* 47, no. 1 (January 2006): 157. To help them understand the difficulties of adjusting to a new environment, astronauts were even encouraged to read *The Great Plains*. Gewertz and Errington, "From Intensive Agriculture to Prairie Heritage," 15.

[84] Bud Kennedy, "'Where the West Begins' Is—120 Miles Past Fort Worth? Now Hold On, Pardner," *Fort Worth Star-Telegram*, June 13, 2017; Mather, "American Great Plains," 245.

[85] George Wolfskill, "Walter Prescott Webb and the Great Plains: Then and Now," *Reviews in American History* 12, no. 2 (June 1984): 298; quoting Webb, *An Honest Preface and Other Essays* (Boston: Houghton Mifflin, 1959), 167.

[86] Jon K. Lauck, "The Prairie Historians and the Foundations of Midwestern History," *Annals of Iowa* 71, no. 2 (Spring 2012): 137–73.

[87] Wolfskill, "Walter Prescott Webb and the Great Plains," 298.

[88] Robert L. Dorman, *Revolt of the Provinces: The Regionalist Movement in America, 1920–1945* (Chapel Hill: University of North Carolina Press, 1993); Wolfskill, "Walter Prescott Webb and the Great Plains," 301. Dobie was known as "Mr. Texas" or "Mr. Southwest." Jeff Dykes, "James Frank Dobie, 1888–1964," *Arizona and the West* 8, no. 3 (Autumn 1966): 203.

[89] Frederick C. Luebke, "Regionalism and the Great Plains: Problems of Concept and Method," *Western Historical Quarterly* 15, no. 1 (January 1984): 33.

[90] Frederick C. Luebke, "Introduction," in Blouet and Luebke, *Great Plains*, xii; Walter M. Kollmorgen, "The Woodman's Assaults on the Domain of the Cattleman," *Annals of the Association of American Geographers* 59 (June 1969): 215–38; Wishart, *Last Days of the Rainbelt*, 7.

[91] Peter Novick, *That Noble Dream: The "Objectivity Question" and the American Historical Profession* (New York: Cambridge University Press, 1988), 201–2.

[92] Wolfskill, "Walter Prescott Webb and the Great Plains," 301; Walter Prescott Webb, *An Honest Preface and Other Essays* (Boston: Houghton Mifflin, 1959), 118–21.

[93] Wolfskill, "Walter Prescott Webb and the Great Plains," 301.

[94] Dan Flores, "Place: An Argument for Bioregional History," *Environmental History Review* 18, no. 4 (Winter 1994): 2.

[95] Flores, "Place," 1.

[96] Flores, "Place," 1.

[97] Flores, "Place," 2 (emphasis in original).

[98] Flores, "Place," 5.

[99] Flores, "Place," 6, 14.

[100] Wallace Stegner and Page Stegner, *American Places* (New York: Penguin Books, 2006 [1980]), 47. The sections of this book quoted herein were written by Wallace Stegner.

[101] Stegner and Stegner, *American Places*, 47. Lincoln, Nebraska, receives about thirty-four inches of rain annually, but Scottsbluff, in Western Nebraska, receives sixteen inches. Rosenberg, "Climate of the Great Plains Region," 27.

[102] Stegner and Stegner, *American Places*, 25.

[103] Jon K. Lauck, *From Warm Center to Ragged Edge: The Erosion of Midwestern Literary and Historical Regionalism, 1920–1965* (Iowa City: University of Iowa Press, 2017), 5.

[104] Stegner and Stegner, *American Places*, 59.

[105] Stegner and Stegner, *American Places*, 61.

[106] Caroline Fraser, *Prairie Fires: The American Dreams of Laura Ingalls Wilder* (New York: Metropolitan Books, 2017), 28.

[107] Fraser, *Prairie Fires*, 45, 69.

[108] Fraser, *Prairie Fires*, 96.

[109] Fraser, *Prairie Fires*, 99. On Wilder as a Midwesterner, see John E. Miller, "Laura Ingalls Wilder as a Midwestern Pioneer Girl," in *Pioneer Girl Perspectives: Exploring Laura Ingalls Wilder*, ed. Nancy Tystad Koupal (Pierre: South Dakota State Historical Society Press, 2017), 145–76.

[110] Fraser, *Prairie Fires*, 98; citing Gilbert Fite, *The Farmers' Frontier, 1865–1900* (New York: Holt, Rinehart and Winston, 1966), 63.

[111] This interpretation is in part explained by the prevalence of the progressive school of history of the early twentieth century. On its influence, see Jon K. Lauck, "The Old Roots of the New West: Howard Lamar and the Intellectual Origins of *Dakota Territory*," *Western Historical Quarterly* 39, no. 3 (August 2008): 261–81.

[112] On the wide variety of viewpoints about the plains available in the nineteenth century, see John L. Allen, "The Garden-Desert Continuum: Competing Views of the Great Plains in the Nineteenth Century," *Great Plains Quarterly* 5, no. 4 (Fall 1985): 207–20. On the detailed maps available to earlier settlers, see John L. Allen, "Patterns of Promise: Mapping the Plains and Prairies, 1800–1860," *Great Plains Quarterly* 4, no. 1 (Winter 1984): 5–28. Only in the 1840s did commentators begin to show some mercy to the plains. See Andrew Menard, "Striking a Line through the Great American Desert," *Journal of American Studies* 45, no. 2 (May 2011): 267–80.

[113] Julie Courtwright, "On the Edge of the Possible: Artificial Rainmaking and the Extension of Hope on the Great Plains," *Agricultural History* 89, no. 4 (2015): 540.

[114] Mary Hargreaves, "Dry Farming Alias Scientific Farming," *Agricultural History* 22, no. 1 (January 1948): 39–40, 52, 56. David Wishart explains that the "degree to which the desert image was contested in the promotional literature suggests that it was a real handicap to overcome" for the boosters of the plains. Wishart, *Last Days of the Rainbelt*, 22.

[115] Bradley H. Baltensperger, "Agricultural Adjustments to Great Plains Drought: The Republican Valley, 1870–1900," in Blouet and Luebke, *Great Plains*, 45.

[116] Allen, "Garden-Desert Continuum," 216.

[117] Athearn, "Great Plains in Historical Perspective," 24.

[118] Quoted in John D. Hicks, "The Western Middle West, 1900–1914," *Agricultural History* 20, no. 2 (April 1946): 70.

[119] Gilbert C. Fite, "'The Only Thing Worth Working For': Land and Its Meaning for Pioneer Dakotans," *South Dakota History* 15, no. 1/2 (Spring/Summer 1985): 1–10.

[120] Wishart, *Last Days of the Rainbelt*, 15 (quotation), 52–55.

[121] Paula Nelson, "Traveling the Hope Highway: An Intellectual History of the West River Country of South Dakota," in *Centennial West: Essays on the Northern Tier States*, ed. William Lang (Seattle: University of Washington Press, 1991), 256.

[122] Jeremy Atack and Peter Passell, *A New Economic View of American History from Colonial Times to 1940*, 2nd ed. (New York: W.W. Norton, 1994), 408–9; John D. Hicks, "The Western Middle West, 1900–1914," *Agricultural History* 20, no. 2 (April 1946): 70. See also Donald L. Winters, "Agricultural Tenancy in the Nineteenth-Century Middle West: The Historiographical Debate," *Indiana Magazine of History* 78, no. 2 (June 1982): 129–30.

[123] Lauck interview of Gilbert Fite, April 2007; Gilbert C. Fite, "'The Only Thing Worth Working For': Land and Its Meaning for Pioneer Dakotans," *South Dakota History* 15 (Summer 1985): 2–25.

[124] Gary D. Libecap, "Learning About the Weather: Dryfarming Doctrine and Homestead Failure in Eastern Montana, 1900–1925," *Montana: The Magazine of Western History* 52, no. 1 (Spring 2002): 32.

[125] Libecap, "Learning About the Weather," 32.

[126] Richard Edwards, Jacob K. Friefeld, and Rebecca S. Wingo, *Homesteading the Plains: Toward a New History* (Lincoln: University of Nebraska Press, 2017), 33–35.

[127] Mary Hargreaves, "Dry Farming Alias Scientific Farming," *Agricultural History* 22, no. 1 (January 1948): 50, 54.

[128] Hargreaves, "Dry Farming Alias Scientific Farming," 50.

[129] Robert Galen Bell, "James C. Malin and the Grasslands of North America," *Agricultural History* 46, no. 3 (July 1972): 415–17; Gary D. Libecap and Zeynep Kocabiyik Hansen, "'Rain Follows the Plow' and Dryfarming Doctrine: The Climate Information Problem and Homestead Failure in the Upper Great Plains, 1890–1925," *Journal of Economic History* 62, no. 1 (March 2002): 107.

[130] James C. Malin, "The Adaptation of the Agricultural System to Sub-humid Environment: Illustrated by the Activities of the Wayne Township Farmers' Club of Edwards County, Kansas, 1886–1893," *Agricultural History* 10, no. 3 (July 1936): 131.

[131] Gilbert C. Fite, "Regionalism: The Historical Perspective," *South Dakota Review* 18, no. 4 (1981): 27.

[132] John T. Schlebecker, "Pliant Prairie: One Plant's Influence on One Prairie State," *Montana: The Magazine of Western History* 8, no. 1 (Winter 1958): 30–41; Wishart, *Last Days of the Rainbelt*, 35. A western South Dakota farmer said, "We will learn much about the crops and their adaptation to conditions that we find here." Paula Nelson, "Traveling the Hope Highway: An Intellectual History of the West River Country of South Dakota," in *Centennial West: Essays on the Northern Tier States*, ed. William Lang (Seattle: University of Washington Press, 1991), 246.

[133] Mary W. M. Hargreaves, "The Dry-Farming Movement in Retrospect," *Agricultural History* 51, no. 1 (January 1977): 164–665; Paul F. Sharp, "The Northern Great Plains: A Study in Canadian-American Regionalism," *Mississippi Valley Historical Review* 39, no. 1 (June 1952): 73; Wishart, *Last Days of the Rainbelt*, 82. On the origins of water wells, see Everett Dick, "Water: A Frontier Problem," *Nebraska History* 49, no. 3 (1968): 215–45. See also A. Bower Sageser, "Windmill and Pump Irrigation on the Great Plains, 1890–1910," *Nebraska History* 48, no. 2 (Summer 1967): 107–18.

[134] W. H. Droze, "Changing the Plains Environment: The Afforestation of the Trans-Mississippi West," *Agricultural History* 51, no. 1 (January 1977): 10.

[135] Droze, "Changing the Plains Environment," 7.

[136] Flores, "Place," 8.

[137] Fraser, *Prairie Fires*, 3.

[138] Pamela Riney-Kehrberg, Geoff Cunfer, R. Douglas Hurt, and Julie Courtwright, "Historians' Reaction to the Documentary, *The Dust Bowl,*" *Agricultural History* 88, no. 2 (Spring 2014): 262–88; Kevin Z. Sweeney, *Prelude to the Dust Bowl: Drought in the Nineteenth-Century Southern Plains* (Norman: University of Oklahoma Press, 2016); Geoff Cunfer, "Scaling the Dust Bowl," in *Placing History: How Maps, Spatial Data, and GIS Are Changing Historical Scholarship*, ed. Anne Kelly Knowles (Redlands, CA: ESRI Press, 2008), 95–121; Geoff Cunfer, *On the Great Plains: Agriculture and Environment* (College Station: Texas A&M University Press, 2005).

[139] David J. Wishart, "The Great Plains Region," in *Encyclopedia of the Great Plains*, ed. David J. Wishart (Lincoln: University of Nebraska Press, 2004), xv.

[140] Elwyn B. Robinson, "An Interpretation of the History of the Great Plains," *North Dakota History* 41 (Spring 1974): 6.

[141] Jon K. Lauck, "Dorothea Lange and the Limits of the Liberal Narrative: A Review Essay," *Heritage of the Great Plains* 45, no. 1 (Summer 2012): 20–29; Amanda Rees, "The Buffalo Commons: Great Plains Residents' Responses to a Radical Vision," *Great Plains Quarterly* 25, no. 3 (Summer 2005): 161–72; Anne Matthews, "The Poppers and the Plains," *New York Times Magazine*, June 24, 1990 (quotation).

[142] Barbara G. Shortridge and James R. Shortridge, "Food and American Culture," in *The Taste of American Place: A Reader on Regional and Ethnic Foods*, ed. Barbara G. Shortridge and James R. Shortridge (Lanham, MD: Rowman & Littlefield Publishers, 1998), 7 (quotation). The Great Plains' "strongest association is with beef—not surprising in an area known for cattle ranching." Barbara G. Shortridge, "A Food Geography of the Great Plains," *Geographical Review* 93, no. 4 (October 2003): 507.

[143] Jon K. Lauck, "How South Dakota Sparked the New Western History Wars: A Commentary on Patricia Nelson Limerick," *South Dakota History* 41, no. 3 (Fall 2011): 353–81.

[144] John R. Hibbing, "Could the People of the Great Plains Have Distinctive Character Traits? Looking to Scientific Research for Clues," *Great Plains Research* 26, no. 2 (Fall 2016): 79–84; Anssi Paasi, "Region and Place: Regional Identity in Question," *Progress in Human Geography* 27, no. 4 (2003): 475–85.

[145] Anne Hyde, "Cultural Filters: The Significance of Perception in the History of the American West," *Western Historical Quarterly* 24, no. 3 (August 1993): 351.

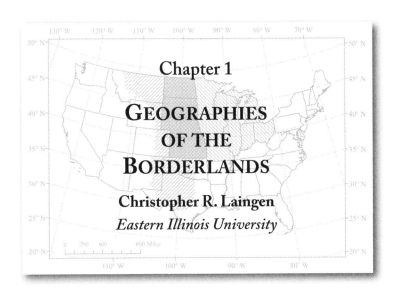

Chapter 1

GEOGRAPHIES
OF THE
BORDERLANDS

Christopher R. Laingen
Eastern Illinois University

An endless plain. From Kansas–Illinois, it stretched, far into the Canadian north, God alone knows how far; from the Mississippi River to the western Rockies, miles without number. . . . Endless. . . . beginningless[1]

Many people who pick up this book might be hoping to finally figure out exactly where the Midwest ends and the Great Plains begins. Prepare for disappointment. Alas, very seldom do regions have actual boundaries. In fact, any region can be, simultaneously, a real place and an intellectual concept.[2] Regions such as the Great Plains and Midwest often exist in the minds of people, and because no two people think exactly alike, it is difficult to determine their precise location. People who claim to be a part of a region base such claims on mutual identities, histories, understandings, and a shared "sense of place" they have with others.[3] This turns any attempt, as futile as it might be, at defining or describing a borderlands between the Great Plains and the Midwest into an exercise in regional geography and, more specifically, into an attempt to visualize the fuzzy, gradual transition between two of our country's iconic regions.[4]

1

A good first step in defining a region spatially, based on its name, is defining what its name means. The Great Plains refers to an actual type of topography (plains), while Midwest, or "middle" and "west," relates to location and direction. Geographically speaking, the Great Plains is a physical, ecological, and even cultural landscape,[5] whereas the Midwest is far more ambiguous and may vary with respect to where a person describing the location of the Midwest is from.

In his 1989 book, *The Middle West: Its Meaning in American Culture*, James Shortridge described how people's affinity for their home state influenced the Midwest's location.[6] Cumulatively, Shortridge's nearly two thousand survey respondents viewed the heart of the Middle West as being the entire states of Nebraska and Kansas, as well as northwestern Missouri and southwestern Iowa. Respondents from North Dakota viewed the region as North and South Dakota, Nebraska, and the western portions of Iowa and Minnesota, while those from Michigan brought the Middle West back toward the east and included western Ohio; the entire states of Indiana, Illinois, Michigan, Wisconsin, and Iowa; southeastern Minnesota; and the northern two-thirds of Missouri. Shortridge's conclusion was that the Middle West's "core" was made up of northwest Ohio; northern Indiana; the northern two-thirds of Illinois; the northern third of Missouri; the eastern halves of Kansas, Nebraska, and South Dakota; the southern half of Minnesota; and a small portion of southern Wisconsin.

The states that I chose to focus on, where the Midwest and Great Plains' borderlands are likely found, are North Dakota, South Dakota, Nebraska, and Kansas—states where most spatial definitions for the Great Plains and Midwest tend to overlap (Fig. 1.1). In particular, I chose these states because of overlapping definitions found in *The American Midwest: An Interpretive Encyclopedia*[7] and the *Encyclopedia of the Great Plains*,[8] along with the *Atlas of the Great Plains*,[9] which uses the same spatial definition as the encyclopedia.

As mentioned, the borderland states (below, in gray), are the product of the overlapping spatial definitions of the Great Plains and the Midwest. The Great Plains' western boundary is the most straightforward to describe thanks in large part to the presence of the Rocky Mountains. If the map would include the Canadian portion of the Great Plains, we would see that the northern boundary is nearly as easy to delineate along the line separating the mixed woodlands and grasslands of the Aspen Parkland ecoregion and the northern boreal forest. The southern boundary is delineated when the Great Plains reach the Rio Grande and converge with the Coastal Plain and the Mexican Highland section of the Basin and Range Province.[10]

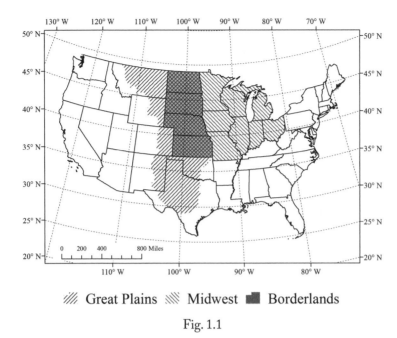

///// Great Plains \\\\\ Midwest ■ Borderlands

Fig. 1.1

As for the regional bounds of the Midwest, Andrew Cayton wrote, "Our Midwest consists of the states created from the original Northwest Territories plus several covered by the Louisiana Purchase of 1803, the states of the upper Mississippi Valley and those parts of Kansas and Nebraska east of the hundredth meridian and of the Dakotas east of the Missouri River."[11] As with the Great Plains, two of the region's three sides have been well-agreed upon over the years. Geography and history helped define the Midwest's northern and southern boundaries—informing topics as disparate as glaciation and slavery. But like the Great Plains' eastern boundary, the Midwest's western boundary has been much more elusive.

Considering that the borderlands we are searching for are probably found somewhere in the Dakotas, Nebraska, and Kansas, one of two approaches to locate them could be used. The first approach would be to use numerous versions of previously published maps of both the Great Plains and the Midwest, overlay them, and find where the greatest consensus of overlap is found. Rossum and Lavin did just this when they compared fifty previously published maps of the Great Plains.[12]

The second approach, and the one used here, was to investigate both regions' human and environmental geographies. Because both human and environmental variables have been used over the years to describe where the borderlands between the Great Plains and Midwest might occur, and because no single, true boundary exists, what follows are a series of ten maps—maps that depict real boundaries, shown as a thick black line with white dashes—of physical and cultural attributes that, when spatially summarized, proximate a location of the borderlands.

Before reviewing the maps, a close look at the landscapes in question is wise. The top photo in Figure 1.2 was taken in western Kansas, and the bottom photo in southern Minnesota. They are meant to be both strikingly similar yet subtly different. In a sense, the photos are a test, in that if someone were asked, "Which photo is from the Midwest, and which is from the Great Plains, and why?" that person would need to give an answer and justify it.

Both images show an unpaved road that stretches off into the distance. However, the Great Plains' road is dirt, and the Midwest's is gravel. The verdant vegetation in the Midwest's road ditch is indicative of an area that receives higher amounts of precipitation, and that it is more "manicured" shows the grass may have been cut and used for livestock hay. The crops themselves are telling. Both photos show corn on the right side of the road, while the Great Plains photo has wheat stubble on the left and the Midwest photo shows soybeans. While both corn and soybeans are grown in greater abundance today in the Great Plains than in the past, wheat has virtually disappeared from most of the Corn Belt.

Signs of settlement, or lack thereof, are also visible. In the top photo, there is no farm in sight, nor are trees evident, while the bottom photo shows not only several tree groves but also a purposefully planted row of twenty-five to thirty trees just above the corn on the right side of the road. The photo is looking to the south, so those trees would have been planted along the farm's northern edge as a protective barrier against the Midwest's cold, northerly winter winds. Cloud formations are also indicative of regional variation. The bottom photo of the more humid Midwest shows an approaching front, evident by the cirrostratus and altostratus clouds off to the southwest, while the photo from the Great Plains includes only fair-weather altocumulus clouds, indicative of a more arid atmosphere.

The Midwest and Great Plains have also been socioeconomically imprinted on America's cultural landscape. People often use familiar or regionally/locally relevant words when naming a business or other cultural institution.[13] Regional identity is an old idea that has gained new importance not only in geography but also in literature, political science, history, anthropology, sociology, and psychology.[14] Cooper, Gibbs Knotts, and Elders used business names to help them build a regional geography of the Appalachians, while others have used themes of place identity to study businesses as disparate as microbreweries and mining.[15]

The Great Plains and Midwest behave no differently. Figure 1.3 shows business names that contain the words "Midwest" or "Midwestern" (top) and those that contain the words "Great Plains," "High Plains," "Central Plains," "Northern Plains," "Eastern Plains," "Western Plains," or "Southern Plains" (bottom). These results were gleaned from a geographic information systems (GIS) software program called Esri ArcGIS Business Analyst, whose educational site-license provides access to a dataset that includes over thirteen million public and private U.S. companies. As of 2016, 10,244 businesses had "Midwest" or "Midwestern" as part of their

Fig. 1.2

name, while 1,335 businesses used "Great Plains," "High Plains," "Central Plains," "Northern Plains," "Eastern Plains," "Western Plains," or "Southern Plains."

I chose to tell this story using maps because I am a geographer, and maps are our currency. The Great Plains and the Midwest are regions that have been created because of natural changes and human actions that occurred in series, over time.[16] These regions are the product of an evolution of patterns and locations of resources, places, and people. Because of this, maps are essential to this inherently geographic quest of locating the borderlands.

The ten variables mapped are not meant to be definitive; they were chosen because I viewed them as items and/or concepts to which most people could relate. Viewing each of the ten boundaries separately, readers will be able to understand what created it and what it means. Readers may have their own ideas on how the Great Plains and Midwest differ, but it is highly likely that these mental maps, like my own, are both highly ambiguous and difficult to explain. Therefore, to illustrate this spatial fuzziness inherent in most regional geography studies—our search for the borderlands being no different—the final map of this chapter will not show a boundary but rather show a borderlands region where the boundary could exist.

It should be noted that regions and their boundaries, even those as amorphous as the Great Plains or Midwest, change with time.[17] If we had been asked to contribute to such a project a century in the past or a century into the future, the borderlands' location might not be the same.[18] As static and foundational as regions seem to be, we must remember that they are indeed dynamic. Another important lesson of this regional exercise is that this imaginary boundary we seek is on the move between and amongst myriad temporal and spatial scales, but also in every person's individual perception of the borderlands idea. As a geographer, it is one of those fascinating, messy problems. However, the very thought of there being a borderlands boundary provides an intellectual structure that allows us to gain a deeper understanding about the human and environmental landscapes of the borderland's parent regions.[19]

Having lived my entire life in either the Great Plains or Midwest, and having traveled across the borderlands many dozens of times, I can assure you that this was one of the most intriguing studies upon which I have ever embarked.[20] The scholar in me wanted so badly to be able to demarcate the singular line that divides these two behemoth American regions. Much of my third decade of life was spent living in and traveling across the Borderlands of South Dakota and Kansas, and, to this day, when traveling across the region on either interstate or minimum maintenance roads, I could not tell you when that magical line is crossed. On westward drives, it dawns on me that I am no longer in the Midwest. How do I know? Well, I can only say to you, the reader, in the words of former Supreme Court justice Potter Stewart: "I know it when I see it."[21] It is my genuine hope that the following maps pique your interests as much as they did mine,[22] for then I have succeeded in what I set out to do.

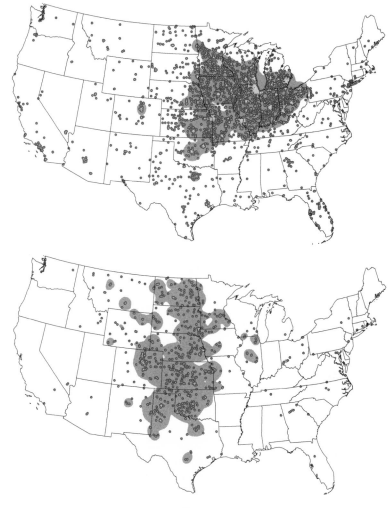

Fig. 1.3

Figure 1.4. Pleistocene Glaciation.[23]

Fig. 1.4. Pleistocene Glaciation

Up to two-miles thick in northern Quebec, though thinner at its edges, the Laurentide Ice Sheet covered most of Canada and stretched south into the United States from the east slopes of the northern Rockies east to the Atlantic Ocean. The southern boundary of glaciation was established by the intermittent glacial episodes of the past 2.5 million years.[24] The advancing ice sheets flattened hills, pulverized bedrock, and gouged valleys. As the glaciers retreated generally northward back into Canada and disappeared twelve thousand years ago, they left behind the topography that we see today— a relatively smooth-to-rolling landscape punctuated by curving moraines (hills of glacial debris) and rivers and their valleys that once helped melting glacial ice find its way to the oceans.[25]

These glacial divides, as will be seen in subsequent examples, help set the stage for the creation of physiographic and ecological regions that scholars have used to help them better understand the environmental processes that occur in those regions. Further, these regions help explain how humans have used those various landscapes in different ways in relation to the regions' underlying bedrock, soils, drainage patterns, and climate.

Figure 1.5. Physiographic Regions.[26]

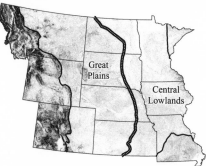

Fig. 1.5. Physiographic Regions

In 1914 Nevin M. Fenneman published a paper where he set about to define and describe twenty-four physiographic "provinces," two of which were part of his "Interior Plains" division: the Great Plains and the Central Lowlands.[27] Fenneman, though trained in both geology and geography, thought like a true regional geographer. He realized that regions were a way to help people visualize the myriad complexities of the planet's physical landscape.[28]

Fenneman's Great Plains/Central Lowlands divide centered on topography, a landscape feature visible in the field. This topographic boundary followed an east-facing escarpment rising three hundred to five hundred feet from east to west. It begins in northwestern North Dakota at the Plateau of the Missouri and follows that topographic break down through South Dakota, along the divide between the James River and Missouri River watersheds. Arriving in Nebraska, Fenneman admits that "the line is almost wholly arbitrary."[29] Citing no abrupt change of altitude or style of topography, or any important differences in underlying bedrock or glacial drift in Nebraska, he simply continues south until he reaches the eastern extent of the outcrop of the Smoky Hills in north-central Kansas, a natural western boundary of the Central Lowlands. This boundary is followed south to the Red Hills of south-central Kansas, where Fenneman's boundary continues into Oklahoma and Texas, but for reasons beyond the scope of this chapter.

Figure 1.6. Twenty-Inch Rainfall Line.[30]

Precipitation amounts have long been recognized as a divide between the Great Plains and the Midwest. The eastern edge of the shortgrass prairie was recognized early as having a close relationship to the twenty-inch isohyet of average annual precipitation.[31] East of that line, the shortgrass prairie transitioned into a mixed-grass and tallgrass prairie environment as precipitation amounts increased due to the influx of moisture moving north

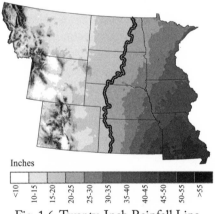

Fig. 1.6. Twenty-Inch Rainfall Line.

from the Gulf of Mexico. Non-irrigated crop-farming west of the twenty-inch isohyet, even with today's drought-tolerant crop varieties, can still be terribly problematic.

The twenty-inch isohyet was often approximated as the 98th meridian, and less frequently the 100th meridian.[32] During the settlement of arid lands west of the 98th meridian during the last decades of the 1800s, land offices launched ad campaigns, backed by statements from leading "scientists" of the day, theorizing that "rain would follow the plow."[33] Co-lin Woodard wrote, "Cyrus Thomas, a noted climatologist, proclaimed, 'As population increases, the moisture will increase.' Rain was said to be trig-gered by smoke from locomotives, by the planting of trees and the plowing of land, even by the vibrations generated by humans and their livestock."[34]

Figure 1.7. U.S. Forest Service Ecoregions.[35]

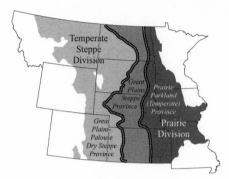

Fig. 1.7. U.S. Forest Service Ecoregions.

The divide being used to dif-ferentiate the Great Plains from the Midwest follows the divide between Domain and Division levels of the U.S. Forest Service (USFS) ecoregion hierarchy.[36] At the Domain level, not shown on the map, the mapped divide splits the United States nearly in half, generally along the 98th merid-ian (the more eastern of the two divides shown), creating the "Hu-mid Temperate" Domain to the east and the "Dry" Domain to the west. At the Division level, and the level used to justify the use of the divide used above, the Prairie Division represents the Midwest while the Temperate Steppe Division represents the Great Plains.

The Prairie Division's climate delivers twenty inches of precipitation along much of the region's western border and as much as forty inches fur-ther south and east. As with all continental climates, summer temperatures are high and winter temperatures are low. The Prairie Division's western border with the Temperate Steppe Division resulted from more days with exceptionally high temperatures and more intense droughts.[37] Soils of the Prairie Division are mollisols, the most productive of the soil groups, and are characterized by thick, black, fertile organic surface layers that allow roots to grow deep into the ground to access nutrients and moisture.

The Temperate Steppe Division's climate is semiarid, where evapo-transpiration rates typically exceed precipitation. As such, the vegetation is a mix of shortgrass prairie and semi-desert conditions. Mollisols are com-mon in steppe environments. However, as precipitation amounts decline further west, the semi-desert shrub soils become aridisols—soils with very little organic content due to the sparseness of the surrounding vegetation.

At the third level of the Domain-Division-Province hierarchy, one could argue that the Great Plains–Midwest divide could be made at the

Province level, and be between the Steppe and Dry Steppe Provinces, moving the divide further west (the more western boundary shown). As with the Divisional breakdowns, Provincial ecoregions are further differentiated by vegetation and other natural land covers.

Figure 1.8. U.S. EPA Ecoregions.[38]

James Omernik—in collaboration with the U.S. Environmental Protection Agency (EPA) regional offices and other federal, state, and international resource agencies—created this structural framework.[39] Criteria include biotic and abiotic phenomena that affect or reflect differences in ecosystem quality and integrity such as geology, physiography, climate, vegetation, hydrology, wildlife, and land use; this spatial framework can be used to help assess and monitor components within and between ecoregions.[40]

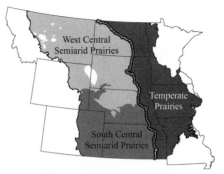

Fig. 1.8. EPA Ecoregions.

A significant difference between the USFS (Fig. 1.7) and EPA (Fig. 1.8) ecoregions is that humans—and their actions, or land uses—are considered part of the biota in the EPA version and are an important factor in determining the spatial extent and existence of some of the resulting regions. For example, three "Corn Belt" ecoregions (Western, Central, and Eastern) comprise much of the Midwest, indicating humans' use of the land as the determining factor above any other criteria in delineating those regions. Like the USFS ecoregions, the EPA's are hierarchical. In the conterminous United States, there are 12 Level I ecoregions (comparable to USFS Domains), 25 Level II ecoregions (USFS Divisions), and 105 Level III ecoregions (USFS Provinces).

Unlike the USFS hierarchy, the EPA's Great Plains Level I region includes the western portion of what most would consider the Midwest, an example of the term "Great Plains" being an actual environmental region whereas the Midwest is a locational description. This difference is caused by the criteria used by the USFS and EPA to delineate their first-order regions. The USFS uses climate thresholds, whereas the EPA takes into consideration other factors such as topography, physiographic processes, natural vegetation, and contemporary land use.

Figure 1.9. Land Resource Regions.[41]

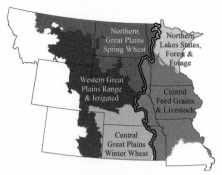

Fig. 1.9. Land Resource Regions.

Social, political, and economic systems are often products of their environmental surroundings.[42] Farmers have long realized that different soils and climates require them to produce certain crop types to be successful and economically prosperous. Land Resource Regions are not unlike ecological regions, in that they consider factors such as physiology, geology, climate, water, soils, and biological resources, but at their core is how the land is being used as a production-based resource.[43]

Using these regions, the Midwest is comprised of the Northern Lakes States, Forest and Forage, and Central Feed Grains and Livestock regions, and the Great Plains are comprised of the Northern Great Plains Spring Wheat, the Western Great Plains Range and Irrigated, and the Central Great Plains Winter Wheat regions. Based largely on environmental factors that determined dominant land uses, a logical Great Plains–Midwest divide places wheat, other small grains, irrigated cropland, and range-livestock in the Great Plains and non-irrigated row-crop (feed grains) farming in the Midwest.

Figure 1.10. USDA Generalized Types of Farming.[44]

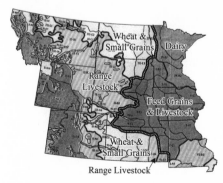

Fig. 1.10. USDA Generalized Types of Farming.

In 1950, to better understand the physical and economic forces influencing agricultural practices, the U.S. Department of Agriculture (USDA) produced a bulletin that described nine farming regions of the United States. These regions were based largely on dominant farming practices that were products of well-defined physical (climate, soils), biological (weeds, pests, disease), and economic forces or conditions (costs of production, consumption demand, prices paid). As with Land Resource Regions (Fig. 1.9), the USDA's "types of farming" regions tend to group themselves into those found within the Great Plains or Midwest. Those regions include the Range Livestock and Wheat and Small Grains regions in the Great Plains, and the Dairy and Feed Grains and Livestock regions in the Midwest.

South Dakota, Nebraska, and Kansas all have transitions from Feed Grains and Livestock farming in their eastern portions that transition to either (or both) the Wheat and Small Grains region and the Range Livestock region.[45] In the drier, but glaciated, portion of eastern South Dakota, wheat and other small grains were grown, as opposed to the unglaciated and more arid western portion of the state. The Nebraska Sandhills and Kansas Flint Hills are home to livestock farming, while the remaining western portions of both states transition back to small grains.

In the first half of the twentieth century, certain types of crops would grow only in certain regions based on precipitation, temperature, and soil types: corn, oats, hay crops, hogs, and beef/dairy cattle, for example, in what we would refer to today as the Corn Belt.[46] Today, the margins of these regions, especially where crops such as corn and soybeans can be grown, have evolved thanks in large part to technological breakthroughs in genetic modification, irrigation, and the proliferation of chemical fertilizers and pesticides.[47] The Corn Belt is now found in portions of southeastern North Dakota, where corn and soybeans have displaced wheat, small grains, and pastureland, and corn, soon after the USDA's 1950 mapping efforts, found a place in portions of the High Plains atop the Ogallala/High Plains aquifer.[48]

Figure 1.11. Farmland Used for Pasture.[49]

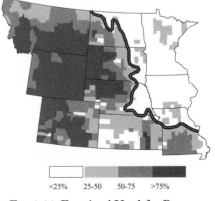

The USDA's Land Resource Areas (Fig. 1.9) and Generalized Types of Farming (Fig. 1.10) regions are descriptive in that they convey the types of agricultural production systems that are in place in each region, but not necessarily what the actual land cover/use might look like or represent to someone as the Midwest transitions into the Great Plains. Where land is not suitable for growing crops, especially in areas

<25%   25-50   50-75   >75%

Fig. 1.11. Farmland Used for Pasture.

not dominated by forests (northern Minnesota), where soils are less fertile, and where less precipitation falls, pastureland is typically found in greater abundance.

The patterns shown on the map generally coincide with glaciation. Where glaciers covered the landscape north and east of the Missouri River, lands are much flatter, and soils are younger and more fertile. Combined with pre-settlement mixed and tallgrass prairie vegetation and a more humid climate, in areas shown as having less than 25 percent of their farmland as pasture, there tends to be a greater probability of encountering highly profitable row-crop (corn/soy) agriculture. In areas where land is less valuable (e.g., hilly, forested, cooler, more arid), pastureland will comprise a greater percentage of the agricultural landscape.

Figure 1.12. Light Pollution.[50]

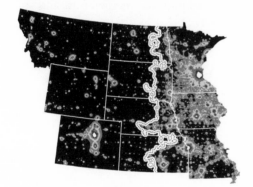

Fig. 1.12. Light Pollution.

Mapping "light pollution" has grown in popularity with initiatives such as the "Dark-sky movement"—a campaign to reduce light pollution and increase the number of visible stars in the night sky, while also seeking to cut down on the amount of energy used to power those lights.[51]

Since the 1960s, Defense Meteorological Satellite Program (DMSP) satellites have been orbiting Earth and obtaining cloud cover imagery and other weather-related data. Though not central to its mission, sensors aboard the satellite have captured light-intensity data that have been used to create the "Earth at Night" images, which have become very popular to simply sit and look at, but also quite useful in myriad scientific applications, not the least of which is measuring "light pollution."

In this application, the above map is meant to be used as a proxy for population density.[52] Using data from the 2010 Census of Population at the county scale, the line shown on the map corresponds approximately to a threshold of ten persons per square mile.

Figure 1.13. Colin Woodard's Americas.[53]

Historian Colin Woodard, author of the book *American Nations: A History of the Eleven Rival Regional Cultures of North America*, explains that the 98th meridian—the imaginary line that runs north-south across the United States, which loosely represents where westward moving Midwestern agricultural practices were stopped due to lack of sufficient rainfall—is where the Midwest ends and the Great Plains begins.

Fig. 1.13. Colin Woodard's Americas.

Woodward writes, "The sheer extremity of the Far Western conditions made it impossible for the other national cultures to take hold here. Greater Appalachia, Yankeedom, and the Midlands each succeeded in adapting to and colonizing the well-watered plains of the Midwest. But as they approached the 98th meridian, each nation came to a halt, its respective social adaptations no longer able to ensure individual or community survival."

Figure 1.14. Ten Boundaries.

This final map depicts the density (number per area) of the ten boundaries discussed in this chapter. Rather than use the actual numeric density values, which because of the mileage involved yield results that are difficult to understand, and because the Borderland itself is a nonquantifiable region, I chose to simplify the map's legend into a continuum from "High" agreement to "Low" agreement. Doing so breaks many rules of good cartography, but this simplified map, nevertheless, does its job.[54]

Regions are rarely discrete physical entities; more often they are conceptualizations that reflect people's perceptions of spatial patterns of how land is organized and used.[55] The Borderland region is no different. The take-home message of this chapter is this:

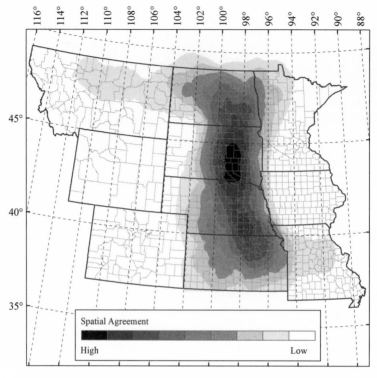

Fig. 1.14

The purpose of regional geography is to understand areas, not merely to draw lines around them. Good regional geography begins in the field, at the grass roots, where we can see things. Exploration is one of our most basic research techniques. Unlike scholars in other disciplines, who can restrict their attention to a limited number of variables, geographers are interested in the totality of places, and we need to see how apparently disparate things fit together in the real world. We cannot understand an area until we have explored it for ourselves.[56]

Notes

1 Ole E. Rölvaag, *Giants in the Earth: A Saga of the Prairie* (New York: Harper & Brothers, 1927). These are Rölvaag's first words of the first chapter of Book II: "On the Border of Utter Darkness."

2 David J. Wishart, ed., *Encyclopedia of the Great Plains* (Lincoln: University of Nebraska Press, 2004), xiii.

3 Tyra A. Olstad, "Understanding the Science and Art of Ecoregionalization," *Professional Geographer* 64 (2012): 303–8.

4 Audrey Kobayashi, "People, Place, and Region: 100 Years of Human Geography in the *Annals*," *Annals of the Association of American Geographers* 100 (2010): 1095–1106.

5 Deborah E. Popper and Frank J. Popper, "The Great Plains: From Dust to Dust," *Planning* 53 (1987): 12–18.

6 James R. Shortridge, *The Middle West: Its Meaning in American Culture* (Lawrence: University Press of Kansas, 1989).

7 Richard Sisson, Christian Zacher, and Andrew Cayton, eds., *The American Midwest: An Interpretive Encyclopedia*, (Bloomington: Indiana University Press, 2007), 5.

8 Wishart, *Encyclopedia of the Great Plains*, xiv.

9 Stephen J. Lavin, Fred M. Shelly, and J. Clark Archer, *Atlas of the Great Plains* (Lincoln: University of Nebraska Press, 2011).

10 Wishart, *Encyclopedia of the Great Plains*, xvii.

11 Sisson, Zacher, and Cayton, *American Midwest*, xxiii.

12 Sonja Rossum and Stephen J. Lavin, "Where Are the Great Plains? A Cartographic Analysis," *Professional Geographer* 52 (2000): 543–52.

13 Derek H. Alderman and Robert M. Beavers, "Heart of Dixie Revisited: An Update on the Geography of Naming in the American South," *Southeastern Geographer* 39 (1999): 190–205. Craig E. Colten, "The Land of Lincoln: Genesis of a Vernacular Region," *Journal of Cultural Geography* 16 (1997): 55–75.

14 Anssi Paasi, "Region and Place: Regional Identity in Question," *Progress in Human Geography* 27 (2003): 475–85.

15 Christopher A. Cooper, H. Gibbs Knotts, and Katy L. Elders, "A Geography of Appalachian Identity," *Southeastern Geographer* 51 (2011): 457–72. Steven M. Schnell and Joseph F. Reese, "Microbreweries as Tools of Local Identity," *Journal of Cultural Geography* 21 (2003): 45–69. John Harner, "Place Identity and Copper Mining in Sonora, Mexico," *Annals of the Association of American Geographers* 91 (2001): 660–80.

16 John R. Borchert, "Maps, Geography, and Geographers," *Professional Geographer* 39 (1987): 387–89.

17 Leonard Guelke, "Regional Geography," *Professional Geographer* 29 (1977): 1–7.

18 Richard Seager et al., "Whither the 100th Meridian? The Once and Future Physical and Human Geography of America's Arid-Humid Divide: Part 1: The Story So Far," *Earth Interactions* (in press), doi:10.1175/EI-D-17-0011.1.

19 John Agnew, "Regions on the Mind Does Not Equal Regions of the Mind," *Progress in Human Geography* 23 (1999): 91–96.

20 Wilbur Zelinsky, "The Geographer as Voyeur," *Geographical Review* 91 (2001): 1–8.

21 See U.S. Supreme Court case *Jacobellis v. Ohio* (1964): https://supreme.justia.com/cases/federal/us/378/184/case.html.

22 Pierce Lewis, "Beyond Description," *Annals of the Association of American Geographers* 75 (1985): 465–77.

[23] Shane A. Lyle, "Glaciers in Kansas," *Kansas Geological Survey Public Information Circular* 28 (2009): 1–6 (http://www.kgs.ku.edu/Publications/PIC/PIC28.pdf).

[24] The thinner line that swoops down into central Iowa, then north toward Minnesota's Twin Cities, indicates the southerly extent of the most recent glaciation approximately twenty-five thousand years ago.

[25] John C. Hudson, *Making the Corn Belt: A Geographical History of Middle-Western Agriculture* (Bloomington: Indiana University Press, 1994), 16–18.

[26] "Physiographic Divisions of the Conterminous U.S.," U.S. Geological Survey, accessed January 26, 2018, https://water.usgs.gov/GIS/metadata/usgswrd/XML/physio.xml#stdorder; GIS data can be downloaded here.

[27] Nevin M. Fenneman, "Physiographic Boundaries within the United States," *Annals of the Association of American Geographers* 4 (1914): 84–134.

[28] Fenneman, "Physiographic Boundaries," 87.

[29] Fenneman, "Physiographic Boundaries," 111.

[30] "30-Year Normals," PRISM Climate Group, accessed January 26, 2018, http://www.prism.oregonstate.edu/normals/; GIS data for the twenty-inch isohyet based on thirty-year (1981–2010) precipitation data can be downloaded here.

[31] W.A. Mattice, "Precipitation in the Great Plains," *Monthly Weather Review* 66 (1938): 117.

[32] Wishart, *Encyclopedia of the Great Plains*, xvii. John Wesley Powell, *Report on the Lands of the Arid Region of the United States with a More Detailed Account of the Lands of Utah* (Washington, D.C.: U.S. Government Printing Office, 1878).

[33] David J. Wishart, *The Last Days of the Rainbelt* (Lincoln: University of Nebraska Press, 2013), xiv.

[34] Colin Woodard, *American Nations: A History of the Eleven Rival Regional Cultures of North America* (New York: Viking, 2011).

[35] "Ecoregions," U.S. Department of Agriculture, Forest Service, accessed January 26, 2018, https://www.fs.fed.us/rm/ecoregions; GIS data can be downloaded here.

[36] Robert G. Bailey, *Ecoregion-Based Design for Sustainability* (New York: Springer, 2002), 33–58.

[37] John R. Borchert, "Climate of the Central North American Grasslands," *Annals of the Association of American Geographers* 40 (1950): 1–39. Charles W. Thornthwaite, *Atlas of Climatic Types in the U.S., 1900–1939*, U.S. Department of Agriculture Soil Conservation Service Misc. Pub. 421, 1941.

[38] "Ecoregions," U.S. Environmental Protection Agency, accessed January 26, 2018, https://www.epa.gov/eco-research/ecoregions; GIS data can be downloaded here.

[39] "Ecological Regions of North America: Toward a Common Perspective," Commission for Environmental Cooperation Working Group, accessed January 26, 2018, http://www3.cec.org/islandora/en/item/1701-ecological-regions-north-america-toward-common-perspective-en.pdf.

[40] James M. Omernik, "Ecoregions of the Conterminous United States," *Annals of the Association of American Geographers* 77 (1985): 118–25.

[41] "Major Land Resource Area (MLRA)," U.S. Department of Agriculture Natural Resources Conservation Service, accessed January 26, 2018, https://www.nrcs.usda.gov/wps/portal/nrcs/detail/soils/survey/?cid=nrcs142p2_053624; GIS data can be downloaded here.

[42] Charles R. Dryer, "Natural Economic Regions," *Annals of the Association of American Geographers* 5 (1915): 121–25.

[43] "Land Resource Regions and Major Land Resource Areas of the United States, the Caribbean, and the Pacific Basin," U.S. Department of Agriculture Natural Resources Conservation Service Handbook 296, accessed January 26, 2018, https://www.nrcs.usda.gov/Internet/FSE_DOCUMENTS/nrcs142p2_050898.pdf.

[44] "Generalized Types of Farming in the United States," U.S. Department of Agriculture Information Bulletin No. 3, accessed January 26, 2018, https://naldc.nal.usda.gov/naldc/download.xhtml?id=CAT87210699&content=PDF.

[45] John Fraser Hart, *The Changing Scale of American Agriculture* (Charlottesville: University of Virginia Press, 2003). Hudson, *Making the Corn Belt*. In North Dakota, one could argue again that the Midwest does not exist in this interpretation, especially if one does not consider northern Minnesota's forests truly to be a part of the Midwest. Shortridge's "core" Middle West does not include the northern forests of Minnesota, Wisconsin, or Michigan. Such a scenario would mean that one would not encounter an east-to-west Midwest/Great Plains transition in North Dakota.

[46] John C. Weaver, "Crop-Combination Regions in the Middle West," *Geographical Review* 44 (1954): 175–200. John C. Weaver, Leverett P. Hoag, and Barbara L. Fenton, "Livestock Units and Combination Regions in the Middle West," *Economic Geography* 32 (1956): 237–59.

[47] Kendra Smith-Howard, "Ecology, Economy, and Labor: The Midwestern Farm since 1945," in *The Rural Midwest Since World War II*, ed. J. L. Anderson (DeKalb: Northern Illinois University Press, 2014), 44–53.

[48] John C. Hudson and Christopher R. Laingen, *American Farms, American Food: A Geography of Agriculture and Food Production in the United States* (Lanham: Lexington Books, 2016), 23–36.

[49] "2012 Census Full Report," U.S. Department of Agriculture, Census of Agriculture, accessed on January 26, 2018, https://www.agcensus.usda.gov/Publications/2012/; GIS data can be downloaded here using the Desktop Data Query Tool 2.0. County-level data for "pastureland" and "land in farms" were downloaded as .dbf tables, input into ArcMap 10.3, and joined to a county shapefile. Dividing acres of pastureland by acres of land in farms results in the values that were used in Figure 1.10.

[50] "Global Radiance Calibrated Nighttime Lights," National Oceanic and Atmospheric Administration, National Centers for Environmental Information, accessed on January 26, 2018, https://www.ngdc.noaa.gov/eog/dmsp/download_radcal.html; the GeoTIFF F16_20100111-20110731_rad_v4 was used to create the image, using ArcMap 10.3, shown in Figure 1.12.

[51] "Who We Are," International Dark Sky Association, accessed January 28, 2018, http://www.darksky.org/about/.

[52] John C. Hudson, "The Other America: Changes in Rural America During the 20th Century," in *North America: The Historical Geography of a Changing Continent, 2nd Edition*, ed. Thomas F. McIlwraith and Edward K. Muller (Lanham, MD: Rowman and Littlefield, 2001), 410. The line in Figure 1.12 generally corresponds to Hudson's map showing fewer than ten people per square mile.

[53] Woodard, *American Nations*.

[54] Philip J. Gersmehl, "The Data, the Reader, and the Innocent Bystander: A Parable for Map Users," *Professional Geographer* 37 (1985): 329–34.

[55] Olstad, "Understanding the Science and Art," 304.

[56] John Fraser Hart, "The Highest Form of the Geographer's Art," *Annals of the Association of American Geographers* 72 (1982): 8, 24.

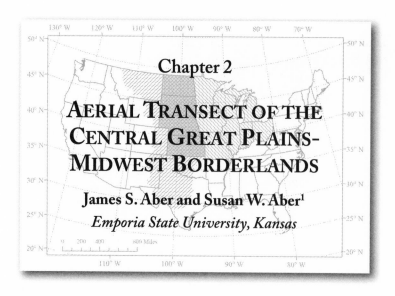

Chapter 2

AERIAL TRANSECT OF THE CENTRAL GREAT PLAINS-MIDWEST BORDERLANDS

James S. Aber and Susan W. Aber[1]

Emporia State University, Kansas

Use a picture. It's worth a thousand words.[2]

Introduction

The flat and almost treeless prairie south of Lake Michigan astonished the first European explorers in the late seventeenth century. This prairie landscape was far richer than anything known in western Europe or the previously explored forested regions of eastern North America.[3] Prior to agricultural, industrial, and urban development, the North American prairie stretched westward to the front ranges of the Rocky Mountains, and prairie reached northward from Mexico to Canada. Once called the Great American Desert, the vast expanse of the Great Plains is now a major agricultural region and produces a wealth of mineral resources.

The concept of a Middle West region appeared in the late nineteenth century and was applied specifically to largely rural society in Kansas and Nebraska to distinguish it from the northern plains and Southwest regions.[4] From the beginning, the Midwest was associated strongly with pastoralism, self-reliance, moral character, and maturity of development. By the early twentieth century, the Midwest had grown conceptually eastward and northward to include twelve states, namely Ohio, Indiana, Michigan, Illinois, Wisconsin, Missouri, Iowa, Minnesota, and the Dakotas in addition to Kansas and Nebraska.[5]

In the mid-twentieth century, the Midwest expanded still farther westward, by some accounts, to encompass the mountain states from the Gulf of Mexico coast to the Canadian border. Only the Pacific coast states of Washington, Oregon, and California were excluded. From this brief discussion, it is clear the expanded Midwest region, however vaguely defined, included all of the Great Plains and prairies east of the Rocky Mountains. Nonetheless, the Midwestern core region has returned toward its original definition, namely Kansas, Nebraska, and parts of bordering states. According to Shortridge, "Americans are now in general agreement that the central-plains region is the perceptual heartland of the Middle West."[6]

The northern boundary of the Midwest region is marked by forestry and mining. The southern fringe is defined by the Ohio River to the east and Arkansas to the west. Oklahoma represents the transition from Midwest to South and Southwest. A current magazine named *The New Territory* describes itself as "the magazine about the Lower Midwest." Based on article content and targeted advertising, the lower Midwest core consists of Missouri, Arkansas, Kansas, Oklahoma, and eastern Colorado. Illinois and Nebraska are also included.

Various Midwest-Great Plains boundaries have been proposed over the years. Among the earliest was John Wesley Powell, who presented a map of the "arid regions of the United States."[7] On this map, the "eastern boundary of the arid region" is a nearly straight line that approximates the 100° W longitude. This boundary corresponds closely with twenty inches (~50 cm) of mean annual precipitation.[8] Other suggestions include the 98th meridian by W. P. Webb and the 100th meridian in Nebraska by M. Sandoz.[9] In this volume, for another example, Lance Nixon argues that the boundary for South Dakota approximates the 99th meridian.

In regard to soils, Marbut classified soils into two major groups known as pedocals (carbonate rich) and pedalfers (aluminum and iron rich).[10] The boundary between these types is essentially the line where mean annual precipitation is equal to evapotranspiration. To the east, excess moisture leads to leaching of carbonates and other soluble compounds from soils; whereas dry conditions westward allow the accumulation of carbonates in soils. This basic wet-dry boundary, known as the Marbut Line, approximates the western Minnesota border (~96° W) in the north and toward the south shifts gradually westward into central Texas (~99° W).

Another approach involves time zones. For many people, the Midwest coincides approximately with the central time zone. National time zones were enacted in 1918, when the central time zone extended from the middle of Ohio (~83° W) to halfway across Nebraska (~100° W).[11] This corresponds to public perception of the Midwest in the early twentieth century, as noted above. Since their establishment, however, time-zone boundaries have changed significantly. In general the boundaries have shifted westward based on local desire and convenience of commerce.[12] The central time zone now stretches from western Indiana (~87° W) to the western boundaries of North Dakota and West Texas (~104° W). This westward migration of the central time zone represents about four degrees of longitude and mirrors the westward shift of the conceptual Midwest during the mid-twentieth century.

Great Plains Gradients and Ecoregions

Three primary physical factors—namely temperature, precipitation, and elevation—exhibit more-or-less continuous gradients across the Great Plains region. Elevation declines from west to east, precipitation increases from west to east, and temperature increases from north to south. These gradients impact the amount of available surface water, soil types, growing seasons, plant hardiness zones, and other factors that influence prairie vegetation, human land use, and ecoregions.

The concept of ecoregions has received widespread support and use for identifying geographic regions and boundaries. Ecoregions are defined as areas of general similarity in ecosystems and in type, quality, and quantity of environmental resources, including past and present human activities in shaping the landscape.[13] For most people, the Great Plains is synonymous with the North American prairie, which spans the terrain between eastern and northern forests and the Rocky Mountains.

The western portion of the prairie region begins around seven thousand feet of elevation at the foot of the Rocky Mountain front ranges and slopes downward to the east to around four thousand feet at the Colorado/Kansas border. Eastward elevation continues to decline to around two thousand feet. Precipitation is generally less than twenty inches (50 cm) per year, and drought is frequent. Perennial water bodies and wetlands are few and far between; only large rivers draining from the mountains provide a reliable source of surface water, which is widely diverted for irrigation.

Shortgrass prairie is the dominant natural vegetation with small groves of trees along water courses or around springs. Agriculture consists of dryland farming in alternate-year-fallow rotation, irrigated crops where surface or ground water is available, and cattle grazing. Human population is generally sparse, dispersed mainly in small towns, although large cities have grown up along the western mountain boundary. Industry is primarily related to mineral-resource extraction (oil, gas, coal, and salt) as well as transportation.

In the central prairie portion, precipitation is mostly twenty to thirty inches (50–75 cm) per year. Drought and flood conditions alternate in cycles that vary from a few years to decades. Perennial water bodies and wetlands are more common than in the western portion. Large parts of the western and central prairies are underlain by the High Plains aquifer, which locally supplies water for irrigation and other uses.[14] During the past decade, the wind-power industry has grown rapidly across the entire prairie region from west to east.[15]

Native vegetation consists of mixed-grass prairie with small groves of trees along water courses. Agriculture is a mixture of dryland and irrigated farming along with cattle grazing. In addition to mineral-resource extraction (oil, gas, and salt) and transportation, manufacturing takes place in some locales, for example the aircraft industry in Wichita, Kansas, and a wind turbine factory in Hutchinson, Kansas. Human population is moderate with several midsized cities within this portion.

The eastern prairie portion is low in elevation, generally less than one thousand feet (300 m), although the Flint Hills escarpment in eastern Kansas reaches sixteen hundred feet (490 m) and the Prairie Coteau in northeastern South Dakota exceeds two thousand feet (>600 m). Precipitation is mostly in the thirty- to forty-inch (75–100 cm) range.[16] Surplus water supports large river systems, drought is rare, and major floods are commonplace events. Wetlands are likewise common. Native vegetation is a mosaic of tallgrass prairie and deciduous woodlands.

Eastern prairies mostly have been converted into cropland except for rocky or sandy portions that are used for grazing. Likewise, much of the original woodland was cleared during the nineteenth and early twentieth centuries for agriculture. Agriculture is dominated by dryland corn along with other row crops. Cattle and hogs are the main livestock. Mineral-resource extraction is less important compared with major manufacturing and transportation industries, and large urban centers have grown up at key transportation hubs.

The ecosystem approach is one utilized mainly by environmental scientists, but it does reflect a combination of climate, soils, and vegetation that has a strong impact on agriculture, water resources, and ultimately human settlement and land use. In a general way, temperate tallgrass prairie relates to public perception of the Midwest region; whereas semiarid mixed-grass and shortgrass prairies correspond with the Great Plains.

As a geographical question, the boundary between the American Midwest and Great Plains regions has sparked debates and various interpretations. Many factors have been considered important, namely landforms and geology, soils, native vegetation and wildlife, climate and water resources, and agricultural practices. Arbitrary boundaries, such as particular meridians, are favored by some, as noted above. Others have emphasized major east-facing escarpments, such as the Flint Hills (Kansas) and Missouri Coteau (Dakotas). But none of these factors individually has achieved universal acceptance.

Laingen (previous chapter) has compiled a cartographic comparison of maps depicting the Midwest-Great Plains borderland. Selected themes include rainfall, ecoregions, agriculture, glaciation, light pollution of the night sky, business names, and other factors. His final summary map depicts the overlapping boundary zone, which lies generally between the 96th and 100th meridians and stretches from central Kansas more-or-less directly northward into central North Dakota. Thus, a combination of several factors, both quantitative and qualitative, is necessary to understand the perceived differences between the American Midwest and Great Plains regions.

Methodology

Among landscape photographers, many have overlooked the Great Plains and Midwest in favor of more obvious and spectacular mountains, sea coasts, deep canyons, coral reefs, and so forth. However, the seeming simplicity of the Great Plains contains rich and diverse environments. In fact, photography has played a key role in shaping public and scholarly impressions of the Great Plains since the mid-nineteenth century.[17] Most such landscape photography is ground based and, thus, presents a frog's-eye view.[18]

Aerial photography adds a third dimension, namely height, which opens new opportunities for imagery and perception. Such elevated vantage points are especially important for the Midwestern landscape that is essentially horizontal over vast distances.[19] Beginning in the 1920s, aerial photographs of the Midwest and Great Plains became increasingly available and were widely adopted by the federal government during the New Deal as a means to survey, evaluate, and reform agricultural practices that had contributed to the Dust Bowl and rural economic problems. High-altitude synoptic views and close-to-earth oblique shots began to transform public perception of the Midwest.

Aerial views of Earth's surface are acquired routinely nowadays from high-flying airplanes and satellites orbiting in space, but a much closer vantage is possible. Small-format aerial photography (SFAP) is a special method to acquire bird's-eye views.[20] SFAP is based on film and digital cameras to acquire low-height aerial photos from manned or unmanned platforms.[21] SFAP has been employed in recent decades for documenting all manner of natural and human resources.[22]

We fly kites to acquire aerial photographs from one hundred to five hundred feet (30–150 m) above the ground using lightweight automatic and radio-controlled camera rigs (Fig. 2.1).[23] For calm days, we also have used a small helium blimp to lift our camera rigs.[24] Such low-height imagery reveals the ground in surprising detail; spatial resolution is typically one to two inches (the diameter of a golf ball). In contrast, conventional aerial photos and commercial satellite imagery have spatial resolutions of two to three feet (the length of a tennis racquet). In addition, nearly all conventional aerial imagery is vertical, looking straight down, a perspective that many people find visually challenging to interpret. SFAP allows also oblique (side-looking) imagery in all directions.

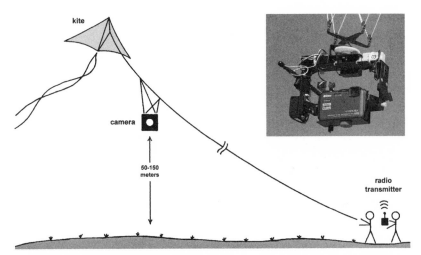

Figure 2.1. Left: cartoon showing typical arrangement for kite aerial photography. The camera rig is attached to the kite line, and a radio transmitter on the ground controls operation of the camera rig. Right: radio-controlled rig for camera operation. The camera pans (rotates) 360° and tilts 0–90°. This rig may be lifted with either a tethered kite or a helium blimp.

Our height limit in the United States is under five hundred feet (~150 m), which is an FAA regulation; manned aircraft should not fly below five hundred feet (one thousand feet in urban areas), and tethered aircraft (kites and blimps) should not exceed five hundred feet. Thus, we collect images from a height interval of airspace that is quite difficult to reach for conventional aerial photography.

Figure 2.2. Little Jerusalem consists of eroded chalk badlands on the southern slope of the Smoky Hill River Valley in Logan County, (west-central) Kansas. This panoramic view is assembled from two wide-angle shots looking toward the southwest (left) and west (right). *Kite aerial photo by JSA and SWA.*

Figure 2.3. Close-up vertical view of Rock City, near Minneapolis, Ottawa County, (north-central) Kansas. Large sandstone concretions resemble giant bowling balls. Most are nearly spherical in shape; some are joined to create double and triple spheres. The single spheres in this cluster are fifteen to twenty-five feet (5–8 m) in diameter. Note the small building and vehicle for scale. *Blimp aerial photo by SWA and JSA.*

With SFAP, we are able to acquire broad panoramas of the landscape (Fig. 2.2) as well as closer shots to illustrate prominent landforms and scenes that portray human land use (Fig. 2.3). SFAP portrays natural and cultural aspects of the Midwest-Great Plains borderland in a way that is readily recognized by most people. Such visual impressions, while subjective, may supplement quantitative measures such as mean annual rainfall, soil types, or time zones.

Bird's-Eye Views—Central Plains Transect

In describing landscapes of the Great Plains and Midwest regions, most people begin on the east and work westward following, perhaps unconsciously, the westward wave of migration, agricultural settlement, and scientific investigations that took place historically. We take the opposite direction, beginning in the western High Plains portion and proceeding eastward.

Typical landscapes are described and illustrated for a transect of the central Great Plains region from southeastern Colorado, stretching across Kansas, and ending in westernmost Missouri (Fig. 2.4). While grassland, agriculture, water, climate, and human activities are certainly themes in many of these examples, they are by no means the only important characteristics, and the reader is left to consider what combination of factors defines the Great Plains as distinct from the Midwest region along this transect.

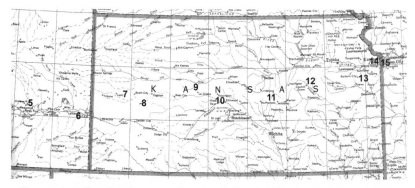

Figure 2.4. Site locality map for the Colorado-Kansas-Missouri prairie transect. The following aerial photographs are identified by figure number. *Base map adapted from USGS.*[25]

Lake Meredith, Colorado. The Arkansas River of southeastern Colorado is the water lifeline for cities and agriculture. Water from the river is diverted via canals that feed a series of reservoirs, notably Lake Meredith, near Rocky Ford. Water from these reservoirs is then distributed via further canals and ditches into irrigated fields downstream. The vicinity is famous for melons, onions, and sugar beets. These reservoirs have become wetland environments with abundant fish and migrating waterfowl.[26] Furthermore, the reservoirs provide recreational activities for the local human population (Fig. 2.5).

Figure 2.5. Overview of Lake Meredith, near Rocky Ford, Colorado. The recreational aspect of the lake is evident with boating and camping during the Memorial Day holiday weekend. *Blimp aerial photo by JSA and SWA.*

Amache Japanese Internment Camp, Colorado. The Amache Japanese Internment Camp (also known as the Granada Relocation Center) was built and operated during World War II to house Japanese-Americans, who were relocated from the west coast far inland to southeastern Colorado. Camp Amache was in operation from August 1942 until October 1945. It reached a peak capacity of more than 7,500 evacuees, two-thirds of whom were American citizens. The camp was a small city with a hospital, post office, elementary and high schools, and stores. But the camp was surrounded by a fence, and guard towers were equipped with machine guns—the Japanese-Americans were virtual prisoners. Today, Amache is a ghost town, in which only building foundations and a cemetery remain (Fig. 2.6).

Figure 2.6. Remains of building foundations at Camp Amache, Colorado. The former high school is marked (*). The town of Granada is visible in the left background. *Kite aerial photo by SWA and JSA.*

Figure 2.7. City of Marienthal on the High Plains in west-central Kansas (top). Nearly the whole town is visible in this view, including an iconic grain elevation to the left and St. Mary's Catholic Church near the scene center. Central Plains Wind Farm (bottom) is just east of Marienthal. Nearly all turbines of the wind farm are visible in this panorama. *Kite aerial photos by SWA and JSA.*

Marienthal, Kansas. The High Plains of west-central Kansas are devoted mostly to crop agriculture, both irrigated and dryland, as well as some grazing. Small towns of the region reflect this agricultural basis (Fig. 2.7). The High Plains aquifer has been severely depleted in this portion, which includes the Western Kansas Groundwater Management District No. 1. Substantial portions of this management district have experienced a 60 percent to more than 80 percent decline in saturated thickness of the aquifer since development began.[27] Nearby, the Central Plains Wind Farm represents development of wind energy, which has taken place at many sites along this transect.

Dry Lake, Kansas. Dry Lake is an ephemeral lake situated in an enclosed drainage basin on the High Plains in Scott County, (west-central) Kansas (Figs. 2.8 a & b). Dry Lake is about three miles (4 km) long and about half a kilometer wide, when full, which is a rare occurrence. This region is semiarid, typically receiving less than twenty inches (50 cm) of precipitation per year. Annual snowfall and rain amounts vary greatly from year to year, and the region is subject to recurring droughts and occasional floods. When dry, salt is present on the lake floor or in brine just below the surface. Dry Lake, thus, represents a salina or salada wetland habitat.[28] When water is present, migrating shorebirds and waterfowl may be seen in abundance.

Figure 2.8a. Dry Lake in Scott County, (west-central) Kansas, displays large changes in water capacity from year to year. The basin was completely full of water in the exceptionally wet spring of 2007. *Kite and blimp aerial photos by JSA and SWA with G. Corley, D. Leiker, C. Unruh, and B. Zabriskie.*

Figure 2.8b. By autumn 2010 the basin was dry and covered with salt deposits. *Kite and blimp aerial photo by JSA and SWA with G. Corley, D. Leiker, C. Unruh, and B. Zabriskie.*

Figure 2.9. View over the town of Liebenthal, Kansas. U.S. highway 183 crosses the scene from left to right, and a county road runs eastward into the distance. St. Joseph's Church stands next to the highway on the right side. Trees follow meandering Big Timber Creek behind the town. *Kite aerial photo by SWA and JSA.*

Liebenthal, Kansas. Liebenthal, a small town in west-central Kansas, was founded by German-Russian emigrants from the Volga region of Russia in 1876. It is the oldest of several similar settlements in Ellis and Rush counties. Because it lacked trees, early settlers quarried chalk beds for fence posts, buildings, bridges, and other structures. As devout Catholics, religion played a large part in the lives of the early inhabitants of these communities, and they built several impressive stone churches (Fig. 2.9). This vicinity is part of the Blue Hills region, which generally has little ground or surface water for irrigation. Dryland farming is practiced, and many oil fields have been developed in the region.

Cheyenne Bottoms, Kansas. Cheyenne Bottoms is the premier wetland of Kansas. Located near the center of the state, it is considered to be among the most significant sites for shorebird and waterfowl migration in the United States.[29] At least 340 bird species have been spotted at Cheyenne Bottoms, some of which are threatened or endangered.[30] The site is an important point for rest and nourishment for hundreds of thousands of birds in their annual migrations between Arctic summer breeding grounds and southern winter ranges along the Gulf Coast, the Caribbean, and South America (Fig. 2.10).

Figure 2.10. Nature Conservancy marsh-pool complex in Cheyenne Bottoms, near Hoisington, (central) Kansas. Cheyenne Bottoms occupies a large enclosed depression and has a variety of pools, marshes, wet meadows, and floodplain environments. *Kite aerial photo by JSA.*

Railroads of Kansas. Kansas is a transportation crossroads, connecting all parts of the United States—north, east, south, and west. Since construction of the Union Pacific began during the Civil War, railroads and later highways, pipelines, electric transmission lines, and airlines have crisscrossed the state. Railroads continue to play a prominent role in the state's economy, and trains are a common sight in many places (Fig. 2.11).

Figure 2.11. Railroads of central Kansas. Top: A Union Pacific train of mixed freight makes its way westward across agricultural land near Hillsboro. *Kite aerial photo by JSA with M. Sprague.* Bottom: BNSF Railroad switching yard and depot at Emporia. Traces of a former roundhouse appear in the lower-right corner. *Kite aerial photo by JSA with D. Leiker.*

Flint Hills, Kansas. The Flint Hills region is one of the most distinctive, picturesque, and best-known landscapes of Kansas. The Flint Hills form a conspicuous east-facing escarpment that rises more than three hundred feet (>90 m) above lower plains to the east. The Flint Hills include the largest tract of tallgrass prairie that still exists in the United States. The grassland is used for cattle grazing, as rocky soils and steep slopes prohibit crop agriculture (Fig. 2.12). Spring burning of the fire-adapted prairie is an annual ritual that ranchers employ to maintain the prairie grasses.[31]

Figure 2.12. The Flint Hills region is characterized by outcropping stone lines in pastures of tallgrass prairie, which is ideal for cattle grazing. The wooded tract in the background is the Neosho River valley, near Council Grove in east-central Kansas. *Kite aerial photo by JSA with J. Schubert.*

Northeastern, Kansas. The rolling landscape presents a mosaic of land covers and human land uses (Fig. 2.13). Rainfall generally exceeds thirty-five inches (>90 cm) per year; floods are frequent and droughts rare. The agricultural methods of the eastern United States were imported by earlier settlers in the mid-nineteenth century and proved successful. Most of the prairie was converted to cropland, and much of the original woodland was cleared. Since the mid-twentieth century, however, woodlands have expanded again.[32]

Kaw Point, Kansas. The junction of the Kansas and Missouri river has been a focal point first for European exploration, then American westward expansion, and finally Kansas City metropolitan urban growth.[33] The Corps of Discovery led by Lewis and Clark was the first explicit U.S. venture into the newly acquired Louisiana Purchase. The Corps arrived at Kaw Point on June 26, 1804, and stayed four days making observations and preparations.[34] These large rivers provided ready transportation routes for riverboats and westward migration prior to the arrival of railroads (Fig. 2.14).

Figure 2.13. Farmstead, agricultural fields, and wooded stream courses near Baldwin City, (northeastern) Kansas. The former Santa Fe Trail and U.S. highway 56 cross the foreground of this scene. This was also the site of the pre-Civil War border skirmish known as the Battle of Black Jack (1856). *Kite aerial photo by JSA with ESU students.*

Figure 2.14. The Kansas River (bottom) joins the Missouri River at Kaw Point, which marks the boundary between Missouri and Kansas. The view is toward the east; the downtown skyline of Kansas City, Missouri, appears in the right background. *Blimp aerial photo by SWA and JSA.*

Kansas City, Missouri. Known as the City of Fountains, Kansas City is famous for its jazz, barbecue, parks, boulevards, museums, and monuments (Fig. 2.15). It services a large portion of the central plains region as a transportation, distribution, manufacturing, science, technology, sports, and cultural hub. Originally two separate cities (in Missouri and Kansas), urban expansion has spread outward to encompass many other smaller cities and towns in the Kansas City, MO-KS, Metropolitan Area with a population of more than 2.1 million people.[35]

Figure 2.15. National World War I Museum and Memorial. Construction on the Liberty Memorial began in 1923; the monument was dedicated in 1926 and finally completed in 1935. A major renovation was undertaken at the turn of this century. Liberty Memorial is in the foreground with Union Station and downtown Kansas City, Missouri, in the background. At one time, the Santa Fe Trail passed over the hill on which the Liberty Memorial is situated.[36] *Blimp aerial photo by JSA and SWA.*

Conclusions

The Midwest, Great Plains, and prairie regions of North America span a vast territory that is characterized by largely agrarian land use, rural landscapes, and long horizontal vistas. Mineral extraction, energy production, transportation, and manufacturing are important human activities that dominate the landscape in many portions. Nonetheless, public impression of the Midwest focuses on agricultural aspects in a traditional approach that applies primarily to the central plains region, as presented in this west-east transect.

Any attempt to draw an arbitrary boundary, such as a particular meridian, between the Midwest and Great Plains regions is complicated by multiple physical and cultural criteria that overlap or intermingle to a considerable extent over substantial west-east distances. From an ecological point of view, the boundary between temperate prairies and semiarid prairies approximates such a division between the Midwest and Great Plains. On our west-east transect, this corresponds approximately to the east-facing escarpment of the Flint Hills. However, this ignores the public perception of the prairie, which stretches to the east, and pastoralism and cropland, which extend farther westward. On this basis, marking a precise Midwest-Great Plains boundary remains an illusory goal.

Sometimes I wasn't sure whether I was on the Great Plains or not. Around the edges it was hard to tell.[37]

Notes

1   We wish to thank the Center for Great Plains Studies at Emporia State University, Kansas, which has supported and encouraged our interest in and travels throughout the Great Plains of North America. Additional financial support was provided by a series of grants from NASA, Emporia State University, and the William T. Kemper Foundation. Over the years, many colleagues, students, and former students from Emporia State University have assisted us with aerial photography. C. R. Laingen and J. Lauck contributed substantially to focusing the coverage and content of this chapter.

2   Gary Martin, "'A Picture Is Worth a Thousand Words'—The Meaning and Origin of This Phrase," *The Phrase Finder*, 2017, https://www.phrases.org.uk/meanings/a-picture-is-worth-a-thousand-words.html.

3   Robert P. Howard, *Illinois: A History of the Prairie State* (Grand Rapids, MI: William B. Eerdmans, 1972), 626.

4   James R. Shortridge, *The Middle West: Its Meaning in American Culture* (Lawrence: University Press of Kansas, 1989), 201.

5   Shortridge, *Middle West*.

6   Shortridge, *Middle West*, 130.

7   John Wesley Powell, *Report on the Lands of the Arid Region of the United States: With a More Detailed Account of the Lands of Utah* (Washington, D.C.: Government Printing Office, 1879), https://pubs.usgs.gov/unnumbered/70039240/report.pdf; Powell, "Arid Regions of the United States Showing Drainage Districts," in *U.S. Geological Survey, Eleventh Annual Report of the Director of the United States Geological Survey, Part 2—Irrigation: 1889–1890*, plate LXIX (Washington, D.C.: U.S. Government Printing Office, 1891), x, https://pubs.er.usgs.gov/publication/ar11_2.

8   Shawn W. Salley et al., "A Long-Term Analysis of the Historical Dry Boundary for the Great Plains of North America: Implications of Climatic Variability and Climatic

Change on Temporal and Spatial Patterns in Soil Moisture," *Geoderma* 274 (2016): 104–13.

9 Shortridge, *Middle West*.

10 Curtis F. Marbut, *Soils of the United States: Atlas of American Agriculture, Part III* (Washington, D.C.: U.S. Government Printing Office, 1935).

11 Dora Whitaker, "U.S. Time Zones in 1918," *The Sound of Shaking Paper* (blog), September 9, 2011, http://papershake.blogspot.com/2011/09/us-time-zones-in-1918.html.

12 "U.S. Time Zones," U.S. Naval Observatory (USNO), last modified November 17, 2015, http://aa.usno.navy.mil/faq/docs/us_tzones.php.

13 G. Griffith et al., "Ecoregions of New England | Science Inventory," US EPA, last modified March 15, 2010, https://cfpub.epa.gov/si/si_public_record_report. cfm?dirEntryId=209857.

14 John B. Weeks et al., *Summary of the High Plains Regional Aquifer-System Analysis in Parts of Colorado, Kansas, Nebraska, New Mexico, Oklahoma, South Dakota, Texas, and Wyoming: U.S. Geological Survey, Professional Paper 1400-A* (Washington, D.C.: U.S. Government Printing Office, 1988), https://pubs.usgs.gov/pp/1400a/report.pdf.

15 James S. Aber and Susan W. Aber, "Kansas Windscape—2016 Status," *Transactions of the Kansas Academy of Science* 119, no. 3–4 (2016): 395–405, doi:10.1660/062.119.0403.

16 "Special Map 9—Ground Water and Precipitation in Kansas," KGS—Water Resources—Ground Water Availability, last modified November 8, 1996, http://www.kgs.ku.edu/Hydro/hydroSheetMap.html.

17 Jon Lauck, "Dorothea Lange and the Limits of the Liberal Narrative: A Review Essay," *Heritage of the Great Plains* 45, no. 1 (2012): 4–37. James E. Sherow and John R. Charlton, *Railroad Empire across the Heartland: Rephotographing Alexander Gardner's Westward Journey* (Albuquerque: University of New Mexico Press, 2014), 212.

18 Kenneth K. Landes, "Scenic Kansas," *State Geological Survey of Kansas, Bulletin of the University of Kansas* 36, no. 18 (1935). John Charlton and Dan Merriam, "Ever Changing Landscape: Recent Topographic Landmark Erosion in Kansas," *Transactions of the Kansas Academy of Science* 106, no. 1–2 (2003): 29–39, https://doi.org/10.1660/0022-8443(2003)106[0029:ECLRTL]2.0.CO;2.

19 Jason Weems, *Barnstorming the Prairies: How Aerial Vision Shaped the Midwest* (Minneapolis: University of Minnesota Press, 2015), 140.

20 William S. Warner, Ron W. Graham, and Roger E. Read, *Small Format Aerial Photography* (Bethesda, MD: American Society for Photogrammetry and Remote Sensing, 1996), 348.

21 Terry Evans and Donald Worster, *The Inhabited Prairie* (Lawrence: University of Kansas Press, 1998), 73.

22 Marvin Bauer et al., *Proceedings of the First North American Symposium on Small Format Aerial Photography* (Bethesda, MD: American Society of Photogrammetry and Remote Sensing, 1997), 218.

23 James S. Aber and Susan W. Aber, *Kansas Physiographic Regions: Bird's-Eye View* (Lawrence: Kansas Geological Survey, University of Kansas, 2009), 76.

24 James S. Aber, Irene Marzolff, and Johannes B. Ries, *Small-Format Aerial Photography: Principles, Techniques and Geoscience Applications* (Amsterdam: Elsevier, 2010), 266.

25 U.S. Geological Survey, *United States of America* [map], 1:3,168,000 (Washington, D.C.: Bureau of Land Management, U.S. Department of the Interior, 1965), https://lccn.loc.gov/gm71000321.

26 James S. Aber, Firooza Pavri, and Susan W. Aber, *Wetland Environments: A Global Perspective* (Chichester, United Kingdom: Wiley-Blackwell, 2012), 421.

27 John J. Woods and B. B. Wilson, "Estimated Percent Change in Saturated Thickness, Predevelopment to Average 2014–2016, of the High Plains Aquifer in Western Kansas GMD No. 1," Kansas Geological Survey, Open-File Report (2016), 2016–19, http://www.kgs.ku.edu/Hydro/Publications/2016/OFR16_19/gmd1_change_st_predv_2014_2016_percent.pdf.

28 Aber, Pavri, and Aber, *Wetland Environments*.

29 John L. Zimmerman, *Cheyenne Bottoms: Wetland in Jeopardy* (Lawrence: University Press of Kansas, 1990), 197.

30 Robert L. Penner II, *The Birds of Cheyenne Bottoms* (Topeka: Kansas Department of Wildlife and Parks, 2010), 156.

31 Jim Hoy, "Pasture Burning in the Flint Hills," *Kansas School Naturalist* 39, no. 2 (1993): 3–7.

32 Rodger D. Applegate, Brian E. Flock, and Elmer J. Finck, "Changes in Land Use in Eastern Kansas, 1984–2000," *Transactions of the Kansas Academy of Science* 106, no. 3–4 (2003): 192–97, https://doi.org/10.1660/0022-8443(2003)106[0192:CILUIE]2.0.CO;2.

33 Charles E. Hoffhaus, *Chez les Canses: Three Centuries at Kawsmouth, the French Foundations of Metropolitan Kansas City* (Kansas City, MO: Lowell Press, 1984), 208.

34 Steven E. Ambrose, *Undaunted Courage: Meriwether Lewis, Thomas Jefferson, and the Opening of the American West* (New York: Touchstone, Simon & Schuster, 1996), 521.

35 "Cumulative Estimates of Resident Population Change and Rankings: April 1, 2010-2016-United States-Metropolitan Statistical Area; and for Puerto Rico," *United States Census Bureau American FactFinder*, last modified March 2017, https://factfinder.census.gov/rest/dnldController/deliver?_ts=527935255188.

36 Gregory M. Franzwa, *Maps of the Santa Fe Trail* (St. Louis, MO: Patrice Press, 1989), 196.

37 Ian Frazier, *Great Plains* (New York: Farrar, Straus and Giroux, 1989), 290.

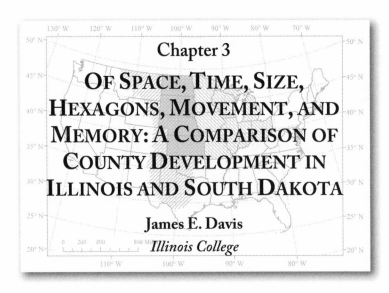

Chapter 3

OF SPACE, TIME, SIZE, HEXAGONS, MOVEMENT, AND MEMORY: A COMPARISON OF COUNTY DEVELOPMENT IN ILLINOIS AND SOUTH DAKOTA

James E. Davis
Illinois College

However defined, the Midwest is the largest region in the United States.[1] Its sheer size, its shape, and its location in North America foster immense variety within the region. Clearly, southeastern Ohio is markedly different from western North Dakota, and Missouri's boot heel is drastically different from Michigan's Keweenaw Peninsula. The Midwest knows yearly temperature variation of 160 degrees Fahrenheit. Near-desert conditions afflict portions of the region's High Plains, but the world's largest collection of fresh water blesses six Midwestern states. Although humid severe-winter continental climates (Dfa and Dfb) cover most of the Midwest, humid mild-winter subtropical climates (Cfa) prevail in the region's extreme southeast, and cold-winter semiarid climates (BSk) dominate the western portions.[2] More than any other region, the Midwest enjoys close ties with Europe via the Great Lakes-St. Lawrence River system and, simultaneously, close ties with Latin America and elsewhere via the Mississippi River system. Canada is still the United States' largest trading partner, the Midwest figuring prominently.

Two comparisons of counties in Illinois's to those in South Dakota help to highlight Midwestern diversity. Macro-comparisons show that the size and shape of Illinois's counties differ markedly from the size and shape of South Dakota's counties. A micro-comparison shows that one county in central Illinois is sharply different from one in western South Dakota in terms of how humans over time arranged themselves spatially. These dual comparisons highlight the distinctions between life in the core of the Midwest and life on the westernmost edge, where the Midwest becomes the Great Plains.

The land that forms new counties comes from one or more sources: unorganized territory; unorganized territory combined with land from an existing county; land lopped off an existing county; land lopped off two or more existing counties; land produced by merging two existing counties. In Illinois, the third and fourth sources produced most counties, the last source producing only one.[3] New counties usually bordered older counties; the few exceptions occurred where mining, military activity, or other anomalous activities attracted surges of people, especially adult males.

The creation of new counties in Illinois and South Dakota caused older counties to shrink. Recently settled regions contained the geographically largest counties. Consequently, poorly drained regions, mostly in north-central and eastern Illinois, contain Illinois's largest counties, which were settled late, largely via surges in the 1840s and 1850s. Arid western South Dakota contains South Dakota's largest counties, which were settled late. Small counties abound in southern Illinois and southeastern South Dakota, regions settled relatively early.

Illinois was settled much earlier than South Dakota, producing significant differences. Illinois attained statehood in 1818, and its last county was formed in 1859. South Dakota attained statehood in 1889, and its last county was formed in 1916.[4] Settlers poured into Illinois far longer (since 1699) than they poured into South Dakota. This helped create a huge population difference: in 2010, Illinois had 12,830,632 residents, while South Dakota had only 814,180.[5] In that year, Illinois had 231.1 people per square mile; South Dakota had only 10.7.

Illinois's counties are generally smaller than South Dakota's. This resulted from Illinois's early settlement and its population being fifteen times larger than South Dakota's. The average county in Illinois is 545 square miles. South Dakota's average is 1,150 square miles.

County size in South Dakota relates to when the counties were established. Older counties tend to be smaller. Thirty-seven counties existed by 1874. They averaged 1,150 square miles. Beginning in 1874, twenty-nine counties were created, their average size being 1,519 square miles. Newer counties were founded in the western part of the state.[6] Western South Dakota is semiarid and arid, with high evaporation rates, uncertain water supplies, and land largely good only for extensive livestock grazing. It never supported many people. Furthermore, unlike counties in southeastern South Dakota, newer counties west of the Missouri River did not enjoy sustained riverboat service.

In Illinois early county creation is not associated with small counties. In fact, older counties are somewhat smaller. By 1830, Illinois had fifty-one counties. They averaged 556 square miles. Fifty-one more counties were founded in 1830 or later, and they averaged 534 square miles. This is a bit surprising. Illinois's unusual settlement pattern influenced this development. Nearly all settlers in Illinois well into the 1840s were from the South. They used southern rivers and trails in Kentucky and Tennessee and the Ohio River to get to southern Illinois, and then they used the Mississippi, Kaskaskia, Illinois, and Wabash Rivers and primitive trails to settle southern Illinois. Significantly, very fertile lands in Illinois's north-central and eastern regions were settled relatively late. Although these counties had fertile soil and although some were created in the 1830s or earlier, the land was poorly drained, greatly inhibiting settlement until the late 1840s and 1850s, when experienced drainers from the Frisian Islands, wetlands ringing the Baltic Sea, and the English Fens arrived. They drained the land.[7] Also, during the 1850s, railroads arrived, shunting livestock and produce to market, enhancing society, and ratcheting settlement.[8]

Six counties in Illinois are larger than 900 square miles. All of them are in east-central or eastern Illinois.[9] However, many small counties founded after 1829 in northern and central Illinois offset these large counties. Of the eleven counties smaller than 300 square miles, six were founded after 1829. Moreover, of eighteen counties between 300 and 399 square miles, twelve were founded after 1829. In short, although the largest counties were founded after 1829, the average size of counties founded after 1829 was smaller than those founded earlier.

Not only are South Dakota's counties larger than those in Illinois, but they are also shaped differently, possibly significantly so. In analyzing county shapes in Illinois and South Dakota, this study excluded counties that border neighboring states. Being on a state line inhibits and distorts county economic and political developments. For example, counties often lose or gain territory from neighboring counties or combine with other counties to form new counties, but this cannot happen across state lines.[10] Accordingly, this study excluded 40 of Illinois's 102 counties, leaving 62; and it excluded 29 of South Dakota's 66 counties, leaving 37.[11]

It is interesting to note that when Illinois was a territory in 1810, it was organized into 2 large counties. In 1820, two years after it became a state, it had only 19, compared to the present number of 102. When South

Dakota was a territory in 1880, it already had 48 counties, compared to the present number of 66.[12]

This macro-comparison of county development in Illinois and South Dakota borrows from location theory, including packing theory.[13] Location theory focuses on the "laws" that influence human activities, including how people arrange themselves and their culture spatially. Packing theory can be understood as a method of analyzing the most efficient manner of fitting items into particular places. Several constraints assist the analysis of these two states. For example, both states are assumed to consist of uniform plains, with a uniform distribution of soils, transportation, population, purchasing power, knowledge, motivation, and other socioeconomic conditions. All conditions being equal, the size and shapes of counties would be identical.[14]

Given these constraints, to maximize administrative efficiency of any county, the county should be, in theory, circular in shape. Moreover, to attain maximum efficiency, county seats should be located at the center of circular-shaped counties. This reduces the distance services in each county seat would have to travel to reach people and reduces the distance for people traveling to the county seat. But circular-shaped counties present a problem: they exclude some regions (see illustration 1). Clearly, no county service reaches people in these excluded regions.

Fortunately, this lamentable problem has a solution: simply keep expanding each circle until every excluded region is included in one or more counties (see illustration 2). This solution, however, creates another problem: the expansion of counties to include everyone necessarily results in previously excluded regions being included in two counties, not one (the shaded regions in illustration 2). This problem also has a solution: bisect longitudinally the overlapped (shaded) regions, and assign half to each of the two counties. This makes each county a regular hexagon of equal size, and all previously excluded regions are included in a county—just *one* county (see illustration 3). This solves the problem of excluded regions, but the solution has a price tag: compared to circular-shaped counties, regular hexagonal-shaped counties are only 80 percent as efficient in providing services to residents. Still, regular hexagonal-shaped regions are nature's most efficient packing shape, excluding nothing that should be included and minimizing travel distance within each region.[15] The dynamics of nature demonstrate this reality.[16]

County shapes and sizes are dynamic. As noted earlier, they change over time, often swiftly. As new counties are cleaved from them, they shrivel and change shape.[17] Some Midwestern counties are not even a tenth of

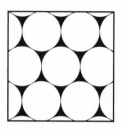

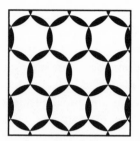

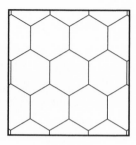

Illustration 1   Illustration 2   Illustration 3

their original size. Rivers and ridge lines form some county boundaries, and such "natural" boundaries resist change. But many newly created counties are rectilinear, often appearing as rectangles or squares. Even those that are not rectilinear have some straight-line boundaries. In general, the older the county, the greater the chance that its residents have arranged for it to border six neighboring counties. Counties bordering six other counties are morphing toward becoming regular hexagons, even if they never become regular hexagons. In short, over decades, counties not adjacent to state lines tend to border six other counties.

Evidence from the history of county development in Illinois and South Dakota supports this idea. In Illinois, sixty-two counties do not border on neighboring states. On the average, they border on 5.76 counties. Three counties border on only three other counties, four border on four other counties, seventeen border on five counties, twenty-four border on six counties, ten border on seven counties, three border on eight counties, and one borders on nine counties. In South Dakota, thirty-seven counties do not border on neighboring states. On the average, these counties border on 5.62 other counties. No county borders on just three neighbors, two border on four counties, fifteen border on five counties, sixteen border on six, two border on seven, one borders on eight, and one borders on nine. The difference between Illinois's average of 5.76 neighbors and South Dakota's 5.62 neighbors may seem relatively slight, but it supports the idea that over time counties tend to assume hexagonal shapes.[18] Since Illinois' counties are in the heart of the Midwest and were settled much earlier than South Dakota's, they have had more time to move toward the theoretical ideal. They thus highlight the distinction between counties in the central Midwest and those on the Great Plains fringe.

While these macro-comparisons show that the size and shape of Illinois's counties differ from the size and shape of South Dakota's counties, the analysis can go deeper. A micro-comparison shows that one county in central Illinois, Shelby County, is sharply different from one in western South Dakota, Meade County, in terms of how humans over time arranged themselves spatially. The macro-comparisons and the micro-comparison highlight Midwestern diversity and differences in geography and social development between the central Midwest and the Great Plains borderlands.[19]

Shelby County was formed in 1827, nine years after statehood, from Fayette County, to the south. It borders on eight other counties and encompasses 759 square miles. In 2010 it contained 22,363 people, giving Shelby County a density of twenty-nine persons per square mile. It is 22 percent urban. Its largest city is Shelbyville, the county seat and home to 4,700 residents in 2010.

Meade County was created in 1889, the year of statehood, from Lawrence County to the west. It borders on five counties and encompasses a whopping 3,483 square miles—South Dakota's largest county. In 2010 it contained 25,434 people, giving the county a population density of only 7.3 persons per square mile, about one-fourth the density of Shelby County. Meade County is 62 percent urban, almost three times more urban than Shelby County. Its largest city is Sturgis, the county seat, with 6,741 residents in 2010.

An examination of the two counties' rural populations reveals sharp differences, most of which are products of Meade County's aridity.[20] Although Shelby County is much smaller in area, it has fourteen unincorporated communities, compared to Meade County's eight. Shelby County has twenty-four townships, six of which have more than one thousand residents. Meade County has only seven townships, the most populous of which has fifty-nine people. None has more than one person per square mile! Meade County is still so close to its frontier origins that much of the western part of the county, stretching from Butte County down to Pennington County, is "unorganized territory."

Impressionistic comparisons of spatial arrangements of human activities in each county reveal much about the counties.[21] Since the mid-1800s, every corner of Shelby County has experienced various forms of sustained human activity. The county has brimmed with towns and hamlets, hundreds of farmsteads, schools and churches, roads and paths, railroad track, timber stands, saw and grist mills, township halls and maintenance sheds, cemeteries, gravel pits, coal mines, bridges, landing strips, drainage tiling, farm ponds, isolated general stores and gas stations, apple and pear orchards, nurseries, pastures for livestock, and tillage of fields of corn, soybeans, wheat, hay, and clover. Some apiary and horticulture undertakings also sprang up. Recent decades have seen the creation of state forests, state parks, county parks, dams, lakes and ponds, fish and wildlife areas and state recreation areas, as well as radio antennae and cell phone towers. A dense network of hardtop township and county roads, state highways, and even a slice of interstate serve motorists. Few residences are farther than a mile from a hardtop road. Gravel roads are few. Lanes connect farmsteads and other dwellings. In short, for decades immensely varied human activities flourished throughout the county.

Due to the systematic surveying mandated by the Land Ordinance of 1785, nearly all roads in Shelby County run north-south and east-west along township lines, section lines, and property lines, almost always crossing at right angles. Exceptions consist mostly of brief stretches of two or three miles of roads following pre-statehood trails, state highways, and Interstate 57 in southeastern Shelby County. A few other exceptions involve roads in rough terrain along Becks Creek, the Kaskaskia River, Richard Creek, and the Little Wabash River, mostly in southern townships. Northern townships contain practically no nonlinear stretches. Moreover, some roads heading diagonally do so in right-angle steps, following property lines, and not in diagonal or curved lines. Right-angle steps are found west and northwest of Herrick, southeast and east of Oconee, and south and northwest of Shelbyville.[22]

Roads changed over time. The checkerboard road system caused nearly all roads to cross at right angles, a product of early surveying via the Land Ordinance of 1785.[23] This arrangement served lumbering wagons well, the wagons making slow right-angle turns in changing directions. With the advent of stagecoaches, however, speed became important, so some right-angle intersections were transformed into curved intersections. And new bridges and improved fords also promoted speed. As railroads replaced stagecoaches, many curved intersections were eliminated, and property that had been appropriated for curves either reverted to original owners or was abandoned. With the advent of carriages and then, more importantly, automobiles shortly after 1900, speed was again important, and roads once again acquired curves. Later, some curves were banked.[24] Some comparable changes were made in compressed fashion in Meade County.

Throughout the Midwest, surveys required by the Land Ordinance of 1785 inevitably produced slight variations in north-south roads. North-south roads paralleled meridians, and meridians converge as they go northward, which meant the roads converged.[25] To compensate for this convergence, every twenty-four miles, north-south roads were doglegged a few hundred feet eastward or westward.

Time diminished or obliterated signs of human activities in Shelby County. For example, the village of Williamsburg, located at the south end of Williamsburg Hill, once contained a blacksmith, a carpenter's shop, a general store/post office, a mill, a church, and some houses. It is now abandoned, vegetation cloaking the ruins. Throughout the county, saw mills, churches, general stores, cemeteries, schools, railroad track, and hundreds of farm houses and farmstead buildings have disappeared, often without a trace. Orchards have vanished, as have hen houses, pastures, oat fields, and clover fields. Now, corn and soybeans constitute the bulk of acreage.

Southern Shelby County contained thick forests, which greatly shrank over the decades, wood being used for houses, buildings, fences, furniture, tools, cooking, heating, and more. Although fields replaced wooded places, tree lines separated fields and provided cover for game. In the late 1900s, as people left the land and farmsteads disappeared, tree lines vanished to allow corn and soybean fields to expand. More recently, however, some pastures and fields have reverted to trash trees or weeds, and in remote places marijuana is a cash crop.

Mechanization drastically reduced the need for "hands," as farm labor was known. Many rural residents now commute to work in Shelbyville, the county seat, or to towns outside the county, including Charleston, Effingham, Vandalia, Pana, Taylorville, Decatur, or even Springfield, the state capital. Some work part-time at home, and many tend gardens. Nurseries employ some. Beginning in the 1960s, ranch-style houses sprang up on the edges of villages and on isolated farmsteads, often replacing abandoned houses.

Similar changes occurred in South Dakota's Meade County, often in accelerated fashion. The county, especially its vast countryside, was never thickly settled.[26] The most intensive human activity in most places in Meade County is, ironically, extensive livestock grazing. Ranches, few and far between, are often tucked downwind from ridge crests, often on south-facing slopes that also host irrigated gardens. Trees windward and sunward of houses provide some shelter.

Three narrow strips encompass nearly all sustained human activity in Meade County, and even these strips have gaps of declining activity or inactivity. Perhaps four-fifths of the county's residents live in these three strips. A highway is each strip's spine, and each meets in or near Sturgis, the county seat in the county's far west. U.S. 212 running from Faith, a community in the county's extreme northeast, to Newell, in Butte County, meets SR 79, which drops south to reenter Meade County before joining SR 34 near Sturgis. SR 34 runs from Howes in eastern Meade County west to Sturgis. And I-90 enters Meade County near Blackhawk and runs by Piedmont and Tilford before reaching Sturgis and heading northwest. (SR 73 runs parallel to Meade County's eastern border, connecting Howes to Faith and traversing extensive grazing lands. Maurine, located on US 212, once boasted a general store/gas station, a post office, a social hall, and some fourteen residents. Perhaps two live there now.) The county's improved road network is thin and sparse, only a fraction as dense as Shelby County's. Many roads are unimproved trails, practically no one living along them.[27] The three strips create an "all-or-nothing" reality. Within the three strips much human activity is possible, but outside the strips little is possible.[28] Shelby County has no such "all-or-nothing" condition. Some South Dakotans practice suitcase farming. Landowners and farm managers commute to farm lands ninety miles or more from the towns in which they live. Some farms have equipment sheds, which sometime serve as dorms for suitcase farmers. Suitcase farmers often "stack demands," shopping and transacting business in county seats or elsewhere while commuting. Illinois has few suitcase farmers, and most make short commutes.

One way to understand Illinois is via its two regions, one region north of I-80 and the other south of I-80. Northeast of where I-80 and I-39 intersect are Chicago and its collar communities. Northwest, rolling hills host dairy farms and struggling towns. Much of America's wheat belt in the mid-1800s lay north of present-day I-80. And the Free Soil Party and then the Republican Party thrived in much of the region and in central Illinois.[29] South of I-80, vast tallgrass prairies roll down eastern and central Illinois to beyond Springfield, trees flourishing in groves and along watercourses. Gentle glacial landforms provide topographical variation. Hills south of Hillsboro, Pana, and Mattoon culminate in rugged, forested lands south of Carbondale, Marion, and Harrisburg. The Corn Belt dominated central Illinois beginning in the mid-1800s. Nineteenth-century Democrats, often of a southern strain, dominated most of downstate Illinois during the Civil War, and Copperhead sentiment flared, sometimes violently. In recent decades Republicans have dominated downstate counties.

South Dakota's basic regional division is the Missouri River. Beginning near Chamberlain, High Plains rise abruptly.[30] The region is unglaciated, semiarid to arid, windswept, and largely devoid of good soil and lush vegetation, the Black Hills being something of an exception. The region orients to Rapid City and Sturgis. If it is still part of the Midwest, it is on its western fringe. The rest of South Dakota, with better soil and sufficient precipitation, is more Midwestern, in general keeping with the farm country of Iowa and Minnesota.

In important ways Meade County and South Dakota are more "modern" than Shelby County and Illinois. Meade County and South Dakota are still gaining population, but Shelby County and Illinois are not. Shelby County had 2,972 residents in 1830, grew to 23,476 in 1870, and peaked in 1900, reaching 32,126. Since then it lost population in eight of the eleven censuses, plunging by 2010 to only 22,363. Farm mechanization produced this decline. After 1960 the county lost only about 1,040 residents, but its downward trajectory continues. Many other downstate counties experienced peak populations in the late 1800s or early 1900s, some then plunging 50 percent or 60 percent by 1910. Moreover, the remaining population is aging.

In 1890, Meade County contained 4,640 people. By 1910 it surged to 12,640. After slumping to 9,367 by 1920, it climbed back to 11,482 by 1930, before tumbling to 9,735 in 1940. Since then, however, it has enjoyed steady growth, reaching 20,717 by 1980 and 25,434 by 2010. It shows no sign of abating. In addition, compared to Shelby County, Meade County has relatively more young residents, relatively fewer elderly, and more Hispanics and other minorities. Shelby County's median age was 43.5 years in 2010, and Meade County's was 35.9 years. Poverty for those under eighteen in Shelby County was almost 17 percent, while in Meade County it was only 12.1 percent. On the other hand, poverty among those over 65 was somewhat higher in Meade County.

Examinations of county sizes, shapes, and populations generate significant understandings. Other examinations—less systematic examinations—of landscapes also have value. Much of north, central, and eastern Illinois is gently undulating and is now largely devoid of forests or even sizable woods, with most existing trees hugging water courses and other low-lying land. Much of hilly southern Illinois and western Illinois is still heavily wooded.

Undulating "seas" of billowing tallgrass and occasional "islands" of timber and peninsular "points" of timber in the grassy "seas" impressed early travelers.[31] Travelers perched on recessional moraines and other glacial land forms and gazed across vast stretches of prairie grass, but few places were sufficiently high for travelers to see great distances. Also, in some places vegetation on glacial landforms and along water courses inhibited views. Moreover, high relative humidity, especially in warm months, and haze from smoke from vast grass fires and other particulate matter from summer to late fall distorted and inhibited vision.

South Dakota offers grand vistas to visitors. Forests and timbered regions are confined largely to the Black Hills, parts of southeastern South

Dakota, and along water courses and other low-lying stretches. Relative humidity in warm months is low, well under 50 percent, especially in the western regions, and relatively few fires greeted travelers. Consequently, splendid vistas abound, enabling visitors to clearly see objects forty miles away. However, frequent sharp winds combine with aridity to reduce visibility by blasting dust and sand across the landscape. This is rare in Illinois.

Still, vistas in South Dakota can deceive, especially in the semiarid region west of the Missouri River. For example, views at Ben Ash in Meade County reveal undulating terrain in all directions. Numerous other sites in that region offer similar spectacular views. But such views can be misleading, deceptive, and even dangerous. Objects forty miles away may be surprisingly clear, but objects forty feet away may be hidden. Wind-whipped grasses and bushes, driven dust and sand, color variations in vegetation and soil, rapidly moving cloud shadows, and eroded undulating terrain conceal much. During the Plains Wars such concealed places spawned many surprise attacks.

Humans and nature shaped the Midwest, but they shaped different regions in varied ways. Since the 1790s, surveyors measured, encompassed, bounded, divided, regularized, and ordered the land. Land offices sold the packaged land. Vast forests and windswept plains were New Edens, places for people to begin anew, and people relentlessly imprinted culture on the land. The Land Ordinance of 1785 and the Northwest Ordinance of 1787, reflecting Enlightenment assumptions and Natural Law realities, were conservative instruments that operated cautiously to produce radical and even revolutionary results: Ordinary people acquired secure titles to land. Political power moved westward with the population. No colonies developed in the West, and no new war for independence was needed. And yet these successes were tempered by contingency, whimsy, irrationality, and misinformation. Moreover, nature was not passive: rivers meandered, hail fell, drought flared, farms failed, towns shriveled, and people moved on, or aged, or died. Illinois and South Dakota developed differently, partly because their dates of settlement were decades apart, their climates and soils were different, available technologies were different, and the country's economy, politics, and society had evolved. At the same time, however, some truths that may be universal operated, causing counties to change size and shape, road patterns to evolve, and rural populations to generally shrink, age, and concentrate. Many of these trends continue.

Notes

[1]   In this study, the Midwest includes the following states: North Dakota, South Dakota, Nebraska, Kansas, Minnesota, Iowa, Missouri, Wisconsin, Michigan, Illinois, Indiana, and Ohio. This region comprises 750,524 square miles, or 21.22 percent of the United States. It is home to 67,745,108 people, or 21.08 percent of the country's population.

[2]   According to the modified Koppen climate classification system, a D type climate is a humid midlatitude climate with severe winters. Shelby County is in a Cfa type climate, just south of the southern border of the D type climate region, and Meade County is in a BSk climate type, just west of it.

In the D type climate, the average temperature of the warmest month is above 50 degrees Fahrenheit, and the average temperature of the coldest month is below 32 degrees. The letter "f" indicates that it has no dry season. The letter "a" indicates that the average temperature of the warmest month is at least 71.6 degrees Fahrenheit. The letter "b" indicates a climate in which the average temperature of the warmest month is below 71.6 degrees, but at least four months have an average temperature of above 50 degrees.

A Cfa climate is a midlatitude climate and dominates the southeastern United States. The average temperature of the warmest month is above 71.6 degrees, and the average temperature of the coldest month is between 64.4 degrees and 32 degrees. The letter "a" indicates that the average temperature of the warmest month is at least 71.6 degrees. The letter "f" indicates there is no dry season.

A BSk climate is a semiarid climate with cold winters. It is cold steppe. The average annual temperature is below 64.4 degrees Fahrenheit, and annual temperatures may range from well over 100 degrees to below -50 degrees.

[3]   For county formation in Illinois, see James E. Davis, *Frontier Illinois* (Bloomington: Indiana University Press, 1998), especially 320–28.

[4]   Several counties in South Dakota were abolished over the decades, becoming part of neighboring counties. Washabaugh County, founded in 1883, was the last to be abolished. In 1983 it was divided into three parts and given to Jackson, Pennington, and Shannon Counties.

[5]   Illinois is shedding more population than any other state, losing 37,508 persons in 2016. The population first declined in 2014, when it lost 11,961 residents. Most go to Sun Belt states. Smaller declines afflicted Michigan, Wisconsin, Indiana, Missouri, and Iowa. Marwa Eltagouri, "Illinois Loses More Residents in 2016 than Any Other State," *Chicago Tribune*, December 21, 2016.

[6]   All of the largest counties, all comprising more than 2,200 square miles, in South Dakota are west of the Missouri River: Butte, Corson, Dewey, Harding, Meade, and Pennington. Conversely, thirteen counties contain fewer than 600 square miles, and all are in southeastern South Dakota: Bon Homme, Buffalo, Clay, Davison, Douglas, Hamlin, Hanson, Jerauld, Miner, Moody, Sanborn, Union, and Yankton.

[7]   Robert W. Frizell, "Reticent Germans: The East Frisians of Illinois," *Illinois Historic Journal* (Autumn 1992). See also, Davis, *Frontier Illinois*, 389.

[8]   Railroad development in Illinois surged in the mid-1850s, after most cities, towns, and even villages were founded. Most early railroads radiated from Chicago, reaching out to existing communities. Occasionally, however, the arrival of the railroad preceded town formation, especially in regions settled during the 1850s in east-central and north-west Illinois. Douglas K. Meyer, *Making the Heartland Quilt: A Geographical*

History of Settlement and Migration in Early-Nineteenth-Century Illinois (Carbondale and Edwardsville: Southern Illinois University Press), 2000, especially 40–41 and 77–79.

9 These counties and their founding dates are as follows: Champaign (1833), Cook (1831), Iroquois (1833), La Salle (1831), Livingston (1837), and McLean (1830).

10 It is possible that "one of the most fruitful areas of research on boundaries was found to be the impact of boundary change." Julian V. Minghi, "Boundary Studies in Political Geography," *Annals of the Association of American Geographers* 53, no. 3 (September 1963): 427. State boundaries rarely change, and the changes are usually slight, but territorial and county boundaries have histories of repeated change, often drastic change.

11 Counties in Illinois: Bond, Brown, Bureau, Cass, Champaign, Christian, Clay, Clinton, Coles, Cumberland, DeKalb, DeWitt, Douglas, DuPage, Effingham, Fayette, Ford, Franklin, Fulton, Greene, Grundy, Hamilton, Henry, Jasper, Jefferson, Johnson, Kane, Kendall, Knox, LaSalle, Lee, Livingston, Logan, Macon, Macoupin, Macon, Marion, Marshall, McDonough, McLean, Menard, Montgomery, Morgan, Moultrie, Ogle, Peoria, Perry, Piatt, Putnam, Richland, Saline, Sangamon, Schuyler, Scott, Shelby, Stark, Tazewell, Warren, Wayne, Washington, Williamson, Woodford.

Counties in South Dakota: Aurora, Beadle, Brule, Buffalo, Clark, Coddington, Davison, Day, Dewey, Douglas, Edmunds, Faulk, Haakon, Hamlin, Hand, Hanson, Hughes, Hutchinson, Hyde, Jackson, Jerauld, Jones, Kingsbury, Lake, Lyman, McCook, Meade, Mellette, Miner, Potter, Spink, Sanborn, Stanley, Sully, Turner, Walworth, Ziebach.

12 G. Edward Stephan, "Variation in County Size: A Theory of Segmented Growth," *American Journal of Sociology* 36, no. 3 (June 1971): 453.

13 Geography is the study of features on or near the surface of the earth and relationships among those features. Location theory in human geography attempts to answer an essential question: "How do we explain the location of features on the surface of the earth?" Another way of putting it: "Why are things located where they are?" In answering these questions, geographers, economists, anthropologists, historians, and others have often formulated "laws," truths that seem to govern processes that account for the location of features. Some laws are highly deterministic, while others are probabilistic. Some are static and ignore changes in reality, while others are dynamic and take changes into account. Packing theory involves finding effective ways to pack objects into finite space, including the number of houses in a subdivision, the number of moving vehicles on a freeway, and the number of people in office spaces.

14 Of course, in reality, one or more of the constraints is not present. They are said to be "relaxed" when they are not present. For example, if population is not uniformly distributed throughout a region, then that constraint is relaxed.

15 August Losch relaxed constraints in *The Economics of Location* (New Haven: Yale University, 1954), *passim*. Arthur Getis and Judith Getis offer a critique of "Christaller's Central Place Theory," giving reasons why it "is not found in the real world" ("Christaller's Central Place Theory," *Journal of Geography* 65, no. 5 [1966]: 224–25). Similar thought is found in Leslie J. King, "The Analysis of Spatial Form and Its Relation to Geographic Theory," *Annals of the Association of American Geographers* 59, no. 3 (September 1969): especially 593–94. Ruth Hottes reveals Christaller's political journey in Germany, joining the National Socialist Party in 1940 and the Communist Party in 1951. His academic reputation in the United

States was established during the 1960s. Hottes, "Walter Christaller," *Annals of the Association of American Geographers 73*, no. 1 (March 1983). Support for Christaller's theory is found in Neil Weber, "A Comparison of the Central Place Hierarchy Pattern of Central Indiana to the Walter Christaller Model," *Proceedings of the Indiana Academy of Science* 79 (1969).

[16] For understanding of the role of regular hexagons in allowing maximum efficiency in packing in a closed area, with minimal movement, see Peter Haggett, *Locational Analysis in Human Geography*. New York: St. Martin's Press, 1966, especially 48-53, Richard L. Morrill, *The Spatial Organization of Society, Second Edition*. Belmont, California: Wadsworth, 1974, especially 73–82, and Arthur H. Robinson, James B. Lindberg, and Leonard W. Brinkman, "A Correlation and Regression Analysis Applied to Rural Farm Population Densities in the Great Plains, *Annals of the Association of American Geographers*, 52:2, June 1961, 214. Walter Christaller, studying regional markets in southern Germany in the 1930s, devised Central Place Theory and the role the hexagon played in understanding the locations and operations of human settlements within an urban system. Nature's creatures and forces have a predilection for hexagons: honeycombs, cooled basalt, soap bubbles in restricted space, snowflakes, and drying mud, to cite some.

[17] The role of politics in influencing county boundaries and, therefore, county shape and size is discussed in C. Edward Stephan, "Variation in County Size: A Theory of Segmental Growth," *American Sociological Review* 36, no. 3 (June 1971): especially 460.

[18] The idea that older and smaller counties in Illinois and South Dakota border on more neighbors than newer, larger counties remains to be studied.

[19] Shelby County is in south-central Illinois, where undulating prairie in the northern quarter of the county meets forested hills that cover about two-thirds of the rest of the county. Meade County is on the High Plains in western South Dakota, well beyond the Missouri River and the 100th meridian.

[20] This aridity is accentuated by summer drought. John R. Borchet, "The Climate of the Central North American Grassland," *Annals of the Association of American Geographers* 40, no. 1 (March 1950): especially 12–18 and 33.

[21] Much of the following stems from personal observations of Shelby County (some of which began in the 1940s) and more recent observations of Meade County. County atlases and other map sources provide context for the personal observations.

[22] *Illinois Atlas & Gazetteer*, 3rd ed. (Yarmouth, ME: DeLorme, 2000), 62 and 70.

[23] The Land Ordinance of 1785 was revolutionary in what it avoided and what it accomplished. In providing a systematic, orderly, and effective way of disposing of public land in the Old Northwest, the ordinance avoided the helter-skelter, inefficient, and inaccurate ways of disposing of public lands south of the Ohio River, where confusion over boundaries produced endless quarrels, lawsuits, hard feelings, and even violence. Suffering from such chaos, Abraham Lincoln's father, Thomas, led his family from Kentucky to Indiana, where the Land Ordinance of 1785 produced relative precision, certainty, and confidence in land ownership. It arranged for the land to be surveyed before sale, creating six-mile-square townships. The land was offered for sale in 640-acre units for $1 per acre. Relatively few people could afford to buy 640-acre units, but land development companies and wealthy individuals often purchased these units and then made portions of them for sale to persons of ordinary means. Congress set aside the sixteenth section in each township for the maintenance of public school. This subsidy for schools and the orderly nature of land

sales via the ordinance generated vibrant nationalism and ties between the central government and settlers. In short, the ordinance got land into the hands of people, money into the federal treasury, and confidence into the public concerning the West. For a thorough discussion of the Land Ordinance of 1785, see Hildegard Binder Johnson, *Order upon the Land: The U. S. Rectangular Land Survey and the Upper Mississippi Country* (New York: Oxford University Press, 1976), especially 37–58.

[24] Davis, *Frontier Illinois*, 365–66, 475.

[25] The problem of converging meridians and its solution are ably discussed in Johnson, *Order upon the Land*, 57–58.

[26] Holdings on the Great Plains were large from the beginning of settlement. Mechanization merely accelerated the formation of large holdings. E. Cotton Mather, "The American Great Plains," *Annals of the Association of American Geographers* 62, no. 2 (June 1972): 254.

[27] *South Dakota Atlas & Gazetteer*, 2nd ed. (Yarmouth, ME: DeLorme, 2007), 27–28, 37–38.

[28] The stark all-or-nothing realities in South Dakota, especially in the region west of the Missouri River, manifest themselves in severe gyrations in weather, grasshopper attacks, railroad developments, and other facets of history. For examples and efforts to resist the gyrations, see Herbert S. Schell, *History of South Dakota*, 4th rev. ed. (Pierre: South Dakota State Historical Society Press, 2004), especially 80, 113–15, 119–21, 161–67, 223–24, 232, 237–38, 255, 257–58, 261–62, 282, 289, 291, 295, 334.

[29] John C. Hudson, *Making the Corn Belt: A Geographical History of Middle-Western Agriculture* (Bloomington: Indiana University Press, 1994), 125–29.

[30] A superb contrast of the region west of the Missouri River to the region east of it in terms of culture, land patterns, economics, politics, attitudes, flora, fauna, climate, and other facets is James D. McLaird's "From Bib Overalls to Cowboy Boots: East River/West River Differences," *South Dakota History* 19, no. 4 (Winter 1989): 454–91.

[31] Allan G. Bogue, *From Prairie to Corn Belt: Farming on the Illinois and Iowa Frontiers in the Nineteenth Century*, reprint ed. (Ames: Iowa State University Press, 1994), 3–5.

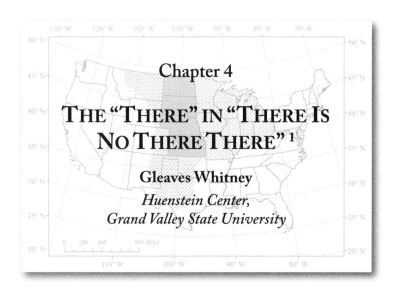

Chapter 4

THE "THERE" IN "THERE IS NO THERE THERE"[1]

Gleaves Whitney

Huenstein Center,
Grand Valley State University

The Significance of the Midwest and Great Plains

With all due respect to Gertrude Stein, if there is any region about which most Americans think "there is no there there,"[2] any region that they feel is "boring,"[3] it is North America's vast interior plains. Described by geographers as "a gigantic undulating swath of land,"[4] the nation's so-called flyover stretches hundreds of miles from the western base of the Appalachians, across the Midwest and Great Plains, to the eastern front of the Rockies. From the north it emerges out of the rock outcrops of the Canadian Shield, down through the great valleys of the Ohio, Mississippi, and Missouri Rivers, to the Ozarks and Balcones Escarpment. Given such an expanse, explorers, geographers, and historians have exquisitely parsed these vast interior plains into evocative identities: Quivira, *pays d'en haut*, Ohio Country, Northwest Territory, Heartland, Midwest, Corn Belt, Wheat Belt, agricultural core, Middle Border, sea of grass, Great American Desert, Coteau des Prairies, Coteau du Missouri, Badlands, High Plains, and Great Plains. Aside from a nod to Chicago, many elites on the east and west coasts are prone to think that the plains has few desirable characteristics, little distinctive identity, no functional center, and no interior borderlands. Thus, there is the tendency to transform the plains from place into space—from meaning to emptiness.[5] The un-California. Plain vanilla.

55

(It doesn't help that the word "plain" conflates topography that is largely nondescript with things that are tediously ordinary and lacking in beauty.)

For many of America's bicoastal intellectuals, especially those who subscribe to "the revolt from the village theory," modernity has turned the plains inside out. It's a remarkable reversal of perception. George Washington believed the plains was tantamount to "the second promised land"; Abraham Lincoln referred to the plains as "one of the most important [regions] of the world"; and Franklin Roosevelt praised the interior during World War II for cradling the "arsenal of democracy." Yet in the postwar decades, this heartland began to feel like a fringe—a fringe of culture, of society, of progress; a place emptied of people and meaning; a place regarded by many, as historian Jon Lauck likes to point out, as the stepchild of the coasts. Lauck reminds us that one of F. Scott Fitzgerald's most memorable characters, Nick Carraway, in describing the decline of his native Midwest, remarked that the region was transformed in the twentieth century from the "warm center" to the "ragged edge of the universe."[6] Yet a middle it remains, existing with adamantine stubbornness in the heart of North America.

Now, the people who live in, travel to, or write about the interior plains usually find something much richer than vanilla. One vicariously experiences that something in the pages of John Steinbeck, Robert Pirsig, and William Least Heat-Moon,[7] all of whose sensibilities vibrate at and even celebrate the middle. These writers experience the American plains as a web of discrete places imbued with meaning—whether it is the modernist vibe of Chicago, the stately bluffs above the Great River Country, or a cultural outpost like Manhattan, Kansas. Midwesterners take political pride in their native sons—in presidents such as Lincoln, Grant, McKinley, Eisenhower, Ford, and Reagan; in other prominent politicians including William Jennings Bryan, Henry Wallace, Arthur Vandenberg, George McGovern, and Robert Dole. Then there are movies set in the interior plains, vivid films like *The Bridges of Madison County*, *Field of Dreams*, *Dances with Wolves*, and *Fargo*, all of which convey a strong sense of place in the heart of the nation. "The case may be overstated," write scholars of regional geography, "but many popular images of America are based on life in the region."[8]

Extensive plains at the earth's middle latitudes tend to be corridors of history. Students of world history know it to be true of the European Plain, Eurasian Steppe, and Indo-Gangetic Plain. Similarly, students of the Midwest and Great Plains know that North America's interior is not meaningless space but contains much of significance to American history.

East of St. Louis lie the ruins of Cahokia, the capital of the oldest Native American civilization north of the Valley of Mexico; in the early twelfth century, Cahokia probably claimed more people than London. A few centuries later, in the western grasslands, Spaniards introduced the horse to Indians whose skill with the animal led to the development of the finest light cavalry on earth.

Near the headwaters of the Ohio are also sites of world-historical significance—at Jumonville Glen, Fort Necessity, Fort Duquesne, and other scenes in a contested middle ground—places where British, French, and Native American warriors waged a fierce imperial struggle that devolved, arguably, into humankind's first world war (1756–1763).[9]

After the United States achieved independence, the nation prosecuted another brutal war—a hundred-year war against the Native Americans who inhabited the interior. This prosecution began in the Ohio Country (1790) and ended at Wounded Knee (1890).

As aboriginal peoples were being forced from the best lands and resettled in the hardscrabble regions, the American project of founding a new republic was launched. The Old Northwest (1787) became our founders' first field of dreams, with Washington, Jefferson, Hamilton, and Adams offering competing views of what the new republic should become. Jefferson's agrarian vision stamped the landscape of the interior plains with the Cartesian grid of township-and-range lines. They would soon stretch from longitude 81° to 105° west—some 1,250 miles from the Pennsylvania-Ohio border to the Colorado Front Range and beyond.

The internal contradictions of the American founding would erupt on a Midwestern stage, not just in the military campaigns against Native Americans, but also in Bleeding Kansas, the dress rehearsal for the Civil War (1857). After abolitionist and proslavery forces suffered the American Iliad to come to Midwestern soil, in haunted places like Marais des Cygnes, the interior plains became the stage for other great icons of American life—the cowboy, baseball, motor car, jazz, Motown. Unfortunately, in recent years, the continent's vast interior plains has been the canary in the mine when it comes to globalization, a barometer of the storms that periodically toss and turn the American Dream. We can see the effects in episodes of depopulation in the High Plains and of deindustrialization in the Rust Belt whose abandoned factories pock the vast megalopolis known as ChiPitts.[10]

So there is lots of "there" there, plenty of thick meaning on the interior plains of North America, scenes of desperate historic struggle in the forging of the new republic.

Early Modern Borderlands, Modern Boundaries, Postmodern Transition Zones

Already in these fugitive observations one can discern that something interesting was happening in North America's interior plains. Here and there arose places of remarkable human agency—places that mixed vastly different Native American peoples, that melded aboriginal peoples with Euro-American colonizers, that mingled Northern and Southern sensibilities, and that merged Midwestern farmers with Western ranchers. Were these human interactions transactional, transformational, or both? To reach for metaphors: Was the geography where these interactions took place transition a zone that gradually blended one thing into another, like colors on an artist's palette? Or sharper, like the hash marks and lines on a football field? Or are they best likened to biological estuaries—the richest biomes on earth—which historians have come to call "borderlands"? Borderlands might be thought of as cultural estuaries. They are places characterized by complex human interactions that involve economic trading, social intermarrying, religious syncretism, cultural clashes, political contestation, creative accommodation, and sometimes bloody conflict in areas that lack a hegemonic power.[11]

To help answer these questions, historian Jon Lauck has proposed an act of rediscovery and recovery, a long-overdue project to revisit the idea of the Midwest vis-à-vis the idea of the Great Plains. The aim is to discover where there might be meaningful transition zones or historic borderlands between these two great interior provinces.

Lauck's project is a daunting act of rediscovery. That's because in recent decades the Midwest has been neglected as a subject of regional inquiry, in large part due to the drive to understand globalization. Likewise, inquiry into possible borderlands between the Midwest and Great Plains has been relatively neglected in the broader borderlands scholarship of North America (in contrast to inquiries into historic borderlands in the Southwest along the Mexican border, in the Great Lakes near the Canadian border, in the border states between the North and South, and in the Lower Mississippi Valley).[12]

Adopting what I call the "heuristic of the borderland" has great potential to cross-pollinate our thinking. It could help us reframe American history and geography in interesting ways, first by disrupting the conventional national narrative, that of the colonizing nation-state whose power radiates out from a core and weakens as it approaches a distant periphery. Such studies are encouraging historians to see the frontier as much more than a one-way process of east-to-west Americanization—the argument of the influential Turner thesis. Scholars have been looking into how frontiers are often borderlands that form cultural cores in their own right. It turns out that borderlands have their own strong sense of place and unexpected narratives of belonging and othering.[13] So the question is an intriguing one: To what extent have borderlands existed between the Midwest's agricultural core and Great Plains? To this question we can add another: How has the possible presence of borderlands in the heartland contributed to a better understanding of the American experience?

In addition to being a daunting act of rediscovery, Lauck's project is also an audacious act of recovery. Reexamining some of the primary sources between 1541 and 1931—from Coronado to John Wesley Powell to Walter Prescott Webb—reveals a host of observers who verbally described, visually depicted, spatially mapped, and historically interpreted perceived changes between the forest parklands and prairie parklands of the Midwest to the mostly treeless Great Plains. Many based their work on ecological and ethnographic criteria.[14]

A good question to ask is whether the ecological and ethnographic changes that Coronado's party observed (1541) amounted to subjective transition zones or to thoroughgoing cultural borderlands. They are different things. When the Spaniards approached the center of the continent from the southwest, they likely penetrated as far east as present-day Lyons, Kansas. Somewhere near longitude 97° or 98° west, they observed new species of flora and fauna as well as a greater variation of lifeways among the aboriginal peoples who were drawn to the proliferating variety of life. It is reasonable to infer that the Coronado expedition's interactions with the Native Americans in Quivira are what started the creation of borderlands deep in the interior of the continent.

Fast forward some 260 years. A good question to ask is whether the ecological and ethnographic changes that the cartographer Perrin du Lac indicated on his "Map of the Banks of the Missouri River" (1802) were transition zones or borderlands. If borderlands, were they waxing or waning at that point? The same questions can be put to Lewis and Clark, whose Corps of Discovery journeyed into the interior from the southeast. Near present-day Yankton, South Dakota, did they find themselves in a mere transition zone or a cultural borderland? Was that borderland waxing or waning?

The same questions hover over Pike's 1806 trek and Long's 1820 expedition; over Karl Bodmer's illustrations and Albert Bierstadt's paintings; and over a number of Oregon Trail accounts from the 1840s and 1850s—for example, those of Francis Parkman and Elizabeth Goltra.

John Wesley Powell certainly made no bones about the existence of a sharp ecological transition with ethnographic consequences. He etched the 100th meridian into the American consciousness. Dividing the more humid East from the more arid West, it was our country's most important longitude. As he explained, in 1890: "Passing from east to west across this belt a wonderful transformation is observed. On the east a luxuriant growth of grass is seen, and the gaudy flowers of the order *Compositae* make the prairie landscape beautiful. Passing westward, species after species of luxurious grass and brilliant flowering plants disappear; the ground gradually becomes naked, with bunch grasses here and there; now and then a thorny cactus is seen, and the yucca plant thrusts out its sharp bayonets."[15]

Examining these sources, historians could plausibly argue that there was a time, between two and four centuries ago, when the rich intersections of the tallgrass prairie parkland and the shortgrass prairie were more than ecological transition zones. Add human agency and they became cultural borderlands. These borderlands would have formed when the Spanish, then the French, and then Anglo-Americans began trading with, marrying, and living among each other as well as among diverse tribes of Native Americans. The encounters gave rise to bloodless and bloody clashes, to be sure, but also to the creative social accommodations that characterize borderlands.

To understand how this process would have unfolded in the prairie between the Midwest and Great Plains, it is helpful to take a detour through the work of such pioneering historians as Herbert Eugene Bolton, who helped launch borderlands studies in the Southwest, and Richard White, who helped establish the "middle ground" historiography in his work on the *pays d'en haut* (i.e., the Great Lakes and Upper Mississippi River Valley). Borderlands and the middle ground are closely related concepts, as historian Bradley Birzer persuasively argues.[16] The labors of Bolton, White, Birzer, and others have documented the complex processes by which borderlands and the "middle ground" come about when people of quite different cultures encounter and live among one another.[17]

The historical pivot in the prairies occurred when the Spanish introduced the horse to Native Americans. The impact was incalculable. Plains cultures evolved in a radically different direction from those who remained in the mostly agrarian woodland tradition. As masters of the horse, the Comanche people transformed not only their own culture—they were known, after all, as the Lords of the Southern Plains—but also others in response to them. Add to these Native American transformations the even more radical encounters between aboriginal peoples on the one hand and a succession of Spaniards, French, and Americans on the other, and it is easy to see how all the elements would have combined to make rich cultural borderlands possible after 1541.[18] Few realize, for example, just how influential French trappers and traders in the interior plains were, well into the 1830s. It is why a city like Fort Collins, Colorado, has the Cache la Poudre River ("The Hiding Place of the Powder") running through it; and that river, before it had a French name, had a Spanish name, as the Long expedition of 1820 discovered.[19]

Yet these cultural estuaries that we are calling "borderlands" did not remain robust. The evidence suggests that early modern borderlands arose in the heart of the prairie; the evidence also suggests that they existed only for a few generations. The most heartbreaking passages in the journals of Lewis and Clark concerned the fate of Indian towns reduced to ruins, wiped out by smallpox epidemics and other ravages. What was decimated first by disease was finished off by empire. All the borderlands in the interior plains were squeezed as the grip of American empire tightened.

There is an important exception to this story of declension. It occurred in the territory immediately south of the region we are studying. Birzer explains that a "fruitful area of middle ground study is nineteenth-century Indian Territory (now Oklahoma). During the 1800s, thousands of Indians moved (mostly forced) there, creating new homes and communities. For the most part, the federal government left them alone, and these 'domestic dependent nations' thrived. Yet, again, few historians have studied these Indians, the sovereignty they enjoyed, or the relative economic prosperity in which they lived. These 'civilized' Indians, living in political limbo, clearly constituted a middle ground. They had significant economic ties to neighboring whites, they were western pioneers, and they served as a buffer to the hostile plains tribes."[20]

However, to the north, in the tier of states from Kansas to North Dakota, remnant borderlands declined earlier, and to a greater degree, than in Oklahoma. As the country's growing managerial and industrial classes imposed the iron cage of rationality across the land, modernity bleached out all but the most resistant colors in erstwhile borderlands. Traces of borderlands remained mostly in locales at the margins of the dominant white culture—near Indian reservations, Exoduster refugee settlements, and Latino migrant camps. By the late twentieth and early twenty-first centuries, globalization was accelerating the integration of North America's interior plains into the world's economy, with the result that erstwhile cultural borderlands between the Midwest and Great Plains all but disappeared.

If the middle ground and cultural borderlands in this part of the world were largely a thing of the past in the late nineteenth and early twentieth centuries, it does not mean that the idea of boundaries lapsed into irrelevance. They are just very different things. Borderlands are the center of something; boundaries, the edge of something.

When Frederick Jackson Turner wrote his landmark 1893 essay, "The Significance of the Frontier in American History," he relied on a scientific consensus that there was a line of demarcation between the Midwest and Great Plains. Turner wrote of "natural boundary lines which have served to mark and to affect the characteristics of the frontiers," especially along "the Missouri [River] where its direction approximates north and south; [and] the line of the arid lands, approximately the ninety-ninth meridian."[21] Yet as Turner's work also implied, the disappearance of the frontier proceeded apace with the diminution of erstwhile borderlands, or the middle ground, in the heart of the country.

Some four decades after Turner, Walter Prescott Webb published his masterpiece: *The Great Plains* (1931). There could be little doubt that a significant transition line was logically necessary to his thesis. Webb called European-dominated areas "the Metropolis," while the rest of the world was "the Great Frontier." In the interior plains of North America, he identified the 98th meridian as a scientifically established boundary, tantamount to an "institutional fault" line. Indeed, "practically every institution that was carried across it [was] either broken and remade or else greatly altered." Thus, "the Great Plains environment . . . constitutes a geographic unity whose influences have been so powerful as to put a characteristic mark upon everything that survives within its borders."[22] This is as powerful an argument for regional differentiation between the Midwest and Great Plains as anything written in the previous four centuries.

Think about it: The fact that conquistadors, explorers, pioneers, settlers, and scholars felt compelled to identify perceived ecological, ethnographic, and institutional transitions between the Midwest and the Great Plains tells us something. To define the places and spaces between the two regions, to discover a middle ground or borderland or transition zone, to experience it and name it in the field—all reflect a persistent quest that goes back many centuries. This perennial human quest of discovery across the meridians—continued by the authors in this volume—defies the quip that there's no "there" there. That the search for transitions and borderlands persists also reveals that the issue is far from settled. Early modern borderlands, like the modern boundaries and postmodern transition zones that supplanted them, are fraught with the same definitional quandaries that other geographic ideas are. Although convention distinguishes between the Midwest and Great Plains around the 98th and 100th meridians—that is, somewhere through the middle or eastern parts of North Dakota, South Dakota, Nebraska, and Kansas—there is no consensus about the boundary. Is it a continuous line, an intermittent line, a continuous transition zone, an intermittent transition zone, a mental construct, all of the above, some combination of the above, none of the above, impossible to determine, or objectively nonexistent? Further, are the transition zones defined principally by the environment, ethnography, institutions, culture, or other criteria? How has globalization impacted the construction and deconstruction of borderlands? The possibilities push Aristotelian logic to the extremes. Writing about the intellectual difficulty of determining where the Midwest ends and the Great Plains begins, geographers Stephen Birdsall, John Florin, and Margo Price come close to presenting students with an unsolvable Zen koan:

> Boundaries between adjacent multifeatured regions [like the Midwest and Great Plains] are seldom sharp and well defined on the landscape. Regions blend into each other, and travelers are often well into a new region before realizing they left the previous one behind. Boundaries between such regions are transition zones, not sharp lines. Because they are transition zones, the boundaries of a multifeatured region are difficult to map. . . . [Since] the boundaries of many regions are fairly broad transitional zones . . . the mix of characteristics is so subtle or complex that it is difficult to assign the area to any one region. The margin between the Midwestern agricultural core and the Great Plains is an example of such a subtle change."[23]

It is not just boundaries and transition zones that are difficult to define; it's the very idea of geographic regions. That regions are regarded nowadays as mental constructs is not the invention of postmodernity. One can already see an expression of the notion almost a century ago in the work of economic geographer J. Russell Smith. In 1925, he wittily observed that no living person has ever visited hell, yet there are plenty of strong opinions about it. Some say it's hot; others, that it's cold. It's all a mental construct.[24]

The rise of postmodern sensibilities since the 1970s has reinforced the notion that there is no objective definition of regions or of the boundaries between them. Nowadays regional transition zones are regarded as intellectual constructs created for cultural, political, institutional, analytical, and pedagogical purposes. To this way of thinking, not just transition zones but the concept of a region like the Midwest is nearly impossible to pin down, as the cultural geographer James Shortridge took pains to argue in his 1989 book, *The Middle West: Its Meaning in American Culture*.[25] What constitutes Midwesternness in this amorphous region has been elusive and changing. Likewise, the Great Plains is often regarded nowadays as an intellectual construct, "an academic invention" of historians like Walter Prescott Webb that answered the contemporary needs of scholars, policy-makers, and novelists facing profound human tragedies during the Great Depression.[26]

So where does the effort to discern the transition between the two great regions leave us? A reasonable compromise that does no violence to common sense would be to acknowledge that nowadays some boundaries can be perceived between the Midwest's agricultural core and the Great Plains. We can describe the Midwest-Great Plains boundary as an inter-mittent line where geographic features warrant—for example, along the east-facing Missouri Escarpment in North Dakota and along the Missouri River in South Dakota; and as a broader transition zone in the gentler topography of central Nebraska and Kansas.

Those who travel through or fly over Kansas know, when they experi-ence it, that the eastern part of the state is not like the western part. Some-thing happened. Archetypal Midwestern scenes pass into High Plains panoramas that look and feel quite different. The former present us with farmlands, silos, and small-town Americana set in pleasant landscapes. The latter make a stronger impression on our sensibilities—this rangeland with its barbed-wire fences, windmills, water tanks, and cowboys on horses or in trucks. The High Plains has a Western feel, and everything on the land is dwarfed by an infinite and often dramatic sky.[27]

Factors That Lend Support to Constructing Transition Zones between the Midwest and Great Plains

When it comes to distinguishing between the Midwest and Great Plains, it is instructive to start with a satellite image of the United States at night. There is a striking transition between the higher density of electrically generated lights in the Midwest and the lower density of lights in the Great Plains. Roughly between longitudes 97° and 99° west—from just west of Grand Forks and Fargo in the north, down through Sioux Falls, to Lincoln, Salina, and Hutchinson in the south—there is an energy transi-tion zone.[28] So prominent is the dark Great Plains in a satellite image of the United States at night that it is tempting to fall back on Major Ste-phen Long's description of the region as the "Great American Desert," a place "almost wholly unfit for cultivation, and of course, uninhabitable for a people depending upon agriculture for their subsistence."[29]

This pattern of night lights accompanies other realities that help in the intellectual construction of a coherent transition zone. For instance, related to energy demand are the region's natural ecology (tallgrass prairie parklands versus shortgrass prairie), land use (farming in the Corn Belt versus ranching on the shortgrass prairie), original homestead size (160 acres versus 640 acres farther west), population density (generally lower as precipitation decreases to the west), less dense transportation networks (highways, railroads, airports), and relative proximity to human services (police, fire, ambulance, health care, post offices, schools).

During a more romantic age, writers translated the passage from the tallgrass prairie parklands of the Midwest to the shortgrass prairie of the Great Plains in terms of psychological states. One can see the different psychological states evoked in the literature and the paintings the region inspired. The picturesque prairie parklands of the Midwest were described as "beautiful" and "cultivated" because they evoked pleasure. By contrast, the dramatic skies and distant horizons of the Great Plains were considered "sublime," even "fearsome," because they could evoke terror.

This romantic distinction between the beautiful and sublime owes its origin to an important work of aesthetic theory by Edmund Burke.[30] One can understand the distinction this way. If a traveler, say, on the Oregon Trail is in the picturesque prairie parkland with its alternating prairies and woodland groves, and a thunderstorm appears, there are places to seek cover. The rain event becomes merely an interesting interlude in the journey. However, if that same traveler is exposed out on the shortgrass prairie of the High Plains, and a thunderstorm suddenly darkens the horizon, there is no place in the land to find cover. The watercourses are dangerous because they are prone to flash floods, and the long slopes are dangerous because of exposure to wind, hail, and lightning strikes. Such a storm inspires awe and terror.

Mari Sandoz described the awe and terror experienced by those with the courage to settle in the harsh Sand Hills of Nebraska. In a biographical passage about her father in *Old Jules* (1935), she noted the pride her father felt in his homestead, especially his orchard. One afternoon a fierce thunderstorm descended: "Suddenly the hail was upon them, a deafening pounding against the shingles and the side of the house. . . . One window after another crashed inward. Jules came in from the garden and sat hunched over a box before the house. All the trees were stripped, bark on the west and south, gone. . . . The corn and wheat were pounded into the ground, the orchard gone, but still they must eat."[31]

In Burkean terms, what Old Jules experienced is related to the land-scape paintings of Albert Bierstadt that overwhelm the viewer with their romantic sublimity. By contrast, the draftsman-like illustrations of Karl Bodmer convey the classical beauty of the region and its aboriginal inhab-itants. Subjectively, then, the transition between the Midwest and Great Plains might be described in terms of an aesthetic and psychological zone where both the beautiful and the sublime, both the pleasant and the terri-fying, are encountered in relatively equal measure: "both-and" not "either-or." This way of grappling with the transition zones of the interior plains merits further study.

Factors That Tend to Deconstruct Transition Zones between the Midwest and Great Plains

The column of states running down the middle of the nation—North Dakota, South Dakota, Nebraska, Kansas—are conventionally viewed as transition states between the Midwest's agricultural core and the Great Plains.[32] Paradoxically, every one of them possesses characteristics that tend to deconstruct both the idea and the reality of transition zones. First, the climate (gradations of mid-latitude continental), combined with signifi-cant rivers (Missouri, Platte, Republican, Kansas, and Arkansas) and the existence of large aquifers (notably the Ogallala), supports both farming and range-and-feedlot agriculture across longitudes that might otherwise be restricted to ranching and dryland farming; it's why the traveler sees cornfields and feedlots from the Scioto Valley in Ohio all the way to the Colorado Front Range.[33] Second, because of the relatively gentle topogra-phy that spans these longitudes, it has been easy to integrate the economic activities of both the Great Plains and the Midwest's agricultural core with the manufacturing core associated with the ChiPitts megalopolis to the east. And third, cultural and economic integration has also been achieved by the startling hydrologic fact that, except for a stretch of the Red River of the North, virtually all the region discussed in this chapter is drained by one river and its tributaries; the vast but unified Mississippi drainage basin lends geographic coherence to a considerable stretch of longitudes that otherwise might develop transition zones associated with watersheds (e.g., like that along the Rio Grande River).[34]

Facts are stubborn things, and scholars have mined plenty of geo-graphic and social data that deconstruct the notion of intellectually coher-ent transition zones between the Midwest and Great Plains. Examination of any good atlas of the interior of the United States readily does the work of deconstruction. For example, a soils map reveals that mollisols stretch well to the east of the 98th and west of the 100th meridians,[35] so a significant transition zone near these longitudes could not reasonably be constructed on the basis of soil orders.

Nor could a transition zone be based on many Euro-American migration patterns. For instance, in the twentieth century, settlers having German ancestry made up similar proportions of the general population in both the Midwest's agricultural core and the Great Plains. The distribution is even more noticeable when Germans from Russia are the focus.

Nor could a transition zone be constructed from the land survey system in use since the 1780s, or the technological adaptations used on the lands divided by that system. Both regions have been imprinted with the Jeffersonian grid. And both regions have seen the transformation of the landscape from "a patchwork of rugged Jeffersonian pioneers" to "a homogeneous grid for industrial agriculture." In other words, both regions now reflect the triumph of Hamilton's vision for the future republic.[36]

The extensive Ogallala Aquifer has likewise weakened the case for borderlands between the Midwest and Great Plains, especially in Nebraska and Kansas. After a devastating drought created the Dust Bowl and began nudging the Great Plains' shortgrass prairie eastward, President Franklin Roosevelt signed an executive order on July 11, 1934, that allocated $15 million for "the planting of forest protection strips in the Plains Region as a means of ameliorating drought conditions." It also stipulated that the U.S. Forest Service, Civilian Conservation Corps, and Works Progress Administration coordinate with local farmers to plant what came to be known as "great walls of trees"—windbreaks on the High Plains. Over the next seven years, the U.S. government and local farmers would plant more than 220 million trees as part of the Prairie States Forestry Project. These human-made shelterbelts led to eighteen thousand miles of windbreaks on some thirty-three thousand Great Plains farms, substantially changing the nature of the landscape where the Ogallala Aquifer could be tapped. Improbably, Kansas would grow its own "national forest."[37] Henceforward, the former transition zone between the mostly treeless shortgrass prairie of the Great Plains and the tallgrass prairie parklands of the Midwest would become blurred or obliterated.

Maps that get at the habits of the heart also tend to obliterate transition zones between the Midwest and Great Plains. What happens on football Saturdays is that Nebraskans in both the Midwest and the Great Plains cheer with equal fervor for the Cornhuskers on the gridiron. The same can be said of Kansans who cheer for the Jayhawks no matter what part of the state they reside in. What happens on Sunday morning is that both Midwesterners and Plainspeople go to church—in equal proportions and in some of the highest numbers in the United States. It matters not which side of the 100th meridian they reside on. What happens on Monday morning is that both Midwesterners and Plainspeople return to work that is directly or indirectly looped into the economic web of the "imperial city" of the interior plains: Chicago, the fourth-largest metro economy in the United States, has long been dominant across the Midwest and Great Plains.[38] What happens on Tuesday is that they vote Republican— very Republican. Only one time since 1940 has the tier of Midwest–Great Plains transition states—from North Dakota down through South Dakota and Nebraska to Kansas—not given its Electoral College votes to the GOP candidate in presidential elections.

What happens after they vote is that these people of the Midwest and Great Plains return to work that is directly or indirectly tied to Chicago's economy. Novelist Frank Norris described Chicago's economic tentacles in *The Pit* (1903): "The Great Grey City, brooking no rival, imposed its dominion upon a reach of country larger than many a kingdom of the Old World. For thousands of miles beyond its confines was its influence felt. . . . Her force turned the wheels of harvester and seeder a thousand miles distance in Iowa and Kansas. . . . It was Empire, the resistless subjugation of all this central world of the lakes and the prairies. Here, midmost in the land, beat the Heart of the Nation."

Case Studies That Obliterate Coherent Transition Zones between the Midwest and Great Plains

If borderlands and the middle ground are early modern, if boundaries are modern, and if transition zones are postmodern, then the notion that transition zones can be exploded is the ultimate in postmodern possibilities. Consider natural and cultural outliers. These outliers defy continuous lines on a map; they disrupt landscapes; they confound the geographer's attempt to create coherent regions.

Prominent examples from the physical geography of the interior plains come to mind. One is the geographic distribution of prairie environments. What does one do with a biome that stretches—here intermittently, there continuously—from the oak openings of Ohio to the prairie peninsula of Illinois, past the shelterbelts of the Great Plains, to the foothills of the Rockies? Another example is the Driftless Area, a northern region of the Midwest that ironically did not experience the most recent episodes of continental glaciation; thus, the landforms in the Driftless Area more closely resemble those in distant unglaciated landscapes south of the Ohio and west of the Missouri rivers than anything in the surrounding Corn Belt. Yet another striking example is the Black Hills whose montane elevations and lifeforms are more akin to the topography and ecology of the Rocky Mountains than to anything in the surrounding sea of grass.

Instances of outliers from physical geography naturally have human consequences. Take the stretch of tallgrass prairie called the Flint Hills. Straddling longitude 97° west in a part of Kansas that would otherwise be considered part of the Midwest's agricultural core, this region of limestone and chert hills was first named by Zebulon Pike (1806) on his trek across the southern part of the Louisiana Purchase. Subsequent generations of farmers did not do well in the Flint Hills unless they cultivated crops in the bottomlands; the poor soils on the higher slopes would not support large-scale corn cultivation, so Colorado and Texas ranchers moved into the region and brought with them the lifeways of cowboys in the American West. The Flint Hills to this day remain an unmovable island of the West—the largest stretch of cowboy country amid the Midwest's corn, soybean, and milo fields.

There are even more striking instances of cultural outliers that obliterate the notion of transition zones in the interior plains. A case in point: On the High Plains near the foothills of the Colorado Front Range are agricultural colonies that were established mostly by Midwesterners following the Civil War. Arguably the most successful of them is Greeley, Colorado, near longitude 104° west. The blueprint for this utopian community was drawn up not in the semiarid Great Plains but in rainy Europe by the French social theorist Charles Fourier (1772–1837). His radical experiments sought to better a society that was being wracked by the transformations of the Industrial Revolution. The aim was to attract men and women of high character, sober agrarians who would help establish a network of independent, self-sufficient "phalanxes." Fourier's idea was attractive to newspaperman Horace Greeley. He used his *New York Tribune* to promote the establishment of these utopian colonies in the open lands of the West.

In the 1860s, Ohio native Nathan Meeker (1817–1879) was moved to act on Fourier's vision and Greeley's editorials. Following the Civil War, he advertised for and selected hardy, morally upright agrarians—mostly Midwesterners, it so happened[39]—to migrate west and establish the agricultural cooperative. It would originally be called Union Colony. In the face of numerous detractors, Meeker's gambit was gutsy. Sensible people thought it a fool's errand. Greeley, after all, is at the margin of the High Plains in the rain shadow of the serrated knife-edge of the Rocky Mountains. Warned an editorial in 1870: the colony's location was "the last place on this terrestial [*sic*] ball any human being should remove to . . . a barren, sandy plain, part and parcel of the Great American Desert."[40]

Against all odds, Meeker and the agrarians who founded the colony successfully reiterated one of the foundational acts of civilization: they embraced the social virtue of cooperation and established a reliable irrigation system for the crops and livestock that were developed in the Midwest. Soon Greeley resembled communities a thousand miles to the east. Because of irrigation, the colony thrived and became a veritable island of the Midwest at the western margin of the so-called Great American Desert.

Other ways transition zones have been obliterated rely on more subjective criteria. A case in point is the work of the historian Charles Beard. In 1921, he wrote utterly without nuance when describing the deadening "uniformity of the Middle West . . . the endless succession of fertile fields spreading far and wide under the hot summer sun. No majestic mountains relieved the sweep of the prairie. Few monuments of other races and antiquity were there to awaken curiosity about the region. No sonorous bells in old missions rang out the time of day. . . . The population was made up of plain farmers and their families engaged in severe and unbroken labor. . . . There was a certain monotony about pioneering in the [Old] Northwest and on the middle border. . . . Happiness and sorrow, despair and hope were there, but all encompassed by the heavy tedium of prosaic sameness."[41] Beard's sentiment already expressed, one century ago, the insouciance the middle of the country has come to expect from elites on the coasts.

Where Borderlands Survive: As a Metaphor for the American Public Square

In this chapter we have examined the complex ways in which people have thought about the lands where the tallgrass prairie parklands of the Midwest intersect with the shortgrass prairie of the Great Plains. We have outlined how early modern cultural borderlands on the prairie originated, grew, and declined. Their demise in the nineteenth century was supplanted by the scientific search—in John Wesley Powell, Frederick Jackson Turner, and Walter Prescott Webb—for modern longitudinal boundaries. In recent decades, postmodern transition zones have been constructed, deconstructed, and even obliterated. Paradoxically, out of the confusion there may arise, once again, novel kinds of borderlands.

Robert Frost said somewhere (I liberally paraphrase): history is a way of remembering what it would impoverish us to forget. Although prairie borderlands have mostly disappeared, we should not forget them. After all, it is quite possible that borderlands are reappearing—new kinds of borderlands—this time, associated with urban areas across the interior plains. At least four significant changes in American life since the 1960s have a bearing on the possible reappearance of borderlands in the interior plains: dramatically different demographics compared to the 1960s, as the once-white majority declines relative to the immigrant population from developing countries; the red-blue political divide seen in most post–Cold War elections, especially in 2016; shifting patterns of urban, suburban, exurban, and rural habitation; and the culture wars that Americans continue to fight. All these factors involve geographic areas of conflict and accommodation that seem to resemble the historic borderlands and middle ground that scholars have been studying for more than a century.

The possibilities for the future of borderlands studies are limited only by our imagination. Take the marketplace of food, perhaps the perfect postmodern expression of the ambivalent and ambiguous. It occurs to me that ethnic restaurants and markets might be characterized as "accordion borderlands," expanding when customers from a variety of backgrounds come to eat and shop, and contracting when they return home. Such fluidity may define the twenty-first century borderland.[42]

I'd also maintain that the idea of borderlands retains potency in our language—as metaphor. Just as Frederick Jackson Turner claimed that the American intellect owed much to the idea and the reality of the frontier,[43] so it is indebted to the idea of borderlands.

Whatever else they are, the transitions that intermittently weave in, out, and through longitudes 98° and 100° west are not so much lines of demarcation as zones of tension—not "either-or" but "both-and"—sharing characteristics of both the Midwest and the Great Plains.

Could such zones of tension help Americans know themselves better? I believe so. The diverse natural and cultural zones between the Midwest and Great Plains unwittingly provide a geographic metaphor for the American experience itself. The notion of a complicated American middle—a contested middle of contrasts, contradictions, ironies, polarities, paradoxes, and tensions—is well known and much commented on. Does this notion not describe the clash of diverse and sometimes irreconcilable values in a vibrant democracy? Whether conservative or liberal, Republican or Democrat, progressive or libertarian, the political challenge Americans perpetually face is how to reconcile such binary values when they clash in the "political estuary" of the public square: republic and empire; natural aristocracy and popular culture; core ("back East") and periphery ("frontier West"); liberty and equality; freedom and order; individual and community; private property and the commons; profit versus that which is priceless; founding families and subsequent immigrants; tradition and novelty; creative destruction vis-à-vis the permanent things.

Historically the majority of Americans have not been ideologues. They have given allegiance neither to the Far Left nor to the Far Right, but reside somewhere in the pragmatic middle, between the proverbial forty-yard lines. As a people we have succeeded in keeping the binary values that clash in the public square in dynamic tension. It is a productive tension not unlike that found in the land and people in the middle ground where the Midwest and Great Plains meet and mingle—these borderlands that generate their own zone of dynamic tension—a cultural estuary, as it were, that enriches our understanding precisely because of its dynamic tensions.

Might the notion of contested and accommodated borderlands be the most characteristic geographic expression of the American idea?

Notes

1   I have lived either in the Midwest or near the Great Plains virtually my entire life. I've attended three universities in the interior plains. Since 1960, I have crossed the 100th meridian by car more than sixty times; by plane, more than forty times. Since that first family vacation to Del Rio, just beyond the 100th meridian, I have been fascinated by the diversity of American landscapes and have wondered much about the subject of this chapter. Indeed, my first book, *Colorado Front Range: A Landscape Divided* (Boulder, CO: Johnson Books, 1983), was about ecological and indigenous borderlands. On the journey I have incurred many debts to people who know more about North American landscapes than I do. It gives me pleasure to acknowledge the generosity of scholars and friends with whom I have spoken and by whose work I have profited: above all, Jon Lauck, who is the historian extraordinaire of the Midwest; also the late Andrew Cayton, John E. Miller, Herbert Krause, Bill McClay, Ted McAllister, Peggy Ford Waldo, Khader Jabbar, Paul Groger, Robert Larkin, J. Stuart Krebs, Elizabeth Wright-Ingraham, staff at the James Michener Library, staff at the Flint Hills Discovery Center, graduate students at Running Creek Field Station, archivists at the University of Kansas, archivists at Colorado State University. I also wish to acknowledge two texts at the outset that were formative to my thinking about borderlands. My good friend Bradley Birzer wrote a brilliant synthesis, "The Middle Ground: Historical Intermixing of Cultures" (http://www.theimaginativeconservative.org/2012/07/the-middle-ground-historical.html), that helped me frame the argument. And one of the formative texts in my geographic education, which I encountered years ago as an undergraduate, is *Regional Landscapes of the United States and Canada* (any edition), by Stephen S. Birdsall, John W. Florin,

and (later) Margo L. Price; they informed my academic understanding of the Midwest's manufacturing core vis-à-vis its agricultural core and the Great Plains, as well as the transition zones between them.

2　Although Gertrude Stein's mordant line refers to the disappearance of her home and transformation of her neighborhood in Oakland, CA, it is subject to much misinterpretation. For a good explanation of what Stein meant, see Wilfred M. McClay, "Why Place Matters," in *Why Place Matters: Geography, Identity, and Civic Life in Modern America*, ed. Wilfred M. McClay and Ted V. McAllister (New York: New Atlantis Books, 2014), 1–4.

3　Stephen S. Birdsall, John W. Florin, and Margo L. Price, *Regional Landscapes of the United States and Canada*, 5th ed. (New York: Wiley & Sons, 1999), 25–26, 271.

4　Birdsall, Florin, and Price, *Regional Landscapes*, 240.

5　For the debate between the humanistic geographers (who argue for the subjective importance of place) and the social science geographers (who advocate pursuing the science of space), see James R. Shortridge, *The Middle West: Its Meaning in American Culture* (Lawrence: University Press of Kansas, 1989), xiii; see also McClay, "Why Place Matters," 1–4.

6　Jon K. Lauck, *From Warm Center to Ragged Edge: The Erosion of Midwestern Literary and Historical Regionalism, 1920–1965* (Iowa City: University of Iowa Press), 1–9; Washington's view of the future Midwest as the "second promised land" is from Gleaves Whitney, "The Upper Midwest as the Second Promised Land," in *Finding a New Midwestern History*, ed. Jon K. Lauck, Gleaves Whitney, and Joseph Hogan (Lincoln: University of Nebraska Press, 2018), 281, 302.

7　John Steinbeck, *Travels with Charlie: In Search of America* (New York: Viking, 1962); Robert M. Pirsig, *Zen and the Art of Motorcycle Maintenance: An Inquiry into Values* (New York: William Morrow, 1974); William Least Heat-Moon, *PrairyErth: A Deep Map* (Boston: Houghton Mifflin, 1991).

8　Birdsall, Florin, and Price, *Regional Landscapes*, 26.

9　Fred Anderson and Andrew Cayton, *The Dominion of War: Empire and Liberty in North America, 1500–2000* (New York: Viking, 2005).

10　See https://www.prb.org/us-megalopolises-50-years/, accessed April 5, 2018.

11　See Birzer, "Middle Ground." For a wide-ranging exploration of the idea of borderlands, see Pekka Hamalainen and Samuel Truett, "On Borderlands," *Journal of American History* 98, no. 2 (September 2011): 338–61.

12　Many historians argue that the field of borderlands studies got its start in the work of Herbert Eugene Bolton in the first decades of the twentieth century; see *The Spanish Borderlands, a Chronicle of Old Florida and the Southwest* (1921). Among the most famous Boltonians was David J. Weber.

13　Hamalainen and Truett, "On Borderlands," 338–61.

14　A highly regarded model of compiling primary sources in the regions under consideration is Paul M. Angle's *Prairie State: Impressions of Illinois, 1673–1967, by Travelers and Other Observers* (Chicago: University of Chicago Press, 1968). Compare Angle's book with John Mack Faragher's *Sugar Creek: Life on the Illinois Prairie* (New Haven: Yale University Press, 1987), a masterful weaving of source materials into a historical narrative.

15　Powell quoted in Wallace Stegner, *Beyond the Hundredth Meridian: John Wesley Powell and the Second Opening of the West* (New York: Penguin, 1954).

16　Birzer, "Middle Ground."

17 Richard White, *The Middle Ground: Indians, Empires, and Republics in the Great Lakes Region, 1650–1815* (New York: Cambridge University Press, 1991, 2011).

18 Birzer, "Middle Ground."

19 See https://history.fcgov.com/explore/poudre-river, accessed April 16, 2018.

20 Birzer, "Middle Ground."

21 Frederick Jackson Turner, "The Significance of the Frontier in American History" (1893), any edition.

22 Walter Prescott Webb, *The Great Plains: A Study in Institutions and Environment* (New York: Grosset and Dunlap, 1931).

23 Birdsall, Florin, and Price, *Regional Landscapes*, 8.

24 See J. Russell Smith, *North America* (1925); for more about Smith's contributions to geography, see Otis P. Starkey, "James Russell Smith, 1874–1966," *Annals of the Association of American Geographers* 57, no. 1 (March 1967): 198–202.

25 James R. Shortridge, *The Middle West: Its Meaning in American Culture* (Lawrence: University Press of Kansas, 1989).

26 Note Birdsall, Florin, and Price, "The Great Plains are a recent addition to popular geographies" (*Regional Landscapes*, 268).

27 See my book that deals with four ecological borderlands (High Plains to juniper-oak transition to montane forests to boreal-subalpine forests to alpine tundra): Gleaves Whitney, *Colorado Front Range: A Landscape Divided* (Boulder, CO: Johnson Books, 1983). As dramatic as is the succession of borderlands in the eight-thousand-foot elevation change along the Colorado Front Range, one can encounter even more dramatic borderlands in the eleven-thousand-foot elevation change from the Colorado Desert at sea level in the Coachella Valley to the alpine summit of Mount San Jacinto in California.

28 See https://www.nasa.gov/sites/default/files/images/712129main_8247975848_88635d 38a1_o.jpg, accessed April 4, 2018.

29 Long quoted in Webb, *Great Plains*, 107.

30 Edmund Burke, *A Philosophical Inquiry into the Origin of Our Ideas of the Sublime and Beautiful*, 2nd ed. (1757).

31 Marie Sandoz, *Old Jules* (1925).

32 Birdsall, Florin, and Price, *Regional Landscapes*.

33 John C. Hudson, *Across this Land: A Regional Geography of the United States and Canada* (Baltimore: Johns Hopkins University Press), 197–201.

34 Birdsall, Florin, and Price, *Regional Landscapes*, 26.

35 See https://www.cals.uidaho.edu/soilorders/mollisols.htm, accessed April 6, 2018.

36 Jason Weems, *Barnstorming the Prairies: How Aerial Vision Shaped the Midwest* (Minneapolis: University of Minnesota Press, 2015), introduction.

37 Wilmon H. Droze, *Trees, Prairies, and People: A History of Tree Planting in the Plains States* (Denton: Texas Women's University, 1970); Thomas R. Wessel, "Roosevelt and the Great Plains Shelterbelt," *Great Plains Journal* 8 (Spring 1969): 58–62; and R. Douglas Hurt, "Forestry on the Great Plains, 1902–1942," presentation at "People, Prairies, and Plains," an NEH Summer Teachers' Institute on Environmental History, Kansas State University, 1996, 1997, at http://www-personal.k-state. edu/~jsherow/lesintro.htm, accessed April 6, 2018.

38 William Cronon, *Nature's Metropolis: Chicago and the Great West* (New York: W.W. Norton, 1992); Gary Brechin, *Imperial San Francisco: Urban Power, Earthly Ruin* (Berkeley: University of California Press, 1999).

[39] Peggy Waldo Ford, *Greeley*, Images of America (Charleston, SC: Arcadia Publishing, 2016); author interview with Waldo, July 27, 2017, Greeley Historical Museum.

[40] Editorial quoted in Ralph C. Morris, "The Notion of a Great American Desert East of the Rockies," *Mississippi Valley Historical Review* 13, no. 2 (September 1926): 199; my thanks to Jon K. Lauck for this reference.

[41] Charles A. Beard, *History of the United States* (New York: Macmillan, 1921), 243–44.

[42] Author interviews with Khader Jabbar, March–April 2018, Grand Rapids, MI.

[43] Turner, "Significance of the Frontier."

Chapter 5

"NEBRASKA IS, AT LEAST, NOT A DESERT": LAND SALES, FALSE PROMISES, AND REAL ESTATE BORDERLANDS ON THE GREAT PLAINS

Matthew S. Luckett
California State University, Dominguez Hills

bservers who read the noted government statistician and econo-mist Joseph Nimmo Jr.'s *Report on the Internal Commerce of the United States* (1885) might be forgiven for concluding that America's Western lands were practically worthless. "By virtue of its characteristics of soil, rainfall, elevation, and natural food supply," Nimmo declared, "this comparatively dry area is especially adapted to pastoral pursuits, and it appears to be probable that a large part of it will never be available for any other purpose." According to Nimmo, this description applied to approximately 44 percent of the nation's territory (excluding Alaska), thus constituting what he termed the "Range and Ranch Cattle Area." He marked its borders on a map, which shaded an expanse stretching from the Sierras to eastern Oklahoma, and from Brownsville (Texas) in the south to Calgary in the north. The Great Plains lies west of the area's eastern border, which waves like a broad stream up from Oklahoma into western Kansas, through central Nebraska, and into the Dakotas just west of the Missouri River. Within this space, the author also pointed out that "the range and cattle business of the Western and Northwestern States and Territories is carried on chiefly upon public lands," implying that for the most part private land acquisitions played a minor role in facilitating and capitalizing the region's chief economic activity.[1]

Joseph Nimmo's 1884 "Range and Ranch Cattle" map.[2]
Reprinted with permission from the Montana Historical
Society Research Center Library, Helena, MT.

Although Nimmo does not specifically attempt to map the Great
Plains, his definition of the "Range and Cattle Area" as a region distinct
from the agricultural lands farther east and along the Pacific coast seems to
preclude the Great Plains from any reasonable geographic interpretation
of the wetter, more fertile Midwest. However, his neatly drawn border did
not add any clarity to the question of where the Midwest ended or where
the Great Plains should start. The absence of a consensus borderline, and
the existence of this book, is due in part to the gradual geographic and
ecological transition zone between the High Plains country and the lowland prairies. This transition zone ensures that areas within it elude easy
categorization, and undercuts efforts to regionalize adjacent states. For
instance, in 1999 the *Nebraska History* journal explored this amorphous

boundary with several articles written in response to the question, "Where is Nebraska?" When Kent Blaser approached the question by evaluating whether Nebraska was a Western, Midwestern, or Great Plains state, he concluded that "there are several different answers" to the question depending on one's vantage point, although his personal preference at the time was to connect Nebraska to the Midwest.[3]

If the "real" interior border is elusive to modern Americans, who can base their determinations on satellite images, personal automobile wanderings, and centuries of accumulated historical and scientific information, it was even more so to settlers, travelers, businessmen, and politicians in the late-nineteenth century. Since regionalizations were less factual and more impressionistic, it was much easier for contemporaries to say and believe whatever they wanted. In a sense, then, the Great Plains was a blank (or, rather, a vast green) canvas for various people's hopes and dreams. For instance, homesteaders believed in the perennial American Dream, which was that yeoman farming provided a path to financial independence and republican respectability. But while yeoman farming required cheap or free land for prospective owners to occupy, agriculture itself required good soil, accessible transportation, and sufficient water—none of which were in ample supply on the Great Plains. Meanwhile, although boosters and businessmen were often cognizant of the perils of plains farming, they underemphasized the distinction between the Great Plains and the prairies. Some ranching firms, including the Bay State Livestock Company in Cheyenne County, Nebraska, cynically appealed to hopeful farmers and aspiring landowners when attempting to liquidate their land holdings.[4] Moreover, the concomitant land boom occurring throughout Illinois and Iowa's prairie belt helped fertilize farmers' optimism and inflate land values farther west, particularly since these flat, mostly treeless prairies closely resembled the homestead reserves in Nebraska in appearance, if not climate.[5] In either case, the borders were muted, and both land buyers and land brokers often based their optimistic interpretations of the plains climate on superstition and false information.

Some cattlemen lied to sell their land, while other ranchers evolved their thinking over time to believe that farming was possible with some help. Prior to the mid-1880s, ranchers minced no words about western Nebraska's aridity. Attempting to capitalize on as much public domain land as possible, ranchers and their investors pushed back against the homesteaders and sheepherders flooding into the region. Most believed that the region would never be cultivated. But the collapse of open-range cattle grazing in the mid-1880s challenged the ranching class as a whole and forced them to reconsider their business practices. Many successful ranchers, like John Bratt of the Equitable Farm and Stock Improvement Company, reconsidered the viability of irrigation, experimental agriculture, and dry farming as those with vast land holdings considered how to dispose of them. By the 1890s, some Nebraska ranchers joined farmers in believing that with the right tools the farming frontier could begin moving west again.

None of these points suggest a concrete border between the Midwest and the Great Plains, but a discussion of the Bay State Livestock Company's and the Equitable Farm and Stock Improvement Company's efforts to sell off their sizeable land holdings reveals something more complex: a sort of real estate borderland where old business models failed, necessitating creative and sometimes contradictory adaptations. The same yeoman farming cultures that dominated the Ohio and Upper Mississippi Valleys following the Northwest Ordinance crashed to a halt in western Nebraska. Meanwhile, although open-range cattle ranching as an economic modality had already conquered Texas and much of Mexico, it was doomed to fail farther north, succumbing ultimately to the climate and ecology of the northern Great Plains. In other words, if there is a true border between the Great Plains and the Midwest, it lies between the former's unpredictability and the latter's governability. The Great Plains tests people's visions of the land and is a place where broken dreams and failed schemes fill the distant horizon like waves of bluestem grass blowing in the wind.

Like many other large ranching concerns, the Bay State Livestock Company was the product of outside capital as a result of the cattle boom. English and Scottish investors infused the firm with over $700,000, and its President, G. W. Simpson of Boston, presumably furnished its geographically confusing name. The company began operating in northwest Nebraska in the late 1870s with nearly a million dollars in capital, which it used to acquire nearly 22,000 head of cattle. With its purchase of the already established Coad Ranch near Scottsbluff, it controlled vast swaths of what is now Banner and Cheyenne Counties, including much of the Sand Hills region. During the 1880s, as homesteaders began eyeing land under company control, Bay State began purchasing much of its range, mostly from the railroad, in hopes of boxing homesteaders out. As late as 1884 the firm grazed over 102,000 cattle on its lands.[6]

Yet by 1887, Bay State was looking for the quickest way to push its Nebraska holdings off its books, and the company rushed to pull up stakes and move farther west. In order to facilitate the process of liquidating its land holdings, the company published a pamphlet in 1887 advertising its

Cheyenne County, Nebraska, lands to prospective land buyers. In addition to land pressure from homesteaders that forced the company's purchase of otherwise free rangeland, the winter of 1886-87 hit Bay State hard. When the snow melted that spring, it revealed hundreds of thousands of frozen cattle carcasses across the region. The dead loss was estimated in excess of a hundred thousand, or about 75 percent of Bay State's herd. After this devastating blow, the Bay State Livestock Company decided to downsize its operations and sell off its vast Nebraska ranch.[7] But since most ranchers were also selling, not buying, Bay State focused its land sales pitch on a target audience long disdained by most of the region's ranchers: prospective farmers.

The allure of "free" homestead land was one thing, but convincing people outside of the region to purchase land in western Nebraska was a tall order. For one, the company fought against the blizzard of bad publicity that followed the disastrous winter earlier that year. The company tried to assuage concerns about the region's frosty climate by denying that the winter was really that bad. "The reported severe winters have done Nebraska much damage," the booklet claimed, but only because the reports themselves had a chilling effect on economic activity in the state. According to the pamphlet, "No report could be more erroneous. It is true severe snow storms sometimes prevail . . . but they are of short duration, and are on average more than five years apart." If that were not convincing enough, the pamphlet continued: "As soon as a reasonable percent of the soil is broken up, in the western part of the state men work in their shirtsleeves during the greater part of the winter months." In other words, Bay State claimed western Nebraska's climate was closer to that of California's Central Valley than to anywhere else in either the Great Plains or the Midwest.[8]

However, fears about the region's aridity dwarfed fading memories of the recent snowstorm. Many Americans simply did not trust the plains as an arable region, and with good reason: most lands west of the 100th meridian received less than twenty inches of rainfall a year, which made farming difficult if not impossible on most non-irrigated plots. Even today, historical markers in South Dakota point out the significance of the 100th meridian as "the EAST EDGE of the Great American Desert" and how "for two generations the Insurance Companies and other world-wide lending agencies would not, as a matter of agreed policy, lend a shiny dime west of this line."[9] To combat these concerns, the booklet focused on proving that Cheyenne County offered enough rainfall for successful farming. "To correct these mistaken ideas," the pamphlet states in the preface, "we have given proof and testimony sufficient to convince the unprejudiced mind that western Nebraska is, at least, not a desert." The pamphlet also addressed the 1877 Desert Land Act, which authorized the sale of 640-acre homesteads to settlers for $1.25 an acre in arid and semiarid Western lands. Perhaps hoping to convince those readers who may not have been otherwise impressed by the available "proof and testimony," the authors declared that they did not include the text of the act because "there is no desert in the state of Nebraska."[10]

The booklet continued to systematically dismantle any notion that the county lacked rainfall. For instance, in spite of a recent and widely publicized drought, the authors claimed that "sod corn was raised in many places that yielded between 25 to 35 bushels an acre . . . [and] potatoes, as large as can be found in any market, yielded from 100 to 250 bushels an acre—all this on upland prairie sod, and without any cultivation whatsoever." Because of this cornucopia of abundance, according to the booklet, "at the Omaha State Fair, 1886, Cheyenne County was awarded first premium on beets, turnips, and potatoes. WHAT A GLORIOUS RESULT!"[11]

If a severe drought could not diminish Cheyenne County's agricultural fertility, then the promise of wetter years in the future could only amplify it. Many prospective farmers (and perhaps even the boosters themselves) subscribed to geologist Ferdinand Hayden's theory that "rain follows the plow"—once farmers begin plowing the land, Hayden argued, the newly exposed soil would release moisture into the air, creating rain. Politicians and businessmen who were interested in selling Western land to a new generation of farmers quickly began to echo this claim.[12] The Bay State Livestock Company was no exception, claiming that "as the soil is broken up the rains increase," and that "it is a common saying among the Indians on the plains, 'White man come, rain come.'" Consequently, "as soon as a reasonable percent of the soil is broken up, the western part of the state of Nebraska will suffer less from drought than any other section of the United States east of the Rocky Mountains."[13] Although Bay State echoed a myth already made prevalent by other railroad companies attempting to sell land and boost ticket sales, widely available writings by John Wesley Powell and other contemporaries provided a less sanguine counter-narrative: that no amount of plowing could kick up a rainstorm.[14]

The pamphlet aggressively targeted other concerns and groups as well. The Bay State Livestock Company alleged that insects in Cheyenne County "seldom do much harm to crops," and it argued that the county's soil is "a deep black loam . . . exactly the same kind of soil which has rendered the valleys of California, Oregon, and Washington Territory so famous." It also directed lawyers and doctors to consider the benefits of owning land as the "basis of wealth," persuaded teachers to consider purchasing it as an investment, and even chided young men who remained unconvinced for their lack of courage. "If you feel, from all that is said, that an investment would be unsafe or unwise," the authors challenged, "then it would be well for you to never leave your home for the West."[15]

For comparison, in 1886, the Chicago, Burlington, and Quincy Railroad Company (CBQ) published a tract entitled *The Broken Bow Country in Nebraska, and How to Get There.* Like ranching firms, railroad companies did not shy away from hyperbole in their advertisements. As part of the Pacific Railway Act, railroad corporations received massive land grants, covering not only the railroad's right of way but also enough on the side for it to pay off its equally massive government loans.[16] These terms incentivized the creation of additional rail routes, oftentimes in areas that did not necessarily require rail service. Thus, in an effort to drum up some business along its new line to central Nebraska, the CBQ Railroad promised readers: "In time this boundless prairie will have a good growth of forest trees and be relieved of its present monotony. Not many years ago Eastern Nebraska was . . . considered almost a desert . . . and yet today it is one of the richest and most prosperous states of the West." The author also argued that rain follows the plow, noting that agricultural improvements "actually increased the amount of rainfall and moisture by the necessary 'give and take' principle of plant life."[17]

Although the CBQ Railroad exaggerated the country's potential and relied on magical thinking to tout its advantages, it also modulated its language more carefully than the Bay State Livestock Company. The booklet argued that the region was "admirable stock country"; recommended growing groves of trees to serve as windbreaks; and noted that while most of the residents lived in sod houses, they were "very cozy." Besides, the author objected, "How many [of you] have ever seen a sod house? It is often a very comfortable dwelling." While honesty is usually the best policy, railroads had one important reason to tell the truth: their future freight revenues depended in part on the area's economic success. Perhaps this is why the tract urged homesteaders to stick it out after reaching the area. "There is no 'kicking' [in Custer County] among the farming classes," the pamphlet claimed, "except those who would fail to be satisfied by wherever their lot may be cast, and who would complain of the golden streets of New Jerusalem because they were not edged with diamonds."[18]

In any case, the Bay State Livestock Company's situation was abysmal, and the subsequent landholders fared little better. For one, few farmers expressed interest in the land, and those who did could barely afford to pay for it. Most of the land sold for about $7 an acre, payable over the course of twenty years. Although this listed price was consistent with what speculators and landlords were charging in east-central Illinois and was actually higher than the average price per acre for railroad land in western Nebraska, the latter state lacked the former's history of successful agricultural production.[19] Suffice it to say the company failed to raise much cash. Moreover, few of the farmers who did purchase Bay State land successfully converted their holdings into profitable farms. Most vacated their plots by 1894, wholly abandoning Cheyenne County's "pure, bracing atmosphere" for better opportunities elsewhere.[20] Meanwhile, the Bay State Livestock Company, having already decided to abandon Nebraska, followed the receding cattle frontier west to Wyoming. They moved tens of thousands of cattle to the Big Horn Basin in 1886, where they continued to operate for another dozen years. Within a decade of their move to Wyoming, however, Bay State downsized to only about three hundred head of cattle. The company dissolved in 1898.[21]

Unlike the owners of Bay State, Nebraska rancher John Bratt ranged cattle in his own backyard. Established in 1870, the John Bratt and Company firm based its operations in North Platte. Bratt founded the firm with investment money from his former employers Isaac Coe and Levi Carter, after having gained their trust during his four-year tenure with their outfit. Bratt himself was an English immigrant, having moved to the United States in 1864. While most of his baggage was lost while en route to Nebraska, his accounting knowledge arrived mostly intact. Consequently, Bratt produced a voluminous set of ranching records that chronicled the growth of his company. Like other ranching firms, he suffered losses during the severe winters of the mid-1880s, but Bratt continued to invest capital and effort in his community, North Platte, and in Lincoln County.[22]

While the Bay State Livestock Company exaggerated the benefits of its land, John Bratt and Company claimed the ethical high ground. After incorporating and rebranding themselves as the Equitable Farm and Stock Improvement Company, Bratt and his partners, General Isaac Coe and Levi Carter, attempted to liquidate their land holdings. They initially focused their efforts on finding other investors who were willing to buy their business, but eventually they established their own real estate firm to help unload their property. John Bratt in particular later embarked on a variety of local projects to augment the land's productivity, funding irrigation canals in the area and encouraging agricultural experimentation. Although Bratt's plans did not succeed entirely, they illustrate a different set of responses to a common problem: the difficulty large landowners on the plains faced when unloading their land assets.[23]

Bratt began to seriously consider breaking up his partnership and selling the firm's land in 1895. He corresponded regularly with William Turpie, a real estate broker based in Columbus, Ohio, and attempted to sell much of the company's holdings to New York investors. Like Bay State, Bratt's company needed to raise some cash, though his liquidity problems were due in part to his partners' financial indiscretions. On New Year's Day in 1895, Turpie informed Bratt that he identified a man in New York, L. F. Davison, who was interested in purchasing the land. "I know [Davison and his partners] cannot help but like it," Turpie cooed. "Just as soon as we get word from you we will get together and get up the company papers. Then they will send a man out with me to look at the property." However, he cautioned, "I would not want to go out when there is a very big snow."[24] Angling for the quick sale, Bratt and his partners lowballed their asking price by January 17, reducing the price of all cattle and horses on hand to $15 a head. They also offered to reduce the investors' risk by offering to assume up to $100,000 of stock in the new enterprise. But Bratt also warned his Midwestern realtor against focusing his efforts on only one prospective seller, and he urged him to make haste:

> As you are aware the property will bear the fullest investigation, and we think taking into consideration the low price asked for the land and stock together with our agreement to assign all our interest in School land leases west of Birdwood Creek; the easy terms of payment, and our willingness to subscribe for a block of the stock equal in quantity to any other subscriber up to $100,000, we think it one of the cheapest properties ever offered for sale, and would seem that you ought not to have to go outside Columbus to market such a valuable property offered as it is, on such easy terms. In frankness to you, judging from his indefinite letter, think you would do well to rely on your own good judgment and your well known good business ability, rather than depend too much on Mr. Davidson.

Bratt later explained his urgency, noting that his "enterprise belongs to a Company of three men, and a portion of the Company are well along in years, and desire to reduce their business. Hence the proposal to sell the property at very low figure." However, according to Bratt's later autobiography, it would seem he was covering for his partners: "After disposing of our [land and cattle, we] did not come out with as much money as we should have owing to some very unfortunate deals made by [Isaac Coe], who seemed bent on a 'rule or ruin' policy, no doubt due to advanced age and broken-down health." In any case, Davidson's hesitation was justified, given that Bratt's "low" figure amounted to $484,422.50 for the company and all of its holdings, including over 123,000 acres of land, three thousand cattle, and four hundred horses. Ultimately the deal fell through, and, in March, Bratt's company settled for exchanging three quarters of its horse herd for real estate lots.[25]

Bratt's efforts to liquidate his firm's holdings—however ill-timed they were, considering the recent panic of 1893's overall effect on real estate speculation throughout the United States—reflected his desire to not only dissolve his former partnership but also reinvest his wealth into the local economy. Unlike the Bay State Livestock Company, whose officers mostly lived outside of the region, Bratt wished to continue living, raising his family, and doing business in western Nebraska. He went on to serve two terms as mayor of North Platte, leveraged his ranching wealth into profitable real estate and insurance businesses, and wrote several reminiscences about his days as a Nebraska cow-puncher turned cattle baron.[26]

Bratt's most lasting mark on the region, however, was geographical. He spearheaded several efforts in the region to build irrigation canals, many of which succeeded in crisscrossing Lincoln County. These projects began as early as 1893, when Bratt filed for permission in Keith County to divert up to 1,500 cubic feet of water per minute from the North Platte River in order to create an irrigation canal stretching east to Lincoln County. According to one news report, Bratt intended to irrigate over two thousand square miles of land with this water. "If Mr. Bratt covers this territory," the report cheekily noted, "he will surely need a big ditch." More importantly for Bratt and his business partners, the canal reached their land holdings along the North Platte River. Bratt believed that his land offered prime opportunities for sugar beet cultivation, and the new canal purportedly added considerable value to their massive ranch. However, since these lands were among those sold with the dissolution of his partnership with Coe and Carter, the canal was never built.[27]

Of those canal projects that were actually completed, Bratt's proudest—and most regrettable—achievement lay closer to home. In his autobiography, he touted the benefits of his Birdwood Canal, which stretched for twenty miles and watered over seventy-five thousand acres. Construction on the canal began in 1894 and concluded the following year. Birdwood Creek, which ran through his ranch in northwestern Lincoln County, supplied the water. "There is no better or purer water than that Birdwood

Creek water," Bratt maintained. "It possesses great medicinal properties and has been known to cure several bad cases of Bright's disease and kidney troubles. It should be piped to the city of North Platte for domestic use." Unfortunately for his neighbors, "schemers and promoters . . . persuaded the owners of land under or adjacent to [the canal] to form an irrigation district and bond it for about $25,000.00." This saddled the community with additional taxes, and Bratt estimated that the perpetrators responsible for creating the district pocketed over ten thousand dollars.[28]

Higher taxes notwithstanding, many local residents believed that the region's economic future depended on irrigation. Between 1889 and 1899, the amount of irrigated land in Lincoln County increased from 3,049 to 22,508 acres. Across Nebraska the number jumped more than tenfold to 145,000 acres, and by the end of the nineteenth century 1,300 miles of ditch stretched across the western part of the state. According to the 1900 Agricultural Census, irrigated farms produced nearly one million bushels of corn on nearly 34,000 acres of land, although the amount of acreage devoted to alfalfa outweighed the total amount of land used to grow corn and wheat combined. In North Platte, excitement over irrigation's successes was on full display when the town hosted the Nebraska Irrigation Association's first annual Irrigation Fair in October 1896. Western Nebraska's farmers showed up in force. "The famous delta of the Nile is no greater in its production of grains, grasses, and vegetables than is the Platte Valley of Nebraska—the Eden of the west," boasted one newspaper report, "and especially is this true of that section where irrigation is applied." Farmers along the Birdwood Canal and other regional irrigated waterways piled and plied their crops on the northern side of the agricultural hall, all fine specimens but "not much above the average of their kind."[29]

Some land buyers still needed convincing, however. In 1902 Bratt and his local real estate business partners published a pamphlet that advertised plots for sale near the Birdwood Canal. Similar in some ways to Bay State's and CBQ's earlier pleas, the booklet contains some familiar refrains: "The climate of Western Nebraska is the most delightful and healthful of any portion of the United States, absolutely free from malaria. . . . Summers have a sufficient amount of warm weather to produce good crops, and the nights are cool and pleasant. The winters are short and dry." Unlike previous attempts, however, this advertisement replaces hyperbolic claims with specific designs for the land in question:

> Experience has demonstrated that these lands are particularly well adapted to the raising of sugar beets and alfalfa, both of which are very profitable crops. An average crop

of beets on these lands will amount to about eighteen tons per acre. The beets sell for $4.50 per ton, making $81.00 per acre, while the cost of raising and harvesting does not exceed $25.00 per acre, and the beet tops that are cut off when harvesting are worth at least $10.00 per acre to feed to either hogs or cattle.

The pamphlet argued that the Platte Valley was also perfect for alfalfa cultivation, which was destined to become "the great money-maker" of the plains. Hardly aimed at capricious young men or naïve investors, Bratt's brochure was carefully, perhaps even sensibly, worded.[30]

Bratt's concern about his land's arability continued unabated. At the turn of the century, he and other locals lobbied for a state-owned sub-experimental (or laboratory) agricultural station to be built in Lincoln County.[31] Completed in 1903, this experimental farm claimed nearly two thousand acres and existed to maximize and optimize local farming outcomes. North Platters raised nearly $3,000 for the project, and Bratt chipped in $250 of his own money. But the station suffered from neglect and underfunding. In 1905, Bratt wrote University of Nebraska professor of agriculture E. A. Burnett in search of support, arguing that the station was necessary to demonstrate what could be grown in the region. "Good, honest, well-to-do citizens intent upon building a home have been continually locating in this belt of our state since 1890," according to Bratt, but only "some few have made a success while a majority lost all. . . . They did not know how or what crops to plant in this section to crown their efforts with success." Bratt demanded that the state further capitalize the project by granting it $50,000 in funds. Although Bratt did not get his wish, by 1920 the state had added a new $6,000 office and a dairy farm to the facility.[32]

The Bay State Livestock Company and the Equitable Farm and Stock Improvement Company represent a range of responses among firms with large, unsalable land holdings in western Nebraska in the late-nineteenth century. On the one hand, the Bay State ranch and similar businesses could publicly deny or confirm their lands' agrarian potential, depending on their needs. In 1885, the United States was better connected and more widely literate than at any previous point in its history, but information was widely suspect. The Bay State Livestock Company could not only lie with impunity—it could also convince possible land buyers with its false promises and, perhaps more significantly, help shape changing public attitudes about the Great Plains climate. "Rain follows the plow" was not just wishful thinking. It became conventional wisdom and was thus difficult to debunk. Even the boasts of the local press, like the report comparing Lincoln County's irrigated lands to the Nile Delta, contributed to this misunderstanding in spite of residents' intimate familiarity with the region's climatological limitations.

On the other hand, John Bratt's attempts to dispose of his land acknowledged and reckoned with the region's legacy of farming failures. He fought against popular misconceptions of the land, believing that real estate in Lincoln County would be inestimably more valuable if plots had water access and if farmers learned how to produce soil- and climate-friendly crops. By 1902, the federal government began to acknowledge the region's promise as well as its perils when President Theodore Roosevelt, himself a one-time rancher in the Dakota Territory, signed the Newlands Reclamation Act into law. This sweeping legislation directed money raised from Western land sales toward dams and irrigation canals in sixteen Western states. Incidentally, if one were to draw a circle around these states and color it in, the shaded area would roughly correspond to Nimmo's original map of the "Range and Ranch Cattle Area" from 1885. But while these lands were no longer worthless, it was by now clear to everyone that they required significantly more than a sharp axe, a sturdy plow, and buckets full of sweat to be productive.

Notes

[1] Joseph Nimmo Jr., *Treasury Department Report on the Interior Commerce of the United States* (Washington, D.C., 1885), part III, 99.

[2] Julius Bien & Co., "The Range and Ranch Cattle Area of the United States: 1884," in Nimmo, *Treasury Department Report*. Creator: Julius Bien & Co.

[3] Kent Blaser, "Where Is Nebraska, Anyway?" *Nebraska History* 80 (1999): 3–14.

[4] Bay State Livestock Company, *Description of the Bay State Livestock Co's Lands in Cheyenne County, Nebraska* (Omaha, NE: Rees Printing, 1887).

[5] Allan C. Bogue, *From Prairie to Corn Belt: Farming on the Illinois and Iowa Prairies in the Nineteenth Century* (Lanham, MD: Ivan R. Dee, 2011), 52–53. For a more recent (and positive) assessment of homesteading and its successes in Nebraska, see Richard Edwards, Jacob K. Friefeld, and Rebecca S. Wingo, *Homesteading the Plains: Toward a New History* (Lincoln: University of Nebraska Press, 2017), 23.

[6] Nellie Snyder Yost, *Call of the Range: The Story of the Nebraska Stock Growers Association* (Denver: Sage Books, 1966), 125–29.

[7] Yost, *Call of the Range*, 140.

[8] Bay State Livestock Company, *Description*, 6.

[9] N. Jane Hunt, ed., *Brevet's South Dakota Historical Markers* (Sioux Falls, SD: Brevet Press, 1971), 157. Historical markers noting the 100th meridian can be found along U.S. Highways 12 and 14 in South Dakota. A quick Internet search shows images of similar markers found from the Dakotas to Texas.

[10] Hunt, *Brevet's*, 4.

11 Hunt, *Brevet's*, 9.

12 Donald Worster, *A River Running West: The Life of John Wesley Powell* (New York: Oxford University Press, 2001), 359–60. For more information on advertising efforts specific to Nebraska itself, see James C. Olson and Ronald C. Naugle, *History of Nebraska* (Lincoln: University of Nebraska Press, 1997), 167–68.

13 Bay State Livestock Company, *Description*, 10.

14 Although Powell did not accept Hayden's reasoning, he did argue that plowing and deforestation increased runoff and erosion, which temporarily led to more water in streams. See Worster, *River Running West*, 346–50, 354–60.

15 Bay State Livestock Company, *Description*, 7, 9, 22–26.

16 For more information on problems plaguing the railroads, see Richard White, *Railroaded: The Transcontinentals and Making of Modern America* (New York: W. W. Norton, 2011).

17 Chicago, Burlington, and Quincy Railroad Company [CBQ], *The Broken Bow Country in Central and Western Nebraska, and How to Get There* (Lincoln, NE: Journal Company, State Printers, 1886), 3–10.

18 CBQ, *Broken Bow Country*, 3–10. By contrast, according to one recent book, Custer County's 324 successful homesteaders (prior to 1908) faced "environmental disasters" in a country that "was long considered a natural grazing land." See Edwards, Friefeld, Wingo, *Homesteading the Plains*, 70–72.

19 Bogue, *From Prairie to Corn Belt*, 61; Olson and Naugle, *History of Nebraska*, 165.

20 See Yost, *Call of the Range*, 143. For more information on the struggles farmers faced in this region, and how they pulled up stakes after only a few years, see David J. Wishart, *The Last Days of the Rainbelt* (Lincoln: University of Nebraska Press, 2013). Meanwhile, as many as one-third of homesteaders with mortgages lost their land to creditors, therefore reflecting the struggles of not just farmers and land sellers but financiers as well. See Allan Bogue, *Money at Interest: The Farm Mortgage on the Middle Border* (Ithaca, NY: Cornell University Press, 1955), 267, 273–74.

21 See Oscar H. Flagg, *A Review of the Cattle Business in Johnson County, Wyoming since 1882 and the Causes That Led to the Recent Invasion* (Cheyenne, WY: Vic Press, 1892), 25.

22 Bratt left behind so many records of his business affairs that they are housed in two different archival collections: one at the Autry Museum of the American West in Burbank, California; and the other at the Nebraska State Historical Society in Lincoln, Nebraska. For the Autry collection, see John Bratt Collection Ranching Records and Biographical Material, Autry Museum of the American West, Burbank, California. For the Nebraska State Historical Society collection, see Bratt, John, 1842–1918, RG4157.AM, Nebraska State Historical Society, Lincoln, Nebraska (hereafter referred to as Bratt MSS). Among published works, currently the best chronicle of Bratt's life and work is his autobiography. See John Bratt, *Trails of Yesterday* (Lincoln: University of Nebraska Press, 1921, 1980).

23 It is important to note that some railroad companies fit within this category as well. For instance, the Burlington's Lines West manager George W. Holdrege supported several dry-farming efforts in western Nebraska. See Olson and Naugle, *History of Nebraska*, 166.

24 William Turpie to John Bratt, January 1, 1895, Bratt MSS.

25 John Bratt to William Turpie, January 26, 1895, and January 28, 1895, Bratt MSS, Box 2, Folder 2; and Equitable Farm and Stock Company to Turpie, March 25, 1895, Bratt MSS, Box 2, Folder 2; Bratt, *Trails of Yesterday*, 292.

[26] Bratt, *Trails of Yesterday*, 290–302.

[27] *North Platte Tribune*, December 27, 1893; Bratt, *Trails of Yesterday*, 291.

[28] Bratt, *Trails of Yesterday*, 290–91; "Irrigation Canals in Lincoln County," *North Platte Semi-weekly Tribune*, December 24, 1901.

[29] U.S. Department of the Interior, *Twelfth Census: Statistics of Agriculture*, 869–70, accessed December 20, 2016, at https://books.google.com/books?id=DdJCAQAAMAAJ&dq; "The Irrigation Fair," *North Platte Semi-weekly Tribune*, October 13, 1896.

[30] "Irrigated Lands under the Birdwood Irrigation Canal, in Lincoln County, Nebraska," Bratt MSS, Box 3, Folder 3.

[31] Sub-experimental stations elsewhere on the plains enjoyed some notable successes in helping adapt commercial agriculture to semiarid climates. For an excellent overview of early dry-farming experimentation in Nebraska and across the plains, see Mary W. M. Hargreaves, "The Dry-Farming Movement in Retrospect," *Agricultural History* 51 (1977): 149–65.

[32] Bratt to E. A. Burnett, January 24, 1905, Bratt MSS, Box 2, Folder 12; Ira L. Bare and William H. McDonald, eds., *An Illustrated History of Lincoln County, Nebraska, and Her People: A Narrative of the Past with Special Emphasis upon the Pioneer Period of the County's History; Particular Attention Also Given to the Social, Commercial, Educational, Religious and Civic Development of the County from the Early Days to the Present Time* (Lincoln, NE: American Historical Society, 1920), 1:89, 297.

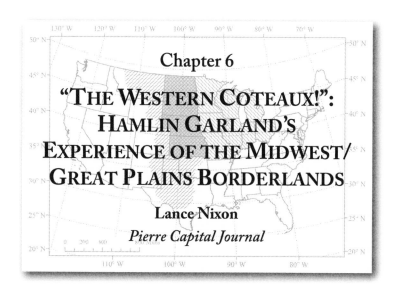

Chapter 6

"THE WESTERN COTEAUX!": HAMLIN GARLAND'S EXPERIENCE OF THE MIDWEST/ GREAT PLAINS BORDERLANDS

Lance Nixon

Pierre Capital Journal

I n 1909, the same year in which the Enlarged Homestead Act spurred a new wave of land claims in Western states by doubling to 320 acres the size of tract a homesteader could claim, the writer Hamlin Garland published a novel about an earlier era of homesteading. It looked back to his own experience nearly three decades earlier in Dakota Territory. Garland's father had been an enthusiastic settler in what is now Brown County in South Dakota, punching down stakes in 1881 when the original 1862 Homestead Act still limited a homesteader's claim to 160 acres. Shortly after his father settled there, Garland himself made a brief attempt at homesteading in the next county to the west, McPherson. The claim was about nine miles south of present-day Leola, South Dakota, on the SW1/4 of section 32, township 125N, range 67W.[1] Garland's fling with the land didn't last long. After experiencing the winter and boredom, dust, and wind that he describes vividly in his memoir, *A Son of the Middle Border*, Garland left Dakota Territory to seek his living as a writer in Boston in 1884, though he returned to what is now South Dakota again in 1887 and 1889.[2] Garland eventually won the Pulitzer Prize for biography in 1922 for *A Daughter of the Middle Border*, and he is probably best remembered today for the agrarian realism of his 1891 short story collection,

Main-Travelled Roads, in which he was already starting to mine his own homesteading experience as material.

Not all of Garland's writing is of the same quality, and his 1909 novel, *The Moccasin Ranch*, is all but forgotten now. But it is interesting for what it tells about homesteading at what is arguably the far western edge of the Midwest. Garland writes:

> And so at last they came to the land of "the straddle-bug"—the squatters' watch dog—three boards nailed together (like a stack of army muskets) to mark a claim. . . .
> It drew toward noon. Bailey's clear voice shouted back, "When we reach that swell we'll see the Western Coteaux." The Western Coteaux! To Burke, the man from Illinois, this was like discovering a new range of mountains.
>
> "There they rise," Bailey called, a little later.
>
> Burke looked away to the west. Low down on the horizon lay a long, blue bank, hardly more substantial than a line of cloud. "How far off are they?" he asked, in awe.
> "About twenty-five miles. Our claims are just about in line with that gap." Bailey pointed with his whip. "And about twelve miles from here. We're on the unsurveyed land now."[3]

There is no doubt that Garland's story is rooted in real geography because his nonfiction memoir refers to "the mysterious plain and a long low line of still more mysterious hills" that he experienced during his own homesteading venture.[4] His 1909 novel echoes the real experience in that *The Moccasin Ranch* also describes the alienation that he and other homesteaders experienced in Dakota in dealing with factors such as wind and drought and cold and the subsequent outmigration. Interestingly, Garland describes the actual landscape of that part of Dakota Territory as a sort of barrier or wall—the physical counterpart of what Garland and other homesteaders, like the people in his novel, experienced on a psychological level as they confronted a new geography where their Midwestern farming techniques and Midwestern lifestyle were no longer sufficient. He writes:

> One day a cold rain mixed with sleet came on, and when the sun set, the Coteaux to the west rose like a marble wall, crenelated and shadowed in violet, radiant as the bulwarks of some celestial city; but it made the thoughtful husband look keenly at the thin walls of his cabin and wonder where his fuel was to come from.[5]

This isn't only figurative language. The "wall" Garland describes is real. It is roughly at the 99th meridian, running in a north-south direction just west of U.S. Highway 281 on either side of the North Dakota/South Dakota border. It is as though Hamlin Garland, with his fascination for "the Middle Border," has blundered across a true border in the interior of the United States at which the middle ends. Here, where the land surges upward abruptly at the west edge of the James River Valley, is one of the few places where it is possible to say precisely where the Midwest ends and the Great Plains begins. At least that is how geographers have dealt with that same range of hills, as in a 1975 photo atlas that includes a satellite image of that same region of the Dakotas. The geographers note:

> The area covered by this photo-map represents portions of the Great Plains and the Central Lowlands. The division between the geologic provinces is apparent just west of Elm Lake and running parallel with the James River. A north-south trending ridge abruptly separates the Black Prairie lowlands to the east from the Missouri Plateau section from the Great Plains.[6]

Even if one did not know this ridge was there, the change is discernible from the elevations of certain towns on either of the North Dakota/South Dakota border that lie on either side of the ridge. At Ellendale, North Dakota, the first town north of the border on U.S. Highway 281, the elevation is 1,453 feet. At Ashley, North Dakota, forty-two miles west, the elevation is more than 500 feet higher—2,014 feet.

A 1978 bulletin on the soils of South Dakota from South Dakota State University agrees that there is a major change in geography at the west edge of the James River Valley. To the east of that line is the Central Lowlands. To the west of that line is the feature Garland describes as "the western Coteaux," or what geographers call, with slightly different spelling, the "Coteau du Missouri." It is part of the Missouri Plateau, which covers roughly the western two-thirds of South Dakota.[7]

John Paul Gries's *Roadside Geology of South Dakota* agrees that there is a major boundary between the Coteau du Missouri and the land to the east, but, in that text specific to South Dakota, Gries's map uses the term "James River Lowlands" to describe the lands immediately to the east.[8] He makes it clear that as far as geographers are concerned, that western coteau that Hamlin Garland saw looming on the horizon is a part of the Great Plains. "Between the James River Lowland and the deep valley of the Missouri River is a sinuous strip of high ground about 25 to 35 miles wide, the

Coteau du Missouri. It is a strip of the Great Plains separated from the plains farther west by the Missouri River."[9]

It is probably more common to think of the Great Plains in North America as beginning at the 100th meridian, which has acquired an almost mystical role in American history as the place where homesteader dreams often fell to ruin in the face of dwindling rainfall and poor soils. Even the Canadian rock band The Tragically Hip, in a song from a 1992 album, spoke of the 100th meridian as the place "where the Great Plains begin."[10]

Canadian writer Candace Savage, in her book about the North American prairie, allows for both of these views, noting that geographers have traditionally divided the prairie region into the Great Plains on the west and the Central Lowlands to the east. As Savage notes, "because there is no clear geographical feature to separate these zones, the boundary between them has never been fixed with precision," leaving some to choose the 100th meridian for the place where the plains begins while others put the line farther east to follow the curves of the Missouri River.[11] Savage solves the problem by using the term "Great Plains" to refer broadly to "the grasslands at the heart of the continent."[12] The curious result is that maps in her book include as part of the Great Plains parts of northwest and southern Minnesota, virtually all of Iowa but for a tiny portion of the northeast, and the northern half of Missouri.[13] More traditionally, the Great Plains would be considered to include North Dakota, South Dakota, Nebraska, Kansas, Oklahoma, Texas, and eastern portions of the four states to the west—Montana, Wyoming, Colorado, and New Mexico. It is a little more unusual for Savage to include parts of Minnesota, Iowa, and Missouri in the Great Plains.

Ian Frazier's far-ranging mediation on this part of the continent's geography notes that it is the eastern boundary of the Great Plains—and thus the western boundary of the Midwest—that is hardest to place: "Many geographers and botanists have said that the Great Plains begin at the hundredth meridian, because that is the approximate limit of twenty-inch annual rainfall. . . . Since the same amount of rain never falls two years in a row, this eastern boundary always changes. Sometimes it happens to coincide at certain points with the Missouri River; the eastern side of the river will be green and lush, and the western side will be a tan and dusty cowboy-movie set."[14]

In South Dakota, the division is a natural one because the 100th meridian happens to run north and south across the state in about the same location as the Missouri River crosses the state on a similar axis. Roughly half of the river's length as it flows from north to south across South Dakota lies on the east side of the 100th meridian, and the other half is on the west side. The river crosses the 100th meridian in Hughes County, at the very center of South Dakota. Thus it was quite natural for the geographer Joseph Nicollet, on a trip as far west as Fort Pierre in 1839, to think of the river as the dividing line where soils become worse and conditions more austere. Nicollet remarks of the high prairies west of the river that "these vast regions, reputed to reach all the way to the mountains, are so sterile that they are referred to as 'the Great American Desert,' and some travelers have compared them to the deserts of Africa."[15]

Nobel Prize-winning novelist John Steinbeck, in his great travelogue of America, felt similarly that the Missouri River when he crossed it in Bismarck, North Dakota, was a great division point between East and West.[16] Later writers who have addressed the issue in the context of South Dakota often couch discussions in the same terms South Dakotans use to speak of their state—East River and West River.[17]

Yet not everyone draws the line in the same place. The scholar John Milton, in his bicentennial study of South Dakota, titles one of his chapters, "Beyond the 99th: Short grass and gold." He explains, "A simplified geographical image of the westward movement during the nineteenth century would consist of three areas, east to west, each with its own occupation: farming, which extended from the moist middle of the nation as far west as the ninety-ninth meridian; cattle-grazing on the immense plains to the foot of the Rocky Mountains; and mining, especially for gold and silver, in the Rockies and the coastal mountains."[18]

Milton is clearly speaking about the westward movement of the entire nation, not just South Dakota. The fact that he uses the 99th meridian as a dividing line may owe something to Frederick Jackson Turner's landmark essay from 1893, "The Significance of the Frontier in American History," in which Turner also settles on the 99th as a decisive marker, one natural frontier of many laid down like glacial moraines: "In these successive frontiers we find natural boundary lines which have served to mark and to affect the characteristics of the frontiers, namely: the 'fall line;' the Alleghany Mountains; the Mississippi; the Missouri where its direction approximates north and south; the line of arid lands, approximately the ninety-ninth meridian; and the Rocky Mountains."[19]

Whatever his influences, Milton is right to draw the line at the 99th meridian in South Dakota instead of the 100th for the reasons discussed here. But the lesson from Midwestern and Great Plains history seems to be—as Frazier suggests about the line of diminished rainfall—that the line is variable. The border between the two regions falls at different points in different states, or even within states, as determined by factors such as terrain and landscape, precipitation, and soil type. Higher, drier, rougher country is part of the Great Plains. The better farmland is more properly a part of the Midwest. Depending on who is arguing the point, and why, there may even be some overlap of geography.

Here is where Walter Prescott Webb's classic study from the Great Plains shows why it is an enduring piece of research. Webb anticipates the problem and allows for its resolution with something like a transition zone. In addition to what he calls "the High Plains," or "the Plains proper," Webb counts everything west of the 98th meridian up to the High Plains as "the prairie plains."[20] It is the 98th meridian, Webb argues, that marks an "institutional fault" line, similar to a geological fault, west of which things do not work as Americans had found them to work in their expansion up to about 1840.[21]

Among other points, Webb argues that the 98th meridian separates the vegetation of the East from the vegetation of the West.[22] It is an interesting argument, and doubtless there are examples of vegetation found east of the 98th but rare west of that line. However, anyone who has lived in the border country between the Midwest and the Great Plains could probably think of plants that would place that border elsewhere. Writer John Madson seems to suggest this vegetation boundary was the 100th meridian when he notes that only the cottonwood, of all the trees known farther east, made it beyond the 100th meridian to the foothills of the Rocky Mountains.[23]

Another possible marker for these prairie plains could be elevation. For example, if 1,500 feet of elevation were taken as the marker, the *Times Atlas of the World* would show the prairie plains beginning in North Dakota at about where Webb believed they did, with a north-south escarpment at the west edge of the Red River Valley that is at about the 98th meridian. But it would be closer to the 97th meridian in Nebraska; the 98th in Kansas; and west of the 99th in Oklahoma.[24]

South Dakota is an anomaly because of another plateau on the east side of the James River Valley, the Coteau des Prairies, which also rises to more than 2,000 feet of elevation, its highest point near Summit. Formed when the separate lobes of a glacier coming down from the north parted and left an upland intact, the plateau is some 900 feet above the Minnesota River trough to the east, and about 400 feet higher than the James River valley to the west.[25] But this plateau is more like an island of high country in the Midwest, not truly a part of the Great Plains, and factors such as rainfall make it a more hospitable region for agriculture than the high country west of the James River Valley.

Elsewhere in the Dakotas, though, rainfall would have been a greater challenge as the country increases in elevation, and farmers used to the agriculture of Eastern states would not be prepared for what they found. In this context it is worth remembering that, as John C. Hudson has noted, the Germans from Russia were "the only settlers in the region preadapted to this way of life," having already adjusted to a climate and Great Plains-like conditions while living for generations as German settlers in Russia. The implication is that the "line of the arid lands, approximately the ninety-ninth meridian" that Turner saw as a natural frontier was less of a frontier to those with experience and perhaps technologies and strategies to adapt to the conditions. By the time those ethnic Germans emigrated from Russia to the Dakotas, they were already innovators in farming a steppe-like environment.[26]

But Midwesterners such as Hamlin Garland, who had previously lived in Wisconsin and Iowa, came equipped with no such experience for farming the plains. He and the homesteaders he had for neighbors in Dakota Territory had pushed beyond the Midwest, where their experience was still valid. It may be in part because that young would-be homesteader was butting heads with a new set of uncertainties presented by the Great Plains that his writing took on such a powerful new note after his failed attempt at homesteading.

On this point it is worth reading the preface Hamlin Garland wrote in 1922 for a new edition of *Main-Travelled Roads*. There he makes it clear that the ugliness, drudgery, and loneliness of the farmer's lot struck him particularly deeply in Dakota in his visits of 1887 and 1889, shortly before he published his landmark collection of short stories. Several of those pieces are inspired by the hardship of that country. The contrast with Chicago and with his former home in Mitchell County, Iowa, stands out to him.

Garland writes: "The farther I got from Chicago the more depressing the landscape became. It was bad enough in our former home in Mitchell County [Iowa], but my pity grew more intense as I passed from northwest Iowa into southern Dakota."[27] Later in the same piece from 1922, Garland qualifies his dislike for Dakota, acknowledging that life on the farms of Iowa and Wisconsin, and "even on the farms of Dakota," has increased in beauty and security since he wrote *Main-Travelled Roads*, though "there are still wide stretches of territory in Kansas and Nebraska where the farmhouse is a lonely shelter."[28]

What is arguably going on here is that Garland is writing about two distinct regions—the Midwest that he knew in Iowa and Wisconsin, and the Great Plains that caused him dismay at the 99th meridian in Dakota. There, life was still a battle against the elements. Simply to acquire fuel to burn to survive the winter cold was a challenge. But as Turner insightfully noted, the peculiarity of American institutions is that they have not been allowed to develop in place but have been forced to develop along with an expanding people. That has meant "a return to primitive conditions on a continually advancing frontier."[29] Garland encountered the frontier ("the arid tract, the current frontier,"[30] Turner says in his 1893 essay) about a decade before Turner wrote those lines. And Garland encountered them at about the longitude Turner said he should—the 99th meridian.

As Webb implies in his study, one way to set the eastern boundary of the Great Plains—and thus the boundary of the Great Plains in the northern states—is by looking at where institutions and technologies that had worked in lands to the east no longer worked. The 99th meridian, when Garland encountered it, was one of those places where institutions failed. Farming no longer worked as it should. Judging by Garland's writing, at the 99th it became a desperate enterprise, fraught with perils such as blizzard and drought for yields that were considerably less than farmers in Garland's old home in Iowa harvested. A single quarter-section of land was not sufficient reward to offset the risks.

Thus, one way to read Garland's *Moccasin Ranch* novel of 1909 is as a footnote to the Enlarged Homestead Act of that year—an ex-homesteader's fiction, based on his own experience, demonstrating why homesteading in 160-acre tracts wouldn't work in some areas beyond the borders of the Midwest where settlers had pushed in the decades after that 1862 legislation. What can easily be missed is the fact that even long before the Enlarged Homestead Act, Congress had been wrestling with this issue of awarding sufficient land to settlers in the Great Plains and other parts of the West. The Timber Culture Act of 1873 and the Desert Land Act of 1877 were also mechanisms to reward settlers who would make improvements to the West such as tree claims or irrigated croplands. Even the Kinkaid Act of 1904, though aimed specifically at thirty-seven counties of northwestern Nebraska's Sandhills and high tablelands, was an acknowledgment that a homestead of 160 acres was not enough; it allowed those Nebraska settlers 640 acres of non-irrigable land. Even after the Enlarged Homestead Act, Congress followed up with the Stock-Raising Homestead Act of 1916 to place larger tracts of land in the hands of producers in the West who wanted to raise livestock and forage crops. Far from ignoring the problem of its Western geography, Congress seems to have figured out about a decade after the Homestead Act that its dry Western country demanded additional tools besides that Midwest-oriented legislation.[31] In this context it is worth noting that one of the great popularizers of a dry-farming "method," Hardy W. Campbell, homesteaded in the same county where Hamlin Garland's father settled—Brown County, in what is now South Dakota—in 1879. In 1890, shortly before Turner's 1893 essay that alludes to the 99th meridian as a frontier, Campbell invented a "sub-surface packer," which he subsequently promoted in Western states as a means of keeping moisture in when used with associated management techniques.[32] What is significant here is not the efficacy of Campbell's method but the fact that he was inventing it at the 99th meridian. Just as Webb suggests, the Great Plains is where many institutions failed, including the Midwestern farm as Garland's generation knew it. In this context, it is worth pointing out that, as biographer Keith Newlin notes, a preoccupation of Hamlin Garland's after he left Dakota was his fervid advocacy of a single tax as a remedy for unequal land distribution and falling wages. That is to say, Garland's experience of living at the 99th meridian in South Dakota had made him aware that the land system, too, in the hands of speculators, had failed.[33]

What Webb seems to have missed in his 1931 study is that there is a temporal frontier as well as geographic; and the failure of institutions that stopped some people at the door to the Great Plains could be overcome in time with new inventions and discoveries beyond the land-taking tools Congress handed its citizens between 1862 and 1916. For example, Mary Hargreaves suggests a major advancement was "acceptance and institutionalization of risk" through such means as crop insurance, forward pricing by means of government supports, and variable payment schedules for amortization of long-term loans developed starting in about the mid-1950s.[34] Surely such tools were as important to agriculture on the plains as the invention of no-till farming in the late decades of the twentieth century.

Are the frontiers of Turner and Webb flexible—reshaped by culture and technology in spite of physical geography? Is it possible that the Midwest's borders expand, and the Great Plains' borders recede, with new technologies that enable farming in regions that previous generations found inhospitable to agriculture? Does the Midwest extend all the way to the Missouri River in South Dakota now when new crop varieties, no-till farming, and climate change have pushed the Midwest's corn and soybean territory all the way to the river? Do technologies such as the Internet help to alleviate the isolation that Garland experienced at the 99th meridian?

Has the Middle Border itself been obliterated? These are questions worth exploring. But at least there is a strong argument to be made that in Hamlin Garland's day (the final two decades of the nineteenth century and the first decade of the twentieth), the Midwest as he knew it ended at the 99th meridian.

Notes

1   Keith Newlin, *Hamlin Garland: A Life* (Lincoln: University of Nebraska Press, 2008), 52. Interestingly, the biographical note about the author in the Signet Classics edition of *Main-Travelled Roads* gets some fundamental details of Garland's experience as a homesteader wrong. It has Hamlin Garland homesteading in MacPherson County, North Dakota, which doesn't exist, instead of in McPherson County, South Dakota. Yet such confusion in itself may help to illustrate the very "borderness" of the area of which Garland was writing. It is so far from population centers that it is hard to keep from confusing the two Dakotas. Hamlin Garland, note about the author, in *Main-Travelled Roads* (New York: New American Library/ Signet, 1962).

2   Hamlin Garland, *A Son of the Middle Border* (New York: Grosset & Dunlap, 1914, 1917), 301–17.

3   Hamlin Garland, *The Moccasin Ranch: A Story of Dakota* (New York: Harper and Brothers, 1909), 5–6.

4   Garland, *Son of the Middle Border*, 303.

5   Garland, *Moccasin Ranch*, 69.

6   *Photo Atlas of the United States: A Complete Photographic Atlas Using Satellite Photography* (Pasadena, CA: Ward Ritchie Press, 1975), 58.

7   South Dakota State University, Plant Science Department/Agricultural Experiment Station, *Soils of South Dakota*, bulletin 656 (Brookings: South Dakota State University, May 1978), fig. 6, p. 11.

8   John Paul Gries, *Roadside Geology of South Dakota* (Missoula: Mountain Press, 1996), iv.

9   Gries, *Roadside Geology*, 21.

10 The Tragically Hip, "At the Hundredth Meridian," from *Fully Completely*, 1992.

11 Candace Savage, *Prairie: A Natural History* (Vancouver, Canada: Greystone Books, 2004), 4.

12 Savage, *Prairie*, 4.

13 Savage, *Prairie*, 6, 23.

14 Ian Frazier, *Great Plains* (New York: Farrar/Straus/Giroux, 1989), 4.

15 Joseph Nicollet, *Joseph Nicollet on the Plains and Prairies: The Expeditions of 1838–39 with Journals, Letters, and Notes on the Dakota Indians*. (St. Paul: Minnesota Historical Society Press, 1976, 1993), 166.

16 John Steinbeck, *Travels with Charley: In Search of America* (New York: Viking Press, 1962), 153.

17 James D. McLaird, "From Bib Overalls to Cowboy Boots: East River/West River Differences in South Dakota," *South Dakota History* 19 (Winter 1989); Maxine Allison Vande Vaarst, "Here Folds the Map: Finding Where the West Begins," *South Dakota History* 46 (Fall 2016).

[18] John Milton, *South Dakota: A Bicentennial History* (New York: W. W. Norton, 1977), 102.

[19] Frederick Jackson Turner, "The Significance of the Frontier in American History," in *The Frontier in American History* (New York: Henry Holt, 1920), 9.

[20] Walter Prescott Webb, *The Great Plains* (New York: Grosset & Dunlap, 1931), 6–7.

[21] Webb, *Great Plains*, 8.

[22] Webb, *Great Plains*, 27.

[23] John Madson, *Tallgrass Prairie* (Helena: Falcon Books, published in cooperation with the Nature Conservancy, 1993), 75.

[24] *The Times Atlas of the World*, 9th comprehensive ed. (London: Times Books, 1994), plates 108–9.

[25] Gries, *Roadside Geology*, 42.

[26] John C. Hudson, "Migration to an American Frontier," *Annals of the Association of American Geographers* 66 (June 1976): 246.

[27] Garland, preface to *Main-Travelled Roads*.

[28] Garland, preface to *Main-Travelled Roads*.

[29] Turner, "Significance of the Frontier," 2.

[30] Turner, "Significance of the Frontier," 9.

[31] David J. Wishart, "Land Laws and Settlement," in *Encyclopedia of the Great Plains*, ed. David J. Wishart (Lincoln: University of Nebraska Press, 2004), 240.

[32] Mary W. M. Hargreaves, "The Dry-Farming Movement in Retrospect," in *Agriculture in the Great Plains, 1876–1936*, ed. Thomas R. Wessel (Washington, D.C.: Agricultural History Society, 1977), 152.

[33] Newlin, *Hamlin Garland*, 109.

[34] Hargreaves, "Dry-Farming Movement," 164.

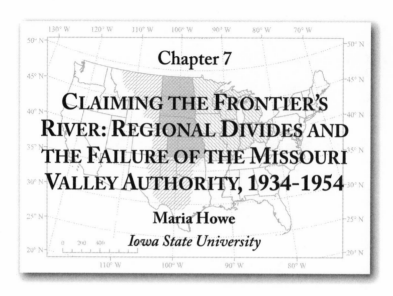

Chapter 7

CLAIMING THE FRONTIER'S RIVER: REGIONAL DIVIDES AND THE FAILURE OF THE MISSOURI VALLEY AUTHORITY, 1934-1954

Maria Howe

Iowa State University

On May 1, 1945, breaking news of Hitler's suicide dominated the press, likely causing many to miss an essay on the Missouri River published the same day in *Harper's Magazine* by the otherwise popular journalist and Western historian Joseph Kinsey Howard. Despite the unlucky timing for publication, Howard's piece, titled "Golden River," was still very germane to readers in the nation's interior—after all, it entered the ongoing debate there over the creation of a Missouri Valley Authority (MVA). The idea to transplant the Tennessee Valley Authority model westward first arose more than a decade earlier, but with increasing anticipation of World War II's end, and attention shifting to postwar job production and infrastructure projects, the MVA proposal was gaining new momentum as well as fresh opposition by the spring of 1945. Howard's article offered a key insight into why the decades long campaign for an MVA would ultimately fail. As he so aptly remarked, "The Missouri is the frontier's river, and it is *still* regarded with the passionate possessiveness the frontier felt for its few immediately available natural resources. And that's just the trouble."[1]

The Big Muddy certainly holds a special place in American memory, especially in connection with our narratives of the early trans-Mississippi frontier. The river notably served as the path of the Lewis and Clark Ex-

102

pedition and later as a primary route west for settlers seeking trapping, mining, ranching, and farming opportunities. Yet westward expansion in the nineteenth century brought a host of challenges in the twentieth century. At approximately 2,340 miles, the Missouri is the longest river not just in the United States but in North America. From Montana's Rocky Mountains to the great confluence in St. Louis, it tracks a watershed that comprises one-sixth of the continental United States. Across this vast basin, agriculture, navigation, hydroelectricity, industry, and growing urban areas all had to compete for the Missouri's rather fickle water supply. And there seemed to be little moderation; the river had become infamous for either devastating droughts or floods. By the 1930s, interests across the watershed and in Washington, D.C., were preparing schemes to address these varied concerns. The MVA campaign, ongoing from 1934 to the mid-1950s, was one such scheme that imagined a new level of federal bureaucratic control to harness the notoriously meandering "Wide Missouri." Like the TVA, the MVA proposed creating a river valley authority, which would establish one large centralized planning agency, tasked not only with providing water management and hydropower generation but also with serving as a regional economic development agency to modernize the watershed. Although the river authority bills varied somewhat over time, the primary purpose was always to create a central forum for coordinated development and water management across the entire watershed. MVA proponents proudly touted the idea of a valley authority for the nation's frontier river as "a job of modern pioneering on a grand scale in the national interest."[2]

The sketch of the MVA debate that follows reveals new dimensions of both this iconic American river and the conceptualization of the interior borderland at midcentury. Much like rivers, frontiers and regional borders are fluid, shifting and forming over time. This chapter focuses less on pinpointing an exact geographical divide between the Midwest and the Great Plains and more on exploring how the real divisions between the two regions affected the twenty-year MVA campaign. It failed, at least in significant part, because of these tense regional divisions combined with that passionate, lingering frontier possessiveness that Howard described. Upstream and downstream identities—formed over the previous half century, perpetuated by robust water and power lobbies, and fueled by the increasingly popular Cold War rhetoric—presented an insurmountable problem for MVA advocates after the war. And in turn, regional divides were reinforced for many in the process. By the mid- to late 1950s, the idea of transporting a TVA-style basin-wide bureaucracy to the Missouri had largely faded. All that was left to manage the Missouri basin was a comparatively flimsy and often contradictory interagency agreement between the Army Corps of Engineers and the Bureau of Reclamation, adopted by Congress in the Flood Control Act of 1944 and packaged as the Pick-Sloan Plan. Critics called it a "shameless, loveless shot-gun wedding."[3]

Senator George Norris of Nebraska was the first to propose an MVA in 1934 while he was still celebrating the passage of his Tennessee Valley Authority bill, which passed the previous year during the frenetic first hundred days of Franklin Roosevelt's presidency.[4] Although far from his constituents, Norris's initial interest in the TVA started with his desire to see the Muscle Shoals Project come to fruition, which had been initially proposed during World War I. As a Republican, Norris may have been an unlikely candidate to propose back-to-back bills for valley authorities, but to him it made perfect sense. As a rural Westerner, he developed considerable wariness of the so-called power trust, and he wanted to help spread affordable electricity. He also witnessed the 1920s agricultural depression firsthand. Combined, these experiences led Norris to embrace many of the progressive government programs of the New Deal, particularly the idea for river valley authorities. Norris thought that Western farmers had already "borne the hardships of the frontier. . . . If they are to be cut off from assistance now while [it's] being given to all other classes of people, it will constitute . . . an injustice that no fair-minded citizen ought to impose."[5]

For Senator Norris, the river valley authority model was about efficient geographies of development.[6] It could provide cohesive planning as well as a feasible cost structure by including navigation and flood control objectives, which he knew had "always been recognized as two things for which the expenditure of public funds was justified."[7] By embracing the multipurpose philosophy, Norris could shrewdly manipulate the perplexing dichotomy between navigation and flood control projects, which were historically a proper government expense, and the irrigation projects that had not been—a dichotomy that also often loosely tracked the boundary between the Midwest and the Great Plains. Interstate river compacts, growing in usage since 1922, demonstrated that basin-wide agreement was theoretically possible. The Hoover, Grand Coulee, and Ft. Peck Dams revealed that large-scale hydroelectric dams were technologically feasible. Together, the compacts and these massive dams meant that large-scale federal water management was a reality; the mood in the 1930s was to dream big.[8]

Senator Norris's big plans for the Missouri largely echoed his TVA legislation from the previous year. From the start, Norris intended that the

TVA would be the "first step in a broad program looking toward complete control of the waters of all streams in the United States."[9] Like the TVA, his MVA plan envisioned a broad, future-oriented, basin-wide scheme that would implement cost-sharing between development interests, limit the market share of the big monopolistic power companies he disliked, and reduce the patronage and "pork barrel spending" of small localized water projects. The MVA plan differed though in that it was not expressly concerned with fertilizer production like the TVA had been; it introduced irrigation as a prioritized use; and it initially anticipated placing administrative authority with the Bureau of Reclamation instead of creating a new government corporation as the TVA did.[10]

In early January 1934, Norris offered his MVA bill, and it was so well received in Washington, D.C., that spring that he expressed concern that it would be "pushed off the bandwagon" by a host of other valley authority proposals.[11] Congress even considered a bill to bring valley authorities to every major watershed from the Atlantic to the Pacific. Despite the warm reception, by 1935 Norris and his collaborators became preoccupied with another passion—rural electrification. Passage of the Flood Control Act of 1936 suggested waning support for the valley authority concept,[12] but Senator Norris did not abandon it. In 1937 he proposed creating seven authorities for each major watershed in the country, which again had the president's support but got delayed. The continued postponement of valley authority legislation in the 1930s seemed primarily the result of a divide within Roosevelt's administration over the appropriate governance structure. Competing bills, as well as objections from power companies, further stymied progress, and the MVA idea could not get out of Washington, D.C. Yet as one of the main skeptics of valley authorities prophetically warned in 1938: "Regional Authority and Planning Bills Not Dead— Only Sleeping!"[13]

By the middle of World War II, Congress was again discussing the Missouri problem, and the nation's interior was eagerly listening. Although Senator Norris was defeated in 1942, the legacy of more than a decade of drought, the fear that depression could return after the war's end, and the major flooding on the Missouri in 1943 all generated public interest in doing something for the Missouri basin. By the spring of 1944, just months before U.S. troops landed on the beaches of Normandy, the discussion over the Missouri reached a fevered pitch. On March 2, the Army Corps submitted a twelve-page report ("Pick Plan") to Congress, calling for levees from Sioux City to the Mississippi confluence; eighteen tributary dams; and a series of five main-stem multipurpose dams above Sioux City. Just two months later, the bureau offered a 211-page plan ("Sloan Plan") to the Senate on May 4, which envisioned more than eighty-five new tributary dams and three main-stem dams, all to irrigate 4.8 million acres. Each agency strongly advocated its own plan, arguing that they were irreconcilable.[14]

Ten days after the Sloan Plan arrived in Congress, the Pulitzer family's *St. Louis Post-Dispatch* led a renewed charge for an MVA by publishing an entire-page appeal to all the editors in the Missouri basin. The *Post-Dispatch* editorial reasoned that even though the Missouri River was nearly four times longer than the Tennessee, it still needed unified planning. The piece argued:

> [The Missouri] is not one thing in Montana and Wyoming, another thing in the Dakotas and Iowa, a third thing in Nebraska, Kansas and Colorado, and a fourth in Missouri. It is not primarily an instrument to be used for irrigation, or for navigation, or for power; nor is it an evil force to be controlled against its repeated and disastrous flooding. It is a synthesis of all of these. Where is the plan that will solve the one big problem of the one big river?

According to the editorial, neither the Pick Plan nor Sloan Plan was enough, because they were focused only on sectional interests. Instead, the *Post-Dispatch* called for visionary leaders in the basin to "transcend the futile rivalries of the past" between regions and federal agencies in the name of overcoming a new "civil war," and finally conquering the "empire of the Missouri."[15]

An editorial war ensued among basin newspapers. Perhaps the editor of the *Miles City Daily Star*, Louis Grill (known as "Montana Lou"), most vividly captured the feelings of those opposed to an MVA. From his desk in Miles City, Montana, on the banks of the Yellowstone River, notably the Missouri's largest tributary, Grill charged that the editors of the *Post-Dispatch* were nothing more than "20th century [Jesse] James" boys who want to make off with the waters of the Missouri River. He suggested that they must have long ears and a tail and go around yelling "yee-haw"—"for no other kind of a person would display such complete ignorance of the subject of irrigation and its relation to the future development of the Missouri River." The downstream interests were said to have no religion, and the *Daily Star* threatened that the "vigilante doctrine" would be used to protect the "God-given waters of the streams of Montana" if this "highway robbery of [their] irrigation water" by "St. Louis pirates" was not stopped. To him, the *Post-Dispatch* really wanted nothing more than "a legalized

Jesse James plundering expedition." In short, Montana Lou did not see "one big river." Instead, he saw downstream Midwestern interests trying to take Montana's scarce water resources, which were so desperately needed for irrigation. The crux of the problem for Montana Lou and others out on the plains was a fear that there simply was not enough flow in the Missouri, despite its grand length, to accommodate their desired diversions for irrigated agriculture and, at the same time, leave enough water in the river for the maintenance of downstream navigation channels or other development.[16]

Montana Lou offered a special warning for those caught in the middle. In an editorial directed to Sioux Falls, South Dakota, the *Daily Star* threatened the owners of stockyards in Sioux Falls that they would withhold Montana cattle and sheep if they did not overtly oppose the MVA. Instead, Montanans could easily ship their livestock to stockyards in St. Paul, where leaders had already come out against valley authorities. Cities like Sioux Falls and Omaha were caught between a rock and a hard place. While flood control and navigation concerns piqued interests there, ranches further out on the plains were still important trading partners to keep happy. Overall, the *Daily Star* editorials were indicative of a problem that could certainly torpedo the MVA's prospects—a perfect storm of regional stereotypes, possessive perspectives on natural resources, and frank blackmail.[17]

All this turmoil occurred before Senator James Murray, a Democrat from Montana, even presented new MVA legislation later that summer on August 18, 1944.[18] The MVA's new crusader was originally from Ontario, Canada, but headed west to Butte, Montana, in 1901. It was not until 1934, later in Murray's career, that he became a senator, but he proved a loyal Democrat and enthusiastically supported Roosevelt's domestic agenda. In reciprocity, Roosevelt was quick to support the MVA idea again, delivering an address to Congress fully endorsing the bill on September 21. Senator Norris's death earlier that month no doubt added to Roosevelt's advocacy.[19]

Murray's bill envisioned the creation of a new government corporation, like the one created by the TVA, that would provide unified basin-wide coordination of the water and other natural resources in the Missouri valley to prevent flooding, generate power, facilitate irrigated reclamation, and improve navigability. Combining Progressive-era ideals of conservation and efficiency with New Deal-size planning, Murray offered a broad vision of "one river, one development, for multiple benefits."[20] He promised that the MVA would eliminate interagency fighting by essentially setting aside the old federal agencies, and it would bypass the circuitous congressional process for appropriations. Murray's bill provided that the MVA was to be based within the watershed, operated by a three-person commission appointed by the president, and charged with managing all dams and other projects across the basin, including Ft. Peck.[21]

In an attempt to halt the growing momentum behind the MVA campaign, in October 1944 the Army Corps and the Bureau of Reclamation brokered the Pick-Sloan Plan, that so-called shotgun wedding. In just two days, the previously irreconcilable differences became reconcilable. C. Girard Davidson, subsequent assistant secretary of the interior, explained that the two federal agencies aligned against the MVA so quickly because they "were interested in protecting and increasing [their own] jurisdiction."[22] Neither agency wanted to be pushed out of the Missouri entirely. Pick-Sloan was essentially just a list of dams. It anticipated that the basin would be simply divided up, leaving the Army Corps to build and operate all the main-stem dams to serve its interests in flood control and navigation, while the Bureau of Reclamation would operate largely on upstream tributaries, focusing on irrigation. Thus, even as Roosevelt signed Pick-Sloan into law in December 1944, he still called for an MVA to fill in the holes left by Pick-Sloan in terms of coordinated governance. In the following congressional session, there were ten bills proposing valley authorities across the nation. In fact, even after Roosevelt died in April 1945, calls for an MVA continued for at least a decade after Pick-Sloan's passage.[23]

For those influenced by Montana Lou's frequent editorials from Miles City, the MVA campaign must have seemed doomed to fail due to the simmering regional tensions, but its eventual failure was actually surprising in several respects. To start, the campaign occurred during decades known for the impressive growth of federal involvement in Western water management—the same decades historian Donald Worster has delineated as the emergence of the "empire stage" of federal water control.[24] The campaign's failure is also ironic when considering how the TVA model led to "democracy on the march" worldwide, with river basin development schemes transplanted across the globe by Bureau of Reclamation officials to newly independent states across the so-called Third World.[25] As geographer Christopher Sneddon recently phrased it, the United States' predilection during the Cold War for encouraging large dam-based river basin development around the globe modeled off the TVA amounted to nothing less than a "concrete revolution."[26]

The failure of the MVA is especially surprising given that advocates were active across the watershed. After all, some of the loudest voices supporting a valley authority were from the plains of Montana, where, according to Montana Lou, Western irrigators were *supposed* to despise the idea of an MVA. Yet the Treasure State yielded the senator who introduced the primary legislation in the 1940s, as well as a large statewide association dedicated to supporting the MVA. While the *Daily Star* declared that "so far as we can learn, no one in Montana asked Senator Murray to introduce such a bill" and that "whatever agitation there was for an MVA arose from the people on the lower end of the Missouri River," the newspaper must have just missed the thirty-one families in town who joined the Montana MVA Association, along with the 813 households statewide that eventually joined the organization's official ranks.[27] Indeed, the Montana MVA Association had members from forty-seven out of fifty-six counties across the state and had members in all of the counties within the Missouri watershed.[28]

Support was not exclusive to Montana though. St. Louis had a strong MVA Association, supported by Raymond Tucker, who became mayor in 1953. A Regional Committee for an MVA was eventually established and headquartered in Omaha and included representatives from across the basin. North Dakota senator Milton Young openly supported the MVA proposal, even though he owed his appointment to Governor Aandahl, who was opposed to a valley authority. The National Farmers Union, led by James Patton from Colorado and representing 141,000 basin farm families, also supported the initiative, along with several labor unions from Butte to St. Louis. A 1946 poll conducted in Iowa by *Wallace's Farmer* found that 57 percent of respondents were in support of an MVA, and the Farmers Union found in a poll the year before that all but seven out of five hundred farmers surveyed across the watershed wanted a valley authority. National publications, like the *Chicago Tribune* and the *Commonweal* (a liberal Catholic weekly), along with academic journals like the *American Political Science Review*, presented favorable analyses. An article in the latter explained that additional valley authorities were "almost a certainty . . . within a few years." When Murray introduced the legislation, he received numerous requests for appointments from across the state and country, including one currently employed engineer named Vernus Pyle, from none other than Miles City, Montana.[29] Despite the widespread support for an MVA and the opportunity for a basin-wide consciousness, influential water and power lobbies fought hard for the continuation of agencies they already knew and liked. The National Reclamation Association (NRA) and its Montana chapter (MRA) loudly defended the Bureau of Reclamation, which had a proven record of supporting Western interests. Playing on opposing regional identities, NRA's publications claimed that no "informed person in the West" could tolerate valley authorities.[30] The MRA produced a series of six radio talks attacking the MVA and then mailed illustrated copies of the talks, printed in color, to approximately twenty thousand voters throughout the state. The show expressed fear that "state lines will be erased" by an MVA.[31] The power lobby was equally vocal. The Montana Power Company, owned by American Power & Light and serving Anaconda Copper and the Milwaukee Railroad, was opposed to an MVA, as this threatened its dominance in the power market. The Montana power interests controlled many newspapers across the state, referred to as the "copper-collar presses," and used them to fan fears that the MVA was a "monstrous super-state" that would condemn all state rights and erode any regional boundaries. One Montanan expressed that negative coverage of the MVA campaign in these papers was "given more prominence than the taking of Berlin by the Russians."[32]

Emerging Cold War politics and the sweeping Republican victory in the 1946 midterm election were also detrimental to the MVA campaign. The *Miles City Daily Star* claimed that the MVA bill and its proposal for one centralized development agency was just one step in a scheme to "socialize the entire nation" by traitors wearing "rose-colored glasses."[33] Republican politicians across the valley began referring to it as the "Murray Dictatorship Bill," or "a gigantic socialistic scheme which would virtually wipe out states' rights and place our affairs in the hands of an autocratic board not responsive to the people."[34] Water and power lobbies eagerly employed the Cold War rhetoric too, arguing that valley authorities were "directly the opposite from the free enterprise system" cherished in the United States. As the MRA put it: "If this isn't **totalitarianism** and **socialism** my knowledge of **Democracy** and **Americanism** is naught." This rhetoric was appealing across the plains, where long-held convictions about individualism and autonomy led many to be suspicious of centralized planning schemes.[35]

Overall, the Missouri Valley Authority debate offers a unique vantage from which to consider the divide between the Midwest and the Great Plains. It lends insight into the process of creating and maintaining regional identities. The arguments against the MVA were strongly colored by the perceived divisions between the two regions—opponents ardently saw either a plains river *or* a Midwestern river. The size of the watershed compounded this tension. The basin linked such disparate places as Denver, Great Falls, the Standing Rock Sioux Reservation, and St. Louis, while collecting rainfall from the northern Ozarks, to the Flint Hills, to the Loess

Hills, to the Black Hills, to the eastern halves of Glacier, Yellowstone, and Rocky Mountain National Parks. Ultimately, during the tumultuous decades of depression, war, and cold war, the lines based on irrigation versus navigation, Bureau of Reclamation versus Corps of Engineers, lobbies versus progressive politicians, wheat versus corn, and Great Plains versus Midwest proved too much for proponents of the MVA. In the end, despite the growth of federal water management across the West, the vibrancy of the TVA model internationally, and the presence of MVA advocates across the watershed, the weaker Pick-Sloan program proved to be the limit of inter-basin coordination. Rivers have certainly played a significant role in shaping regional identities, but, as the MVA debate revealed, those identities are sometimes fluid, much like the Missouri River itself.

Notes

1   Joseph Kinsey Howard, "Golden River: What's to Be Done about the Missouri?" *Harper's Magazine*, May 1, 1945, 511 (emphasis added). Howard was the author of the classic Montana history *Montana: High, Wide and Handsome* (New Haven: Yale University Press, 1943).

2   Statement by Senator James E. Murray of Montana, quoted in Howard, "Golden River," 518.

3   H.R. REP. No. 4485, 78th Cong., 2nd sess. (1944) (Pick-Sloan / Flood Control Bill of 1944). James Patton, president of the National Farmers' Union, decried the Pick-Sloan Plan as a "shot-gun wedding" at a press conference in December 1944. See Henry C. Hart, *The Dark Missouri* (Madison: University of Wisconsin Press, 1957). For more background on Patton, see Michael W. Flamm, "The National Farmers' Union and the Development of Agrarian Liberalism, 1937–1946," *Agricultural History* 68 (Summer 1994).

4   U.S. Congress, Senate, *A Bill to Improve the Navigability of the Missouri River . . .* , S. 1973, 73rd Cong., 2nd sess., 1934 (Norris Bill).

5   See Richard Lowitt, *George W. Norris: The Triumph of a Progressive, 1933–1944* (Urbana: University of Illinois Press, 1978), 19–20; and "Letters Reveal 'Power Trust' Fight on TVA: Norris, 'Not Surprised,' Assails Utilities on Senate Floor," *Washington Post*, April 3, 1934. For more consideration of the "power trust," see Gifford Pinchot, *The Power Monopoly: Its Make-up and Menace* (Milford, PA, 1928); and Albert Williams, *The Water and the Power* (New York: Duell, Sloan and Pearce, 1951). Norris to Harold Ickes, November 24, 1933, George William Norris Papers, Nebraska State Historical Society, Box 1 / Folder 18 ("Norris Corresp. 1933"), 2.

6   See generally, Christopher Sneddon, *Concrete Revolution: Large Dams, Cold War Geopolitics, and the US Bureau of Reclamation* (Chicago: University of Chicago Press, 2015).

7   Norris to W. V. Hoagland, April 29, 1933, Norris Papers, Box 1 / Folder 18 ("Norris Corresp. 1933"), 2.

8   For more consideration of the so-called "Big Dam Era," multipurpose dams, and improving technologies, see David P. Billington et al., *The History of Large Federal*

Dams: Planning, Design and Construction (Denver: U.S. Bureau of Reclamation, 2005); Karin D. Ellison, "The Making of a Multi-purpose Dam: Engineering Culture, the U.S. Bureau of Reclamation, and Grand Coulee Dam, 1917–1942" (Ph.D. Diss., MIT, 1999), 10–11; and Donald C. Jackson, *Building the Ultimate Dam: John S. Eastwood and the Control of Water in the West* (Lawrence: University Press of Kansas, 1995). Regarding interstate compacts, see generally Edella Schlager and Tanya Heikkila, "Resolving Water Conflicts: A Comparative Analysis of Interstate River Compacts," *Policy Studies Journal* 37 (2009): 367–92, 369, 374; and Daniel Tyler, *Silver Fox of the Rockies: Delphus E. Carpenter and Western Water Compacts* (Norman: University of Oklahoma Press, 2003).

9   "Statement of Senator George W. Norris with reference to development of Missouri," copy dated December 18, 1933, Norris Papers, Box 6 / Folder 3 (Manuscripts, Speeches, 1931–36), 1–2.

10 See "Norris to Urge Huge Missouri Valley Project: Muscle Shoals Sponsor Warns of 'Pork'; Awaits New Power Battle," *Washington Post*, December 26, 1933; and Lowitt, *George Norris*, 45. For more on Norris' motivations for the TVA specifically, see Richard Lowitt, "'Present at the Creation': George W. Norris, Franklin D. Roosevelt and the TVA Enabling Act," in *East Tennessee Historical Society Publications* 48 (1976), 116.

11 Norris Bill; Lowitt, *George Norris*, 44–49.

12 Karen M. O'Neill, "Why the TVA Remains Unique: Interest Groups and the Defeat of New Deal Planning," *Rural Sociology* 67 (2002): 164.

13 See "Norris to Push TVA Project at Ft. Peck Dam: Believe Congress to Select Missouri Valley as Power Site," *Washington Post*, December 16, 1934; and William E. Leuchtenburg, "Roosevelt, Norris and the Seven Little TVAs," *Journal of Politics* 14 (1952): 418–41. While President Roosevelt supported the valley authority idea, Secretary of Agriculture Henry Wallace and Secretary of War Harry Woodring objected to the bill as proposed because it granted the authorities too much power. Patrick Kline and Enrico Moretti, "Local Economic Development, Agglomeration Economies, and the Big Push: 100 Years of Evidence from the Tennessee Valley Authority," *Quarterly Journal of Economics* 129 (February 2014): 275–331. National Reclamation Association, "New Bulletin No. 24" (June 23, 1938), 21, National Water Resources Association Papers, Colorado State University's Archives and Special Collections, available at https://dspace.library.colostate.edu/handle/10217/31642.

14 Michael L. Lawson, *Dammed Indians Revisited: The Continuing History of the Pick-Sloan Project and the Missouri River Sioux* (Pierre: South Dakota State Historical Society, 1985), 14–16.

15 "To the Editors of the Missouri Valley: One River, One Problem," *St. Louis Post-Dispatch*, May 14, 1944, 2D; see generally Lawson, *Dammed Indians Revisited*.

16 "Jesse James Boys Ride Yet—Not Again," *Miles City Daily Star*, April 9, 1944, 4. According to the *Miles City Daily Star*'s historian, Lou Grill was the editor in 1944. See correspondence with Amorette F. Allison, October 7–13, 2016, on file with author.

17 "The Kansas City Gentry," *Miles City Daily Star*, June 4, 1944, 4.

18 U.S. Congress, Senate, *A Bill to Establish a Missouri Valley Authority . . .* , S. 2089, 78th Cong., 2nd sess., 1944 (Murray Bill).

19 See Donald E. Spritzer, *Senator James E. Murray and the Limits of Post-war Liberalism* (New York: Garland, 1985); and "F.D.R. Pitching: Some Missouri Valley Governors Charge Fast Curve in President's Message Asking for TVA-Model River Authority,"

Business Week, September 30, 1944. By the end of September 1944, three additional proposals for an MVA were before Congress, including bills offered by Rep. John Cochran of Missouri, Rep. John Rankin of Mississippi, and Sen. Guy Gillette of Iowa.

20 James E. Murray, "Speech of Honorable James E. Murray of Montana in the Senate of the United States, August 18, 1944" (Washington, D.C.: U.S. Government Printing Office, 1944), Jerome K. Walsh Papers, Box 3 / Subject File 1931–1966, Personal Papers Collection, Harry S. Truman Presidential Library, Independence, MO.

21 See Murray Bill.

22 Oral history interview with C. Girard Davidson, Washington, D.C., July 17, 1972, conducted by Jerry N. Hess, transcript available at https://www.trumanlibrary.org/oralhist/davidsn1.htm#16.

23 Murray introduced a second bill in 1945. U.S. Congress, Senate, *A Bill to Establish a Missouri Valley Authority* . . . , S. 555, 79th Cong., 1st sess., 1945. For a discussion of the continued push for an MVA despite Pick-Sloan, see Lawson, *Dammed Indians Revisited.*

24 See Donald Worster, *Rivers of Empire: Water, Aridity and the Development of the American West* (New York: Pantheon Books, 1985), chapter 6.

25 See David E. Lilienthal, *TVA—Democracy on the March* (New York: Harper and Bros., 1944). Lilienthal's pro-TVA analysis was translated into twenty-one different languages.

26 Sneddon, *Concrete Revolution*, 1–27.

27 "Who in Montana Wants a Missouri Valley Authority," *Miles City Daily Star*, September 3, 1944, 4.

28 Membership cards, Boxes 4–5, Marian Covington Papers, 1896–1976, Montana Historical Society, Research Archives, Helena, MT.

29 "How Can We Harness Missouri Floods?" *Wallace's Farmer and Iowa Homestead*, April 6, 1946, 311–18. For Farmers Union poll results, see Edward Skillin Jr., "MVA: America's Greatest Single Peace Project," *Commonweal* 42, no. 19, August 24, 1945, Jerome K. Walsh Papers, Box 4; Wesley C. Clark, "Proposed 'Valley Authority' Legislation," *American Political Science Review* 40 (1946): 62–70; "Applications & Appointments—Missouri Valley Authority, 1944–48," Box 108 / Folder 3, James E. Murray Papers, University of Montana, Mansfield Library, Archives and Special Collections, Missoula, MT.

30 National Reclamation Association Bulletin, vol. 9, no. 6 (February 28, 1945), 2, National Water Resources Association Papers, available at https://dspace.library. colostate.edu/handle/10217/31747.

31 Radio show pamphlet, Montana Reclamation Association, Subject File, 1943–1954, Buffalo Rapids Irrigation Project Records, Montana Historical Society.

32 Letter by Fred Huntington to Senate Committee on Irrigation and Reclamation (April 1945), Box 376 / Folder 3, James E. Murray Papers.

33 "Boys, We Have Uninvited Guests in the House," *Miles City Daily Star*, October 1, 1944, 4.

34 "A Report of the State of Missouri's Commission Studying the Tennessee Valley and the Missouri Valley: Presenting Conclusions and Recommendations," November 28, 1945, 50, pamphlet 802, Montana Historical Society.

35 Radio show pamphlet, Montana Reclamation Association, Subject File, 1943–1954, Buffalo Rapids Irrigation Project Records (emphasis in original); Thomas Biolsi, "New Deal Visions v. Local Political Culture: The Agony of the South Dakota State

Planning Board, 1934–1939," in *The Plains Political Tradition: Essays on South Dakota Political Culture*, ed. Jon K. Lauck et al. (Pierre: South Dakota Historical Society, 2014), 2:79.

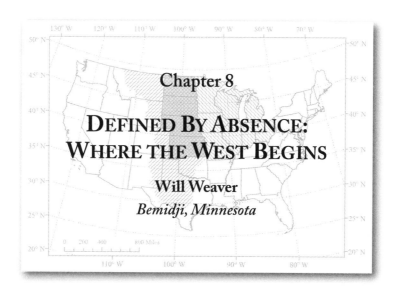

Chapter 8

DEFINED BY ABSENCE: WHERE THE WEST BEGINS

Will Weaver

Bemidji, Minnesota

Introduction

As a small boy eavesdropping on my parents late one summer night—something was afoot—I heard we might be taking a road trip "out West." This was beyond exciting. From our farm in Minnesota, I had never been past Fargo, and I always imagined that the fabled West began somewhere past it. Our family trip did not disappoint. Packed in our 1963 Chevrolet, we left in purple dawn (my father believed in getting a "good start"). In the backseat my sister quickly fell asleep, but I was too excited to close my eyes. After we passed through Detroit Lakes, the pine forests withdrew, and the landscape opened its arms into impossibly wide and rolling fields. Approaching Fargo, the treeless land fell into the flatness of a giant tabletop.

"The Red River Valley," my father remarked.

I did not see a valley of any kind, but soon came Fargo and a large sign that said, "Welcome to North Dakota."

I leaned forward with excitement; my mother smiled.

Not far beyond Fargo the flat fields began to rise and swell again, and speckle themselves with brown cattle. A black-and-white bird with a very long tail fluttered across the highway.

"Magpie," my mother said. "We don't have those."

115

The odd-looking bird lit alongside a mostly dried-up waterhole that carried a wide ring of white.

"What's that white stuff?" I asked.

"Alkali," my father said. "It's like salt. They don't have good water like we do back in Minnesota."

At that moment, like a switch flipped inside my head, it happened: we had arrived! We were in the West.

Years later, in college, I came across a literary term that made all the sense in the world because it named that felt sensation I had as a boy. It was T. S. Eliott's "objective correlative," which he described as "a set of objects, a situation, a chain of events which *shall be the formula* of a particular emotion."[1] We all have such "formulas." When I hear a train whistle, I think of my grandfather's farm. When I smell patchouli, I think of a long-ago summer trip to San Francisco. These emotions are deep-set personal truths, and they are not subject to change. Nowadays, when I drive west from Minnesota, my feeling of crossing into the West comes from the same wellsprings, though with some additional currents. Cowboy hats begin to pop up at truck stops near West Fargo. Local radio stations include feeder cattle prices per hundredweight. Farm—make that *ranch*—pickups carry dual tandem rear wheels plus a supplemental fuel tank with a hose at ready. On the open range, occasional Western Meadowlarks perch on what fence posts remain.[2] But all those emblems aside, if I had to choose a single object as my "formula" for the West, it would be one of absence rather than presence. To me, the West is about water—or lack thereof.

I

John Wesley Powell (1834–1902), a pioneering explorer and scientist, was an environmentalist before there was a such word. While he was too late to be among the first wave of hardy adventurers who "opened" the West (that is, to white settlers), his reputation is cemented as one of the first to articulate the need for new ways of thinking about where the West begins, how the West fits into the American vision, and what the future of the West might be—especially when it comes to water resources.

Powell—a United States soldier, geologist, and professor at Illinois Wesleyan University—led various expeditions into what he called the "arid regions." He defined these as beginning at the 100th meridian, sometimes called the "dry line," which runs from Rugby, North Dakota, south to the Texas-Mexico border, passing just west of San Antonio. From this north-south line, the "arid regions" extended west to the front range of the Rockies. Wallace Stegner, born in Iowa, though later known as a writer and scholar of the West, wrote a book called *Beyond the Hundredth Meridian: John Wesley Powell and the Second Opening of the West*. In it Stegner cements how Powell came to see the beginning of the West: "The inflexible fact of aridity lay like a fence along the 100th meridian."[3] (Stegner himself would come to see that "fence" closer to the 98th meridian, which he and others called "the humid line.") Much of Powell's work focused on the Colorado area, including the Grand Canyon; however, no western state or territory from Montana to Arizona was unaffected by his growing conservationist bent toward the mapping and management of water resources and orderly settlement based thereon.

At first from intuition, then from the science of observation and measurement, Powell came to a clarity of belief. The rapid settlement of the West could not—should not—be business as usual. The scarcity of water called for a new approach. The western land rush following the Civil War was in full bore with Dakota prairie schooners and Oklahoma Sooners, and Powell viewed this enormous, chaotic migration with alarm. Beginning in 1867, he led a series of western expeditions that increasingly codified his sense that caution was needed in the rush west. However, his advocacy of cautious, planned settlement ran afoul of prevailing, powerful metaphors of unfettered American expansionism: "free land,"[4] "homestead," "taming of West," and of course America's self-proclaimed "manifest destiny." What ensued was a textbook case of science versus sloganeering.

II

My family's history is entwined, past and present, with matters of water. Aridity along the 100th meridian was precisely the reason why my grandfather settled up north in Minnesota "where there was plenty of good water." His father had brought the family west from Pennsylvania, where they were washed out by the Johnstown Flood, to Chamberlain, South Dakota, where land was cheap and wild game abundant: pheasants, prairie chickens, ducks, antelope, deer. But, in the end, South Dakota was too hot. Too dry. Fragments of family stories remain about drought (they pronounced it "drowth"), waves of grasshoppers, and a cistern that was always low on water—water that smelled bad. In 1914, my family gave up on South Dakota. They backtracked east to Iowa and then north into Minnesota where there was good water everywhere. My grandfather homesteaded in Hubbard County near Park Rapids, now a popular summer destination for tourists, largely because of its bounty of water. There are four hundred lakes (among Minnesota's more than ten thousand) within a twenty-mile radius of Main

Street; outside of town, if a country road curves and bends, it is because of a lake or stream just beyond the trees.

Growing up in pine and lake country, I never thought much about water. It was always there. A given. However, it took a stint of living in California to make me appreciate water resources. Flying across the Great Plains, and looking down at the unending brownness of the land; driving through California's green, verdant (and irrigated) Central Valley; and living in an apartment in the Bay Area where water was metered and expensive—all were an eye opener to me: I had always taken water for granted. After graduate school, I eventually returned to Minnesota, and, for the past twenty-some years, I have lived and taught and written from my home just east of Bemidji on the Mississippi River, which flows past my dock.

The river is a throughway for waterfowl and wildlife as well as canoeists and kayakers. The Mississippi headwaters start at Lake Itasca, Latin (generally) for "true head," about twenty-five miles upstream from my house. However, "upstream" is mostly south, and I take no small pleasure in saying that where I live the Mississippi River flows north. On a map, the upper Mississippi looks like a giant, inverted fishhook; it trickles out of Lake Itasca with Hudson Bay on its mind, grows in stalwartness from the cold springs and smaller streams along the way, then hits an understated but effective continental divide just north of Bemidji. This encounter tilts the Mississippi River eastward (past my dock) and then into a wide, curling turn to the south. As it turns out, I live almost exactly at the northernmost point of the Mississippi, a fact that I do not take for granted. Without the river's understated collision of hydrology and geology, America would be greatly diminished. No "mill city" of Minneapolis. No barges full of wheat and coal. No St. Louis. No Mark Twain. No Mississippi Delta. No New Orleans. Without this grand river, we would have none of the vibrant river commerce and cultural energy of the Mississippi Valley, which stretches south through Illinois, Missouri, Arkansas, and Louisiana, and its river cities with millions of people. The heart of America would be missing—when it comes to settlement and civilization, water is everything.

III

Powell understood this, but his cautious approach to settlement was in direct contrast to one of the leading proponents of unregulated, water-be-damned inhabitation of the West. William Gilpin (1813–1894) believed that the Great Plains was America's grand future of commerce and settlement—even more promising than the Mississippi Valley. As with John Wesley Powell, Gilpin was a veteran of the Civil War (Powell himself lost an arm at Shiloh), but Gilpin had a knack or just plain luck to be at the center of American events: he was a friend of Andrew Jackson and a volunteer bodyguard (one of a hundred men) who protected Abraham Lincoln when he assumed the presidency in 1860; and it was Lincoln himself who dispatched Gilpin west to "secure" Colorado, where Gilpin became the first territorial governor.[5] It was there that Gilpin developed his evangelical belief in the continuation of America's westward movement. Wallace Stegner describes Gilpin's vision:

> He saw the West through a blaze of mystical fervor, as part of a grand geopolitical design . . . and his conception of its resources and its future as a home for millions was as grand as his rhetoric, as unlimited as his faith, as splendid as his capacity for inaccuracy. . . . He had joined the politicians and the railroad [barons], eager for settlers, in finding most of the plains region exuberantly arable.[6]

It was Gilpin who codified the phrase "Rain follows the plow." That is, forget about the facts of western aridity. With settlement comes sod breaking and tree planting, both of which, by creating more humidity in the air, will cause rain. While it is true that changes in forestation can cause minor changes in weather patterns, Gilpin's exaggerations became a popular truth. As a slogan for the masses, "rain follows the plow" had it all: strong imagery, active voice, and compact construction, and it was easy off the tongue. What was easy to say became easy to believe, and Gilpin developed a following of zealous adherents.

On July 4, 1868, Gilpin was in the territorial capital of Colorado orating this extravagant vision of the West to a large, holiday crowd. Onto his "rain follows the plow" he had grafted new "facts." True, there were few trees, he said, but, through the beneficence of nature, there were sufficient old-growth roots just beneath the surface of the sod—settlers need only dig for their firewood. Agriculture was "effortless" because there were no bothersome trees as there had been in the eastern stretches of the Midwest, and a farmer need not even employ a plow, so ready were seeds to germinate and take hold in this promised land.[7] Yes, he exhorted, the plains seemed arid in some places; however, there was plenty of pure snowmelt to come down from the mountains, plus ample underground artesian waters just below the surface. In Edenic, soaring language Gilpin went on to predict that the Great Plains would support far more population than even the Mississippi Valley to the east. All it needed was people! More settlers! Powell could only counter Gilpin with science, with the facts of aridity, most of which fell on deaf ears.

IV

East of Bemidji, where I live, the Mississippi is still small. It is about eighty yards wide and twenty feet deep in the main channel, though even that breadth and volume is swelled unnaturally by a small power dam a mile downstream; otherwise, the river might be only fifty feet wide and six or eight feet deep. The water is clear and clean—it would not hurt you to drink it. The current is a bit more than one mile per hour, barely notice-able when swimming upstream, but clearly directional when lazing on an inner tube (my choice, to stay warm). If you swim, swim briskly in the top thermoclines warmed by the sun; if you pause and let your legs hang down, your ankles will turn blue. My house sits on the tip of a peninsula from which the Mississippi is visible from every room. Underneath my house, the water table rises up to within twenty or thirty feet of a layer of clay; then a stratum of large rocks and yellow gravel; and, finally, a slim carpet of loamy topsoil good for pines, aspen, and wild blueberries. Our well is sixty feet deep, the drillers going the extra yards to find the "sweet water" (their term), with the strongest cubic feet per minute flow up the four-inch steel well pipe. While we soften water for bathing, we and most everyone around these parts keep a separate tap for "raw water," as it is coming to be called nowadays, which has no odor, no color, no arsenic, and no lead. Yes, it has minor levels of iron ("Good for your bones," my father always said), and some lime (coffee pots need the occasional vinegar treatment), but it is likely some of the best drinking water in the United States.

Because we are swimming in water, we could use it with impunity. We can water our lawn like a golf course. Take half-hour showers. But while it is nice to have all that water, I never take it for granted. Those deep-bone memories of dry-land farming in South Dakota, plus my time in drought-ridden California, rise up inside me. I remember a cheerful, water-use re-minder sign hung above the toilet at a friend's house in San Jose: "If it's yellow, let it mellow. If it's brown, flush it down."

V

On the very same day in 1868, when Gilpin, in Colorado, was exhorting his fanciful vision of western settlement, Major Powell was leading an ex-pedition into Wyoming territory. The group included his wife and sister, scientists and college students from Illinois, and a guide or two. Powell's research was beginning to challenge everything that Gilpin asserted about the West—challenging him "coolly and on evidence."[8] But western maps still contained much uncharted territory, and Powell was firm enough in his scientific training to let facts lead to conclusions even if that method was slow going. Before Powell would directly confront Gilpin and his fellow travelers of expansionism, exploitation of resources, and raw capitalism, he saw the need for serious, extensive, and orderly mapping of the West. First, he addressed overlooked geologic features, including basins and ranges, but gradually Powell became fixated on the need for another kind of map: water resources. The hydrology of the West.

From his expeditions on the ground (as opposed to Gilpin's orations at chautauquas and political rallies), it became clear to Powell that the processes of settlement that had occurred east of the 100th meridian simply would not do west of it. Utah author Bernard DeVoto (1897–1955) concurred. As writer of *Across the Wide Missouri* plus an expert on Lewis and Clark as well as Mark Twain, DeVoto argued:

> In general, historians have been content to postulate that American institutions, orientations, and habits of thought developed east of the 100th meridian maintained their form and retained their content after reaching the West, whereas in fact a good many important ones did not.[9]

DeVoto goes on to address the imagined know-nothings (such as Gilpin) with an amusing "the-West-for-idiots" primer:

> Well, there isn't much rain out west. There is not enough rain to grow crops and so additional water has to be brought to them for irrigation. That additional water falls as snow on the mountains, it melts, and it flows down the brooks and creeks and then into rivers. If you build dams, you can hold the runoff for when you need it . . . and build canals can bring water to town mains, and to fields that won't grow crops without it.[10]

Pulling away from his "address" to idiots, DeVoto summarizes what Powell had come to believe: "The historical process which we called the westward movement shattered against these facts."[11]

VI

There are signs even in my water-rich northern Minnesota that stressors have come to our hydrologic resources. One of the flashpoints is agricultural irrigation—industrial farming—of potatoes. Beginning in the 1970s, a new phenomenon began to appear on the flat, quarter-section fields around Park Rapids: the central pivot irrigator. Powered by a deep well pumping millions of gallons per field, the long-armed pipe on stilts and wheels slowly circled the field, sprinkling the sandy loam that was ideal for heavy water and fertilizer usage. Ironically, farmers who irrigated this "lighter" soil had better horticultural control and more consistent yields—therefore a stronger business model—than farmers with richer soil in southern and northwestern Minnesota. Irrigation acreage surged. This required the obliteration of the pine plantations and of single-family farms, usually with livestock, whose owners quickly sold out to the "big farmers." A giant French fry plant came to Park Rapids, bringing jobs and new prosperity—but at a price. Trout streams near Park Rapids began to shrink and warm. Recently, the municipal well, which pumps water for almost three thousand people, began to show high concentrations of nitrates—so much so that a water emergency was declared. According to the *Star Tribune*:

> Decades of fertilizer use in neighboring agricultural regions are starting to produce dangerous results in local drinking water. In Park Rapids, located in the potato and corn region of southwest Hubbard County, water is showing rising levels of nitrates from nitrogen fertilizer, which can cause a potentially lethal condition in infants called blue baby syndrome. Park Rapids plans to install new, deeper wells and a water treatment plant that will cost $2 million.[12]

And so my hometown had run up against that most American of dilemmas: the promise of prosperity versus the stewardship of natural resources. A new town well was hastily dug, and the city's water has been restored to acceptable drinking quality; however, many residents believe that the damage has been done, and that they are powerless against the interests of Big Agriculture—in this case, our addiction to cheap French fries.

VII

The arrival of Big Potatoes in my home county in the 1970s meant the end of the line for an entrenched American metaphor: the quarter-section farm. It is what I grew up on and harks back to Thomas Jefferson, who saw 160 acres as the perfect amount of land with which to support one family. His surveyor's vision (mostly realized) was a national checkerboard grid of survey lines—a precise, orderly layout of farms each with four square corners. As DeVoto writes, "The 'quarter-section' had acquired mystical significance in American thinking . . . [as] the basis of a yeoman democracy, the buttress of our liberties, the cornerstone of our economy."[13] But the myth of the quarter-section farm had been broken far earlier by Powell.

It was clear to him that settlement of the West based on this Jeffersonian ideal would mean, for settlers, deprivation if not starvation.

This was the heart of Powell's 1878 paper, "Report on the Lands of the Arid Region of the United States." In its specifics, Powell suggests that, because of aridity, the individual farmer would need as much as 2,900 acres of land in order to create a viable agricultural business model. But more than that, he proposes policy: federal management and control. Stegner explains:

> Powell wanted to close . . . a great part of the remaining public domain ["free land" for homesteading], and bring to a close, except with the irrigable lands, the agricultural expansion which had been part of the national experience for over a century. . . . Settlers should be limited in their archaic personal rights, and brought up sharp against a thing that until now few had bothered to consider: the common interest.[14]

In short, Powell was saying, "Let's slow down and think about the West. Let's let the facts determine our path forward in the West. Let's make the best possible use of this great natural resource." But this measured approach to expansionism collided head-on with the American ideal of Manifest Destiny and Rugged Individualism. To be clear, Powell was not talking about turning the West into one giant, federally controlled national park. As Stegner reminds us, Powell had "the full hope and expectation [that] the American West would become one of the great agricultural regions of the world, but the hope was predicated on wise use of water."[15]

VIII

In my hometown there is now an environmental activist group called "Toxic Taters." They are a citizen's watchdog organization dedicated to monitoring chemical drift from crop spraying as well as water quality. In the schools, student groups keep track of water clarity in key lakes via use of the Secchi disk, a white standardized disk lowered to gauge the transparency of water by measuring the depth at which the disk ceases to be visible. Unfortunately, in many lakes that depth appears to be shortening. But local governing bodies have taken note, and now home septic systems close to lakes have far more stringent requirements than even five years ago. The Minnesota Pollution Control Agency is newly focused on water quality, which is also a good sign. And on the national (western) scene, the "water protectors" of Standing Rock, North Dakota, are opposed to the construction of an oil pipeline beneath the Missouri River; these activists, like Powell, find themselves on the frontlines of the "water wars," a new American metaphor that is not going away any time soon.

IX

Luckily for Powell, "Report on the Lands of the Arid Region" was not the most engaging of titles, and so, at first, most politicians were not paying attention. His research continued, as did his government-funded expeditions; all the while his influence grew in direct relationship to his political skills. It became clear to him that development of the West was best done not by "arbitrary political lines drawn on a map" but rather by water resources. He proposed to organize the new state of Montana by "hydrographic basins" (watersheds) rather than by the Jeffersonian construct of section and quarter-sections. Scientifically, this made all the sense in the world, but Powell's "irrigation legislation" in 1890 finally kicked the hornet's nest.[16]

Politicians on the side of runaway, more-is-good settlement and expansionism in the West suddenly saw Powell as a serious enemy. Even some scientists, perhaps jealous of Powell's growing influence, turned against him. Newspapers blared headlines about this "bitter warfare" among scientists and trumpeted fantastic "charges" against Powell: that his personal learning was fake; that Powell had stolen the work of state geological surveys; and that he had blocked the work and publications of other scientists. As Stegner writes, "They were laying for him when he appeared before the House Appropriations Committee [in June of 1890]" looking for more funding for his work. First, the senators wanted to know who had defined the "arid regions" (not the most inviting of descriptors), and they "implied that it was a fiction of Powell's own, designed to get him extra powers."[17] The grilling went downhill from there, to personal insults and innuendo, all of it intent on denying Powell any more funding for further study of western hydrology. The senators raised a general chorus of objection—objection to any government control; let nature and "man" take their course in the West. Surely that was best?

Powell's reply: "I think it would be almost a criminal act to go on as we are doing now, and allow thousands and hundreds of thousands of people to establish homes where they cannot maintain themselves."[18] Here, Powell was referring to the ongoing, observable facts related to the willy-nilly settlement of the West and the dangers of ignoring the science of climate. "A cycle of unusually wet years, which encouraged the settlement of much semi-arid land, was followed by a return to more conditions of drought over the higher plains, which brought disaster to the Middle Border."[19] The late 1880s became a period of "bitter adjustment," brought on by crop failures followed by a "deluge" of mortgage foreclosures that "sent demoralized settlers returning with their pitiful sticks of furniture to start again in some kinder, more easterly neighborhood."[20] As the historian Fred Shannon writes, "Half the population of Kansas moved out between 1888 and 1892, and large portions of the plains from Kansas to North Dakota were virtually depopulated [from drought]. . . . At least eighteen thousand prairie schooners entered Iowa from Nebraska" as they fled crop failure and aridity.[21] As it turned out, rain had not followed the plow.

In the end, the scientific, hydrologic approach to settlement of the West by Major Powell was derailed by the forces of sloganeering and populism. "Powell underestimated the capacity of the plain dirt farmer to continue to believe in myths even while his nose was being rubbed in the unpleasant facts."[22] Powell's plan was crushed by Congress when he was "within a year of introducing an utterly revolutionary—or evolutionary—set of institutions into the arid West . . . and saving that West from another half century of exploitation and waste."[23]

This triumph of populism over science was very possibly on Frederick Jackson Turner's mind in 1893. Turner, a professor of history the University of Wisconsin and long a writer focused on the American Experiment, published an attention-getting scholarly paper, "The Significance of the Frontier in American History." It was a work that would dominate thinking about the West for decades to come. As Turner theorized:

> Democracy born of free land, strong in selfishness and individualism, *intolerant of administrative experience and education* and pressing individual liberty beyond its proper bounds, has its dangers as well as its benefits. Individualism in America has allowed a laxity in regard to governmental affairs which has rendered possible the spoils system and all the manifest evils that follow from the lack of a highly developed civic spirit.[24]

And Turner's words were never more prescient than when applied to what Stegner called "the triumph of the Gilpins"—that is, the victory of short-term thinking over long-term; the victory of emotion over facts; the victory of sloganeering over science.

X

It is hard not to see our current debate over natural resources and the environment in similar terms. Nearly all scientists maintain there is little question about climate change: it is real, and we have the facts to prove it. But politicians—fretting about short-term economic growth and limits on individual enterprise, not to say getting reelected—often duck and cover. "I don't know," they say about climate change, "because I'm not a scientist," at the same time as they ignore and/or suppress reports like Powell's from real scientists working today. In the current Trump era, political discourse on the use of America's natural resources is eerily similar to that of Powell versus Gilpin, and once again "the Gilpins" seem to be winning.

But past my dock the Mississippi River continues to flow. Its course will likely never change in my lifetime, and I feel lucky for that. Next summer will come the usual "through-paddlers," who vary by age and craft, but I can tell their intent. Their canoes and kayaks run low in the water from the weight of food and gear. Many sport miniature solar panels that power wireless technology. They are loaded for a long trip, which usually means "all the way," that is, to New Orleans. If I am on my dock, I am happy to hail them, hand down some fresh cookies or a cold beverage, and wish them well. But what they do not seem to know, or what they perhaps believe does not apply to them, is that danger lies ahead.

This stretch of river is the easy part. A week downstream are locks and dams, and the thunderous flow under the Stone Arch Bridge in Minneapolis. Below the Twin Cities, in Wisconsin, Illinois, and beyond, are the barges—giant beasts of the river, their bellies filled with iron ore, corn, or gravel, barges so large they appear to be hardly moving when in fact they are rolling up a muddy, curling wake six feet tall. Have these paddlers in their small crafts read their Mark Twain, about "snags" and "deadheads" and "boils" in the current? Do they know how to read the river? Probably not because these paddlers are Americans—intrepid, never short on optimism, sometimes incautious—who often have to learn the hard way.

"Good luck," I call to them as they head downriver. "I hope you make it."

Notes

1   T. S. Eliot, "Hamlet and His Problems," in *The Sacred Wood* (New York: Alfred A. Knopf, 1920), 87–94 (emphasis added).

2   Lark species themselves are part of the demarcation of the West. Any lark sighted west of a north-south line from Warroad to Fairmont, Minnesota, is likely a Western

(versus Eastern) Meadowlark. Both species are in decline from intensive farming practices resulting in loss of grassland habitat.

3 Wallace Stegner, *Beyond the Hundredth Meridian: John Wesley Powell and the Second Opening of the West* (New York: Penguin, 1954), 229.

4 A novel by Rose Wilder Lane, *Free Land* (New York: Longman, Green, 1938), focused on homesteading in South Dakota in the 1880s.

5 Stegner, *Beyond the Hundredth Meridian*, 8.

6 Stegner, *Beyond the Hundredth Meridian*, 2.

7 Stegner, *Beyond the Hundredth Meridian*, 4.

8 Stegner, *Beyond the Hundredth Meridian*, 6.

9 Bernard DeVoto, introduction to Stegner, *Beyond the Hundredth Meridian*, xviii-ix.

10 DeVoto, introduction, xix.

11 DeVoto, introduction, xix.

12 Josephine Marcotty, "In Central Minnesota, Potatoes Are Pushing Out Forest Land," *Star Tribune*, October 26, 2013, http://www.startribune.com/in-central-minnesota-potatoes-are-pushing-out-forest-land/229339381/.

13 DeVoto, introduction, xix.

14 Stegner, *Beyond the Hundredth Meridian*, 219.

15 Stegner, *Beyond the Hundredth Meridian*, 314.

16 Stegner, *Beyond the Hundredth Meridian*, 328.

17 Stegner, *Beyond the Hundredth Meridian*, 330.

18 Stegner, *Beyond the Hundredth Meridian*, 333.

19 Frank Thistlethwaite, *The Great Experiment: An Introduction to the History of the American People* (Cambridge: Cambridge University Press, 1967), 196.

20 Thistlethwaite, *Great Experiment*, 196.

21 Fred Shannon quoted in Stegner, *Beyond the Hundredth Meridian*, 409, note 3.

22 Stegner, *Beyond the Hundredth Meridian*, 336.

23 Stegner, *Beyond the Hundredth Meridian*, 338.

24 Frederick Jackson Turner, "The Significance of the Frontier in American History," in *The Annual Report of the American Historical Association* (Washington, D.C.: Government Printing Office, 1894), 119–227 (emphasis added).

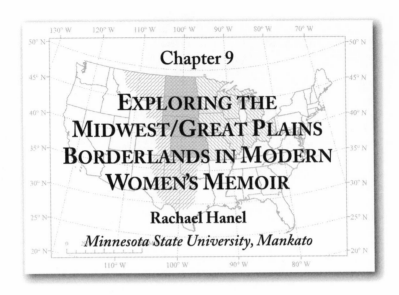

Chapter 9

EXPLORING THE MIDWEST/GREAT PLAINS BORDERLANDS IN MODERN WOMEN'S MEMOIR

Rachael Hanel

Minnesota State University, Mankato

Introduction

One way to discern the differences between the Great Plains and the Midwest is to see how people from those regions describe them. To get a better sense of how the Midwest and Great Plains are defined in the modern world, I will specifically look at examples of recent women's memoir. I have chosen three examples from each region. Representing the Great Plains are Julene Bair's *The Ogallala Road*, Mary Clearman Blew's *Balsamroot: A Memoir*, and Tracy Seeley's *My Ruby Slippers: The Road Back to Kansas*. The Midwestern books are Barrie Jean Borich's *Body Geographic*, Nicole Helget's *The Summer of Ordinary Ways*, and Gayla Marty's *Memory of Trees*. I recognize this is a small sample size, which therefore prevents the extrapolation of sweeping generalizations about each place. However, in examining these books, clear differences emerge in how these women write and what they write about. The results may serve as a guide to examine how people from the Great Plains and Midwest see themselves and how they interact with their regions, but as with any guidelines there will always be exceptions.

The dividing line between the Great Plains and the Midwest in these memoirs is more emotional than geographic. The line falls between writing from outside the place versus writing from within it; between landscape as the driving narrative versus landscape as a background character; and between the need to explore the larger world versus the need to explore the place where one lives. The women writing of the Great Plains leave the area in order to reinvent themselves; the women writing of the Midwest reinvent themselves in order to stay.

Writing from Within / Writing from the Outside

Lack of geographic security in Great Plains states—with their vulnerable, open spaces and windstorms that blow away topsoil—translates into lack of emotional security the women writers face. As a result, these writers tend to leave the Great Plains and write about it from a different (safer) place. But in the Midwest, with its security represented by deep tree roots that keep soil from escaping, the women writers are more likely to stay and write about where they live.

All three of the Great Plains memoirists—Bair, Blew, and Seeley—had moved away from their places of origin at the time they were writing their memoirs. Bair and Seeley were raised in Kansas, and Blew comes from Montana. Bair wrote most of *The Ogallala Road* while living in Wyoming and Colorado. Seeley taught writing at the University of San Francisco while working on *My Ruby Slippers*, and Blew lived in Idaho while writing *Balsamroot*.

Bair has never considered herself rooted, moving away from Kansas when she was eighteen years old to live in San Francisco. She spent time living in the Mojave Desert before relocating to Wyoming to teach. She briefly returned to Kansas to help her father farm after she went through a failed relationship, but she found Kansas much different than the one of her youth.

Bair attended the Iowa Writers' Workshop, where she received a master of fine arts in creative writing. She thought she would write about her experiences in San Francisco during its revolutionary heyday in the 1960s and 1970s, and also her unique experience living alone in the desert. But it was her original home on which her memories centered. "My fingers kept typing out stories about the place I was born," she said in an interview.[1] Even though she hadn't lived in Kansas for years, her family still had ties to the land. Like many farm families, they struggled with issues like water rights and the legacy of who gets to farm the land after a parent dies. Bair realized that Kansas is part of her "fundamental identity. Everything that made us who we were was on the farm."[2]

Seeley also found herself in San Francisco after moving away from Kansas. But unlike Bair, Seeley stayed in the city and settled into a comfortable Bay Area life. But thoughts of home kept returning to Seeley, too. In the early 2000s, after a relationship dissolved and she was diagnosed with cancer, Seeley traveled to Kansas in an attempt to discover the meaning of home and the hold it had upon her.

In San Francisco, she thought she had left the Great Plains behind forever: "Nearly everyone I meet here has escaped Kansas or somewhere like it, and no one dreams of going home. Who would give up her sparkling ruby dancing shoes for a farm house in the middle of a desiccated nowhere? We've flown the flyover zone. Our migration has saved us. Reinvented, reeducated, recoiffed, and redeemed, we live fascinating, urbane lives. Or at least that [is] what we tell our satisfied selves."[3] Seeley writes how others she met when she moved away saw Kansas as "flat, dull, and culturally backward."[4] She incorporated that mythos into her own understanding of home. So she went to another plains state, Texas, to get her education. Texas in terms of topography was a lot like Kansas, but it also had a "panache, a national myth that made it rise above geography and hickdom like a lone, shining star."[5]

What initially drove Bair and Seeley away? For one thing, the land could not sustain a way of life they had remembered. Bair witnessed dramatic changes to her family's farm. When she was sixteen years old, her family became "town people." For farmers, it was a sign of prosperity to be able to afford a home in town. Bair saw her dad commute every day to work, just like a suburbanite. She did not know it then, but the farm already was changing. Irrigation allowed her father to raise crops like corn, which naturally cannot grow in the dry, sandy soil of Kansas. Millions of gallons of water were pumped from the ground every year to nourish the crops. But how long could that practice last?

Bair could not project into the future when she was young, but Blew knew as a girl that she would not have a future on her family's Montana ranch. She left to go to school, eventually settling in Idaho to teach, much to her father's disappointment. "When I left home, it was a serious economic blow to my family. They had been counting on me to come back from college after a year or two with a teaching certificate and help support the ranch. I was looking for intellectual challenge? It wouldn't have been a concept my father understood. The very notion would have angered him, as did so much else. He allowed little margin in his world for deviance."[6]

On the contrary, Gayla Marty would have given anything to be able to stay on her family's rural Minnesota farm. When her parents decided to sell the farm, Marty and her husband wanted to buy it, but ultimately they could not afford the property. Marty was living only sixty miles away in Minneapolis when her parents sold the farm. In *Memory of Trees*, she recalls the anguish over her missed opportunity: "Riding home, I cried with rage and grief. For many nights, I woke up in the darkness, crying, exhausted, looking down on my own bowed head in a bed on the second floor of a house that was not my home in the middle of Minneapolis. I felt unmoored, wandering, and found no consolation in my husband's arms. The farm was my home, the place I'd always counted on, my refuge and comfort, the anchor I'd needed to raise my children."[7]

Marty's book is not the only example of Midwestern women writing from within the place they are writing about. They have stayed instead of leaving. It is as if the Midwest imprinted upon them something so strong that they could not escape even if they wanted to. Borich, in *Body Geographic*, takes this imprint literally. She opens the book by recounting the day a tattoo artist worked on her back. "The artist inks a dual city skyline. My Chicago in the center. My Minneapolis to either side."[8] Borich was raised in Chicago, attended school in rural Illinois, then decamped to Minneapolis where she spent almost three decades living, writing, and teaching. She is now back in Chicago.

Both Marty's book and Borich's book are like odes to the places where they live. Helget's book is no exception. *The Summer of Ordinary Ways* reads like a love letter to the rural Midwest. Throughout the book, Helget describes the way of life in this place:

> Mom's creative mind went to work on her garden and in her meals and in food preservation. Clear jars with gold rims for our garden tomatoes, crushed and whole, lined full rows in the basement canning room. Purple beets lay sliced and stacked in wine-colored juice. Two rows of pickled cucumbers stood straight in brine just right. Mom chose the most uniform jars and sent me off to the county fair with them. She stood a few feet from the judge and listened to me talk about choosing the best sized and best textured and best flavored cucumbers from the vine. . . . I earned Grand Champion and was sent to the state fair. The state fair judges slapped a purple ribbon on my jars, too, and the newspaper snapped my picture, which Mom cut out and taped to the refrigerator.[9]

Helget was not living far away from Sleepy Eye while writing *The Summer of Ordinary Ways*, still surrounded by the cornfields, barns, and gravel roads of her childhood. More than a decade later, that rural landscape continues to provide inspiration for writing. Though she lived for a time in Mankato, southern Minnesota's regional center, she sought to return to a rural haven. She now lives and writes on a farmstead outside of Mankato. "I love the trees," she says. "I love to go down to the creek to see what I can find. I think about history, I think about current politics, I think about relationships, and I like to do that by myself."[10]

The Role of Landscape

The role landscape plays in these memoirs relates to the aforementioned living within the space or living outside of it. In the Great Plains memoirs, the landscape is treated with a sense of awe. As Bair writes: "It was the kind of low-key vista that could thrill only a native Kansan whose eye had not been jaded by mountains or the sensational. 'Thrill' is probably the wrong word. 'Satisfy' might be better, or 'fulfill.'"[11] Bair further describes what it is like to see the Great Plains: "There's something about being able to see far that instills the spirit with a sense of grandeur."[12]

In Bair's book, the Kansas landscape is the heart of the story. She also weaves in a thread about the beginning and ending of a romance with a Kansan, but the land plays an important role in their relationship. In one of their early conversations, Bair and her boyfriend, Ward, talk about place:

> "But that's what intrigues me about you," I said. "You stayed."
>
> "And that's what intrigues me about you. You didn't."[13]

Place is a main reason why the relationship failed. Bair and Ward could not agree where to live if the relationship were to progress. Did Bair really want to move back to Kansas to live with him? Did Ward want to move to Wyoming to be with Bair? They decided neither would be happy—not if Bair went home or if Ward left home.

Leaving home for many years, and then returning, also sparks a sense of wonderment and seeing the place with fresh eyes. In Seeley's book, the primary narrative is her return to Kansas through regular visits as an adult. Because Seeley had moved around so much throughout Colorado and Kansas as a child, she didn't have a good sense of what "home" was. The entire book takes place as she moves through the landscape. That landscape helps her rediscover the pride she has in her roots in the heartland: "Little by little, with every conversation, every museum, every mile, I take Kansas more deeply into myself. Driving the long straight roads or the hilly crooked ones, I settle into the comfort of knowing and belonging, slowly losing my fear of the plains' empty reaches and relishing the different textures of the wind. I have finally shucked my stereotypes and city condescension, the snobbishness of a lucky escapee, and can appreciate the people I meet, not dismiss them for what they think or wear or know about the world. They have a rooted experience I envy."[14]

The landscape draws Seeley back again and again. After that initial sojourn, she returns to Kansas every year for a few years: "At the end of my two weeks on the road, I had fallen in love with Kansas. Or let myself admit I'd loved it all along. Every spring for the next five years, I got the itch. Kansas. I still feel the pull, not of nostalgia, but of long horizons and open sky, tall grass and wheat fields, of wind and the smell of ozone before a summer storm."[15]

While Bair's and Seeley's books are primarily about the landscape, Blew's central narrative is her relationship with her ailing Aunt Imogene. But still, the importance of a Great Plains backdrop as a driving force is evident. Like Blew, the aunt also left the desolation of Montana to start a new life. She started a new life as far west as she could get, Port Angeles, Washington, overlooking the Strait of Juan de Fuca, a place where one needs a ferry to arrive. Escaping the wide-open space of Montana set the aunt's new life in motion. She escaped not only the wildness but also her family. In Washington, Blew's aunt could have a fresh start. Nothing was left for her in Montana, only a life of hardship: "What kind of ending would we write for Imogene if we could? Do we want to see her married and stuck on some godforsaken ridge or coulee ranch in Fergus County, spending her days scrubbing and baking and helping with the harvest and the cattle? Holding together a few depleted acres? Or not even that much—to work for wages on somebody else's acres?"[16]

The Midwestern memoirs, on the other hand, treat the landscape almost as just another facet of life that contributes to self-development. The landscape is respected but not elevated. Readers do not get the sense that the authors are in a state of wonderment or awe by living in this land. It just "is." The authors put it on equal footing with family relationships or experiences that shape the self. "People writing from and about the Midwest," says Kent Ryden, "pay close attention to the subtle histories and cultures that are everywhere in the landscape, perceiving and describing the world as its residents see it, collectively writing and inscribing regional identity from the materials at hand."[17]

While the family's farm is an important component of *The Summer of Ordinary Ways*, Helget concentrates more on local history, family dynamics, and her change from a child to a young woman. The farm could have been anywhere and her family would have had the same dramas and conflicts. The fact that it is a southern Minnesota farm is not entirely important to the story; it just happens to be where she lives. Few people are in awe of how the Midwest soil produces corn and soybeans. Likewise, the Midwestern authors recognize that they and others around them also spring from the soil without fanfare or reverence. In this passage where Helget describes a neighbor of the farm, she is focusing on those subtle histories and characters of the Midwest: "Moonshine farmed the eighty to the east of us. He had bought that eighty, some of the richest soil north of the Little Cottonwood River, off Henry Fischer but only after Moonshine agreed to marry his oldest daughter, Clara, a solid-hipped German girl whose cooking apologized for the temper she inherited from her dad. Moonshine set aside three of those acres for growing potatoes and made the corn, soybean, and alfalfa farmers wonder about his sanity."[18]

In Marty's book, the farm is a central character. It is almost a living, breathing thing, just like Marty's parents. Throughout the book, Marty provides short meditations on the landscape in the form of trees. These meditations—on elms, maples, oaks, pines, and others—are interspersed throughout the book: "In the fall, maples make our woods dazzle. One Sunday, Mama and Daddy take the twins and me for a walk up the lane. Daddy takes pictures of us under the gold maples glowing in the sunlight. We walk through Applegate's, cross the highway, meet up with the creek, and follow it all the way to the farm where Mama grew up, where we surprise Grampa and Gramma Anderson."[19]

The land is something to be passed down, if not physically, then in spirit. Marty raises her children in Minneapolis but still tries to bring a bit of the farm life to them: "Every spring, I bend over the garden with Claire, teaching her to plant black-eyed Susans while I mark off rows for green beans. She waters, sprinkles dirt, tamps it down. She comes behind me, watering, pushing the row closed, tamping it down with the hoe. She gathers green beans in August, snapping them open and eating them as she squats by the row."[20]

In *Body Geographic*, too, geography is the backdrop to a larger life. Borich is well-known in creative nonfiction circles for her lyric essays, the hallmarks of which are poetic language and metaphor. She takes the concept of geography and Midwest and uses it as a metaphor for her own life. The publisher says the book "turns personal history into an inspired reflection on the points where place and person intersect, where running away meets running toward, and where dislocation means finding oneself."[21]

Borich writes of her time in Urbana, Illinois, as a young undergraduate, surrounded by flat farmland, where corn and soybeans protrude from the earth. She recalls the time she was taken back to the farmhouse of a university professor, who took advantage of her while she was drunk. This was the time before concepts like "date rape" and "consensual sex" were part of the college conversation. She looks back upon that time through the lens of geography: "That my fundamental landscape—my body and the body of the prairie, the body of my whole Midwestern home, made of all I would do and have done to me in this formative time and space, the map I'd make all my later maps against—could be for me, or for anyone, a utopian construction of chosen elements, like a city planner's chart of the perfect city, all rounded edges and proportionate balance, free of any overgrown patches that thirty years later would be impossible to fully survey."[22]

Exploration

For the women growing up in the Great Plains, one gets the sense that the landscape was a launching pad for physical adventure and exploration. The women do not seem to be able to stay on the land where they were raised. It is not so much a forced ejection, but perhaps has its parallel in what grows naturally on the land. The plains is the land of prairie grasses, the sandy soil not supporting much else. Native Americans relied on bison for food and grew fewer domesticated crops compared to their counterparts in other regions. The soil, the droughts, the storms, and early frost in the upper Great Plains made growing crops an unsure proposition. But with technical advances in agriculture, the Great Plains in the twentieth century became the country's breadbasket, with vast amounts of irrigation supporting corn and soybeans—crops that naturally grow better in the rich soil of the Midwest. Independent, family-run farms, like the Bair farm, involved a high degree of risk and loss. Just as corn and soybeans do not naturally fit on the plains, the women memoirists of the plains have a need to go elsewhere to find a place where they belong. As Norma Elia Cantu says, "The areas that western literature reflects are definitely place-bound and have to do with migrations and with movement as well as with home, a home that is not ever really secure, but something ephemeral."[23]

For Bair, growing up in a place of wide vistas and tremendous sky launched a quest to find the same in other places. She felt at home in the desert, when she lived for a time in the Mojave: "Imprinted on my memory were the conical peaks of the Pinto Mountains, dappled in juniper. They and the craggy sandstone pinnacles of the New York range beyond them spoke the layered language of geology. To float in that valley had been to float on the sea of time."[2] Indeed, whenever Bair went to the Midwest, she found the landscape stifling. She attended graduate school in Iowa and made the trip between Iowa and Kansas often. Something happened to her after she crossed the 100th meridian: She wanted to turn around and go back to the plains. "It took all I could do to turn east on I-80," Bair says.[25] In *The Ogallala Road* she writes of driving to Iowa: "As the Rocky Mountain rain shadow dissipated, the land got greener, the skies diminished in both height and breadth, and I saw the sun less often. I felt like a child going inside after recess. No pale vistas. No vaulting, translucent blue. As hills and cornfields multiplied, my sun-dependent, distance-dependent soul shriveled to a nubbin of yearning."[26]

Seeley found a renewed connection to the home of her youth in *The Ruby Slippers*, but she did not find a need to permanently return. Instead, she continued to move and explore new places. At the end of the book, Seeley has moved to Los Angeles, almost as far away from the Great Plains as one can get, if not physically, then psychologically and emotionally. But she saw herself as belonging in this new place: "My work is here, becoming native to the place where I find myself. Finding and nurturing the green world inside my city life. Letting the place teach me. Peeling back the layered accretions of history, culture, and migration; gathering those stories as I go. . . . Learn what geology, weather, and soil can teach me."[27]

The Midwestern memoirists exhibit a stronger sense of belonging where they were raised. Like the strong roots of oaks and maples, or the roots of corn and soybeans that reach into the Midwestern soil and grab hold, plants in the Midwest are not easily uprooted and neither are these memoirists. Indeed, one of Helget's chapters is titled "Rooted Here." In *The Music of Failure*, Minnesota writer Bill Holm says, "I meant not to write autobiography, but to use myself as example, duplicated many times in southwestern Minnesota, of attempted escape from these unlikely prairies, and the discovery, usually after years passing, that for better or worse, you belong in a place, and grow out of its black soil like a cornstalk."[28]

The Midwestern memoirs exhibit a willingness to discover the place where they live, whether it be southern Minnesota, east-central Minnesota, or the urban landscapes of Chicago and Minneapolis. The majority of Helget's memoir is written through the eyes of a child. Readers get a sense of innocent wonderment of the small pocket of Minnesota prairie and the people who inhabit that place. Helget's childhood was marked by curiosity. She was the oldest of six children growing up on a farm in the 1970s and 1980s, and nature was their playground. Helget and her sisters ran in and out the farm buildings, the creeks, the ditches, the garden. With so much to see, and with each of the four seasons always bringing a new view to the same place, why go anywhere else?

The exploration also comes in the form of history. The landscape satisfied Helget, but there was also so much to learn in terms of local legends. She writes of a young girl, Annie Mary Twente, who supposedly was buried alive in the late nineteenth century, near where Helget grew up: "A terrible death lends itself to a restless existence. . . . It's only natural the girl's spirit can't stay quiet, that she can't stop roving these hills and this river valley. And, like you, other people want to see her. . . . You pick ditch flowers and fashion bouquets for the dead girl. You leave barrettes, miniature Strawberry Shortcakes, fancy erasers that sit alongside the nickels, necklaces, shiny rocks, and other trinkets the little township girls of the past century have left for Annie Mary."[29]

Borich also takes a dive into Midwestern history. She writes of the 1893 World's Fair in Chicago and her family's immigrant history from Croatia to Chicago. Of her grandfather, Petey, she says: "He will learn the new American fox-trot and marry Rose, that beautiful American doll training to be a nurse. He will run into his American life, toes twitching, wind stinging his eyes. He will make his American babies, buy his American house on Blackstone Avenue."[30]

Marty's writing, too, intently explores the farm where she grew up and the history behind it. These "little things" are what defines the Midwest, as Kent Ryden argues. Regions such as the East and the South are defined by "big" events—colonialism, the Revolutionary War, the Civil War—that give residents there a common background. The Midwest (and I would add the Great Plains) lack a big historical event that happened region-wide. "In the Midwest, such events seem less obvious and available, less urgently remembered and reinforced over time; instead, individuals and communities and institutions decide who they are by looking first at how they live in the present and how their lives connect to the locally grounded past."[31]

Marty, Helget, and Borich wrote their memoirs while living in close proximity to the places they were writing about. While working on a last revision of *Memory of Trees*, Marty left her Minneapolis home to stay three nights a week with her mom, just a mile or so from where Marty was raised. She was in that place, surrounded by mementoes of history, like stones in a fireplace that had been taken from the foundation of an old family homestead: "All around me were the pieces of my former life that were being repurposed. I could see that we go on, we take the building materials from past life and build new life."[32]

Conclusion

By definition, memoir is the story of a self. But for these Great Plains and Midwestern memoirists, the story of self is tied closely to place. The books become "a collection of places where [one] has lived, worked, played, gone to school, visited family."[33] While there is no agreed-upon clear boundary between the Great Plains and the Midwest, these memoirs suggest subtle differences in how writers perceive their regions. But one thing the writers have in common: the need to attach meaning to a place the rest of the world tends to ignore. To give this place credibility, to breathe life into it in order to offset stereotypes or broad generalizations. The incredible love these writers hold for the places they are from is impossible to miss.

As Ryden says: "Viewed from the level of the landscape itself, read about in the pages of its nonfiction chroniclers, traveled through with eyes and ears and mind wide open, the region's inscrutable surface refracts and resolves into a rich and complex world of individual places and locally grounded histories, an overlooked and undiscovered country continually thought and written into being."[34]

Notes

[1] Julene Bair, interview by author, telephone, December 9, 2016.
[2] Bair, interview by author.
[3] Tracy Seeley, *My Ruby Slippers: The Road Back to Kansas* (Lincoln: University of Nebraska Press, 2011), xi.
[4] Seeley, *My Ruby Slippers*, xii.
[5] Seeley, *My Ruby Slippers*, xii.
[6] Mary Clearman Blew, *Balsamroot: A Memoir* (Norman: University of Oklahoma Press, 1994), 144.
[7] Gayla Marty, *Memory of Trees: A Daughter's Story of a Family Farm* (Minneapolis: University of Minnesota Press, 2010), 200.
[8] Barrie Jean Borich, *Body Geographic* (Lincoln: University of Nebraska Press, 2013), 8.
[9] Nicole Helget, *The Summer of Ordinary Ways* (St. Paul: Borealis Books, 2005), 163.
[10] Nicole Helget, interview by author, St. Peter, MN, December 13, 2016.
[11] Julene Bair, *The Ogallala Road: A Story of Love, Family, and the Fight to Keep the Great Plains from Running Dry* (New York: Penguin, 2014), 64.
[12] Bair, interview by author.
[13] Bair, *Ogallala Road*, 77.
[14] Seeley, *My Ruby Slippers*, 112.
[15] Seeley, *My Ruby Slippers*, 105.
[16] Blew, *Balsamroot*, 174–75.
[17] Kent C. Ryden, "Writing the Midwest: History, Literature, and Regional Identity," *Geographical Review* 89 (1999): 522.
[18] Helget, *Summer of Ordinary Ways*, 42.
[19] Marty, *Memory of Trees*, 39.

[20] Marty, *Memory of Trees*, 229.

[21] "*Body Geographic*: About the Book," University of Nebraska Press, accessed December, 16, 2016, http://www.nebraskapress.unl.edu/product/Body-Geographic,675632.aspx, paragraph 1.

[22] Borich, *Body Geographic*, 174.

[23] Julene Bair, Mary Clearman Blew, Norma Elia Cantu, Patricia Hampl, John Price, and Kathleen Boardman, "Western Autobiography and Memoir: A Panel of Writers," *Western American Literature* 37 (2002): 160.

[24] Bair, *Ogallala Road*, 110.

[25] Bair, interview by author.

[26] Bair, *Ogallala Road*, 141.

[27] Seeley, *My Ruby Slippers*, 174.

[28] Bill Holm, *The Music of Failure* (Minneapolis: University of Minnesota Press, 1985), 40.

[29] Helget, *Summer of Ordinary Ways*, 96–97.

[30] Borich, *Body Geographic*, 56.

[31] Ryden, "Writing the Midwest," 514.

[32] Gayla Marty, interview by author, telephone, December 30, 2016.

[33] Ryden, "Writing the Midwest," 527.

[34] Ryden, "Writing the Midwest," 528.

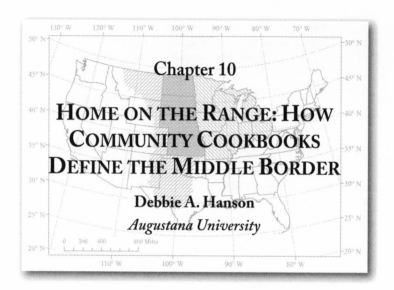

Chapter 10

HOME ON THE RANGE: HOW COMMUNITY COOKBOOKS DEFINE THE MIDDLE BORDER

Debbie A. Hanson

Augustana University

While the borders of some geographical areas of the United States, such as New England or the Deep South, are generally accepted, neither the Midwest nor the Great Plains is typically seen as such a well-defined region. Surely the difficulties in defining these regions are partly due to the vast sizes of them both, but perhaps the problems that lie in delineating what Hamlin Garland referred to as the middle border might be seen differently if viewed through a greater number of lenses, including those available in community cookbooks. While not generally viewed as texts with much to contribute to geographic study, compiled cookbooks produced in the Midwest and on the Great Plains provide an insider's perspective that illuminates what joins these distinctive regions as well as what divides them.

Lynne Ireland has described the community cookbook as a hybrid form that may be viewed as a popular culture medium that is also basically folkloric and can function as a collective autobiography[1] as well as allow for the financial support of causes.[2] Indeed, during the Civil War, community cookbooks were second only to charity fairs in their ability to raise funds for the war effort, and their popularity increased as the popularity of charity fairs declined.[3] In fact, by the end of the nineteenth century, more than two thousand community cookbooks had been published in the United

140

States[4] with 1,051 produced between the end of the Civil War and the beginning of World War I by Presbyterian, Methodist, Methodist Episcopal, Congregational, Baptist, and Episcopal churches.[5] While it is impossible to gauge precisely how much money such cookbooks have raised since the Civil War, it is estimated that since 1990, the hundreds of books submitted to the Tabasco Community Cookbook Awards committee have raised millions of dollars, and the books granted Hall of Fame status by Tabasco have collectively raised more than twenty-nine million dollars.[6]

Beyond their ability to raise money, community cookbooks have been referred to as "memorial texts"[7] and "multi-authored auto-ethnographical accounts" that provide the "perspective of a community written from inside that community."[8] More simply, they have been called "community biographies."[9] That the communities in question are invariably parts of larger regions makes it inevitable that community cookbooks also indicate how those who provide the recipes for these volumes view their place within that greater geography. If, as Amy Bentley has suggested, no national American cuisine exists because American cuisine exists only at a regional level, community cookbooks may well be exceedingly useful in showing how those who live within particular regions define them for themselves.[10]

In terms of this study, forty-five cookbooks from eleven states, including those generally described as Midwestern or Upper Midwestern—Illinois, Michigan, Wisconsin, Minnesota, and Iowa—were examined along with those from states more typically associated with the Great Plains or the West, including Nebraska, Montana, Colorado, and Washington and those from states like South Dakota and North Dakota. These states sometimes fall in the grey, ambiguous area between the Midwest and the Great Plains, at least in terms of how they are viewed by geographers and the general public. The largest number of cookbooks considered came from South Dakota and Minnesota, partially because they are adjoining states that do not necessarily always see themselves as being part of the same region and partially because they were easily accessible to a researcher working in South Dakota who's originally from Minnesota. The cookbooks themselves came from library book sales, church bazaars, used bookstores, antique shops, various charity sales, and this academic's own shockingly large collection of such books. The books' publication dates covered roughly the last fifty years, a large span of time for a fairly limited survey of cookbooks, but given that community cookbooks are frequently kept for decades, reprinted, and handed down from one generation to the next, one that is also reflective of how the books actually function in everyday kitchens. Similarly, the cookbooks were produced by a variety of groups, including churches, civic groups, service organizations, tribes, extended families, and occupational organizations. Cookbooks published by groups promoting the use of a particular ingredient or product, such as bison, were not included in order to avoid skewing the study toward recipes that included that ingredient.

What, then, did the analysis of these texts indicate? Lucy Long has called the typical Midwestern diet meat-and-potatoes cuisine.[11] A reading of more than eight hundred questionnaires regarding Midwestern eating habits conducted by Barbara G. and James R. Shortridge yielded results that support Long's contention. According to the Shortridges' research, a typical Midwestern meal "consists of beef (roast or grilled steak), with potatoes (mashed with gravy or baked), corn on the cob, green beans, and apple pie," though they also noted preferences for turkey in Minnesota and pork chops in central Illinois, Iowa, and eastern Nebraska, as well as a "Jell-O and casserole belt in the Dakotas."[12] Indeed the cookbooks examined for this study proved these descriptions to be at least somewhat accurate as their recipes often emphasized the use of meat, potatoes, Jell-O, and cream of mushroom soup—but not always. Asian, Mexican, and Italian recipes were also extremely popular, though what was defined as belonging to those cuisines by the contributors to the cookbooks often did not resemble what might be considered Asian, Mexican, and Italian recipes elsewhere. For instance, "Chinese Coleslaw"[13] and "Crispy Taco Turnovers"[14] are fairly obviously not traditionally associated with Asian or Mexican cuisines, and "Italian Dunkers"[15]—made with hot dog buns, cheese, and whipped butter or garlic butter spray—are surely not eaten regularly in Rome or Milan. Unusual fusions of such cuisines were in evidence as well, such as "Chilighetti Casserole"[16] and "Swedish Spaghetti."[17]

Recipes identified as originating in California, Texas, or Hawaii, also universally popular in the cookbooks, did not seem necessarily representative of these states either. In particular, the appellation "Hawaiian" was apparently considered appropriate for any recipe to which pineapple or coconut, or both, had been added. Recipes regarded as having German, Norwegian, Swedish, and Danish roots were generally more reflective of traditional recipes from these countries, though recipes for *lefse* that involved instant mashed potatoes or tortes that used cake mixes and pre-packaged puddings were not uncommon. Across all the states, German recipes were the most popular, although some individual cookbooks—such as Grace Lutheran Church of Watertown, South Dakota's *Cooking with Grace*— had a heavy concentration of Norwegian recipes. In all cases, German and Scandinavian recipes were those most often included in "heritage" sections of these cookbooks. Recipes bearing the names of individual contributors or those originally associated with particular recipes were also popular in all the cookbooks examined. Marion Bishop has referred to recipes named by contributors as sending a "life-validating second message" that connects the "recipe writer to [the] cook."[18] For these cookbooks, they also validated a community connection that crossed regional boundaries, while the ingredients, cooking styles, and names of other recipes emphasized instead distinct differences between the Midwest and the Great Plains.

While any number of ingredients appear in recipes across the selected cookbooks, some, such as wild rice and various types of wild game, help indicate just where the dividing line between these two regions may be. Recipes featuring wild rice, or boxed wild rice blends, were featured most heavily in cookbooks from Minnesota, then Iowa, North Dakota, South Dakota, and Nebraska; but not at all in the cookbooks from Illinois, Michigan, Wisconsin, and Washington used for comparison; and only once in a Montana cookbook. That Minnesota cookbooks contained the most recipes for wild rice makes sense, as wild rice is Minnesota's state grain, but it is still significant that the cookbooks from states the farthest west referred to it less frequently and that the North Dakota cookbooks that most often mentioned wild rice were from towns or cities in the northeastern sections of the state, such as Fargo, which is frequently linked to Moorhead, Minnesota, its nearest geographic neighbor. If wild rice was more heavily tied to Minnesota than either of the two Dakotas, so were wild game and fresh-caught fish, though if two cookbooks from northeastern Minnesota, including one from the Fon Du Lac reservation, were disregarded, Nebraska and South Dakota were more heavily tied to these ingredients, both in terms of numbers of recipes involving wild game and in terms of the variety of types of wild game mentioned, from pheasant and duck to deer and antelope.

Barbecue—a cooking style associated with the West as well as the South and Southwest, primarily due to the iconic image of cowboys roasting their meals over open fires—was also given a more prominent place in cookbooks from the states more likely to be thought of as part of the Great Plains, with North Dakota volumes including the most barbecue recipes, followed by Iowa, Nebraska, South Dakota, and Minnesota. Iowa having the second-most barbecue recipes was due primarily to a large number of recipes for sandwiches involving barbecued hamburger, which are popular in the Midwest but might not be viewed as having much to do with barbecue elsewhere. If cookbooks from Iowa were left out of the equation, the frequency with which barbecue was stressed in the cookbooks of Nebraska,

North Dakota, and South Dakota as opposed to states farther east indicates that there may be a separation of geographical cuisines somewhere between Minnesota and the two Dakotas, as is further emphasized by the recipes included in *Pine to Prairie Cookbook: Volume IV*, a cookbook published jointly by the Minnesota and North Dakota chapters of the Telephone Pioneers of America. *Pine to Prairie Cookbook* had ten recipes for wild rice and only a single recipe for wild game, which would make it seem to share more similarities with Midwestern cookbooks. However, the single recipe for wild game calls for rattler, a snake more strongly connected to the Great Plains, and the cookbook had a six-page section on barbecue, which would also make it more Western than Midwestern. Perhaps this split focus is simply indicative of the fact that *Pine to Prairie Cookbook* is in the unusual position of including contributions that span a regional dividing line as well.

Ingredients and cooking styles, of course, are not the only indicators of regionality. Regional attributions tie recipes to specific locations, too, and help to identify distinctive regional cuisines.[19] This indicator of regional distinctiveness is particularly clear in community cookbooks from the Midwest and Great Plains. Specifically regional names of recipes in cookbooks from Iowa primarily referred to the states of Iowa and Minnesota, as in "Iowa Chili"[20] and "Minnesota Wild Rice Salad"[21]; meteorological conditions, as in "Cold Weather Chili"[22] and "Jewels in the Snow"[23]; and agriculture or regional agricultural products, as in "Farmer's Salad"[24] and "Baked Soybeans."[25] Recipes in Minnesota community cookbooks also referred often to local areas or places in their titles, such as "Chicken Breast from New Ulm"[26] or "Park Point Rabbit Stew"[27]; geographical features, such as "Prairie Honey Mustard"[28]; and occupations associated with the state's history and legends, such as "Lumberjack Hamburger."[29] In North Dakota, however, while some recipes might reference agriculture, such as "Farmer's Dessert,"[30] many more stressed the state's connection to the Great Plains, including "Big Country Breakfast Casserole,"[31] "Buffalo Chip Cookies,"[32] "Chuck Wagon Peanut Butter Cookies,"[33] "Western Mac,"[34] and "Ranch Style Chicken."[35] A similar trend was evidenced in South Dakota cookbooks, which included recipes like "Farmer Brownies"[36] and "Farmer's Breakfast"[37] but included more recipes with titles featuring traditionally Western imagery, such as "Cowboy Cookies,"[38] "Camp Potatoes,"[39] "Mesquite Beans,"[40] "Beef and Cheese Round-Up,"[41] "Bunkhouse Chili,"[42] "Rancher Steak Tips,"[43] and "Trail Ride Eggs."[44]

Beyond the two Dakotas, cookbooks from Nebraska might contain recipes mentioning agriculture or the state itself like "'End of Garden' Uncooked Relish"[45] and "Nebraska Birthday Frosting"[46] but more frequently featured recipes with westward-leaning titles such as "Pioneer Lemon Pie"[47] and "Pioneer Wild Plum Butter,"[48] "Rancher's Short Ribs,"[49] "Western Barbecued Spareribs,"[50] "Ranger Cookies,"[51] and "Cowboy Cookies."[52] Recipes from North Dakota, South Dakota, and Nebraska stressed Western imagery that linked them more closely to recipes in cookbooks from Colorado, a definitely Western state, too. While references to specific locations in Colorado were extremely popular in cookbooks from the state, recipes connected to farming virtually disappeared, replaced by those tied to more Western images like "Dude Ranch Whole Wheat Biscuits,"[53] "High Country Rhubarb Coffee Cake,"[54] "Prospector Potato Salad,"[55] "Bronco Bread,"[56] and "Hiker's Hot Dogs."[57] Sometimes, common recipes were simply Westernized as well, such as "Crowded Canoes," a recipe that differs little from the typical Ants on a Log recipe except in its name.[58] Renaming also happened in other cookbooks, such as Faulkton, South Dakota's *Kitchen Delights*. Two recipes in *Kitchen Delights* —"Pioneer Beans"[59] and "Ranch-Style Beans and Beef"[60]—are simply versions of Calico Beans, a recipe popular in Midwestern cookbooks that was given a Western twist primarily by changing its name. Still, that contributors to a South Dakota cookbook would feel the need to change that name ought not to be overlooked, as it emphasizes a desire to identify a recipe from the state, and thus possibly the state itself, as more a part of the Great Plains than the Midwest.

In 1825, French epicure Jean Anthelme Brillat-Savarin famously declared, "Tell me what you eat and I will tell you what you are." Much more recently, Mike Petrik called private collections of recipes "significant cultural symbols in their own right" that prove connections among cooking, culture, memory, and identity exist.[61] Cookbooks, however, stress separations as well as connections, as they serve as "active sites of the production of differences" too.[62] Thus, examining community cookbooks produced by and for residents of the Midwest and the Great Plains may make the dividing line between these regions, as seen by those who inhabit them, more distinct, if not completely clear. Maybe these cookbooks can help explain not only what these people eat but who and where they believe they are.

Notes

1   Lynne Ireland, "The Compiled Cookbook as Foodways Autobiography," *Western Folklore* 40 (1981): 112–14.
2   Ireland, "Compiled Cookbook," 107.

3   Barbara Kirshenblatt-Gimblett, "The Moral Sublime: The Temple Emmanuel Fair and Its Cookbook, Denver, 1888," in *Recipes for Reading: Community Cookbooks, Stories, Histories*, ed. Anne L. Bower (Amherst: University of Massachusetts Press, 1997), 142.

4   Rebecca Sharpless, "Cookbooks as Resources for Rural Research," *Agricultural History* (Spring 2016): 197.

5   Janice Bluesmen Longone, "'Tried Receipts': An Overview of America's Charitable Cookbooks," in *Writing Food History: A Global Perspective*, ed. Kyri W. Claflin and Peter Scholliers (London: Berg, 2012), 18.

6   Longone, "Tried Receipts," 27.

7   Rosalyn Collings Eves, "A Recipe for Remembrance: Memory and Identity in African-American Women's Cookbooks," *Rhetoric Review* 24 (2005): 285.

8   Traci M. Nathans-Kelly, "Embracing Compiled Cookbooks as Historical Documents," in *The State We're In: Reflections on Minnesota History*, ed. Annette Atkins and Deborah L. Miller, Nook ed. (St. Paul: Minnesota Historical Society Press, 2010), 257.

9   Jane Stern and Michael Stern, foreword to *Up a Country Lane Cookbook*, by Evelyn Kirkby (Iowa City: University of Iowa Press, 1993), xi.

10 Amy Bentley, "Sustenance, Abundance, and the Place of Food in U.S. Histories," in Claflin and Scholliers, *Writing Food History*, 83.

11 Lucy M Long, "Culinary Tourism: A Folkloristic Perspective on Eating and Otherness," in *Culinary Tourism*, ed. Lucy M. Long (Lexington: University Press of Kentucky, 2004), 36.

12 Barbara G. Shortridge and James R. Shortridge, "Food and American Culture," in *The Taste of American Place: A Reader on Regional and Ethnic Foods*, ed. Barbara G. Shortridge and James R. Shortridge (Lanham, MD: Rowman & Littlefield Publishers, 1998), 7.

13 Grace Lutheran Church of Watertown, South Dakota, *Cooking with Grace* (Watertown: n. pub., 1996), 57

14 David Fitz, ed., *First Lutheran Choirs' Favorite Recipes 1985* (n.p.: n. pub., 1985).

15 All-School Reunion Committee of Garretson, *2009 Garretson School Lunchroom Favorites* (Garretson: Sanders Printing, 2009), 46.

16 Bethany Lutheran Church—WELCA, *Celebrating 110 Years 1885–1995: A Book of Favorite Recipes Compiled by Past and Present Members of Bethany ELCW Relatives & Friends, Rural Selby, SD* (Selby, SD: n. pub., 1995), 64.

17 American Cancer Society, Nebraska Division, *Cornhusker Cupboards* (Memphis: Wimmer Brothers Books, 1982), 89.

18 Marion Bishop, "Speaking Sisters: Relief Society Cookbooks and Mormon Culture," in *Recipes for Reading: Community Cookbooks, Stories, Histories*, ed. Anne L. Bower (Amherst: University of Massachusetts Press, 1997), 97.

19 Sharpless, "Cookbooks as Resources," 204.

20 Le Mars Area Chamber of Commerce, *All Aboard: Le Mars Quasquicentennial Cookbook* (Le Mars, IA: Red Printing / Audubon, IA: Jumbo Jacks, 1994), 67.

21 Le Mars Area Chamber of Commerce, *All Aboard*, 160.

22 Le Mars Area Chamber of Commerce, *All Aboard*, 64.

23 Le Mars Area Chamber of Commerce, *All Aboard*, 12.

24 Waverly Lutheran Church Women, *"Adventures in the Kitchen" II* (Audubon, IA: Jumbo Jack's Cookbooks, 1999), 142.

25 Waverly Lutheran Church Women, *Adventures*, 145.

26 *Come to the Table: A Collection of Recipes by Christ the King Lutheran Church New Brighton, Minnesota 2011* (Kearney, NE: Morris Press Cookbooks, 2011), 66.
27 Park Point Community Club, *Bridged: A Collaboration of Recipes from the Park Point Community: Duluth MN,* 2nd. ed. (Duluth: n. pub., 2005), 93.
28 *Come to the Table,* 136.
29 Immanuel Ladies Aid of Galena; Ormsby, Minnesota, *Centennial Cookbook: 1885–1995* (Pleasanton: Fundcraft Publishing, 1985), 350.
30 *Hanson Family Favorites* (Lenexa: Cookbook Publishers, 1997), 116; and Christian Mothers' Society of LeFor, North Dakota, *What's Cookin'? in LeFor,* 13th ed. (Lenexa: Cookbook Publishers, 1981), 163.
31 *Hanson Family Favorites,* 45.
32 *Hanson Family Favorites,* 139.
33 Christian Mothers' Society, *What's Cookin'?,* 160.
34 Zonta Club of Fargo-Moorhead, *Zonta International All Time Favorites* (n.p.: n. pub., 1985), 87.
35 Zonta Club of Fargo-Moorhead, *Zonta International,* 107.
36 The Cookbook Committee of St. Paul Lutheran Church of Java, South Dakota, *Favorite Recipes: St. Paul Lutheran Centennial 1900–2000* (Cicero: Project Cuisine, 2000), 33.
37 "Starfires" (Elton, S.D. Firemen's Wives), *Come Cook with Us....* (Waverly: G&R Publishing, n.d.), 1.
38 South Dakota Ambassadors of Excellence, *Celebrity Cookbook: A Showcase of South Dakota Talent* (Kearney, NE: Cookbooks by Morris Press, 1991), 62–63.
39 South Dakota Ambassadors of Excellence, *Celebrity Cookbook,* 16.
40 South Dakota Ambassadors of Excellence, *Celebrity Cookbook,* 29.
41 Willow Creek WELCA Cookbook Committee, *Willow Creek Lutheran Church 120 Years: Cherish the Past, Embrace the Present, Proclaim the Future, 1874–1994* (Hills: Crescent Publishing, 1994), 110.
42 Willow Creek WELCA Cookbook Committee, *Willow Creek,* 162.
43 Zonta Club Cookbook Committee, *Inspirational Cooking with Zonta: Zonta Club of the Black Hills* (Kearney, NE: Morris Press Cookbooks, 2008), 76–77.
44 Bethany Lutheran Church—WELCA, *Celebrating 110 Years,* 57.
45 Catherine J. Hillegass, ed., *A Nebraska Centennial First Ladies' Cookbook,* comp. Maxine Morrison (Lincoln, NE: Cliff's Notes, 1966), 35.
46 Hillegass, *Nebraska Centennial,* 157
47 Hillegass *Nebraska Centennial,* 29.
48 Hillegass, *Nebraska Centennial,* 31.
49 Hillegass, *Nebraska Centennial,* 222.
50 Hillegass, *Nebraska Centennial,* 223.
51 American Cancer Society, *Cornhusker Cupboards,* 144.
52 Osceola Good Samaritan Center of Osceola, NE, *Traditions: You Cooked with the Rest, Now Cook with the Best* (Kearney, NE: Cookbooks by Morris Press, 1996), 134–35.
53 Colorado Dietetic Association, *Simply Colorado: Nutritious Recipes for Busy People* (Denver: Colorado Dietetic Association, 1989), 111.
54 Colorado Dietetic Association, *Simply Colorado,* 35.
55 Junior League of Denver, *Colorado Cache Cookbook,* 23rd ed. (Denver: AB Hirschfeld Press, 1995), 94.
56 Junior League of Denver, *Colorado Cache Cookbook,* 232.
57 Junior League of Denver, *Colorado Cache Cookbook,* 315.

[58] Colorado Dietetic Association, *Simply Colorado*, 240.

[59] Faulkton Area Medical Center Foundation, *Kitchen Delights* (Kearney, NE: n. pub., 2011), 37.

[60] Faulkton Area Medical Center Foundation, *Kitchen Delights*, 63.

[61] Mike Petrik, "Cooking Books for More than Cooks," *Missouri Review* 38 (2015): 161.

[62] Eric Mason, "Cooking the Books: Jewish Cuisine and the Commodification of Difference," in *Edible Ideologies: Representing Food & Meaning*, ed. Kathleen LeBesco and Peter Naccarato (Albany: University of New York Press, 2008), 119.

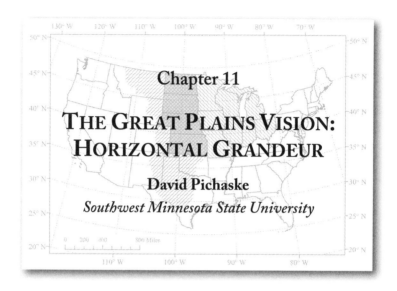

Chapter 11

THE GREAT PLAINS VISION: HORIZONTAL GRANDEUR

David Pichaske
Southwest Minnesota State University

In an oft-quoted essay titled "Horizontal Grandeur," Southwest Minnesota native Bill Holm talks about ways of seeing . . . and thinking. "There are two eyes in the human head," he writes:

> the eye of mystery, and the eye of harsh truth—the hidden and the open—the woods eye and the prairie eye. The prairie eye looks for distance, clarity, and light; the woods eye looks for closeness, complexity, and darkness. The prairie eye looks for usefulness and plainness in art and architecture; the woods eye for the baroque and ornamental. . . . One eye is not superior to the other, but they are different. To some degree, like male and female, darkness and light, they exist in all human heads, but one or the other seems dominant.[1]

"I have a prairie eye," he adds.[2]

This prairie eye and brain have several characteristics that Holm shares with older writers from this region (although they are not so prominent among younger, postmodern prairie writers): reliance on experience over theory; preference for the visual, and usually horizontal; attention to small details; a voice that reflects the place (idiomatic, often quiet, unostentatious); a vague sense of lost pastoralism; an awareness of and even an affection for the dark side, which can be dangerous but opens the door to imagination, strength, and adventure.

Holm owes his prairie eye to years spent on his parents' farm in Swede Prairie Township in Yellow Medicine County, a fringe area promoted on page 4 of the 2009 Dex/Qwest Minnesota Southwest telephone directory as "Northern Tall Grass Prairie." That's how the "area attractions" page pitches this region, with advertisements for the Minnesota Farm Machinery Museum, the Pipestone County Museum and Monument, and the Redwood County Museum. Both Holm and Paul Gruchow—whose family farmed section 28, Rosewood Township, Chippewa County, thirty miles north of Holm—saw the region as ecologically splendid but intellectually arid. Gruchow writes, "I had not imagined, or been encouraged to imagine, that it was possible to live in the country and write books, too. Nor did I suspect that it was possible to write books about our countryside."[3] But this prairie countryside—Holm's and Gruchow's homeland—produced a spate of fairly well-known writers who seem to share Holm's prairie eye and thinking. To this flyover country, a hundred-mile radius around Swede Prairie Township, belong Gruchow and Holm, Ole Rölvaag, Fred Manfred, Herbert Krause, Robert Bly, Leo Dangel, Tom Hennen, Faith Sullivan, David Jauss, Kent Meyers, and younger writers like Leif Enger, Gene Stark, and Forrest Peterson. They're out there.

Minnesota Highway 23, just north of Green Valley. *Courtesy David Pichaske.*

Although they recognize "The Middle West" as a place and a set of values, most of these authors identify themselves as "prairie" or "plains" writers. "All of our writers have at least one foot in the Great Plains," notes the postscript of Leo Dangel's 2013 *Saving Singletrees*, part of the William Kloefkorn Series published by WSC Press at Wayne State College in Nebraska. "If you head west from my house near the western border of Minnesota, you will begin at the western edge of the tallgrass prairie," writes Gruchow.[4] Thomas Dean remembers meeting Gruchow at a writers' festival in Marshall, Minnesota, on "the imposing flatness of the Great Plains edge, a beautiful but forbidding landscape, especially in early fall."[5] Gene Stark, whose *Flyover Seasons* landscape includes "prairie wetlands," titles one poem "Tall Grass Days."[6] Although Thomas R. Smith labels Morris native Tom Hennen "one of the Midwest's best and most underappreciated poets,"[7] Hennen himself never once uses the word "Midwest," while mentioning "prairie" at least five times.[8]

Writers on this western edge of the Corn Belt would like to claim Sinclair Lewis and Garrison Keillor as co-conspirators: Gopher Prairie (it is "Gopher *Prairie*") and Lake Wobegon are just up the road. Can they too be prairie writers? Or is the difference between "Middle West" and "prairie" the point at which—for reasons of agriculture or settlement—small towns fade from the map? Lewis is traditionally identified not as a prairie writer but as a "Midwest Writer" (and sometimes just a satirist of "American" life), but Carol and Will Kennicott seem happy only when hunting pheasants, doctoring farmers, or hanging out at a cottage in the country, so perhaps Lewis is at heart more prairie than Middle West. Perhaps any 1920s writer who is critiquing the Middle West at a time when, as Paul Gruchow points out, the region was shucking its agrarian traditions and converting prairie vistas to small towns and even manufacturing centers is really a prairie writer.[9]

Or is the divide between Midwest and prairie that point, not too far from Minneota, where attention shifts from woodland and lake to farm and field? A Middle West writer like John Calvin Rezmerski might give us a long Minnesota river poem titled "Cataloging the Flow: Elegy," but although lakes do exist in Southwest Minnesota, and wooded valleys and even rivers trickling down from the Coteau des Prairies to the Minnesota, they do not figure prominently in the work of prairie writers. Their eyes focus on sky and earth.

And if—as so many writers assure us—place shapes personality, and spending a lot of time in one place means that place spends a lot of time in you, what does the prairie eye see that the Midwestern eye might not?

First, and perhaps most important, the prairie eye sees what it sees, not what the brain behind the eye imagines. Many of these writers are deep imagists, and most are political activists; they are not, however, postmodernists. Holm advises readers to accept experience as our teacher, mother, state, church, "even, or perhaps particularly, if it comes into conflict with the abstract received wisdom that power always tries to convince you to live by."[10] If the current political agenda contradicts or is not in alignment with your own experience, disregard it. Power, as Holm fully understood, could be the national government or the current academic agenda coming at you from places far away. These writers see experience in place as the touchstone of knowledge. It has its own reality, which shapes your thought and material. Kent Meyers writes, "When you make your living off the land and belong to it, you come to feel it as something with force and presence."[11] Blurbing Fred Manfred's *The Chokecherry Tree*, Wallace Stegner writes, "Few writers ever achieve so sure a sense of place and of how human beings are shaped by it." In his introduction to that book, Delbert Wylder writes, "They have settled on the land and are close to the land, and the land has settled in them."[12] "I don't care anymore how the world thinks," writes Tom Hennen: "I only know that the snow / Has reached my knees."[13] Speaking of Hennen's poetry, Thomas R. Smith mentions "those who, chosen by a place, return the favor, forsaking other 'higher' ambitions that might call them elsewhere."[14]

Plains writers do indeed tend to dismiss life elsewhere. Fred Manfred writes from his plains experience, even if that means—to quote again Wylder's introduction—his characters "have neither the craving for excitement found in the city people of a Dos Passos novel . . . nor the sophistication."[15] Hennen writes disparagingly of "airplanes and power plants, all the machinery that surrounds us" in a city.[16] Stark recalls life in Minneapolis during his college years: "always a sooty, abrasive smoke in the air. The city also sounded different with constant traffic and the sound of never-ending commerce and perpetual movement. The view was constantly obstructed by buildings."[17] (Holm dismisses those "dark old brownstones on Summit Avenue" as the work of a woods eye.) "The city's just a jungle, more games to play," sang Hibbing's Bob Dylan in his song "Mississippi."

Nor do these plains writers invent in the postmodernist manner of, for example, Don DeLillo, whose novel *White Noise* is set in the Midwest. DeLillo's "College-on-the-Hill" and its Hitler Studies Program are divorced from place in a manner that a prairie university would not have been . . . at least in 1985, when Southwest State in Marshall was heavy into rural-regional studies, headquartered in the History and English Departments.

Maybe that's the difference between DeLillo's town of Blacksmith in "the Middle West" and Manfred's Chokecherry Corner on "the Plains": one admits of invention; the other does not. (Significantly, after moving into globalism and postmodernism in the DeLillo manner, Southwest State University closed first its Rural-Regional Studies Program and, in 2015, its English Department!) The essence of DeLillo's Midwestern-borrowed-from-New-York postmodern dislocation is the *White Noise* tale of THE MOST PHOTOGRAPHED BARN IN AMERICA, elevated to that remarkable status by nothing more than the words of aggressive advertising. "We see only what the others see," one of DeLillo's characters tells another. "We've agreed to be part of a collective perception."[18] This is not the way plains writers see . . . or write. Maybe DeLillo misread the Middle West, or maybe the Middle West admits of more imagination, but the notion that idea is reality does not play well on the prairie, just as prairie realism troubles a more Middle West imagination. Of a Middle West man relocated to a prairie nursing home in *Simon's Night*, Jon Hassler writes, "Simon paused to look out over the prairie to the point where the plowed fields dissolved into the gloomy sky. Simon detested the prairie. He had lived all his life among hills where the eye—the mind—was not expected to take in so much at once, where more was left to the imagination."[19]

These writers not only tell us what they've seen; they show us: you'll find prairie photos in Bill Holm's first book, *The Music of Failure* (the original 1985 Plains Press edition), and Paul Gruchow introduces each season of *Journal of a Prairie Year* with a picture. The photos are usually horizontal: a line of land below enormous sky above. Gruchow, who credits photographer Jim Brandenburg with teaching him to see the prairie,[20] writes, "The prairie landscape is so completely dominated by its skies that sometimes there seems to be no middle ground between us and the firmament."[21] Introducing *The Chokecherry Tree*, Deb Wylder notes, "The prairie provides a horizon impossible to encompass."[22] Way back when, Ole Rölvaag opened *Giants in the Earth* with the line of the landscape: "Bright, clear sky over a plain so wide that the rim of the heavens cut down on it around the entire horizon. . . . Bright, clear sky, to-day, to-morrow, and for all time to come."[23]

Holm's prairie eye, however, sees both "magnitude and delicacy."[24] Prairie writers often focus on the minutest details of their landscape and lives. One of Robert Bly's most quoted poems runs in its entirety: "How strange to think of giving up all ambition! / Suddenly I see with such clear eyes / The white flake of snow / That has just fallen on the horse's mane."[25] Tom Hennen notices the lone monarch butterfly that has landed on the dry corn tassel[26] and the blue jay disappearing into the black folds of the spruce tree.[27] Leo Dangel focuses on "the old plow rusting in the grove."[28] There is beauty in detail, although outsiders might find it just "small potatoes," as Garrison Keillor dismisses that prairie vision in *Lake Wobegon Days*.[29]

The ears as well as the eyes of these writers are tuned to their prairie place. We can be casual about describing that prairie voice—I recommend *How to Talk Minnesotan*, by Cottonwood's Howard Mohr—or we can be rigorously analytical. I recommend Harold Byron Allen's *Linguistic Atlas of the Upper Midwest*, the basis of my analysis of Bob Dylan's language in what has proven to be the most interesting chapter of *Song of the North Country*. Dialect is vocabulary and idioms as well as pronunciation, and we recognize the voice of the prairie even when we are just reading it in a book. Fred Manfred was criticized for writing in the prairie voice he heard outside his Roundwind retreat; prairie writers like Garrison Keillor convert it into literary capital.

In general, that prairie voice is Anglo-Saxon peasant plain rather than Anglo-Norman nobility elegant. As prairie pronunciation is flat, prairie vocabulary is sparse. Nothing fancy or overstated. Mohr writes, "Rattling on and on is bad enough in Minnesota."[30] With a former student, I recently tracked Bill Holm's revisions in 1985 manuscripts of *The Music of Failure*, and for the most part movement was in the direction of simplicity, informality, and colloquialism: "hind end" for "rear end," "growth" for "luxuriant vegetation." This guarded, understated prairie voice opens one of Leo Dangel's most popular poems, "After Forty Years of Marriage, She Tries a New Recipe for Hamburger Hotdish":

> "How did you like it?" she asked.
> "It's all right," he said.

So, then. What kind of a mentality does this great immensity of land and sky plant in the minds of these prairie writers? First, as we have noted, it is a curious affection for their not-very-much of a place over the opportunities of elsewhere. Almost all of these writers (Holm, Bly, Gruchow) have seen elsewhere. Like Dorothy in *The Wizard of Oz* they got O U T, but they came quietly B A C K, because there's no place like home. Little is okay. Faith Sullivan's characters in Harvester, Minnesota, have been repeatedly described as absolutely ordinary, but that's just fine. Garrison Keillor writes of small-potatoes Lake Wobegon, "Lake Wobegon, whatever its faults, is not dreary."[31] "Whatever failure is," Bill Holm famously remarked in closing his essay on the subject, "Minneota is not it. . . . The heart can be filled up anywhere on earth."[32] Paul Gruchow suggests that we just "stay at home and plant some manner of a garden." Foreigners often denigrate this view as antiquated, ignorant, primitive, "hillbilly" or "peasant."[33] Carol Bly, from the city of Duluth, definitely saw "the lost Swede towns" of Southwest Minnesota as failures.

Carol Bly's husband, Robert, probably the most successful of all Southwest Minnesota authors, thought otherwise. Raised (like Holm and Gruchow) on a prairie farm, Bly (like Holm and Gruchow) made a career out of his home near Madison. "That place, that way of life, has always been, I think, at the core of his identity," said Michael Quan.[34] Meridel Le Sueur called him a "poet of prairie horizon . . . to pit and bloom in Dakota dark,"[35] and Wayne Dodd writes, "*The spirit of the American prairie* . . . is what Robert Bly discovered for us in *Silence in the Snowy Fields*."[36] Titles in the table of contents in *Selected Poems* (1986) provide an extended inventory of Bly's rural markers: "A Home in Dark Grass," "Hunting Pheasants in a Cornfield," "Snow Geese," "Driving toward the Lac Qui Parle River." It's all "barns, farmhouses, fields," writes Louis Jenkins, "ordinary Midwestern landscape, dull as dirt."[37]

But Bly, a deep-image poet, reads the world in those dull-as-dirt details. And what most interests Bly about his prairie place is a dark side that, unlike his wife, he accepts and even promotes. "I wanted the poems in *The Man in the Black Coat Turns* to rise out of some darkness beneath us," he notes in *Selected Poems*.[38] Bly repeatedly says that we find redemption in

Swedes Forest Township, Redwood County, Minnesota, west off Harvest Avenue at Boiling Spring Creek. *Courtesy David Pichaske.*

the loss, in the dark side that is so prominent in his prairie culture. A late afternoon snow falls in the last poem of *Silence in the Snowy Fields*, and the barn—filled with corn—moves on its own toward the living people: "Like a hulk blown toward us in a storm at sea; / All the sailors on deck have been blind for many years." Bly suggests that what our cultural elite—misinformed, misguided, and misguiding—really need is a prairie snowstorm and a barn full of nourishing corn. The problem with John Kennedy, Bly told Bill Moyers in an interview, is that he lived too much on the light side.[39] He would repeat this theme in his analysis of the story of Iron John in his best-selling book by that same title: Iron John lives in the fearful, dangerous wild, but he offers a vision that transforms the boy into a man, a husband, a king. Precisely because it is pagan, uncultured, not "Minnesota nice," the dark redeems us.

Even Bly, however, would admit the prairie darkness can be dangerous and annihilating. In the prairie's "most minimalist of all landscapes, a place with which not even the simplicity of the sea can compare,"[40] Kent Meyer writes, "freedom of movement has its own accompanying fears."[41] Paul Gruchow writes in *Journal of a Prairie Year*, "The fundamental fact of life on the wild prairie is danger"[42]—real danger, not crime novel danger. In *The Necessity of Empty Places*, he writes, "A journey into the wilderness is a test of the will against the odds. Going into the wilderness, any wilderness, is a way of opening yourself to the possibility of danger and to the likelihood of discomfort, at the least. There is the possibility of getting lost, of being trapped in a storm, of confronting an angry animal, or falling."[43] Compare Dorothy as the twister hits Kansas.

On the other hand, as Gruchow goes on to say, "to confront the unknown and to meet its challenges is to be admitted into a permanently enlarged world . . . so our encounters with the wilderness widen and free us."[44] The Kansas tornado set Dorothy on her journey to Oz. Prairie annihilation—"giving up all ambition," as Bly put it—is in the long term beneficial. For all the prairie evils that confront Jim Heynen's farm boys in *The One-Room Schoolhouse*—ice, snow, skunks, head lice, ringworm, coyotes, tornadoes, the disasters of stillborn calves and castrated pigs—there are blessings: newborn pigs, dandelions, butterflies, fireflies, the swimming hole. Most importantly, it is the challenge of dealing with the dark side that tweaks the boys' ingenuity into the games and cons that make Heynen's stories so entertaining.

Prairie-eye writers see the enormous resounding emptiness of the prairie, at night or in the day, at sunrise or high noon or midnight, as a boon, as a blessing. As Dorothy's challenges along the way to Oz strengthened her into the princess she became, the expanses of the prairie set her to dreaming. "To live on the prairie is to daydream," Gruchow notes,[45] explaining that when we are smallest, our dreams come quickest. Individual items, which might get lost in a more complex woodland environment, expand and receive more attention. They might be the small flake of snow that has just fallen on the horse's mane, or our own selves. Close attention might even produce a vision worthy of the postmodernists. Leo Dangel has one farmer wearing a lilac shirt[46] and another painting words on all his animals and sitting on the porch "watching his words eat and mate."[47] Jim Heynen's country boys fly-fish for bats,[48] spin stories about the big bull that "clumb right up the haymow."[49]

So the prairie eye and the prairie voice are like a dialect, a set of traits, none of which are unique, but that in combination define a particular vision and thought. Has this always been the prairie vision, the prairie voice of Southwest Minnesota writers? Certainly elements of the Bly-Holm-Gruchow prairie vision antedate Bly, Holm, and Gruchow. But today, thirty years after the heyday of the 1980s, is this still the voice and the vision of writers in this area—or have younger writers spent so much time online that they have lost the horizon?

Herbert Krause was born in 1905 on a small farm near Fergus Falls, a hundred miles north of Robert Bly's Madison, farther yet from the quarter-section homesteaded by Ole Rölvaag's Per Hansa, but in the region of which we speak. "Pockerbrush," Krause named his home place in his novels, a place of "wide acres in stubble stretching out until they washed around an island of trees in which a huddle of buildings and a bulge of yellow straw were nearly hidden."[50] In his introduction to *Poems and Essays of Herbert Krause*, Arthur Huseboe identifies this as "the northern prairie plains," a region "Krause at first called the Middlewest but latterly called the West."[51] In *The Thresher* it's "the prairie,"[52] although the landscape is hilly and some of it is timber.[53] The first ("early") poem of Krause's *Poems and Essays* is titled "Sun upon the Skyline." There is plenty of prairie place in the writings of Herbert Krause, which also exhibit some of the other prairie-eye traits I've identified. Introducing the 1967 edition of *Wind Without Rain*, Fred Manfred—admittedly not an unbiased source—writes, "when *Wind Without Rain* came out [Krause] had a lot of criticism for its realism. In Luverne, for example, a friend of mine tells me that when he asked the librarian for it, she wasn't sure he should read it. She warned him that it was terribly brutal and frank." Manfred goes on to recall that after the publication of *The Oxcart Trail*, Krause received a letter from a woman who "blistered him for his raw realism."[54] Not surprisingly, Krause's announced goal as an academic was "to found a school of writing at Augustana College, where, as he wrote to President Clemens Granskou, young writers could learn 'to appreciate their own cultural heritage, to regard it with the sympathy and understanding necessary for true artistry, and to preserve it with the realization that it is truly worth saving.'"[55]

That preservation involves descriptions of the land in various stages of the year—scenic vistas like: "Clouds like a great smoke rolled their black bellyings against the dull reddish sky. 'Gonna be a ripper,' someone said."[56] It involves observing tiny details like "little white snowflakes turning to gold," reminiscent of Bly's snowflake on the horse's mane.[57] That preservation extends to the idiom and language of his characters and narrator. Echoes of his characters' German heritage abound, as do Manfred-like echoes of the local vernacular: "sirrup," "fellers," "growed up," "doodads," *would* reduced to a simple *'d* (to pull but a few examples from *Wind Without Rain*). Krause wrote what he heard, as well as what he saw. He also wrote what he did not hear: "No one I ever met had less to say, except Father—few words to say and those were short."[58]

A new wave of writers associated with Southwest Minnesota began publishing books in the late twentieth and early twenty-first centuries. One of them is Faith Sullivan, who grew up in Lakefield and attended Pipestone High School and Mankato State University before departing for twenty years to New York and Los Angeles—thus the dichotomy in her writing: the landscape of Harvester, Minnesota, seems on target, but Lark Erhardt, Sullivan's precocious narrator in *The Cape Ann*, speaks in a voice not quite from around here. Another younger writer with Southwest Minnesota connections, Mary Bly (pseudonym Eloisa James), grew up on a farm near Madison, Minnesota. But Mary Bly sets her own mystery novel *When the Duke Returns* far, far from Southwest Minnesota, in England, 1784. The only landscape vision to color this novel is the landscape of the Duchess of Cosway's dress. David Jauss, who grew up in Morris, Minnesota, but taught in Little Rock, Arkansas, writes (in his own words) his way into "many characters whose lives I know nothing, or next to nothing, about."[59] Neil Smith came to Southwest Minnesota from the Mississippi Gulf Coast to write his noir detective novels. His 2008 novel *Yellow Medicine* is actually set in my house in Granite Falls, along the Minnesota River, which Smith had rented for a year. The geographical markers are there, and his main character, who has moved to Minnesota from New Orleans, understands the voice he hears ("the soundtrack of Minnesota—heavy on the vowels"),[60] but the voice of the narrator is not the voice he hears. Nor is the vision. My own autographed copy reads, "Apologies for all the slams against Minnesota. It was a dark time."The novel, and the dark time, could have happened anywhere, any place. These writers have spent more time in front of a computer screen than outside on the prairie.

Lyon County, 130th Avenue, west of Minneota, Minnesota, circa 1985.
Courtesy David Pichaske.

How about Steve Linstrom, from Marshall; Leif Enger, from Sinclair Lewis's Sauk Centre; Forrest Peterson, from Willmar, Minnesota, forty-five miles south of Sauk Centre and sixty miles from Madison and Minneota? Linstrom sets his novel *The Last Ram* in the Badlands of South Dakota: place plays a role here, but there is no Middle West–Prairie debate. Leif Enger and his brother Lin early on wrote mystery novels set in North Dakota. Then Leif wrote and published his own mystery novel set west of Sauk Centre. *Peace Like a River* opens in a hospital, but the characters are soon goose hunting on the plains. The landscape occasionally intrudes on the action, but the vision of horizontal grandeur is lost in this book written by a man who works for Minnesota Public Radio. So is the prairie voice. What we hear is the Minneapolis *Star Tribune*: "August's judiciousness cost him transient glory,"[61] and "the superintendent made the most fitful transformation—his neck compressed into his shoulders, his hands clawed and shrunk upward into his sleeves, he stamped his foot like the maladjusted."[62] This don't sound too Great Plains, too Nort Dakoter to me.

The dust jacket tells us that Forrest Peterson's first novel, *Good Ice* (2007), is set in "a small town in the Midwest" in the middle fifties, portraying "a Midwestern town, its people, and the measure of tolerance and bigotry in facing racial and cultural differences." It is, in short, mortgaged to the Politically Correct agenda (and the promotion of World War II) of the late twentieth century, projected half a century backward. The book opens on a stage, not on the landscape, a perfect metaphor for the book. Peterson's second novel, *Buffalo Ridge*, references exactly that 150-mile rise of glacial drift upon which Bill Holm discovered horizontal grandeur, and it opens on the ridge itself. Or inside of a truck turning into an eighty-acre organic farm "in the middle of nowhere."[63] The geography is here, and perhaps the vision, but the language is that of National Public Radio, which drones from the radio at the end of the trestle table. The prairie language, like the prairie vision, has been adjusted for Y2K, not as dramatically as the language of Leif Enger, but definitely adjusted.

Marty Seifert's *Sundown at Sunrise* is a work of historical fiction "based on one of the most notorious ax murders in American history."[64] In researching the murder—which occurred on a farmstead six miles outside of Morgan, Minnesota—Seifert studied old plat maps, letters, church records, microfilm newspapers from two years before to two years after the events he describes, and museum materials relevant to the times (1909–1917). Seifert catches the eastern plains landscape at a moment when it has been subdivided into 160-acre farms, but already the landscape is dotted with aging farmhouses and old barns. He has Manfred's ear for dialect, and his characters think like folks from around here. Here is Great Plains realism reborn.

In most of these books, however, the influence of place upon vision and language and thought is largely lost. And distinctions between the Great Plains and the Middle West are lost on authors who sit indoors in front of a computer screen. The distinctions are irrelevant as well to their audiences, who also spend their lives in front of a computer screen—until, that is, a storm hits, the power goes out, and we confront once again Nature in all her duplicity. The day-to-day landscape shaped and continues to shape the prairie vision and the prairie experience—even if today's writers (and readers) pay it little attention, and the distinction between Great Plains and Middle West has been lost.

Notes

1 Bill Holm, *The Music of Failure* (Marshall, MN: Plains Press, 1985), 17.

2 Holm, *Music*, 2.

3 Paul Gruchow, *Grass Roots: The Universe of Home* (Minneapolis: Milkweed Editions, 1995), 134.

4 Paul Gruchow, *The Necessity of Empty Places*, 1st ed. (Minneapolis: Milkweed Editions, 1988), 59. In opening his meditation on horizontal grandeur, Holm is returning from the city of Willmar; in opening *Journal of a Prairie Year*, Gruchow is returning from the city of Winnipeg. But the prairie amplitude is what has imprinted itself on his mind and eye.

5 Thomas Dean, *The Grace of Grass and Water: Writing in Honor of Paul Gruchow* (North Liberty, IA: Ice Cube Press, 2007), 2.

6 Gene Stark, *Flyover Seasons* (St. Cloud, MN: North Star Press, 2011), 23.

7 Thomas R. Smith, ed., *Walking Swiftly* (St. Paul, MN: Ally Press, 1992), 159.

8 Tom Hennen, *Darkness Sticks to Everything: Collected and New Poems* (Port Townsend, WA: Copper Canyon Press, 2013), 20, 74, 75, 81, 134.

9 Paul Gruchow, *Journal of a Prairie Year* (Minneapolis: University of Minnesota Press, 1985), 128.

10 Holm, *Music*, 12.

11 Kent Meyer, *The Witness of Combines* (Minneapolis: University of Minnesota Press, 1998), 69.

12 Frederick Manfred, *The Chokecherry Tree*, reprint (Albuquerque: University of New Mexico Press, 1975), viii.

13 Hennen, *Darkness*, 39.

14 T. Smith, *Walking Swiftly*, 173.

15 Manfred, *Chokecherry Tree*, viii.

16 Hennen, *Darkness*, 70.

17 Stark, *Flyover Seasons*, 13.

18 Don DeLillo, *White Noise* (New York: Viking Penguin, 1985), 12.

19 Jon Hassler, *Simon's Night* (New York: Ballantine Books, 1979), 10.

20 Gruchow, *Journal*, vii.

21 Gruchow, *Journal*, 61

22 Manfred, *Chokecherry Tree*, vii.

23 Ole Rölvaag, *Giants in the Earth: A Saga of the Prairie* (New York: Harper & Brothers, 1927), 3.

24 Holm, *Music*, 18.

25 Robert Bly, *Selected Poems* (New York: Harper & Row, 1986), 34.

26 Hennen, *Darkness*, 3.

27 Hennen, *Darkness*, 144.

28 Dangel, *Home from the Field*, 38.

29 Garrison Keillor, *Lake Wobegon Days* (New York: Viking Penguin, 1985), 7.

30 Howard Mohr, *How to Talk Minnesotan*, 2nd ed. (New York: Penguin, 2013), 249.

31 Keillor, *Lake Wobegon*, 22.

32 Holm, *Music*, 87. When that final line of *The Music of Failure* became the title of an anthology of Bill Holm essays published by Milkweed Editions Press of Minneapolis, publisher Emily Buchwald—or one of her editors—deleted the "up" from Holm's declaration, so that the heart could be filled, but not filled up, in a prairie place like Minneota. Thus the Twin Cities views Southwest Minnesota.

[33] Gruchow, *Grass Roots*, 3.

[34] T. Smith, *Walking Swiftly*, 34.

[35] T. Smith, *Walking Swiftly*, 61.

[36] Wayne Dodd, "Back to the Snowy Fields," in *Critical Essays on Robert Bly*, ed. William V. Davis (New York: G. K. Hall, 1992), 107 (italics in original).

[37] T. Smith, *Walking Swiftly*, 36.

[38] Bly, *Selected Poems*, 142.

[39] Bill Moyers, *Bill Moyers' Journal: A Conversation with Robert Bly*, directed by Mark Kolgan (WNET/Thirteen, Educational Broadcasting Network, 1979).

[40] Meyer, *Witness*, 70.

[41] Meyer, *Witness*, 73.

[42] Gruchow, *Journal*, 20.

[43] Gruchow, *Necessity*, jacket.

[44] Gruchow, *Necessity*, jacket.

[45] Gruchow, *Journal*, xi.

[46] Leo Dangel, *Home from the Field* (Granite Falls, MN: Spoon River Poetry Press, 1997), 98.

[47] Dangel, *Home*, 104.

[48] Jim Heynen, *The One-Room Schoolhouse* (New York: Knopf, 1993), 59.

[49] Heynen, *One-Room Schoolhouse*, 14.

[50] Herbert Krause, *The Thresher* (New York: Bobbs-Merrill Company, 1946), 1.

[51] Arthur R. Huseboe, ed., *Poems and Essays of Herbert Krause* (Sioux Falls, SD: Center for Western Studies, 1990), 32.

[52] Krause, *Thresher*, 2.

[53] Krause, *Thresher*, 5.

[54] Herbert Krause, *Wind Without Rain* (Sioux Falls, SD: Brevet Press, 1967), 10.

[55] Huseboe, *Herbert Krause*, 14.

[56] Krause, *Wind*, 175.

[57] Krause, *Wind*, 15.

[58] Krause, *Wind*, 27.

[59] David Jauss, http://davidjauss.com/ (accessed November 5, 2016).

[60] Anthony Neil Smith, *Yellow Medicine* (Madison, WI: Bleak House Books, 2008), 103.

[61] Leif Enger, *Peace Like a River* (New York: Atlantic Monthly Press, 2001), 15.

[62] Enger, *Peace*, 79.

[63] Forrest Peterson, *Buffalo Ridge: A Novel* (St. Cloud, MN: North Star Press, 2012), 45.

[64] Marty Seifert, *Sundown at Sunrise* (Edina, MN: Beaver's Pond Press, 2016).

Chapter 12

FINDING THE SUBREGIONAL DIVERSITY IN THE AMERICAN WEST: HISTORIANS AND THEIR SEARCH FOR THE AMERICAN INTERIOR BORDERLANDS

Nathalie Massip

Université Côte d'Azur

The historiography of the American West is characterized by attempts at definitions. Following the success of Frederick Jackson Turner's "Significance of the Frontier in American History" (1893), the notion of a frontier had to be defined, so hazy was the term in a document that nonetheless remains a landmark in American history. Later, when regionalists started questioning Turner's interpretation and suggested the West ought to be studied not in terms of "process" but instead as a "place," the West as a region had to be delineated. The debate between the West as process and the West as place seems to have reached its climax in the early 1990s with the much-publicized emergence and development of the New Western History. Even though this debate has waned, attempts at defining the West continue and remain a trademark of Western historiography.[1]

The subregions of the American West themselves have been defined differently depending on the historians. Turner, whose research interest drifted away from the frontier soon after he published his seminal article, thought that both the Midwest and the Great Plains were sections. Walter Prescott Webb, who is credited with launching a regional interpretation of the West and its components, provided a clearer definition. The New Western History, whose uppermost concern was to discard the notion of frontier, further developed the regionalist reading of the American West, emphasizing its external limits and intrinsic characteristics.[2]

In this chapter, I argue that regionalist historians' efforts at delimiting and defining the West have hindered their analysis of the internal subdivisions and borderlands of the region. Most notably, New Western Historians' insistence on delineating the West as a place, as opposed to the Turnerian theory of a moving frontier, has led them to overlook the heterogeneity of the West and to ignore its subregions. First, I intend to show that a lack of consensus on defining the West is a key feature of a regionalist reading of the West. I will then argue that New Western Historians' insistence on regionalizing the West has resulted in its homogenization, thus annihilating its dynamism. Finally, I will show that, ironically, their claim to a "new" Western history has prompted these scholars to neglect their predecessors'—including Turner—pioneering work on sections, internal divisions, and borderlands.

Analysis of the West as a region with clear limits and distinctive characteristics has always been a challenge for historians. Even though Turner is considered the father of Western history, his use of the words "frontier" and "West" as synonyms considerably slowed down this examination. In 1934, historian Bernard DeVoto called for a clear mapping of the West, stating:

> Much energy has been spent in an effort to determine where the West begins. The definitions of poetry and the luncheon clubs are unsatisfactory: vagueness should not be invoked when a precise answer is possible. The West begins where the annual rainfall drops below twenty inches. When you reach the line which marks that drop— for convenience the one hundredth meridian—you have reached the West.[3]

The West truly entered the realm of regionalism thanks to historian Walter Prescott Webb. In 1957, Webb published "The American West: Perpetual Mirage" in *Harper's Monthly Magazine*. By then, he had already written extensively on the Great Plains, on his native Texas, and on the frontier. His *Harper's* article remains a landmark document in Western historiography. Webb defined the West as follows:

> Fortunately the West is no longer a shifting frontier, but a region that can be marked off on a map, traveled to, and seen. Everybody knows when he gets there. It starts in the second tier of states west of the Big River. A line drawn

> from the southern tip of Texas to the farther boundary of
> central North Dakota marks roughly its eastern bound-
> ary. It starts almost in the tropics; it reaches almost to the
> northern limits of the Temperate Zone. Hemmed in by
> Canada on the north and Mexico on the south, it runs
> with the sun to the Pacific.[4]

The distinction between frontier and region could not be any clearer. Even though Webb's delineation remains hesitant—as evidenced by the words "roughly" and "almost," as much as by the very unscientific "Everybody knows when he gets there"—Webb truly endeavors to give the West a concrete location on a map. Associated with his analysis of what he sees as the major characteristic of the West—its aridity—the mapping Webb offered launched the study of the West as a region.

Following in DeVoto's and Webb's footsteps, the New Western Historians of the 1980s-1990s have striven to locate the West on a map and to draw its limits. Justifying a regionalist reading of the West in opposition to the frontier interpretation, Patricia Nelson Limerick remarked that the frontier was too abstract a concept to convey a full picture of the West and, along with New Western Regionalists, banished the "f-word" entirely.[5]

From the moment historians started considering the West as a region, their first and most difficult task was to determine its boundaries. The most common delimitation of the West can be found in Michael Malone's introduction to his 1983 *Historians and the American West*. To Malone, the eastern limit of the region is the 98th meridian—that is, "the line of diminishing rainfall." This definition echoes Walter Prescott Webb's, who first acknowledged the 98th meridian as a useful tool in a regional analysis of the West. In the same way, New Western Historian Donald Worster considers that the West starts with the Dakotas, Nebraska, Kansas, Oklahoma, and Texas. As for Limerick, the first item of her "What on Earth Is the New Western History? (Not a Manifesto)" reads: "New Western Historians define the West primarily as a place—the trans-Mississippi region in the broadest terms, or the region west of the hundredth meridian." Similarly, very early in his seminal *"It's Your Misfortune and None of My Own": A New History of the American West*, published in 1991, historian Richard White undertakes to situate the West on a map. Yet he distances himself from the use of the 98th meridian to locate the eastern boundary of the region. When discussing the limits of the West, history and politics seemingly matter more to him than geology or physiography:

> The geographical boundaries of the American West were
> not naturally determined; they were politically deter-

mined. The American West is that contiguous section of the continent west of the Missouri River acquired by the United States, beginning with the Louisiana Purchase of 1803; continuing through the acquisition of Texas, the Oregon Territory, and the Mexican Cession in the 1840s; and ending with the 1853 Gadsden Purchase of the lands between the Gila River and the present Mexican boundary.[6]

Clearly, determining the limits of the American West is not an easy task and, as Albert Hurtado contends, "perhaps the West . . . is too riven with historical, cultural, and environmental differences to allow for boundaries that are equally satisfying to all surveyors in the field." The eastern limit of Malone's definition does not correspond to White's (the Missouri River) or to Limerick's (the Mississippi River). The western limit has been the topic of much debate—White excludes Alaska and Hawaii; others, such as the authors of the *Atlas of the New West*, dismiss the Pacific Rim states. The northern and southern limits themselves are not as obvious as one could expect. For instance, in *Many Wests*, historians David Wrobel and Michael Steiner include British Columbia, Alberta, Saskatchewan, Manitoba, and Mexico, in addition to the U.S. West. Assuming that capitalism knows no border, William Robbins includes the Canadian West and northern Mexico in his analysis of the economic transformation of the West.[7]

Moreover, there is no real consensus on the characteristics that best define the West, either. Aridity is most often mentioned and considered as the most salient trait of the West. To Donald Worster, it is what distinguishes the West from the other American regions and thus makes it unique. William Cronon believes it would be more appropriate to speak of "a climate of extremes" or, as Susan Rhoades Neel puts it, "an environment of profound variability and extremity." Considering the difficulty in defining where and what the West is, it is no wonder, then, that distinguishing its subregions and internal borderlands is a very daunting task.[8]

However, despite these numerous variations, what these studies have in common is a desire to study the West as a region, as a distinct place with limits—however blurry these may be—and intrinsic characteristics. This insistence on a regionalist perspective is a trademark of the revisionist school of the late twentieth century, known as the New Western History. To New Western Historians, the West is neither some moving line advancing westward nor "a mental image, an undefined generality," but a region. According to them, the West is as much a fixed entity as the South and the Northeast, not some vague process.[9] Yet, paradoxically, this very insistence on depicting the West as a region and singling out its specific characteristics has led to a fossilization of the West. In discarding the Turnerian frontier, New Historians have stifled the dynamism of the West; in looking for specific characteristics for the whole region, they have overlooked its interior borderlands and its subregional diversity.

Edward Ayers, a specialist of the South, has warned against the dangers of "essentializing" when studying regions: "[When] the South is portrayed as a 'culture' or 'society,' even a 'civilization,' that stands as the binary opposite of the North, a relative situation tends to become an absolute characteristic; Southern differences with the North are transformed into traits that mark the very soul of the Southern people."[10] Even though Ayers's statement is about the South, one could easily replace "South" with "West," so relevant is his analysis in a regionalist reading of the West. A depiction of the latter in opposition to the other American regions results not only in an overemphasis of certain characteristics—which may be prevalent in some areas but not in others—but also in neglect for other, more marginal ones. Aridity, for instance, which is unquestionably a major trait of New Mexico and Arizona, can hardly be said to define the Pacific Rim. Regionalizing the West thus runs the risk of generalization.

Undoubtedly, the regionalist outlook of the New Western Historians has emphasized, if not promoted, a Western identity. Members of the movement are intent on rehabilitating a region whose history has not received the same attention as the colonial past of the East and the slavery heritage of the South. Their plea for the American West to be recognized "as a real place, as a region of significance with a serious history" conveys their "'ferocious,' regional pride."[11] Yet their regionalist perspective may also be seen as a double bind or, as historians David Wrobel and Michael Steiner put it, "a double-edged sword":

> Deemphasizing the frontier process and focusing on the West as a definable place marked by certain characteristics—such as aridity, conquest, Native Americans, racial and ethnic diversity, and boom-bust economic cycles—has amounted to a double-edged sword for western historians. On one level, it has bolstered the West's regional identity by applying to it characteristics that move beyond frontier-centered notions of the area as the final stage in a heroic process of Euro-American settlement. But on another level, by emphasizing defining regional characteristics for the whole of the West, the new revisionism has to

some extent overlooked significant differences within this
vast region.

New Historians' efforts to define the West in opposition to Turner's frontier have been counterproductive: the incomparable diversity of the West,
its dynamism and variety, have been flattened by the historians' will to
study and present the West as a monolithic region distinct from the other
American regions. As a result, the heterogeneity of the subregions of the
West, these Wests within the West, not to mention its various internal
borders and borderlands, have been ignored, if not erased. As specialist of
the U.S. Southwest, David Weber noticed that "by abandoning the idea of
the frontier and making the West *as place* the *center* of [their] focus, [New
Western Historians have] drained away some of the drama of life on the
edges where people and places meet."[12]

Ironically, had they paid more attention to Turner's other writings and
less to his frontier thesis and its flaws, New Western Regionalists might
have been tempted to look into these various "sub-Wests" a little more
closely—for Turner, who is mostly known for his frontier thesis, also wrote
about "sections" to the point that, as historian Michael Steiner contends,
"geographical sectionalism eventually dominated his thought and overshadowed the frontier as a causal force." Early in his career, Turner en-
deavored to go beyond the frontier thesis and study what was left now
that the frontier was gone. To him, the frontier was a temporary stage in
the development of the nation, a "fleeting process," while the section was
a lasting component of American history. Once the frontier had gone, the
section took over: "[As] the frontier advance drew to a close, as these provinces were no longer regions to be crossed, or merely to be exploited, but
home-sections of permanent settlers, the final stage was reached." Therefore, Turner urged scholars to go beyond the study of sections in terms of
conflict between North and South. To him, sectionalism was to be seen as
"involving all the various geographic provinces of the United States and
the regions within them, and exhibiting itself in economic, political, and
cultural fields." This is the reason why he saw both the Midwest and the
Great Plains as sections, on a par with New England or the Southwest:

> We must also remember that each of the sections of this
> continental nation—New England, the Middle States,
> the Southeast, the Southwest, the Middle West, the Great
> Plains, the Mountain States, the Pacific Coast—has its
> own special geographical qualities, its own resources and
> economic capacities, and its own rival interests, partly

determined in the days when the geological foundations
were laid down.[13]

Contrary to New Western Regionalists, then, Turner saw the West not
as *a* region but as a *group* of regions worthy of historians' attention. Not
only did he observe variety within the West, but he also suggested ways to
dissect and analyze it. In an 1896 letter addressed to Walter Hines Page,
one of the editors of *The Atlantic,* Turner makes a list of the states compos-
ing the West. Yet he also expresses his dissatisfaction with such a division
of the West into states and suggests "a more scientific method, [which]
would be to ignore state lines" and, instead, to use "natural physiographic
divisions." Referring to John Wesley Powell's *Physiographic Regions of the
United States,* Turner praises this method, which "revolutionizes the study."
And indeed, the physiographic division he suggests for the Old Northwest
allows for a map that is different—that is, less rigid and artificial—from
the traditional partition of the region into states:

> 1. Alleghany Plateaus, which include the strip along the
> Ohio—(and run back to the Appalachian Ranges)
>
> 2. Prairie Plains, which include the middle of Ohio, nearly
> all of Indiana, Illinois, and western Wisconsin—running
> also to the Great Plains on the West, and so including
> western Minnesota, eastern Dakotas, Iowa, northern Mis-
> souri, and eastern Nebraska and Kansas
>
> 3. Lake Plains, including Michigan, eastern and northern
> Wisconsin, and northeastern Minnesota.[14]

As for the Middle West, a division into physiographic lines results in the
"Prairie Plains and Great Plains, with the Ozark Mt. region (in southern
Missouri, northwestern Arkansas and eastern Indiana) breaking the area."
The purpose of an analysis of the internal divisions of the West along physiographic lines was, according to Turner, "to divide the West into its proper
regions and describe the spirit of each." The boundaries Turner suggests
within the West may seem blurry, yet his partition reflects and allows for
more complexity than New Western Historian Patricia Nelson Limerick's
delineation of the West:

> Allowing for a certain shifting of borders, the West in this
> book will generally mean the present-day states of Cali-
> fornia, Oregon, Washington, Idaho, Utah, Nevada, Arizo-
> na, New Mexico, Colorado, Kansas, Nebraska, Oklahoma,
> Texas, Montana, Wyoming, North Dakota, and South

Dakota and, more changeably, Iowa, Missouri, Arkansas, and Louisiana. (Many patterns explored here apply also to Alaska, but limits of space and time have prohibited its full inclusion.)[15]

Drawing on geography and geology, Turner made historical inquiry more complex by suggesting a method to study the West according to its internal, physiographic divisions. Not only did he inspire the "Prairie Historians" to pursue the study of the history of the Midwest, but his work was also more pioneering than the New Western History, which seems to "draw boundaries between things we call cultures and then fill in those boundaries with something to make the boundaries meaningful." The New Western Regionalists, who rejected him outright, may have unfairly simplified Turner. Of course, one should add that, since they always have a purpose, revisions often lack in subtlety, and critics have pointed out how the New Historians are not any different from other revisionists.[16]

Yet, it is also surprising that they did not pay more attention to Walter Prescott Webb's attempt to divide the West up into its subregions. Indeed, not only did Webb offer a clear definition of where the West was and what it consisted of, but he also delineated three subregions: "Internally the West is divided into three strips, laid one beside the other on a north-south axis—a mountain strip in the center flanked by the Great Plains strip to the east and the Pacific slope strip to the west." Like Turner, Webb does not offer a clear picture as to where the internal borderlands stand, but he does try to distinguish various "sub-Wests" within the larger West.[17]

Needless to say, the New Western Historians' neglect of the subregions of the West has not prevented the publication of a number of studies on these subregions per se, by scholars from various disciplines, from environmental history to biology. Yet it seems that none has attempted to study the dividing line between the American Midwest and the Great Plains, despite historians Michael Steiner and David Wrobel's call to study the "many Wests" that make up the larger region.[18]

The very concept of "borderlands" provides a relevant tool for an analysis of the internal divisions of regions and is particularly suited to the diversity of the West. Historian Herbert Eugene Bolton, who had been Turner's student yet disagreed with the frontier thesis, popularized the concept in the early twentieth century, defining it as "the meeting place and fusing place of two streams of European civilization, one coming from the South, the other from the North." Focusing on the American Southwest, Bolton was less interested in American exceptionalism than in the characteristics and consequences of the long-lasting presence of the Spanish Empire in

North America, thus "[hoping] to forge a Hispanic counterpart to Frederick Jackson Turner's foundational narrative of the U.S. frontier." Due to Bolton's numerous students, the Spanish borderlands remained the focus of attention for most of the rest of the century.[19]

The field of borderlands studies was revamped in the 1970s in the wake of the new social history and has grown steadily since. As a result of its use in a comparative approach from the 1990s on, the borderlands concept has encompassed much more than analyses of the United States-Mexico border area, and its flexibility attests to its relevance for various regions, periods, and topics. It is particularly fruitful when dealing with the American West. Following Bolton in "The Epic of Greater America," historian Stephen Aron has resurrected some of the dynamism of the Turner thesis through the concept of a "Greater Western History," which sees the West as a series of "wests."[20]

Even though historians "now find borderlands everywhere," the concept remains particularly meaningful when applied to the transitional area between the Midwest and the Great Plains. It is no longer the Boltonian borderland, in the sense that it does not separate empires or nations, yet it makes it possible to study the porous area where two of the nation's understudied subregions meet and interact, thus highlighting the "paradoxical character" of borderlands: "Borders create political, social, and cultural distinctions, but simultaneously imply the existence of (new) networks and systems of interaction across them."[21]

Defining and locating a region is probably one of the historian's most difficult tasks. It is all the more daunting when one adds the psychological factor to the geographical, physiographic, historical, and political components. As Martin Ridge contends, historians may spend their time and energy debating and arguing over the boundaries of the West, yet only its inhabitants may have clear and definite answers:

> There is a location on the Plains of the West where, for some undetermined reason, people think of themselves as being westerners and not middle westerners or southerners. It would be convenient if it were at the one-hundredth meridian—the so-called line of semi-aridity—but it is not. There is a psychological and not a physiographic fault line that separates regions.

However, the fight the exercise may trigger and the limits of the endeavor should not prevent historians from trying.[22]

In their attempts at both reviving interest in the past of the region and defining a collective Western identity, New Western Historians have failed to acknowledge the West's internal variations and borderlands, and they have ended up eliding them. Their eagerness to do away with Turner and his legacy has led them to overlook some of his pioneering work, and it is tempting to conclude that, as Jon Lauck contends, "[this] new wave of history . . . was too much of a myth-busting exercise and not enough of a good-faith attempt to understand the American West as a region and map its subregions." One can only hope that the "newest," "next," or "post" Western history will remedy the failings of the New Western History and offer a more complex study of the subregions, internal borders, and border-lands of the American West.[23]

Notes

[1] See, for instance, Stephen Aron, "What's West, What's Next," *OAH Magazine of History* 19, no. 6 (November 2005): 22–25; or Maria E. Montoya, "Onward to the Next Western History," *Western Historical Quarterly* 43, no. 3 (Autumn 2012): 271–73.

[2] Frederick Jackson Turner, "Sections and Nation," in *Rereading Frederick Jackson Turner: "The Significance of the Frontier in American History" and Other Essays*, ed. John Mack Faragher (New Haven: Yale University Press, 1998), 182. Walter Prescott Webb, *The Great Plains* (Lincoln: University of Nebraska Press, 1981), 3. It is important to distinguish two groups among the New Western Historians, as advocated by Kerwin Lee Klein: "students of the Greater West and New Western Regionalists." While the former study frontier processes in order to write a "Greater Western History," the latter discard the frontier and think the West should be studied not in terms of process but as a place. Klein, "Reclaiming the 'F' Word, or Being and Becoming Postwestern," *Pacific Historical Review* 65, no. 2 (May 1996): 180. The present chapter deals mostly with the "regionalist" perspective of the New Western History, whose members have been particularly vocal in rejecting the frontier thesis and advocating a regionalist reading of the West.

[3] Bernard DeVoto, "The West: A Plundered Province," *Harper's Monthly Magazine* 169, no. 1011 (August 1934): 356.

[4] Walter Prescott Webb, "The American West: Perpetual Mirage," *Harper's Monthly Magazine* 214, no. 1284 (May 1957): 25.

[5] Patricia Nelson Limerick, *The Legacy of Conquest: The Unbroken Past of the American West* (New York: W.W. Norton, 2006), 26. Banishing the "frontier" concept: see Limerick, "The Adventures of the Frontier in the Twentieth Century," in *The Frontier in American Culture*, ed. James R. Grossman (Berkeley: University of California Press, 1994), 72. "'F' word" reference: see Klein, "Reclaiming the 'F' Word," 179–215.

[6] Michael P. Malone, ed., *Historians and the American West* (Lincoln: University of Nebraska Press, 1983), 1–2. Webb, *Great Plains*, 8–9. Donald Worster, *Under Western Skies: Nature and History in the American West* (New York: Oxford University Press, 1992), 24. Patricia Nelson Limerick, "What on Earth Is the New Western History?" in *Trails: Toward a New Western History*, ed. Patricia Nelson Limerick, Clyde A. Milner, and Charles Rankin (Lawrence: University Press of Kansas, 1991), 85.

Richard White, *"It's Your Misfortune and None of My Own": A New History of the American West* (Norman: University of Oklahoma Press, 1991), 4.

[7] Albert L. Hurtado, "The Proffered Paradigm: Finding the West in Time and Space," *Western Historical Quarterly* 25, no. 4 (Winter 1994): 469. William E. Riebsame, ed., *Atlas of the New West: Portrait of a Changing Region* (New York: W.W. Norton, 1997). David M. Wrobel and Michael C. Steiner, "Many Wests: Discovering a Dynamic Western Regionalism," in *Many Wests: Place, Culture, and Regional Identity*, ed. David M. Wrobel and Michael C. Steiner (Lawrence: University Press of Kansas, 1997), 12. William Robbins, *Colony and Empire: The Capitalist Transformation of the American West* (Lawrence: University Press of Kansas, 1994). The Census Bureau makes a clear distinction between Midwest and West, with the latter's eastern limit corresponding to the states of Montana, Wyoming, Colorado, and New Mexico. "Census Regions and Divisions of the United States," Census Bureau, accessed October 29, 2017, https://www2.census.gov/geo/pdfs/maps-data/maps/reference/us_regdiv.pdf.

[8] Worster, *Under Western Skies*, 23. William Cronon, "Kennecott Journey: The Paths out of Town," in *Under an Open Sky: Rethinking America's Western Past*, ed. William Cronon, George Miles, and Jay Gitlin (New York: W.W. Norton, 1992), 32. Susan Rhoades Neel, "A Place of Extremes: Nature, History, and the American West," *Western Historical Quarterly* 25, no. 4 (Winter 1994): 498.

[9] For more on the New Western History, see Nathalie Massip, "The Role of the West in the Construction of American Identity: From Frontier to Crossroads," *Anglophonia/Caliban* 31 (2012): doi:10.4000/caliban.486. "Mental image" reference is in Robert G. Athearn, *The Mythic West in Twentieth-Century America* (Lawrence: University Press of Kansas, 1986), 16. A fascinating essay on how and where to locate the West is Walter Nugent's report on a survey ("Where Is the American West?") carried out among members of the Western History Association, journalists, editors, publishers, and Western writers in 1991. Unsurprisingly, the survey reveals a lack of consensus regarding the limits and characteristics of the West. It also exposes very personal, even passionate reactions to the questions asked. Walter Nugent, "Where Is the American West? Report on a Survey," *Montana: The Magazine of Western History* 42 (Summer 1992): 2–23.

[10] Edward Ayers, "What We Talk About When We Talk About the South," in *All over the Map: Rethinking American Regions*, ed. Edward L. Ayers, Patricia Nelson Limerick, Stephen Nissenbaum, and Peter S. Onuf (Baltimore: Johns Hopkins University Press, 1996), 65.

[11] Patricia Nelson Limerick, "The Trail to Santa Fe: The Unleashing of the Western Public Intellectual," in Limerick, Milner, and Rankin, *Trails*, 70. "[Ferocious] pride" reference by Western historian Howard R. Lamar is cited in Richard Bernstein, "Unsettling the Old West," *New York Times Magazine*, March 18, 1990, sec. 6, p. 34.

[12] Wrobel and Steiner, "Many Wests," 10–11. David Weber, quoted in Donald Worster, Susan Armitage, Michael P. Malone, David J. Weber, and Patricia Nelson Limerick, *"The Legacy of Conquest*, by Patricia Nelson Limerick: A Panel of Appraisal," *Western Historical Quarterly* 20, no. 3 (August 1989): 316 (emphasis in original). The point here is not to reproach New Western Historians with ignoring the heterogeneity of the West. They have consistently acknowledged this major characteristic. Responding to critics considering that the West is too diverse an area to be called and studied as a region, Patricia Nelson Limerick rightly remarks that regions are, by definition, heterogeneous. Limerick, "Trail to Santa Fe," 70. However, acknowledging the

diversity of the West, as Limerick and others do, is one thing; but actually studying this diversity, and the various subregions that compose the West, is another.

[13] See Frederick Jackson Turner, *The Significance of Sections in American History* (New York: Henry Holt, 1932). "Geographical sectionalism" and "fleeting process" quotes are in Michael C. Steiner, "The Significance of Turner's Sectional Thesis," *Western Historical Quarterly* 10, no. 4 (October 1979): 440, 448. Section as final stage quote is in Turner, "Geographic Sectionalism in American History," *Annals of the Association of American Geographers* 16, no. 2 (June 1926): 88. Sections in terms of conflict between North and South is in Turner, "Sections and Nation," 184; Turner, "The Significance of the Section in American History," in Faragher, *Rereading*, 205. "[Geographic] provinces" quote is in Turner, "Geographic Sectionalism," 85. Middle West and Great Plains quote is in Turner, "Sections and Nation," 182.

[14] Turner and the West as a set of regions is in Frederick Jackson Turner, "The West as a Field for Historical Study," *Annual Report of the American Historical Association* (1896): 282. Frederick Jackson Turner, "Letter to Walter H. Page" (August 30, 1896), quoted in Fulmer Mood, "The Origin, Evolution, and Application of the Sectional Concept, 1750–1900," in *Regionalism in America*, ed. Merrill Jensen (Madison: University of Wisconsin Press, 1952), 94–96.

[15] Turner quoted in Mood, "Origin," 94-96. It is to be noted that Turner does not see a dividing line between Midwest and Great Plains, since, to him, the Great Plains is a subregion of the Midwest. Limerick, *Legacy of Conquest*, 26.

[16] "Prairie Historians" quote is in Jon K. Lauck, *The Lost Region: Toward a Revival of Midwestern History* (Iowa City: University of Iowa Press, 2013), especially 29–52. Ayers, "What We Talk," 66. On how the New Western History used Turner as a foil, see Jon K. Lauck, "How South Dakota Sparked the New Western History Wars: A Commentary on Patricia Nelson Limerick," *South Dakota History* 41, no. 3 (Fall 2011): 353–81.

[17] Webb, "American West," 25.

[18] Wrobel and Steiner, "Many Wests." The expression "many Wests" was first used by Frederic Logan Paxson, in his 1929 *When the West Is Gone*. Geographers have also expanded on this theme. In 1972, Donald W. Meinig observed how geographers were more interested in the West as "a *set* of regions" than in the West "as *a* region." Meinig, "American Wests: Preface to a Geographical Interpretation," *Annals of the Association of American Geographers* 62, no. 2 (June 1972): 159 (emphasis in original).

[19] Herbert Eugene Bolton, "Defensive Spanish Expansion and the Significance of the Borderlands," in *Wider Horizons of American History*, ed. Herbert Eugene Bolton (Notre Dame, IN: University of Notre Dame Press, 1939), 98. "Hispanic counterpart" quote is in Samuel Truett and Elliott Young, "Making Transnational History: Nations, Regions, and Borderlands," in *Continental Crossroads. Remapping US-Mexico Borderlands History*, ed. Samuel Truett and Elliott Young (Durham, NC: Duke University Press, 2004), 3. The authors estimate that Bolton had 104 Ph.D. and 323 M.A. students throughout his career.

[20] The Association for Borderlands Studies was created in 1976. Among various examples of works using the borderlands concept in a comparative approach, see Michiel Baud and Willem Van Schendel, "Toward a Comparative History of Borderlands," *Journal of World History* 8 (Fall 1997): 211–42; Kate Brown, *A Biography of No Place: From Ethnic Borderland to Soviet Heartland* (Cambridge, MA: Harvard University Press, 2003); or Eric Tagliacozzo, *Secret Trades, Porous Borders: Smuggling and States along a Southeast Asian Frontier, 1865–1915* (New Haven: Yale University Press, 2005).

Herbert Eugene Bolton, "The Epic of Greater America," *American Historical Review* 38, no. 3 (April 1933), 448–74. Stephen Aron, "Lessons in Conquest: Towards a Greater Western History," *Pacific Historical Review* 63, no. 2 (May 1994): 136.

[21] Pekka Hämäläinen and Samuel Truett, "On Borderlands," *Journal of American History* 98, no. 2 (September 2011): 339. Baud and Van Schendel, "Toward a Comparative History," 216.

[22] Martin Ridge, "The American West: From Frontier to Region," *New Mexico Historical Review* 64, no. 2 (April 1989): 139–40. Adam Arenson contends: "Give a group of historians (or regular citizens) a map and ask where the regions of the country start and end, and you are asking for a fight; add a historical dimension and it gets even more complicated." Arenson, "U.S. History's Regional Associations—Shaped by Geography or Driving Questions? And Does It Matter?" *U.S. Intellectual History Blog*, November 11, 2015, https://s-usih.org/2015/11/u-s-historys-regional-associations-shaped-by-geography-or-driving-questions-and-does-it-matter-guest-post/.

[23] Jon Lauck, "Finding the Rural West," in *Bridging the Distance: Common Issues of the Rural West*, ed. David D. Danbom (Salt Lake City: University of Utah Press, 2015), 20. For the "newest" Western history, see Stephen Aron, "Convergence, California, and the Newest Western History," *California History* 86 (September 2009): 4–13. For the "next" Western history, see Aron, "What's West, What's Next?" For the "post" Western history, see Klein, "Reclaiming the 'F' Word."

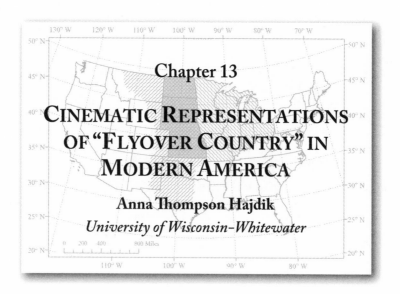

Chapter 13

CINEMATIC REPRESENTATIONS OF "FLYOVER COUNTRY" IN MODERN AMERICA

Anna Thompson Hajdik

University of Wisconsin–Whitewater

To the traveller, who for several days traverses these prairies and barrens, their appearance is quite uninviting and even disagreeable. . . . No pleasant variety of hill and dale, no rapidly running brook delights the eye, and no sound of woodland music strike the ear; but in their stead, a dull uniformity of prospect, spread out immense.[1]

These recollections of early nineteenth-century historian/archeologist Caleb Atwater were published almost two hundred years before the box-office success of the 2009 film *Up in the Air*. Yet the quote reflects a cultural attitude about the Midwest that is enduring and pervasive. In the film, George Clooney portrays Ryan Bingham, a corporate downsizer who logs countless air miles across America's midsection. His travels are frequently portrayed in the film, as he scans the vast rural landscape from above. Audiences too are given a bird's-eye perspective of the region, as the director, Jason Reitman, incorporated several shots of "flyover country" from the air. Bingham's job consists chiefly of entering drab boardrooms and firing people as he works to maintain a minimal personal life until romance intervenes. Against the backdrop of the Great

Recession, the film was a critical and commercial success. It stands as just one popular example of a complex depiction of "flyover country," a term of "playful condescension toward rural America from an urban perspective."[2] Such depictions almost always include the Midwest and/or the Great Plains.

This chapter explores how a number of popular films like *Up in the Air* effectively collapse the boundaries between the Great Plains and Midwest. While *Up in the Air* in particular conveys problematic ideas at times by imbuing "flyover country" with a kind of placelessness, other filmmakers working today like Joel and Ethan Coen and Alexander Payne have developed a decidedly Midwest aesthetic that simultaneously celebrates and derides the places and characters they seek to portray. However, I first delve into the field of art history in order to further illuminate the phrase "flyover country" by looking backward to the late nineteenth and early twentieth centuries. Ultimately, the boundaries of flyover country, much like the boundaries between the Great Plains and the Midwest, are nebulous at best.

The phrase "flyover country" first appeared in the 1970s. Working within a much simpler media landscape, entertainment executives sought to create television programs that appealed to Midwestern audiences, but those executives also derisively dismissed those same viewers as they constantly shuttled back and forth between New York City and Los Angeles, flying over the nation's midsection in the process.[3] As Anthony Harkins notes in more depth about the phrase, it became increasingly prominent and more politicized after the 2000 presidential election, with a noted spike in its usage during the 2008 presidential election campaign.[4] In the wake of the 2016 election, "flyover country" was everywhere, even becoming the title of a weekly national public radio program.[5]

The dismissal of America's midsection as barren, unexciting, or a vast wasteland stretches back to the age of scientific exploration at the dawn of the nineteenth century. As Joni Kinsey and C. Elizabeth Raymond have shown, the perception of the Midwest as a homogenous, empty landscape has its roots in the writings of early American explorers.[6] Zebulon Pike referred to the Great Plains as "internal deserts" in the published accounts of his 1806–1807 expedition to the Rocky Mountains.[7] Many of these early explorers mistakenly thought the Great Plains in particular to be infertile, and thus not worthy of attention.

By the late nineteenth century, the phenomenon of "prospect pictures," a precursor to aerial photography, began in earnest throughout the region. These "bird's-eye" images of small towns or plots of land were used to publicize and promote small towns in the region, and they led to a general uptick in civic pride as boosters sought to carve out unique identities for their little corners of the world. Especially popular were "panoramic views" of these young, gridded communities across the region. Inexpensive lithographic prints were sold by the thousands throughout the United States.[8] The dawn of commercial flight however had a more considerable impact on how the Midwest came to be perceived by the public, and perhaps it is most directly responsible for the development of the phrase "flyover country." As Jason Weems observes, during the 1920s and 1930s, "the agricultural landscape, particularly the vast gridded landscapes of the American Midwest, came into sight as a locus for the construction of new cultural outlooks that were intricately tied to emergent practices for aerial looking and thinking." As Weems further notes, the "airplane became an apparatus for new ways of looking, from paintings and photographs to movies and popular media, a plethora of aerial images of landscapes entered the American, and more specifically, the midwestern scene."[9] This new way of visually conceptualizing the region had far-reaching impacts, but I argue it was especially influential in art and cinema of the 1930s.

The emergence of the Regionalist Art Movement of the 1930s was a significant slice of visual culture that impacted how coastal elites thought of the nation's midsection. Artists like Grant Wood, John Steuart Curry, Harvey Dunn, and Thomas Hart Benton asserted an American modernist vision through the lens of agrarian landscapes. Furthermore, as Michael Steiner argues, these Midwestern painters articulated a notion of "the primal basic America, a desire for stable communal identity, and a reverence for the past—especially the memories that could bring a sense of order and certainty to a tumultuous present."[10] In other words, their work reclaimed a nostalgic, seemingly close-knit regional identity at a time when urban America was frequently visualized as impersonal and disorienting.

Wood often utilized an aerial perspective in many of his works. This viewpoint "enabled him to conjure landscapes that exuded a romanticized picture of rural culture that tended to comfort his fellow midwesterners by confirming the personalized and affective bonds shared between the land and its inhabitants."[11] While many of Wood's paintings fit into this framework, perhaps none are as notable as *Stone City, Iowa*. The rolling hills of this northeastern Iowa community are the very definition of American pastoral in Wood's representation. The vantage point is from above, looking down at homes, farms, plowed fields, and a river that cuts through a valley. A palette of vibrant shades of green fills the canvas, and, from above, all seems to be in perfect harmony: a seamless blend of town and country.

At the same time, however, the aerial view provides a kind of distance. There is an almost cinematic or panoramic pleasure in seeing this idyllic scene from far above, yet it also provides distance from the sometimes more negative details of small-town life that had been so bitingly critiqued by novelists like Sinclair Lewis who gave rise to the "revolt from a village" a decade earlier. Intriguingly, no people appear in *Stone City, Iowa*, although their presence is certainly made clear. A year later, Wood's *Birthplace of Herbert Hoover* again used an aerial perspective to imbue the president's hometown of West Branch, Iowa, with pastoral themes, articulating a romantic vision of the community.[12]

By the end of the 1930s, Hollywood's adaption of L. Frank Baum's *The Wonderful Wizard of Oz* became an important cinematic template for conceptualizing the Midwest as flyover country. While much scholarly attention has been given to the book's many allegories to populism at the turn of the twentieth century, less scholarly attention has been paid to the film version as its own significant text in relation to the cultural, political, and international turmoil of the 1930s. *The Wizard of Oz* (1939) became an almost instant classic when it was released. The stark contrast between Dorothy Gale's home in sepia-toned Kansas and the vivid Technicolor of Oz would certainly have been noted by Midwestern audiences in 1939. Audiences might also have identified with Dorothy's restlessness. In the lyrics of "Over the Rainbow," Dorothy clearly yearns for something beyond Kansas. Indeed, Oz is portrayed as an exciting, thrilling escape from the mundane drabness of the farm. Moreover, Dorothy reaches Oz only because she's flown there. The house is picked up by a cyclone, Dorothy watches as key symbols and markers of her rural upbringing float by her bedroom window, and then the house is dropped in this new, exotic landscape. But of course once she's in Oz, she pines for home. Her eager return provides order to a chaotic world, and, against the backdrop of looming world war, audiences also likely found solace in an ending that touts the importance of home while reifying the Midwest as a stable bulwark against chaos. Here, flyover country becomes reimagined as the wholesome heartland.

The Wizard of Oz solidified the idea of the nation's midsection as America's heartland, and it became one of the most enduring stereotypes of the cinematic Midwest. In the decades that followed, films like *State Fair* (1945), *The Best Years of Our Lives* (1946), *Oklahoma!* (1955), and *The Music Man* (1962) helped to cement the region's association with values and virtue, even if the films themselves continued to be made on a distant Hollywood sound stage. Southern California further cemented itself as a repository for the imagined, mythic heartland when Walt Disney opened Disneyland in 1955. Against the backdrop of the Cold War, Disney sought to recreate his hometown of Marceline, Missouri, through the design of Main Street, U.S.A., an idyllic simulation of the small town circa 1900.[13] As media scholar Victoria Johnson argues, the heartland is a presumed, shared "commonsense" norm:

> Middle America becomes a preferred place—the core, au-thentically American locus of genuine affect and of the presence of divinity . . . the mythic American Pastoral, site of time-bound values of expressed belief in God, pio-neering self-sufficiency, "knowable" community and het-erosexual/nuclear-familial ideals.[14]

Furthermore, the idea that the heartland (and the people residing within its nebulous borders) is somehow more authentically American continues to wield cultural power, especially in essays and news stories that seek to make sense of a nation that is now so polarized politically. A recent *New York Times* essay on the geographic and cultural boundaries of the heartland noted:

> The heartland can also be defined by what it's not—the coasts. And in many ways its cultural values have been framed in opposition to that Other America. "The suspicion persists," wrote the English professor and critic Barry Gross in 1977, "that what goes on at either coast is the extreme, the perverse and bizarre, the grotesque and the Gothic, unreal and worse, unAmerican."
>
> The center of the country is the normal against which the coasts are abnormal, or merely peripheral.[15]

At the same time, the notion of the Midwestern gothic—the region as home to a special brand of darkness uniquely suited to its seemingly banal landscapes—has shown up in a range of creative works, from Michael Lessy's lurid catalog of dysfunction, *Wisconsin Death Trip*, to Truman Capote's horrifying nonfiction novel *In Cold Blood*, to Terence Malick's grisly, bleak film *Badlands*. Critic Dave Kehr wrote of *Badlands*: "Malick's 1973 first feature is a film so rich in ideas it hardly knows where to turn. Transcendent themes of love and death are fused with a pop-culture sensibility and played out against a midwestern background, which is breathtaking both in its sweep and in its banality."[16] The film tells the story of a pair of young lovers on a cross-country murder spree, loosely based on the lives of Charles Starkweather and Caril Ann Fugate. It is an incredibly dark vision of flyover country (primarily South Dakota and Montana) that in many ways laid the foundation for Joel and Ethan Coen's masterpiece, *Fargo* (1996).

While the 1980s saw its share of films and associated popular culture that romanticized rural life against the backdrop of the Farm Crisis (*Witness* [1985] and *Field of Dreams* [1989] are just two that found both critical acclaim and box-office success), I argue that the release of *Fargo* (1996) was a pivotal contribution in both positive and negative ways in relation to the concept of flyover country. Set and filmed throughout Minnesota, *Fargo* is a quirky but dark tale about a kidnapping-for-hire plot that quickly goes awry. The Coen brothers, also Minnesota natives, wrote the screenplay and directed the film. Upon its release, it immediately received positive reviews across the United States, and critics often cited the movie's Minnesota locale as one of its most noticeable traits. Janet Maslin, writing for the *New York Times*, noted, "The Coens are at their clever best with this snowbound film noir, a crazily mundane crime story set in their native Midwest."[17]

Fargo went on to become the independent darling of film critics and moviegoers in 1996. The film won two Academy Awards, one for best original screenplay and another for actress Frances McDormand, who portrayed police chief Marge Gunderson. It was also nominated for best picture, cinematography, best supporting actor, and best director. It performed well at the box office, costing only $7 million to make and grossing $25 million.

Perhaps the most indelible element of *Fargo* is the landscape, or the lack thereof. The flat, vast whiteness that opens the film is the very definition of what Joni Kinsey calls "the aesthetics of absence." Early American writers often described the Great Plains in particular as a "sublime void." Kinsey then defines the sublime as characterized by "scenes that provoke fear or awe by their vastness, immensity, extraordinary roughness, or other such pronounced qualities."[18] As *Fargo* opens, a frigid, white sublimity immediately envelops the screen. The snow is essentially its own character and is used to set an ominous tone. Production designer Rick Heinrichs and cinematographer Roger Deakins worked with the Coens on the challenge of making the film's Midwestern landscape look simultaneously bleak, boring, and laden with dramatic possibilities and, according to William Luhr, "worthy of Dante in its potential for immanent horror." Heinrichs also concocted the Paul Bunyan statue that towers eerily over the town of Brainerd (ironically replacing the town's actual more cheerful Bunyan mascot) with its axe murderer stance and mad, glaring eyes.[19] The Bunyan statue in *Fargo* is symbolic of something sinister in the air.

In the essay *"Fargo,* or the Blank Frontier," Christopher Sharrett also identifies the film with an overwhelming sense of emptiness, but of a slightly different kind. Sharrett argues that emptiness of the landscape is reinforced by the "overly sanitary feel of the thoroughly bourgeois, commodified, fast-food civilization of postindustrial America."[20] In the small town of Brainerd, the chief protagonists Marge and Norm Gunderson are shown leading dull but content lives. They enjoy a big night out at the local all-you-can-eat buffet from time to time, and both of them would be perfectly happy if they never left the familiar surroundings of Brainerd. *Fargo* offers an at once exotic and provincial representation of the American Midwest. The Minnesota of *Fargo* is filled with a collection of eccentric, heroic, and dangerous people, but it is also constructed as a parochial place. Marge Gunderson, the police chief who solves the heinous crime and shoots the bad guy at the film's climax, is intelligent, effective, but also wide-eyed, innocent, and incorruptible. She's an update of Dorothy Gale but in a much darker cinematic universe.

In the 1990s, the independent film industry flourished. The Coen brothers were in the good company of edgy directors like Quentin Tarantino, Jane Campion, and Danny Boyle who pushed the boundaries of cinema and made intelligent, thought-provoking films that appealed to a range of audiences. Another director in the 1990s who was just beginning to build a reputation as a purveyor of dark humor combined with a modicum of heartland sentimentality was Alexander Payne. A native of Omaha, he has consistently explored the cinematic landscape of the American Midwest in satirical, heartbreaking, and ultimately uplifting ways. The three films I discuss here—*Election* (1999), *About Schmidt* (2002), and *Nebraska* (2013)—share more than just their Nebraska setting. Each film centers on a white male protagonist searching for redemption or, at the very least, vindication for his life and the choices he has made along the way. *Election* (1999) places a young go-getter named Tracy Flick at the center of the narrative, but the film is really about her high school government teacher, Jim McAllister, living and working in the Omaha suburbs. It is chiefly through Jim's eyes we come to know Flick and what she symbolizes in his life. Ambition is what drives Flick's desire to become the student body president, but Jim resents her polished image of perfection. *Election* is the first of Payne's Nebraska-set films, although its landscape is not overtly a part of the story. But it increasingly takes on an oppressive and stifling tone as Jim becomes aware of Tracy's seemingly inevitable path to victory while, simultaneously, his marriage collapses. Eventually, Jim is disgraced and fired when it is revealed that he rigged the election to favor Flick's opponent. He finds redemption however when he leaves the drab, oppressive surroundings of Omaha, moves to New York City, and restarts his life. He also discovers that Tracy has left Omaha behind for the greener pastures of Washington, D.C. In the end, both characters find a future on the East Coast, making *Election* Payne's most critical film in its treatment of the Midwest.

Released several years later, *About Schmidt* (2002) expands upon the theme of redemption through its chief protagonist, Warren Schmidt. Once again set in Omaha but also incorporating a western road trip, the film begins with scenes of drab landscapes as the main character's seeming life of mediocrity begins to unfold for the audience. It opens with Schmidt's retirement from a midlevel career in the insurance industry, his wife dies soon after, and he then learns of a long-term affair she had with a close friend. Feeling utterly alone, Schmidt signs up to sponsor a poor orphan in Africa and begins to send the boy letters and money through the aid society associated with the orphanage. Schmidt's various narrations of his letters to the orphan are juxtaposed against that cross-country road trip from Omaha to Denver in a Winnebago as he travels to his estranged daughter's wedding. Along the way, he visits his hometown in far western Nebraska and makes several other pit stops as well.

About Schmidt is a deep character study, but the film would not be the same without its Midwestern setting. Critic Stephen Holden noted its "expansive, impressively even-handed vision of life in contemporary Middle America" and praised the film for striking the difficult balance between satire and sentimentality. He further observes, "While one eye gazes satirically at the rigid institutions and shopworn rituals that sustain a sense of order and tradition in the heartland, the other views those same institutions with a respectful understanding of their value."[21]

Moreover, the landscape of the Great Plains serves as an important backdrop to the deeper emotional themes in the film. Schmidt's alienation, regret, sadness, and isolation feels especially profound as the vast, open spaces of western Nebraska roll by. However, a major turning point in the film involves Schmidt sitting on the roof of his Winnebago as a shooting star flashes across the endless night sky. The rural setting allows for a kind of intimacy in that moment that imbues the scene with pastoral romanticism as the film shifts to a more redemptive tone.

Payne's third film set in the Midwest, *Nebraska* (2013), led the *New Yorker* to dub the director the "High Plains Auteur," and, to date, it is his most critically acclaimed film.[22] The stark yet vivid visuals of the rural landscape along with an intimate story of a father and son road trip from Billings (Montana) to Lincoln (Nebraska) capture both the vivid beauty and the mundaneness of the region. Bruce Dern for his portrayal of Woody, the father on a quest for validation and recognition in the twilight of his life, earned an Academy Award nomination for best actor, while the film was also nominated for best picture, original screenplay, and cinematography, along with Payne for directing.

Nebraska is shot entirely in black and white, which adds a kind of cinematic drama to the scenery that vacillates between flat, open farm fields and the vast rolling hills of the Great Plains. This landscape is juxtaposed against that of the small town of Hawthorne, Nebraska, the hometown of Woody, the grizzled, alcoholic father in search of redemption. Father and son stay over in the small town of Hawthorne for several days, a farming community that seems to have been preserved in a time capsule but has also clearly hit hard economic times.

Art reflects reality or, at the very least, is a barometer of it. Payne's *Nebraska* is beautiful but austere. Hawthorne in particular has been left behind by the economics of globalization, ongoing country-to-city migration, and a pervasive provincialism. In this vein, as a cultural representation of flyover country, Payne's depiction of Hawthorne becomes politically relevant. Ten days after the 2016 presidential election, Texas senator and former GOP presidential candidate Ted Cruz declared, "This election can well be understood as the revenge of flyover country."[23] The statement cut to the heart of the current political reality of America, a polarized country with divisions that are geographic, economic, intellectual, and, perhaps most significantly, cultural in their various dimensions. Earlier in 2016, a journalist writing for *National Geographic* eerily foreshadowed the major role "flyover country" resentment would play in the presidential campaign and its outcome:

> As a concept, flyover country can exist almost anywhere in the United States. As a phrase, it's become almost a dare, a way for Midwesterners to cajole the coastal elites into paying attention to a place they might otherwise overlook. But it's also a bond for Midwesterners—a way of forging an identity in a place they imagine being mocked for its lack of identity. It's a response to an affront, real or imagined, and a way to say "Well, maybe we don't think that much of you, either."[24]

But the fissure between the coasts and America's midsection is hardly unique to 2016. As Jon Lauck notes, "The Midwest reveals the evolution of interior resistance to the coastal dominance of politics and culture, which begat forms of populism that still persist and resonate in American political culture, and explains the history of capitalism in the United States, over which the debate will long endure."[25] The media coverage of the presidential campaign exposed these divisions to some degree before the election, but there were also pronounced efforts on the part of major news outlets to better understand flyover country voters. The *New York Times*, for example, "embedded" several of their top political reporters in Iowa for a year preceding the Iowa caucuses. One essay exhorted its readers to "Go Midwest, Young Hipster" in order to more equally distribute left-leaning voters across the country.[26]

In the wake of Donald Trump's election, however, it is an open question as to whether the film industry might begin to depict narratives set in the Midwest that represent the region as not merely landscapes to cross quickly or escape from (like *Up in the Air* or *Election*), sentimental bastions of heartland virtue as in decades past, or quirky but isolated curiosities filled with eccentrics and criminals (*Badlands* and *Fargo*), but instead imbue the region with a sophisticated cosmopolitanism that Hollywood tends to reserve for the coasts. The entertainment industry's issues with diversity more broadly have been well chronicled in the past few years as executives have been encouraged to cultivate talent that includes more women and people of color. Might we see more diversity of regional identity as well if more Midwestern filmmakers brought a wider array of stories to the big screen and, like the Coen's and Payne, made the Midwestern landscape an integral part of their storytelling?

In all the films analyzed for this essay, the relationship between Midwestern place and identity is at the forefront of these narratives. From *Up in the Air*, where the chief protagonist's very placelessness defines him and his complicated relationships to others, to the Nebraska-set films of Alexander Payne, where the stark bleakness of the prairie landscapes are simultaneously stifling and redemptive to the characters, these various representations further the flyover country stereotype, but also offer unexpected depth. For the time being, from a political vantage point we are indeed the divided states of America. Perhaps it is up to the culture industry to foster a greater degree of understanding among regions by producing entertainment that is more nuanced and intelligent in its portrayal of the nation's midsection.

Notes

[1]   Caleb Atwater, "On the Prairies and Barrens of the West," *American Journal of Science* 1 (1818): 124; available at https://books.google.com/books?id=rChGAAAAcAAJ (accessed December 26, 2016).

2   Richard Sisson, Christian Zacher, and Andrew Cayton, eds., *The American Midwest: An Interpretive Encyclopedia* (Bloomington: Indiana University Press, 2007), 66.

3   Ben Zimmer. "After the Election, the Concept of 'Flyover Country' Rises," *Wall Street Journal*, November 22, 2016, http://www.wsj.com/articles/after-the-election-the-concept-of-flyover-country-rises-1479830039.

4   Anthony Harkins, "The Midwest and the Evolution of Flyover Country," *Middle West Review* 3, no. 1 (Fall 2016): 111.

5   Corrine Grinapol, "MPR Is Highlighting the Voices of 'Flyover' Country with a New Call-in Show," *Ad Week*, August 9, 2017, http://www.adweek.com/digital/mpr-is-highlighting-the-voices-of-flyover-country-with-a-new-call-in-show/.

6   C. Elizabeth Raymond, "Middle Ground: Evolving Regional Images in the American Midwest," in *"Writing" Nation and "Writing" Region in America*, ed. Theo D'Haen and Hans Bertens (Amsterdam: VU University Press, 1996), 95–114.

7   Joni Kinsey, *Plain Pictures: Images of the American Prairie* (Washington, D.C.: Smithsonian Institution Press, 1996), 15.

8   Kinsey, *Plain Pictures*, 18.

9   Jason Weems, *Barnstorming the Prairies: How Aerial Vision Shaped the Midwest* (Minneapolis: University of Minnesota Press, 2015), ix–x.

10 Michael Steiner, "Regionalism in the Great Depression," *Geographical Review* 73, no. 4 (October 1983): 432.

11 Weems, *Barnstorming the Prairies*, 128.

12 "Grant Wood: Iowa's No. 1 Artist Who Died Last Winter Gets Big Retrospective Show in Chicago," *Life*, January 18, 1943, 52–57.

13 Steven Watts, *The Magic Kingdom: Walt Disney and the American Way of Life* (Boston: Houghton Mifflin, 1997), 4, 7.

14 Victoria E. Johnson, "Welcome Home? CBS, PAX-TV and 'Heartland' Values in a Neo-network Era," *Velvet Light Trap* (Fall 2000): 43.

15 Emily Badger and Kevin Quealy, "Where Is America's Heartland? Pick Your Map," *New York Times*, January 3, 2017, http://nyti.ms/2hNv2LM.

16 Dave Kehr, "Badlands," *Chicago Reader*, http://www.chicagoreader.com/chicago/badlands/Film?oid=2769609.

17 Janet Maslin, "Film Review: Deadly Plot by a Milquetoast Villain," *New York Times*, March 8, 1996, https://www.nytimes.com/1996/03/08/movies/film-review-deadly-plot-by-a-milquetoast-villain.html.

18 Kinsey, *Plain Pictures*, 11–13.

19 William G. Luhr, "Fargo: Far Removed from the Stereotypes of . . . ," in *The Coen Brothers' Fargo: Cambridge Film Handbooks*, ed. William Luhr (Cambridge: Cambridge University Press, 2004), 104–5.

20 Christopher Sharrett, "*Fargo*, or the Blank Frontier," in Luhr, *Coen Brothers' Fargo*, 55–74.

21 Stephen Holden, "Film Festival Review: An Uneasy Rider on the Road to Self-Discovery," *New York Times*, September 27, 2002, http://www.nytimes.com/movie/review?res=9E00E5D91139F934A1575AC0A9649C8B63.

22 Margaret Talbot, "Home Movies: Alexander Payne, High Plains Auteur," *New Yorker*, October 28, 2013, https://www.newyorker.com/magazine/2013/10/28/home-movies-4.

23 Zimmer, "After the Election."

24 Gabe Bullard, "The Surprising Origin of the Phrase 'Flyover Country,'" *National Geographic*, March 14, 2016, http://news.nationalgeographic. com/2016/03/160314-flyover-country-origin-language-midwest.

25 Jon K. Lauck, *The Lost Region: Toward a Revival of Midwestern History* (Iowa City: University of Iowa Press, 2013), 14; and for a more current perspective on this topic, also see Lauck, "Trump and the Midwest: The 2016 Presidential Election and the Avenues of Midwestern Historiography," *Studies in Midwestern History* 3, no. 1 (January 2017): 1–24.

26 Alec MacGillis, "Go Midwest, Young Hipster: If You Really Want Democrats to Win in Iowa, Move There," *New York Times*, October 22, 2016, http://www.nytimes. com/2016/10/23/opinion/campaign-stops/go-midwest-young-hipster.html.

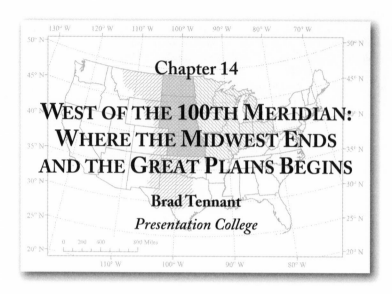

Chapter 14

WEST OF THE 100TH MERIDIAN: WHERE THE MIDWEST ENDS AND THE GREAT PLAINS BEGINS

Brad Tennant

Presentation College

A s the U.S. Senate debated the ratification of the 1803 Louisiana Purchase Treaty, Federalists argued against the acquisition that would double the size of the United States. Delaware's Senator Samuel White, along with other Federalist opponents of the purchase, favored American access to the Mississippi River and New Orleans, but he questioned the need for such a "new, immense, and unbounded world." According to White, it would be only a matter of time before American citizens would enter Louisiana and thus distance themselves by two or three thousand miles from the country's government, becoming alienated from the eastern United States.[2] Similarly, Rufus King, who served as American foreign minister to Great Britain at the time, expressed concerns that Louisiana would be "too extensive" to govern effectively.[3] On the contrary, President Thomas Jefferson viewed the Louisiana Purchase favorably as a region that held vast promises for the future of the United States. As far as Jefferson was concerned, Louisiana Territory, along with the American West as a whole, would take one hundred generations of Americans to settle and to determine the possibilities that the region held. Jefferson theorized that, once Americans fully understood its potential, the West's sustainability would last for a thousand more generations.[4] If Jefferson could have personally seen the West a century later and then again two centuries beyond his time, he would have likely revised his views more than once. More specifically, he would have recognized that the most notable demographic changes and questions regarding economic potential have arguably been in the area known as the Great Plains, that is, the region lying to the immediate west of the 100th meridian. It is at this point that the Midwest begins its transition to the American West, where factors such as climatic conditions, vegetation, and animal life affected the lifestyles of peoples past and present.

Throughout the nineteenth century, the West experienced the ebb and flow of nonindigenous peoples bent on bringing Manifest Destiny to fruition. For many, however, the challenges of the West outweighed its potential. Nonetheless, while many Americans ventured westward only to later retreat to the eastern United States, others stayed and endured.[5] It is important to note that, although Manifest Destiny and western settlement are related, they are not the same. The doubling of the United States gave reason for citizens of the young country to envision continued expansion and the eventual settlement of the West, but those who went west did so with both eagerness and trepidation.

Those who embraced the country's seemingly inevitable future were encouraged by individuals such as newspaper editor John O'Sullivan, who made the now-renowned comment that it was the United States'"manifest destiny to overspread the continent allotted by Providence."[6] Americans quickly accepted this notion that God's divine nature guided the country's future, and thus Manifest Destiny became the justification for westward expansion and settlement throughout much of the second half of the nineteenth century. Even in the early 1900s, artist Edwin Blashfield designed murals such as *Westward* (1905) and *Spirit of the West* (1910) for the Iowa and South Dakota state capitols, respectively, in which Providence is depicted by female spirits. In *Westward*, the angelic "Spirits of Enlightenment" guided pioneers, while, in *Spirit of the West*, South Dakota is portrayed by a woman clasping a Bible to her chest who is guided by a female spirit who floats above her.[7] Such images of God's divine intervention were popular; author Dee Brown states that the role of Providence was simply "the self-conscious creation of political propaganda" that became known as Manifest Destiny.[8]

The expansion of the United States from the Atlantic to the Pacific under the label of Manifest Destiny is one matter; settlement of the region west of the 100th meridian remains an issue unto itself. When historian Frederick Jackson Turner presented his paper "The Significance of the Frontier in American History" to the American Historical Association in 1893, he began by quoting the superintendent of the census report that stated that the American frontier experience concluded during the 1880s. As a result, the census bulletin stated that by 1890 there was no longer a frontier demarcation and the frontier would no longer "have a place in the census reports."[9] Since then, many have refuted the notion of a bygone American frontier. Still, there is much to consider about the events of the time that give credence to the census report. The *expansion* of the United States from coast to coast did not mean that *settlement* progressed in a similar East Coast to West Coast pattern. In fact, there is a great deal to be noted about the northern Great Plains—the region ranging from the 100th meridian to the Rocky Mountains—in connection with the end of the frontier proclamation. After all, the northern plains was the last real Indian Country with the Sioux Nation retaining its venerable images as plains warriors and buffalo hunters. As a result, settlers often quickly passed through or around the region as they headed to destinations farther west, making the northern Great Plains the last major area of settlement during the nineteenth century.[10]

Turner argued that, historically, settlement consisted of four frontier experiences—trading, mining, ranching, and farming.[11] Although each of these affected the northern Great Plains in its own way, challenges peculiar to the region disrupted the continuity from one frontier to another more than in other parts of the country. For instance, the Arikara may very well be the most underestimated Indian nation of the northern plains especially when it comes to the trader's frontier. William Nester points out that the Arikara War of 1823 was not only the first Plains Indian war but the first war fought between the United States and an Indian nation west of the Mississippi River.[12] The Arikara resistance to the American fur trade on the upper Missouri River Valley impeded early American control and settlement of the northern plains. As a result, the Arikara opposition helped to shift much of the American trade from the upper Missouri River to the South Pass of the Rockies.[13]

Although the Arikara provided the greatest resistance to American trade and control of the northern plains in the early 1800s, the Sioux became the United States' main rival during the second half of the nineteenth century. The 1862 Dakota War in Minnesota marked the beginning of conflict between the United States and the Sioux, which included on-again and off-again clashes until 1890.[14] With the 1862 Dakota War coming only a year after the creation of Dakota Territory, it is not surprising that the newly created territory—a region comprised of what is now North Dakota, South Dakota, and the eastern portions of Montana and

Wyoming—did not experience the influx of settlers often associated with the opening of new lands.[15]

Furthermore, the gold rush to Montana in the 1860s and to the Black Hills in the mid-1870s only increased tensions with the Sioux. Sioux opposition to those traveling by way of the Bozeman Trail to Montana resulted in Red Cloud's War, preventing many hopeful prospectors from taking the risk. Although the United States attempted to provide protection by maintaining troops and military forts along the Bozeman Trail, the government finally succumbed to Sioux resistance and agreed to the 1868 Fort Laramie Treaty. In addition to giving up the forts and closing the trail to the Montana mines, the Fort Laramie Treaty also established the Great Sioux Reservation consisting mainly of present-day western South Dakota.[16]

After Lieutenant Colonel George Custer's 1874 expedition to the Black Hills returned with news verifying the presence of gold, a wave of miners flooded the region. Since the Black Hills were part of the Great Sioux Reservation, the federal government sent troops to keep miners from encroaching. Despite intercepting and escorting numerous trespassing miners off the reservation, estimates put the number who avoided the military patrols at more than eight hundred by the summer of 1875.[17] When negotiations for the Black Hills ended without compromise, federal officials decided to discontinue its enforcement of no trespassing. This, in turn, meant that beginning in October 1875 the Black Hills gold rush was open for any prospectors willing to take the risk of invading Sioux lands. Increased tensions led to the Sioux War of 1876, which resulted in Congress ratifying an agreement for the Black Hills in February 1877—an action that has since been declared illegal. Since earlier gold rushes skipped over the northern Great Plains/Black Hills region and took place farther west, frontier historian Ray Allen Billington states that the Black Hills gold rush marked the end of the "eastward advance" of the mining frontier.[18] Still, the Montana and Dakota gold rushes' immediate contribution to nonindigenous settlement paled in comparison to other notable mining frontiers such as in California and Colorado, due primarily to the presence of the Sioux Nation.

In the latter months of 1890, government officials became increasingly concerned about the spread of the Ghost Dance among the Sioux because the ceremony would create the hope that the buffalo would return and that the white man would disappear. Such fear eventually led to events in December 1890, resulting in the death of the Lakota leader Sitting Bull and the Wounded Knee Massacre. Many regard the massacre at Wounded

Knee as the last major U.S.-Indian confrontation, marking the final conquest of the American Indian in United States history.[19]

In 1889, the year before these last acts of subjugation over the Sioux (and American Indians as a whole), the United States welcomed four new states to the Union—North Dakota, South Dakota, Montana, and Washington—which were followed by the states of Idaho and Wyoming in 1890.[20] With the exception of Washington and Idaho, the other four states included lands located in the northern Great Plains. Given the circumstances of newly created states and the military conquest of the Sioux, it is not surprising that the superintendent of the census felt that the American frontier had indeed passed. Yet, long-avoided by ranchers and farmers who chose to continue their travels to the far western reaches of the United States, the northern Great Plains remained the one geographic region that upset the progression of frontier settlement. Just as the northern plains' trading and mining frontiers provided challenges to would-be settlers, so, too, did its ranching and farming frontiers. Regardless of reports that the United States succeeded in both its Manifest Destiny and the settlement of the American frontier, significant demands lay ahead for those who sought to make the northern plains west of the 100th meridian their home.

In Emerson Hough's 1903 book *The Way to the West*, Hough devoted his first four chapters to the ax, the American rifle, the birch-bark canoe, and the horse, each of which he credited in its own way with the conquering of the West. In fact, Hough went so far as to say, "Without the ax, the rifle, the boat and the horse there could have been no West."[21] These might be easily replaced with the plow, barbed wire, the wagon, and oxen as perhaps the most significant influences on the prairies west of the 100th meridian. Whereas the ax was necessary in the woodlands east of the Mississippi River, its value was less appreciated on the relatively treeless plains where farmers used the plow and ranchers grazed their livestock. And although there are numerous stories of tensions between farmers and ranchers, the main weapon was not the rifle; rather, it was barbed wire. Patented in 1874 by Joseph Glidden, barbed wire became increasingly popular as homesteading farmers, cattle ranchers, and sheepherders began to merge and clash throughout the Great Plains.[22] Meanwhile, farm wagons, often covered by canvas (creating the iconic prairie schooner image), replaced the birch-bark canoes used so commonly by early traders and trappers.[23] Teams of oxen commonly served as beasts of burden pulling the supply-laden wagons.[24] Indeed, the plow, barbed wire, wagon, and oxen were among the most notable influences of the plains.

As settlement of the plains began slowly but surely, historians and geographers attempted to define the Great Plains as a region. Although some general consensus has existed, there have also been a fair number of nuances that continue to blur the distinction between the Midwest and the West or the central plains and the Great Plains. For instance, Frederick Jackson Turner regarded the "Middle West" as including the twelve states of Ohio, Indiana, Michigan, Wisconsin, Minnesota, Illinois, Missouri, Iowa, Kansas, Nebraska, South Dakota, and North Dakota.[25] Meanwhile, it is commonly understood that the ten Great Plains states predominantly include North Dakota, South Dakota, Nebraska, Kansas, Oklahoma, Texas, and portions of New Mexico, Colorado, Wyoming, and Montana.[26] It is important to note that the four states that are included in the subset from both groups are South Dakota, North Dakota, Nebraska, and Kansas, thus making them the transitional states between the Midwest and the West, as well as from the central plains to the Great Plains, a transition that is reflected in its aridity and shortgrass prairie and that becomes more noticeable beginning at the 100th meridian.

As previously noted, there are subtle differences used by those who attempt to divide the Midwest from the West by describing the starting point of the Great Plains.[27] Despite these differences, geographer Edward Patrick Hogan, author of *The Geography of South Dakota*, stated that the more traditional beginning of the Great Plains has been generally "associated with the 100th meridian of west longitude."[28] Although the starting point of the Great Plains has been somewhat of a gray area, the one key factor in defining the Great Plains is that it typically receives less than twenty inches of rainfall per year. This arid nature of the region is what led to Zebulon Pike's 1810 report in which he described much of the region between the Missouri River and the Rocky Mountains as a Great American Desert, a depiction that has endured off and on since then.[29] Even today, historical markers in South Dakota point out the significance of the 100th meridian as "the EAST EDGE of the Great American Desert" and how "for two generations the Insurance Companies and other world-wide lending agencies would not, as a matter of agreed policy, lend a shiny dime west of this line."[30] Edwin James, in his report from the 1820 Long expedition, described the region as a "dreary plain, wholly unfit for cultivation" and unsuitable for people who depend on agriculture. For Wallace Stegner, the 100th meridian served as a figurative fence that marked the eastern boundary of the arid Great Plains.[31]

The Pike, Long, and James views of the Great Plains as a dreary, uninhabitable territory likely contributed to the limited expansion of westward settlement in the region. Consequently, their gloomy assessment of the Great Plains helped alleviate the earlier concerns expressed by Rufus King and Samuel White, who feared that the acquisition of Louisiana Territory would make it difficult for the United States to govern such a large domain. In the words of historian Walter Prescott Webb, such a negative perception actually prevented "too great an extension of our population westward."[32] In hindsight, there was some truth to their belief since the northern Great Plains would be the last major region to be settled. On the other hand, others came later who felt that the concept of the Great American Desert was an exaggeration. One such individual was John Wesley Powell, whose time, energy, studies, and efforts focused on disproving the misconceptions of the West, especially the region directly beyond the 100th meridian.[33]

To Powell, the image of a Great American Desert was nonsense. After all, this "desert" supported millions of bison and dozens of Indian nations who did more than merely survive, but, in fact, thrived.[34] Furthermore, numerous poems, novels, and histories commonly noted the image of the prairie as a sea of grass. Depending on the time and place, the Great Plains image can easily vary from the prairie as a grass sea, as a garden, or as a desert.[35] Many who have traveled across western South Dakota and other Great Plains states have compared the motion of blowing prairie grasses to the waves of a sea. During July and August, there may be other areas where the natural grasses have been replaced with gardens of grain waiting to be harvested. Yet periods of drought and blowing topsoil remain common enough to maintain the perception of a desert.

Webb stated that the combination of land, water, and timber were essential to American civilization east of the Mississippi River; however, only one of these—land—existed adequately between the Mississippi and the Rockies. Given the arid nature beyond the 100th meridian, along with other challenges, not even the abundance of land could prevent the region's sporadic failures.[36] Without question, the challenges of the northern Great Plains were considerable, yet for many who endured tough times, there are few places where they would rather reside.

David Lavender, in his book *The Great West*, noted the concern over whether the average annual rainfall of the plains would be enough to support agriculture. According to Lavender, once farmers ventured into Kansas northward to Dakota Territory, they crossed what he called the "danger line," that is, the point at which dry farming becomes unreliable. Given the lack of annual precipitation, gaining access to water was essential for both the rancher and the farmer. A truly fortunate newcomer was the man who had a creek or river nearby. Even then, the task of hauling water from creek to dwelling required a great deal of physical exertion. For the less fortunate, they may have been forced to carry water several miles.[37] Beyond the 100th meridian, annual rainfalls become unreliable to the point where droughts occur more frequently and severely. Even creeks that seemed sufficient in the spring might very well run dry by summer.[38] For others, digging wells was an option as long as the water was not too deep. Eventually, machines pushed pipes deep into the ground; however, it took windmills above ground to pump the water that existed below the surface. Meanwhile, some hopefuls endorsed the theory that increased rainfall would follow the plow, but this proved to be a relatively short-lived belief.[39] Samuel Aughey, a University of Nebraska biology professor during the 1870s and 1880s, became a highly proclaimed advocate of both planting trees and increased plowing as means to increase rainfall. Aughey's theory involved cultivating more land, which would then increase the soil's absorption of rain. In the long run, Aughey and his supporters believed that the soil's moisture would then gradually return to the atmosphere generating more rain.[40] Over the years, sporadic droughts led to the decline of the "rain follows the plow" theory and the realization of the region's natural aridity. Even today's more recent large circular fields watered by pivot irrigation systems face occasional decreases in the supply of water below.[41] Despite the dry years, many farmers and ranchers west of the 100th meridian maintained a positive outlook. According to Kathleen Norris, this optimism is still shared by many who hang onto the hopes of "next year country."[42]

Whether from a nearby stream, below the surface, or from the skies above, the availability of water for households, livestock, and agriculture can vary greatly from year to year. In the drier years, the waves of prairie grasslands could easily become a frightening wall of fire pushed to great speeds by the incessant winds of the plains. For many plains homesteaders and townspeople, the red horizon of a rapidly approaching prairie fire often meant loss of one's belongings—home, livestock, and possibly loved ones.[43] The wind by itself is a feature that, combined with other factors, becomes a notable characteristic of the Great Plains. Kathleen Norris noted that "the western Dakotas are the windiest region" of the forty-eight contiguous states and that it is the sound of the wind that makes her most often compare the plains to the open sea.[44] It is the wind that can take a gentle snowfall and turn it into a blinding blizzard; the wind that takes a cold day and makes it even more dangerous by creating life-threatening wind chills; the wind that can blow the topsoil high above the ground as was often the case with the black blizzards of the Dirty Thirties.[45] It is not particularly surprising that, given the propensity of wind on the plains, today's technology is now harnessing wind power as a viable source of energy.

For early settlers, the immediate concern was shelter—temporary at first and a more substantial structure eventually. Just as Walter Prescott Webb noted the settlers' concern for water on the Great Plains, he also noted the lack of timber for housing. Given the lack of wood, pioneers made do with what they had. This meant that, in most cases, housing options included shanties, sod houses, and dugouts. None of these were especially large, but the intent was to use them as temporary shelter until a larger, sturdier dwelling could be built, at which time the original temporary shelter was often turned over to the livestock.[46] With such challenges existing beyond the 100th meridian, it is understandable why Watson Parker, a longtime Black Hills and American West historian, recounted that dejected homesteaders often sang,

> It's fifteen miles to water,
> And twenty miles to wood;
> To hell with this damned country
> I'm going home for good![47]

From the 1890 perspective, it is understandable how the settling of the northern Great Plains allegedly marked the end of the frontier in American history, but, over the years, it is also easy to acknowledge why the frontier never really disappeared. Given the circumstances west of the 100th meridian, agricultural historian Gilbert Fite is undoubtedly correct to point out that the thousands of land-seeking settlers who seemingly brought an end to the frontier were only half of the story—"thousands more were conquered by it."[48] Furthermore, many view the attempted settlement of the Great Plains as creating negative changes that contributed to the image of a Great American Desert. Dayton Duncan and Ken Burns emphatically state that the Dust Bowl "was the worst man-made ecological disaster in American history."[49] Timothy Egan stated that much of the Great Plains never fully recovered from the Dust Bowl years.[50] In the same vein, geographers Frank Popper and Deborah Popper contend that attempts to settle the Great Plains resulted in the "longest-running agricultural and environmental miscalculation in American history," a mistake that is evidenced by the depopulation of numerous towns and counties.[51]

As renewed interest in the Midwest builds, there will undoubtedly be a wave of new political, economic, social, and environmental studies that examine the region. Considering the vastness of the twelve-state Midwest region, however, considerable differences between the eastern Midwest states and those of the Great Plains will persist. Whereas Ohio and Michigan mark the start of the region historically known as the Midwest,

Kansas, Nebraska, South Dakota, and North Dakota on the western edge of this region will always be notable for their own historical perceptions and environment. It is with the northern plains states that we see the transition from the central plains to the Great Plains and from the Midwest to the American West, and, specifically, this transition becomes more evident when one travels west of the 100th meridian.

Notes

1 This essay is based on a paper originally presented at the Forty-Seventh Dakota Conference on the Northern Plains, Center for Western Studies, Augustana College, Sioux Falls, SD, April 24–25, 2015. The conference solicited papers focusing on the theme "Where the West Begins?" The *Studies in Midwestern History* online journal of the Midwestern History Association published it, with the exception of a few additions, in vol. 1, no. 6 (June 2015).

2 Junius P. Rodriguez, ed., *The Louisiana Purchase: A Historical and Geographical Encyclopedia* (Santa Barbara, CA: ABC-CLIO, 2002), 419–20.

3 Jon Kukla, *A Wilderness So Immense: The Louisiana Purchase and the Destiny of America* (New York: Alfred A. Knopf, 2003), 289.

4 Clyde A. Milner II, ed., *Major Problems in the History of the American West* (Lexington, MA: D.C. Heath, 1989), 661.

5 Dee Brown, *The American West* (New York: Charles Scribner's Sons, 1994), 25–26.

6 Thomas R. Hietala, *Manifest Design: American Exceptionalism & Empire* (Ithaca, NY: Cornell University Press, 1985), 255.

7 Bailey Van Hook, *Angels of Art: Women and Art in American Society 1876–1914* (University Park: Pennsylvania State University Press, 1996), 126; Doane Robinson, *South Dakota Historical Collections, Vol. V* (Pierre, SD: State Publishing, 1910), 245. Although Blashfield originally titled the mural *Spirit of the West*, it has also been known as *Progress of South Dakota* and is currently covered from view with a small plaque noting a legislative name change to *Only by Remembering Our Mistakes, Can We Learn*. For more information about this controversial mural, see the South Dakota Bureau of Administration website "The South Dakota State Capitol: The Decorated Capitol" at https://boa.sd.gov/divisions/capitol/CapitolTour/blashfield.htm.

8 Brown, *American West*, 80.

9 Frederick Jackson Turner, *The Frontier in American History* (Tucson: University of Arizona Press, 1986), 1.

10 Wallace Stegner, *Beyond the Hundredth Meridian: John Wesley Powell and the Second Opening of the West* (Boston: Houghton Mifflin, 1954), 174, 217. See also Derek R. Everett, *Creating the American West: Boundaries and Borderlands* (Norman: University of Oklahoma Press, 2014). Everett further states that the development of Dakota Territory "veiled a sobering realization—that the opportunity to mold vast tracts of land into new states was ending."

11 Turner, *Frontier in American History*, 12.

12 William R. Nester, *The Arikara War: The First Plains Indian War, 1823* (Missoula: Mountain Press, 2001), 1.

13 Brad Tennant, "The Arikara: Roadblock to the American Fur Trade on the Northern Great Plains," *Heritage of the Great Plains* 44, no. 2 (Winter 2012): 37.

[14] Brown, *American West*, 81, 83.

[15] Herbert S. Schell, *History of South Dakota*, 4th ed., rev. John E. Miller (Pierre: South Dakota State Historical Society Press, 2004), 78. In addition to the hostilities associated with the Dakota War, the Civil War waged back east also contributed to Dakota Territory's slow settlement.

[16] Alvin M. Josephy, Jr., *The Indian Heritage of America* (Boston: Houghton Mifflin, 1991), 338; Schell, *History of South Dakota*, 86, 88–89.

[17] Schell, *History of South Dakota*, 130, 132. In its negotiations with the Sioux, the U.S. government offered to pay the Sioux Nation $400,000 per year for mining rights or to buy the Black Hills for a total of $6 million. The Sioux refused both offers.

[18] Schell, *History of South Dakota*, 138–39, 363; Ray Allen Billington, *Westward Expansion: A History of the American Frontier* (New York: Macmillan, 1967), 633–34.

[19] Josephy, *Indian Heritage of America*, 342.

[20] Gerald D. Nash, *Creating the West: Historical Interpretations 1890–1990* (Albuquerque: University of New Mexico Press, 1991), 103.

[21] Emerson Hough, *The Way to the West and the Lives of Three Early Americans: Boone— Crockett—Carson* (Indianapolis: Bobbs-Merrill, 1903), 25.

[22] Billington, *Westward Expansion*, 689, 691–92.

[23] David Lavender, *The Great West* (Boston: Houghton Mifflin, 1987), 239.

[24] Joe Koller, "This Was Homesteading in Dakota," in *Dakota Panorama*, ed. J. Leonard Jennewein and Jane Boorman, 3rd ed. (Sioux Falls, SD: Dakota Territory Centennial Commission, 1973), 222.

[25] Jon K. Lauck, *The Lost Region: Toward a Revival of Midwestern History* (Iowa City: University of Iowa Press, 2013), 8.

[26] R. Douglas Hurt, *The Big Empty: The Great Plains in the Twentieth Century* (Tucson: University of Arizona Press, 2011), xii.

[27] In Zebulon Pike's official report of his 1806–1807 expedition to the Southwest, he described regional changes generally beginning west of St. Louis. Stegner, *Beyond the Hundredth Meridian*, 215. Dr. Edwin James, who served as the naturalist and official recorder for Stephen Long's 1820 expedition that followed the Platte River toward the Rockies, noted that a gradual environmental change began around the 96th meridian. American historian Walter Prescott Webb, writing in the first half of the twentieth century, viewed the 98th meridian as the start of the Great Plains. Webb, *The Great Plains* (Lincoln: University of Nebraska Press, 1981), 7–8, 146, 157. Likewise, geographers Frank Popper and Deborah Popper also placed the 98th meridian as the starting point. Deborah Epstein Popper and Frank J. Popper, "The Great Plains: From Dust to Dust," *Planning* (December 1987): 12. John Wesley Powell, who led several exploratory expeditions across the plains to the Rockies, concluded that a subarid zone existed between the 97th and 100th meridians, but, beyond the 100th meridian, the characteristics of the Great Plains became more evident. Stegner, *Beyond the Hundredth Meridian*, 224.

[28] Edward Patrick Hogan and Erin Hogan Fouberg, *The Geography of South Dakota*, rev. ed. (Sioux Falls, SD: Center for Western Studies, 1998), 162.

[29] Stegner, *Beyond the Hundredth Meridian*, 214–15. An exhibit at the Timber Lake (SD) and Area Museum shows monthly and yearly precipitation totals from the town's founding in 1910 through 2014. During this 104-year period, only thirty-one times has the annual precipitation exceeded twenty inches.

[30] N. Jane Hunt, ed., *Brevet's South Dakota Historical Markers* (Sioux Falls, SD: Brevet Press, 1971), 157. Historical markers noting the 100th meridian can be found along

U.S. Highways 12 and 14 in South Dakota. A quick Internet search shows images of similar markers found from the Dakotas to Texas.

31 Stegner, *Beyond the Hundredth Meridian*, 215, 229.

32 Webb, *Great Plains*, 156–57.

33 Stegner, *Beyond the Hundredth Meridian*, 176.

34 Stegner, *Beyond the Hundredth Meridian*, 216.

35 Lauck, *Lost Region*, 242–43.

36 Webb, *Great Plains*, 9.

37 Lavender, *Great West*, 396. As with Webb, the Poppers, and others, Lavender noted the 98th meridian as the point at which the climate changes, resulting in the shortgrass prairies in contrast to the tallgrass prairies east of this point.

38 David J. Wishart, *The Last Days of the Rainbelt* (Lincoln: University of Nebraska Press, 2013), 30.

39 Billington, *Westward Expansion*, 693; Robert V. Hine and John Mack Faragher, *Frontiers: A Short History of the American West* (New Haven: Yale University Press, 2007), 136. The slogan "rain follows the plough" became a popular catchphrase used to encourage new town sites in Nebraska and is attributed to Charles Dana Wilbur, who used the phrase in his 1881 publication *The Great Valleys and Prairies of Nebraska and the Northwest*.

40 Wishart, *Last Days of the Rainbelt*, 21, 35–36. Wishart explains the "Rainbelt" as a notion in which human activity, such as planting trees and increased plowing, would increase rainfall in the Great Plains region.

41 Hogan and Fouberg, *Geography of South Dakota*, 168.

42 Kathleen Norris, *Dakota: A Spiritual Geography* (Boston: Houghton Mifflin, 2001), 18. *Dakota* served as the 2014 North and South Dakota One Book Selection to commemorate the quasquicentennial of statehood for South and North Dakota.

43 Brad Tennant, "Red Horizons: South Dakota Prairie Fires," in *18th Dakota History Conference Papers*, comp. H. W. Blakely (Madison, SD: Dakota State College, 1987), 646.

44 Norris, *Dakota*, 40.

45 Lavender, *Great West*, 396; Timothy Egan, *The Worst Hard Time* (Boston: Houghton Mifflin, 2006), 5–6. For photographs and more information about black blizzards, see Dayton Duncan and Ken Burns, *The Dust Bowl: An Illustrated History* (San Francisco: Chronicle Books, 2012); and the 2012 PBS documentary *The Dust Bowl*, directed by Ken Burns and produced by Dayton Duncan, Ken Burns, and Julie Dunfey. The debate regarding the causes of the Dirty Thirties include the perception of the Great Plains as a desert in which such events will naturally occur, a human-made disaster generated by plowing the prairie grassland, and the combination of both as contributing factors. For critiques of Ken Burns's *The Dust Bowl* documentary, see Pamela Riney-Kehrberg, Geoff Cunfer, R. Douglas Hurt, and Julie Courtwright, "Historians' Reaction to the Documentary, *The Dust Bowl*," *Agricultural History* 88, no. 2 (2014): 262–88.

46 Schell, *History of South Dakota*, 176. The typical shanty consisted of a nine-by-twelve-foot structure made of pine boards covered by tarpaper, whereas a sod house took advantage of sod strips cut from the prairie and supported by a simple wooden frame. The third option, a dugout, required digging into a hillside.

47 Watson Parker, "A Westward Heritage," *South Dakota History* 6, no. 3 (Summer 1976): 331.

[48] Nash, *Creating the West*, 78. Fite's article appeared in the October 1966 issue of *Agricultural History*.

[49] Duncan and Burns, *Dust Bowl: An Illustrated History*, 5.

[50] Egan, *Worst Hard Time*, 309.

[51] Popper and Popper, "Great Plains."

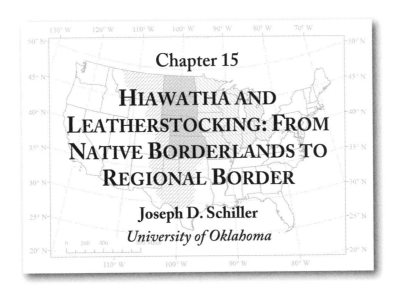

Chapter 15

HIAWATHA AND LEATHERSTOCKING: FROM NATIVE BORDERLANDS TO REGIONAL BORDER

Joseph D. Schiller

University of Oklahoma

The year 1825 is, admittedly, an odd time to find the Midwest-Great Plains border. The nineteenth century's most popular authors, however, turned the experiences of American explorers and Indian agents from that moment into some of our most durable cultural productions positing a change in peoples and landscapes as the young nation-state carried its aspirations into open country toward the center of the continent. In that year, Michigan territorial governor Lewis Cass and Indian Agent William Clark convened the Native peoples west of the Great Lakes at Prairie du Chien, the mixed-heritage French and Native post where the Wisconsin River pours into the Mississippi. They planned to end by treaty intertribal warfare that endangered white settlers and flew in the face of U.S. authority, gained ostensibly at the end of the War of 1812. Misunderstanding the conflict to be about tribes not knowing their boundaries, Clark and Cass allowed the Native people to negotiate and settle their own borders, asking for no tribal land. They called it their "paternal interposition" into Native life, reporting to Washington: "We appeared as the representatives of their great father, to reconcile and adjust their conflicting claims, to terminate their hereditary hostilities, and to remove all probable cause of future difficulties." According to Clark and Cass, "Such a spectacle has not been witnessed since the white and the red

201

man have been brought into contact with each other."[1] Of course the treaty did not achieve its high billing—treaties seldom have, and the agents expected it to fail—but the lines it drew had important consequences along the interior border.

The 1825 council dealt with nine Native groups and a large area, but the American agents were most concerned—as I am here—with the country far to the north and west of Prairie du Chien, along the upper Mississippi River. There they perceived a borderland between what they called the "Chippewas" and the "Sioux," Ojibwe and Dakota. The Americans were cognizant of some relation between the Ojibwe and other groups at the council, and that the Dakota's exclusion from this larger union made them a common enemy.[2] In this far northwestern stretch, the Ojibwe shared the longest boundary with the Dakota, and were embroiled in long-standing animosity—the "hereditary hostilities" to which the Americans referred but little understood. No tribes, they believed, were more in need of parsing their boundaries to avoid offending one another's property.

Property, though, was a problematic word. Ojibwe and Dakota would have scarcely recognized the notion of owning land as property like the Americans understood it. Still, Clark and Cass seem to have missed the irony in allowing Indians to draw their own borders while believing that the problems stemmed from the Indians' ignorance or lack of boundaries. As a growing scholarship has shown, indigenous people in early North America well understood their claims to specific locations, in this case wild-rice lakes, stands of maple forest for sugar production, or hunting territory.[3] They knew who could reasonably lay claim to what, but instead of ownership they honored usufruct, the rights of individuals to use resources on collectively possessed land or water, with the injunction against selling or exploiting it in ways that would hinder future use of the resource. Such a posture toward land and resources often transcended what we understand as tribal affiliation, as in the case of the Dakota, Ojibwe, and other groups assembled at Prairie du Chien.

This landscape of possession and resource use changed almost constantly through conflict, diplomacy, and kinship. As even the earliest Americans to the region understood, Dakota and Ojibwe had not always lived in the locales they inhabited in 1825 but were dynamic and adaptable peoples. Those Americans did not, however, seem to understand the Native peoples' shared, overlapping history. Each had been moving west, perhaps for centuries, as the result of a complex set of geopolitical and social circumstances. Old interpretations posited that Ojibwe access to European guns sent the Dakota west to their kin and the buffalo chase. Recent reassessments have found a more complex likelihood that economic opportunity also pulled the Dakota onto the plains.[4] Some have even found a less antagonistic relationship between the groups. For fifty years after 1679, the Ojibwe and Dakota peoples shared an alliance that served both economic and defensive purposes; groups beyond even Ojibwe and Dakota could see the attraction of upper Mississippi resources, and Ojibwe access to French trade goods meant also Dakota access to the same. The alliance broke down long before 1825, yet it had produced intertribal kin connections that fostered periods of détente for many years thereafter.[5] The "hereditary hostilities" the American agents hoped to stem in 1825 were neither an all-out offensive by Ojibwe warriors pushing Dakota west nor a similarly coherent counteroffensive by the Dakota. Instead, they were small-scale skirmishes around ritualized revenge for previous isolated offenses, like murders. They were the small conflicts of people so close as to be kin, and often they were over the privileged access that kinship connections could grant a person or family to contested environmental resources.[6]

Regardless of the push or pull factors at work, the Dakota had vacated their easternmost haunts by 1825. The places most sacrosanct to the Ojibwe, the river and lake country near the head of the Mississippi and the foot of Lake Superior, were thus also cherished seats in the Dakota past.[7] These were places like Leech Lake, Mille Lacs, and Sandy Lake in present north-central Minnesota. Still in 1806 some Dakotas mounted an attack to regain control of wild-rice beds at Mole Lake in present northeast Wisconsin.[8] The Sioux moniker, which conjures an equestrian people on the plains, obscures the history written by these different peoples upon the same landscapes. The eastern Dakota at Prairie du Chien were, like the Ojibwe, harvesters of wild rice and maple sap. They represented only a couple of the "Seven Fires of the Dakota," the larger "Sioux" Nation.[9]

At Prairie du Chien in 1825, the Dakota-Ojibwe boundary created a different picture for American agents. Transmitted to wide audiences, that picture has had lasting consequences for the ways that a new settler society would envision Native peoples. The line separating Ojibwe from Dakota claims ran from the Chippewa River in present Wisconsin, northwest across modern Minnesota, and into the Red River Valley. It followed almost perfectly a regional ecotone, the transition zone between biological communities, in this case between prairie and forests. Suddenly the Dakota belonged to open country, and the Ojibwe to the forested landscapes. Furthermore, the treaty process forced the groups to constitute themselves as discrete bodies with exclusive territories, something more like the American nation-state.[10] This grated against attendees' assertions that they enjoyed the use of one another's lands without trouble.[11] Where Ojibwe and Dakota had shared a long history of migration, conflict, and kinship, bounding the territory foreclosed a continued contingent history, at least in American imaginations.

Of course, along the upper Mississippi in 1825 the American state had hardly any presence at all, so intertribal conflict and indigenous autonomy went on. Clark and Cass were experienced Indian diplomats and likely knew the ramifications of the paternalist language in which they dealt. Euro-Americans generally would have understood the father-child relationship in terms of dominance and subservience, descending from a tradition of absolute monarchy. But these American agents probably understood that, to the Native peoples, the child's role meant ritualized humility, to appear purposely pitiful. Such a condition was not meant to garner derision or mockery, "but rather represented a condition or status that deserved positive intervention and protection" by the father.[12] In a case like the 1825 treaty, that meant the American father would be responsible for holding accountable any parties that transgressed the border and broke the peace. Clark and Cass, however, also knew their nation-state's weakness in the region.

Government exploration from Zebulon Pike in 1805 and thereafter had been driven by, among other things, the desire to find suitable locations for forts, so that the territory could actually be administered.[13] Only Fort Snelling, at the confluence of the Mississippi and Minnesota Rivers, had been built by 1825. This desire to show authority also motivated the treaty talks, as the Americans hoped to remedy their failure in bringing to justice an Ojibwe war party that had killed American traders in 1824.[14] If Cass and Clark understood their paternal role as peacekeepers, and equally understood their weakness in the region, then they probably knew quite well that the American state would fail as father to the peoples assembled at Prairie du Chien, at least in the short term. Indeed it was the built-in obsolescence of the treaty, the understanding that it would be broken, that justified a continued and expanded American presence in the region.

This setting up of dominoes, this creation of boundary lines from which future land cessions could be extracted, is the most visible aspect of the "paternal interposition." The American model to settle the region was merely an aspiration in the interior borderlands of 1825. The fur trade was still robust, its conventions deeply inflected by Native norms. If American agents knew they could not enforce the treaty, then what purpose did it serve but to erode Native resource bases and autonomy?[15] We could recognize this impulse by tracing the region's subsequent treaty history down to the reservation era and beyond.[16] We might also find it by following the Euro-American cultural output from that time and place, a settler-colonial process that is more insidious, less visible.[17] Knowledge created about Native people near this interior border around 1825 found fast transmission to wide audiences in the East and beyond, with consequences not only for Dakota, Ojibwe, and other groups in the region but also for wider Native history.

The tension is between a real Native history that continued beyond 1825 and fictional productions set in that moment, whose narratives disallowed the continuation of that history. Most critical to this process was the presence at Prairie du Chien of Henry Rowe Schoolcraft, agent to some of the Michigan Ojibwe at the council. A household name in studies of the Native people in the region, Schoolcraft remains a hard paternalist to crack. Married into a prominent Ojibwe family, and already a published author, in the years surrounding the Prairie du Chien council Schoolcraft was collecting ethnographic material on the Ojibwe. His official duties in the years following 1825 were critical to that research. In the early 1830s, Lewis Cass, still governor of Michigan Territory, dispatched Schoolcraft to the Mississippi headwaters country to explain the Prairie du Chien treaty to his charges, especially "that the Sioux now freed from the pressure in other quarters, can direct their whole force against [the Ojibwe]."[18] That is, Cass hoped Schoolcraft might raise the specter of an organized Sioux attack since the Prairie du Chien council had created peace along other borders. Those, at least, were Cass's directions. But Schoolcraft had his own goals, encouraged by the commercial success of his earlier publications. Since his was an Indian Affairs assignment on public money, he couldn't publicize the exploratory nature of his real mission: to find the true headwaters of the Mississippi River and, subsequently, publish an account of the discovery.[19] Still, Schoolcraft and his small cadre of soldiers satisfied their orders, claiming that they impressed upon the Indians "their true relation to the United States," and "destroyed the charm of their seclusion."[20] One only wonders how awed were the Ojibwe as they guided the Americans, who couldn't find their way alone. The travels also allowed Schoolcraft to make a census of the Indians in the region. He found an enterprising, growing population well aware of its advantages—so aware, Schoolcraft believed, that their young men were haughty and prone to continuing the warfare that Prairie du Chien was supposed to quell. Paradoxically, success at their chosen lifestyle kept the Ojibwe from engaging in what Schoolcraft considered more sensible pursuits that would ensure their long-term survival, like sedentary agriculture.

It is this mismatch between Schoolcraft's evidence and conclusion that makes him and so many others of his period difficult to peg. His intellectual proclivities, though, ran beyond nonfiction; he also saw in America's indigenous people the opportunity for a national literature. For a time he even published a journal, *The Literary Voyager*, from his remote post at Sault Ste. Marie. Imagine how Schoolcraft's literary pretentions were bolstered when, in 1827, he encountered an Ojibwe youth in the forest, which he captured in verse: "What warms thy bosom this relentless day, / Amidst the rigors of an arctic storm? / What lights thy visage with a smile so gay? / Plays there some occult intellectual charm?"[21] The answer to those questions was that the Ojibwe youth was carrying a copy of the *Literary Voyager*. Whether real or imagined, the encounter betrays Schoolcraft's desire for a "folk" literature based on indigenous history and myth. The *Literary Voyager* ran poems, stories, biographies of prominent Ojibwe men, and other works. Schoolcraft authored many of them under his own name and various pseudonyms, while his wife, Jane Johnston Schoolcraft, and others wrote some pieces.[22] The journal—like much of Schoolcraft's work—was an attempt to record Ojibwe culture before its carriers disappeared, something Schoolcraft believed was imminent.

Perhaps it was Schoolcraft's literary pretensions that explain his inability to recognize the future in a society seemingly thriving. Indeed, engagement with the period's literature meant encountering assumptions about vanishing primitive peoples the world over. No matter how one felt about indigenous peoples, these stories went, they were bound to disappear in the face of oncoming white, European civilization. This was equally evident in soldiers bent on wiping Indians out, and among humanitarians or poets lamenting their passing. At both of these ends, and all points in between, few people in the nineteenth century questioned the assumption that so-called primitive races were waning. Most importantly, in the words of literary theorist Patrick Brantlinger, such ideas set a "temporal hierarchy or limit" for peoples, "assigning primitive races to a futureless past."[23] White people had a history, a present, and a future, while primitive peoples inhabited only a past. Especially for those predisposed to romanticize the indigenous passing, like Schoolcraft, this idea manifested itself in the "proleptic elegy," preemptive mourning for something that isn't actually gone yet.[24] Schoolcraft and his fellow Americans could not square the evidence before them of Native people painfully, dynamically, and inconveniently still in the way of white society in the Native borderlands.

It has not been any secret that Schoolcraft's ethnography became the primary source material for Henry Wadsworth Longfellow's epic poem

The Song of Hiawatha.[25] Their correspondence was not extensive—mostly Longfellow simply used Schoolcraft's works and acknowledged him later—but clearly they joined the wider conversation about vanishing peoples and about an indigenous, nationalist literature for the young United States.[26] Happily for Longfellow, he need not be encumbered by the actual vitality that Schoolcraft had seen among the peoples assembled at council in 1825. Longfellow chaired an Eastern literary establishment that could understand its regional Natives to be long dead (or removed to invisibility, anyway). He also published *Hiawatha* thirty years after Prairie du Chien and more than twenty years after Schoolcraft's work that motivated the poem. Much had changed along the interior border; Wisconsin had recently gained statehood, with Minnesota Territory well on its way amid a settler explosion during the 1850s. *Hiawatha* met popular success beyond even Longfellow's imaginings and became a character whose story was (and is) recognizable to generations of schoolchildren. The story expressed, as the historian Michael Witgen has put it, "an understanding about the meaning of America so familiar it was almost invisible," that Hiawatha and his people were disappearing simply as the result of spreading civilization.[27] This was the American empire of liberty extending democracy and Christianity across a virgin land that had been ceded nobly by such Indians as Hiawatha. Living its own teleology, the interior border of the 1850s made that story even more intelligible than it was in Schoolcraft's world that bore it.

The cultural historian Alan Trachtenberg has written that nobody approached the success of Longfellow and James Fenimore Cooper at melding Indian stories into usable American histories.[28] Less recognized is how their stories—noted for turning specific Native cultural material into something generically "Indian"—were born in the interior borderlands. Cooper, like Longfellow, derived the sources for some of his most durable work from around the 1825 Prairie du Chien council. When Cooper moved his famous Leatherstocking character west for *The Prairie: A Tale* in 1827, he likely wrote with the account of Major Stephen H. Long's western expeditions open on his desk.[29] Long had encountered at least one Dakota who spoke at the Prairie du Chien council and probably many more who had attended. And he had certainly encountered and described the landscapes to which those people belonged. Long is the chief coiner of the "Great American Desert" descriptor for what we now call the Great Plains. He wrote the oft-cited lines about the region being "almost wholly unfit for cultivation, and of course uninhabitable by a people depending upon agriculture for their subsistence." Thankfully, he thought, it would "prove an insuperable obstacle in the way of settling the country." It might actually save the union from overextension westward and the "incursions of an enemy that might otherwise be disposed to annoy us in that part of our frontier."[30]

As with Longfellow, Cooper's fictional Indian story of the interior borderland conjured up an ecotonal transition not only of vegetation or precipitation but also of people. He saw American prairies in two varieties. They were divided by the Mississippi River, a marker close to the ecotone and the Ojibwe-Dakota border in the river's upper reaches. Those prairies east of the Mississippi, Cooper related, "are comparatively small, are exceedingly fertile, and are always surrounded by forests." "West of the Mississippi, at a distance of a few hundred miles from that river," were "the Great Prairies," almost entirely deficient of fuel and water for serious settlement (what was in those intervening hundreds of miles is anybody's guess).[31] For his westering Americans, all was well until they encountered just this environment and the savage people that inhabited it. Indeed, "the Great Prairies," according to Cooper, "appear to be the final gathering place of the red men."[32] For the author of *The Last of the Mohicans* fame, vanishing Indian stories were stock-in-trade. Even the savage "Sioux" that threatened Cooper's pioneers would disappear eventually, the "self-exterminating savage" as romantic counterpart to the noble Indian, in Brantlinger's conception.[33]

Taken together, these images—of a noble Indian ceding territory to civilization in the woods and lakes and of vicious savages challenging civilization in the open country—admittedly, form a fuzzy borderline. It is not a river or a line of longitude, not an argument about aridity or land use. In fact the border's creation so temporally and geographically distant from its source material makes it hardly defined at all. The interior border was, to the Eastern or European reader, as it was to its authors, somewhere "out there." Eventually, though, to so many Yankee and foreign immigrants, the border became less distant. It became home and, as such, needed defining.

I found my copy of *The Prairie* at a touristy antique shop in Galveston, Texas. Who knows its whole provenance, but it bears a hand-written inscription to "Austin . . . with wishes for a Merry Christmas, 1914." It was published by M. A. Donahue & Co. of Chicago, maker of inexpensive editions of popular stories for a mass market, especially children's books.[34] The back of the book has advertisements for their other offerings: the Boy Scout Series, the Horatio Alger Series, *Woodcraft for Boy Scouts and Others*, "Donohue's Plays, Dialogs, Readings, Recitations, Etc.," and other long-forgotten series "for boys." The press's educational bent demands that we ponder what *The Prairie* was meant to teach its reader in the early twentieth century. The increasingly professional academic establishment, with the rise of anthropology and ethnology, was headed for a cultural relativism that valued indigenous life in new ways. But much of the impetus to these sciences derived from the same persistent belief that drove Schoolcraft, Cooper, and Longfellow: that they were recording cultures before they melted away forever. And ever more readers came into contact with vanishing Indian stories. As the historian Robert Berkhofer has described, from Cooper on down, from so-called high literature to popular literature like *Hiawatha*, to the dime novel, access to vanishing Indians was democratized through the nineteenth and into the twentieth century.[35] Clearly, Cooper's books were still selling. And even in the 1990s a sixty-two-year-old Lakota recalled how *Hiawatha* would be "beat into you" in school, but also that even as a fourth-grader he "thought it was a lot of bullshit."[36] What about for non-Indians?

The 1914 publication of my copy of the book is propitious for thinking about regionalism along the interior border. It was almost precisely then that "Middle West" became widely used to describe the region as we know it. Contemporary writers styled the region as youthful, but not brash. Not so young (like the West) as to be untrustworthy, but not so old (like the East) as to be stodgy. It was vibrant, the favored region.[37] It was realizing its rural ideology, the "stable agricultural democracy," in geographer James Shortridge's words.[38] The Texas recipient of my copy of Cooper's *The Prairie* surely continued an examination of American regions he was probably beginning to understand, experiencing the "public awareness of differentiation of place" so central to regionalism.[39] The phenomenon was characterized nationwide by an increased "pride of place" amid Progressive Era concern about rapid change and discontinuity. That anxiety induced nostalgia, and history and myth became more intertwined in American culture than perhaps ever before. If works like *Hiawatha* and *The Prairie* were born of a nationalist impulse, in the early twentieth century they could be wed in readers' minds to ossifying American regional pride. Imagine how the youthful reader of *The Prairie*, with its depiction of Native peoples, might have learned their regionalism and the rightness of the American pioneering project.

Certainly the 1825 treaty mattered for Native history along the interior border, but what of the poems and books born of that historical moment? Even assuming that settlers read or discussed the stories of vanishing peoples, does it matter that Indians of the open country were colored "savage" and those of the woodlands painted "noble"? I think it does. To the historian, not a whole lot from the human past looks inevitable, so even demographic takeover by white Euro-Americans need not have turned out the way it did. It was contingent, in part, upon the arrival of a people well schooled in vanishing Indian stories, ones inflected by differences in the landscapes and the peoples. Conquest set Ojibwe and Dakota, understood as woodlands and plains peoples, respectively, on different paths toward the reservation and allotment eras. It left Ojibwe on reservations in tribal homelands, while removing most Dakota to reservations near the Missouri River. Yet both were dispossessed utterly.

The stories matter because of persistent notions of the temporal limits of Indianness. The action around Prairie du Chien in 1825 helped write narratives that survive in perceptions about the place of Native people in modernity.[40] These "glorification[s] of the national past" are no less important to the regions of their nativity than they are to the larger national story.[41] People want to recognize the contributions of their place to the national narrative. No doubt that impulse undergirds the ongoing and admirable work to revitalize Midwestern studies. Through these stories we might imagine how early Midwesterners perceived their place at the center of these fictions framed as histories at the very moment the region became self-aware. Midwesterner Frederick Jackson Turner was the preeminent early theorist of how brushes with landscape and people operated on Euro-Americans. He wrote in the tradition of 1825 at Prairie du Chien: "Geographically the Middle West is almost conterminous with the Provinces of the Lake and Prairie Plains." The original people were divided there between the "horsemen of the plains and the canoemen [sic] of the Great Lakes."[42] By his time, though, immigrants carrying "Pioneer Democracy" had achieved "the dreams of their youth."[43] We might wonder only if they were dreamt after reading *Hiawatha* or *The Prairie* by candlelight. As so many historians are only recently revealing, Turner acknowledged that the United States did not just take on an empire with the Spanish War. The nation had one from the beginning, "hidden under the phraseology of 'interstate migration' and 'territorial organization.'"[44] These stories contribute to that history.

More than a decade after Turner published these sentiments, the Federal Writers Project of the Works Progress Administration set out to define all kinds of regional diversity and distinctiveness in the face of Great Depression anxiety. For the project, each state produced a guidebook with general descriptions of history, industry, culture, and prescribed road tours (and, in Minnesota's case, canoe trips!). The guides for Minnesota and the Dakotas strongly emphasized their pioneer heritage as the spirit that allowed them not only to settle the country but also to persist in their recent Depression troubles. They all highlighted the youth of their states and, especially in the Dakotas, their Westernness. Tellingly, they all followed a standard format where a section on "Indian Life" immediately preceded that on "History," another episode in the perceived temporal boundaries of Native peoples. The guides for the Dakotas especially further demonstrated this tendency. The "Sioux" added color. Or, as Western historian David Wrobel describes in *North Dakota: A Guide to the Northern Prairie State*, Native people with many thousands of years in the state received fewer words than Theodore Roosevelt, who spent only a couple years there.[45] The South Dakota guide, similarly, mentioned contemporary Indians scantily, calling its large Native population mostly "descendants of the highly developed Sioux," as though modern Sioux had regressed. The Sioux also "*were* a virile race," in the past tense, "splendid specimens physically."[46] The guide diminished Native peoples in the face of a hardy white civilization.

The Minnesota guide, for its part, devoted a surprising amount of space to Native people within the state's white history. It lacked denigrating language about their savagery or backwardness, and even displayed some nuance in describing exploitative treaties that led to the 1862 Sioux War. Still, predictably, "New Englanders, Germans, and Scandinavians—probably as hardy as the world has produced"—were the ones who carried out the state's triumphs of civilization, not indigenous peoples.[47] Whether or not the differences between state guides point to one state being more hospitable to its indigenous residents in the twentieth century is a fraught question. More certainly, the processes of conquest detached the Dakota from the lands to which they had tied much of their identity. This has, as Gwen Westerman and Bruce White point out, made it more difficult for Dakota to harness the cultural revitalization that has taken root in many Native communities in recent years.[48]

Although the Midwest and Great Plains are place names born of Euro-American settlement, they demand their Native histories to ensure that the regional past remains realistically complicated. It was more than a story of the most American section extending democratic principles and ultimately uniting disparate immigrants. Fealty to such a narrative would be to ensconce something in the middle of the United States that New Western historians confronted a generation ago: myths of civilization and savagery "struggling quaintly in the wilderness."[49] These would ignore the history of conquest in the region and hide especially the insidious ways that the seemingly innocuous development of American ideals actually depends upon it.

As these cultural products show, immigrants to the Midwest need not take Eastern stories and extrapolate them to their new places; through *Hiawatha* and *The Prairie*, Midwesterners and plains people viewed in their own recognizable landscapes the fictional process of Indians nobly ceding land to a higher order of civilization, or savagely resisting and still submerging beneath it. Regional differentiation, though, was not fictional. Regionalism is by nature a settler endeavor, made clear by some regions' names—the West, Midwest—taken as they are from their location relative to some metropolitan core. It is a product of knowledge, differentiation, and the settler imperative to name one's place. Settlers' collective understanding or misunderstanding of indigenous forebears and neighbors, disseminated in fiction based on primary experience in these landscapes, affected how they enacted their colonial project.

Notes

1   "Ratified Treaty No. 139, Documents Relating to the Negotiation of the Treaty of August 19, 1825, with the Sioux, Chippewa, Sauk and Fox, Menominee, Iowa and Winnebago Indians and Part of the Ottawa, Chippewa, and Potawatomi of the Illinois Indians," accessed April 27, 2015, http://digicoll.library.wisc.edu/cgi-bin/History/History-idx?type=article&did=History.IT1825no139.i0001&id=History.IT1825no139&isize=M. Hereafter cited as "Ratified Treaty 139."

2   The Ojibwe, Ottawa, and Potawatomie share a related language and oral tradition, in a larger union described by the historian Phil Belfy's title: *Three Fires Unity: The Anishinaabeg of the Lake Huron Borderlands* (Lincoln: University of Nebraska Press, 2011).

3   Cary Miller, *Ogimaag: Anishinaabeg Leadership, 1760–1845* (Lincoln: University of Nebraska Press, 2010), 111; Juliana Barr, "Geographies of Power: Mapping Indian Borders in the 'Borderlands' of the Early Southwest," *William and Mary Quarterly* 68, no. 1 (January 2011): 5–46; Jacob Jurss, "Contested Authority: Indigenous Borderlands of the Western Great Lakes" (Ph.D. diss., Michigan State University, 2017).

4   Gary Clayton Anderson, "Early Dakota Migration and Intertribal War: A Revision," *Western Historical Quarterly* 11, no. 1 (1980): 35; Richard White, "The Winning of the West: The Expansion of the Western Sioux in the Eighteenth and Nineteenth Centuries," *Journal of American History* 65, no. 2 (1978): 322.

5   Michael Witgen, *An Infinity of Nations: How the Native New World Shaped Early North America* (Philadelphia: University of Pennsylvania Press, 2012), 143–51; Jurss, "Contested Authority," 85–89.

6   Jurss, "Contested Authority," 6, 51–53.

7   Gwen Westerman and Bruce White, *Mni Sota Makoce: The Land of the Dakota* (St. Paul: Minnesota Historical Society Press, 2012), 15.

8   William W. Warren, *History of the Ojibway People*, Second Edition, ed. Theresa Schenck (St. Paul: Minnesota Historical Society Press, 2009; orig. 1885), 223n12.

9 Westerman and White, *Mni Sota Makoce*, 22. It is worth noting how Dakota band names carry meanings that place them "by the water" and "in the forest," with only the Teton being "dwellers of the plains."

10 Bethel Saler, *The Settler's Empire: Colonialism and State Formation in America's Old Northwest* (Philadelphia: University of Pennsylvania Press, 2015), 105, 107.

11 Ratified Treaty 139. Iowa chief White Cloud elaborated most clearly upon this theme, and Native resistance to drawing boundaries in general: "I go upon the lands of our friends the Sacs and Foxes. We alternate [*sic*] go upon each other's land. Why should we quarrel about lands when we get enough on what we have."

12 Ratified Treaty 139, 52.

13 Jared Orsi, *Citizen Explorer: The Life of Zebulon Pike* (Oxford: Oxford University Press, 2014).

14 Jurss, "Contested Authority," 135.

15 For this line of thinking I'm indebted to audience comments, and especially those by panel chair and commenter Cary Miller, on the panel "The Treaties of Prairie du Chien: Research Reports and Response," presented at the 2016 Western History Association meeting at St. Paul, MN.

16 Jurss, "Contested Authority," 141. Jurss asserts that one "unintended consequence" of the treaty's boundaries was that Americans found it easier, subsequently, to engage fewer Native leaders and groups to negotiate or coerce land cessions.

17 Historians are increasingly recognizing a cultural dimension to empire, one attraction of the settler colonial framework that recognizes processes that occur outside of battlefields and include more intimate spaces. Ann Laura Stoler, "Tense and Tender Ties: The Politics of Comparison in North American History and (Post) Colonial Studies," *Journal of American History* 88, no. 3 (December 2001); Margaret D. Jacobs, *White Mother to a Dark Race: Settler Colonialism, Maternalism, and the Removal of Indigenous Children in the American West and Australia, 1880–1940* (Lincoln: University of Nebraska Press, 2009).

18 Philip P. Mason, ed., *Schoolcraft's Expedition to Lake Itasca: The Discovery of the Source of the Mississippi* (East Lansing: Michigan State University Press, 1958), 109.

19 Mason, *Schoolcraft's Expedition*, 134–35.

20 Mason, *Schoolcraft's Expedition*, 146, 128.

21 Henry Rowe Schoolcraft Papers, Manuscript Division, Library of Congress, Washington, D.C., Reel 53. See: Gertrude P. Kurath, review of *The Literary Voyager or Muzzeniegun*, by Henry R. Schoolcraft, ed. Philip P. Mason, *Midwest Folklore* 13 (Winter 1963–1964): 261–63.

22 Alan Trachtenberg, *Shades of Hiawatha: Staging Indians, Making Americans 1880–1930* (New York: Hill and Wang, 2004), 64. Further complicating our understanding of Schoolcraft's fidelity to his Ojibwe objects of study, Trachtenberg asserts that he little recognized the degree to which his wife's influence allowed him into the world of Ojibwe custom.

23 Patrick Brantlinger, *Dark Vanishings: Discourse on the Extinction of Primitive Races, 1800–1930* (Ithaca, NY: Cornell University Press, 2003), 1–2.

24 Brantlinger, *Dark Vanishings*, 4.

25 Trachtenberg, *Shades of Hiawatha*, 60. According to Trachtenberg, other sources included the artist George Catlin, John G. Heckewelder, Mrs. Seth Eastman, and John Tanner, a white man known for the narrative of his captivity with the Ojibwe and other Native peoples.

26 Trachtenberg, *Shades of Hiawatha*, 65.

27 Witgen, *Infinity of Nations*, 9; Brantlinger, *Dark Vanishings*, 60.

28 Trachtenberg, *Shades of Hiawatha*, 60.

29 James Fenimore Cooper, introduction by Henry Nash Smith, *The Prairie: A Tale* (New York: Rinehart, 1953; orig. 1827), vi.

30 Edwin James, *Account of an Expedition from Pittsburgh to the Rocky Mountains, Performed in the Years 1819 and '20, by Order of the Hon. J. C. Calhoun, Secy of War: Under the Command of Stephen H. Long* (Philadelphia: H. C. Carey & I. Lea, 1823), 20.

31 James, *Account of an Expedition*, 4.

32 James, *Account of an Expedition*, 5.

33 Brantlinger, *Dark Vanishings*, 3.

34 *Wikipedia*, s.v. "M.A. Donahue and Co.," last modified November 9, 2017, https://en.wikipedia.org/wiki/M.A._Donohue_%26_Co.

35 Robert F. Berkhofer Jr., *The White Man's Indian: Images of the American Indian from Columbus to the Present* (New York: Knopf, 1978). We can think about this process from an even earlier point, as Cary Miller points out, with ideas about peoples and the "state of nature" from Locke, More, Rousseau, and others. Miller, *Ogimaag*, 239.

36 Quoted in Roy Rosenzweig and David Thelen, *The Presence of the Past: Popular Uses of History in American Life* (New York: Columbia University Press, 1998), 168.

37 Jon K. Lauck, ed., *The Midwestern Moment: The Forgotten World of Early-Twentieth-Century Midwestern Regionalism, 1880–1940* (Hastings, NE: Hastings College Press, 2017).

38 James R. Shortridge, *The Middle West: Its Meaning in American Culture* (Lawrence: University Press of Kansas, 1989), 8.

39 Shortridge, *Middle West*, 17.

40 See Philip J. Deloria, *Indians in Unexpected Places* (Lawrence: University Press of Kansas, 2004). Deloria's essays use situations of Native people doing "unexpected" things in the twentieth century like driving cars, playing sports, or performing on the stage and in Western shows, to interrogate why such activities appear "anomalous" to the modern viewer.

41 Berkhofer, *White Man's Indian*, 87.

42 Frederick Jackson Turner, *The Frontier in American History* (New York: Henry Holt, 1958; orig. 1920), 128, 130.

43 Turner, *Frontier in American History*, 339.

44 Turner, *Frontier in American History*, 127.

45 David M. Wrobel, *Global West, American Frontier: Travel, Empire, and Exceptionalism from Manifest Destiny to the Great Depression* (Albuquerque: University of New Mexico Press, 2013), 179; Federal Writers' Project of the Works Progress Administration, *North Dakota: A Guide to the Northern Prairie State* (Fargo, ND: Night Printing, 1938).

46 Federal Writers' Project of the Works Progress Administration, *A South Dakota Guide* (Pierre, SD: State Publishing y, 1938), vii, 20 (emphasis added).

47 Federal Writers' Project of the Works Progress Administration, *Minnesota: A State Guide* (New York: Viking, 1938), 3.

48 Westerman and White, *Mni Sota Makoce*, 8.

49 Patricia Nelson Limerick, *The Legacy of Conquest: The Unbroken Past of the American West* (New York: Norton, 1987), 19.

Chapter 16

EXPLORING MIDWESTERN V. GREAT PLAINS REGIONAL VARIATION BY WAY OF THE JEWISH IMMIGRANT EXPERIENCE

Mara W. Cohen Ioannides

Missouri State University

Regionalists and regional historians wisely caution that sweeping, all-encompassing terms for regions can disguise the idiosyncrasies of each region.[1] Broad categorizations can create a belief in a homogeneity that does not exist.[2] This chapter will examine the Jewish experiences in the region we broadly call the Midwest in an effort to dispel myths about Midwestern homogeneity. Through this study an understanding of why American Jewish Studies scholars have divided the Great Midwest into the Midwest and the Upper Midwest will be developed, which is a different understanding of Midwestern sub-regions than other scholars have. Particular notice will be given to how the Jewish experience in the central states of the Midwest differs from the Midwest's western borderlands.

The early American demographic of the Midwest was: Native Americans, who were considered outsiders by the Europeans; citizens of the United States, who viewed themselves as the insiders; slaves and former slaves, who were outsiders; and immigrants to the New World, who were new to the idea of being outsiders. However, Jews are set apart from others who migrated to the Midwest because they have always viewed themselves as outsiders and the communities in which they lived kept them as outsiders. As Amy Hill Shevitz, professor of Jewish studies, notes:

215

Jews have been in perpetual encounter with other peoples, experiencing changing patterns of accommodation and conflict. In a way, Jews have always lived in a borderland and have had to create Jewish identity in part through a definition of themselves relative to their experience of the non-Jewish world.[3]

Scholars of American Jewish studies are aware that the regions where Jews live affect the American Jewish experience. They suggest that more than region, the local environment and the kind of local Jewish community are factors in the development of the Jewish community.[4] Jews who immigrated to the Midwest had varying experiences based on their chosen occupation, the local environment, and the size of both the local Christian and Jewish communities—all of which affected their understanding of being American.

First Wave

The First Wave of Jews to North America began in 1624 when twenty-three Jews fled the Inquisition in Brazil and sought safety in New Amsterdam. Jews were permitted to live in those parts of North America owned by England and later by the United States. After these refugees arrived and the British took over New England, Jews from England and Germany came to the New World because of trade opportunities. However, until 1763, when the French ceded much of their claims in North America to the British, Jews could not legally enter the Ohio River Valley.[5] The *Code Noir* (Black Code), introduced to French North America in 1724, required French "officers to chase from our . . . [lands] all the Jews who have established residence there." The Ohio River was crucial to opening the west in the seventeenth and eighteenth centuries. It connected Pittsburgh (Pennsylvania) to Cairo (Kentucky) and the Mississippi River. Already by 1750, European communities were scattered along the river, and, once the French government left, more communities grew.[6] The Northwest Ordinance of 1785 promised "the fundamental principles of civil and religious liberty," which made the region appealing to Jews who were deprived of the economic operations.[7] For immigrants who came from enlightened countries where those who did not follow the state religion were citizens, this equality was appealing as they were often second-class citizens.

Illinois's and Missouri's Jewish history also began with the First Great Wave of Jewish immigrants to the New World. John Hays, whose grandfather arrived in New York in 1742, migrated to Cahokia, Illinois, a community on the eastern bank of the Mississippi River, in 1793. At first he worked as a trader, then turned to agriculture, and then became a civil servant (acting as sheriff and then Indian agent in Indiana).[8] Just across the Mississippi River in 1764, Pierre Laclede Liquest established a post he named after King Louis IX of France: Saint Louis. After the Louisiana Purchase, Americans arrived daily; in 1807, Joseph Philipson, a Philadelphia merchant, arrived.[9] He was quickly followed by his brothers, Jacob and Simon.[10] It did not take long for the Block family, an extensive group who had started settling in the United States after its founding, to move to the region and settle in various communities along the Mississippi.[11] In 1811, Joseph Philipson moved south to St. Genevieve, where he opened another store[12] in his wife's, a Block, hometown.[13]

Other Midwestern states have similar stories. The first Jew in Wisconsin was the Canadian Jacob Franks who, in 1794, opened a fur-trading station in what is now Green Bay. Michigan's Jewish history too starts in the First Great Wave with Ezekiel Solomon, who arrived in Detroit in 1761 and set up a fur-trading station.[14] In the 1820 census, only five Jewish men were listed as living in Indiana. One was Samuel Judah, a prominent lawyer from New York, who settled in Vincennes in 1818 and became a member of Indiana's House of Representatives.[15]

These First Wave Jews were important to the region for many reasons. They were as American as their Christian neighbors. They and their Christian neighbors were immigrants or first or second generation—immigration was living memory. They were part of the community creating American culture. Because they were a small minority of the American population, three thousand[16] of the 9,625,734 counted in the 1820 census,[17] or 0.03 percent of the country's population, they were often overlooked as outsiders, especially at a time when whites were considered equal citizens. Thus they not only opened the frontier, they created a positive or neutral feeling toward Jews among the Christian frontier families.

Second Wave

While many of the first Jewish immigrants were English and Dutch who became established Americans, the tide was turning, as Germans, Jewish and Christian, began arriving in the 1820s, fleeing economic depression and social repression in Europe. These immigrants moved west because of the economic opportunities available in the lands of the Louisiana Purchase. When the United States became owner of the middle of North America in 1803, the land opened to more than just Americans and Catholics. Most of these German Jews were merchants in the Old Country and so continued in that path. However, before many of these business-men developed brick-and-mortar businesses, they peddled. Hasia Diner, professor of American Jewish history, speculates that "it may not be at all outrageous to suggest that every European Jew would have known ped-dlers as family members and neighbors,"[18] which would explain the easy choice of occupation in the New World. Peddling created a customer base, a knowledge of local culture and tastes, and a chance to build savings to open a store.[19] Becoming a merchant brought middle-class respectability, something denied Old Country merchants and, thus, entry into the town's society regardless of religion, also something denied European Jews.[20] In Europe, religion and family background were just as important in entry into a social group as economic standing. German Jews came to America to flee not just a poor economy in Germany but also the strict rules that inhibited non-firstborn German Jewish men from marrying.[21] The ability to marry, be economically prosperous, and practice their religion freely was an opportunity too great to ignore for these German Jewish immigrants.

The first Jew in Cincinnati, Joseph Jonas, arrived in the community in 1817, a few months after arriving in the United States. There were al-ready about six thousand people in the city.[22] At this point, there were not quite 2,600 Jews in the United States.[23] Jonas was a watchmaker and silversmith.[24] All the Jewish men who followed him to Cincinnati during this period were businessmen.[25] Within five years, the Jewish community in Cincinnati had grown enough to form a congregation.[26] The first Jew in Cleveland, Phillip J. Joachimssen, was an Austrian immigrant who ar-rived in 1836 and opened a grocery store when the town boasted around six thousand inhabitants.[27] By 1840 there were twenty Jewish families (the majority Austrian) in the city, and by 1850 nearly five hundred fami-lies.[28] There were only about fifteen thousand Jews in the United States in 1840,[29] but by 1850 the estimate is between fifty thousand and one hun-dred thousand Jews.[30] With a national population of 23,191,876,[31] Jews were between 0.04 percent and 0.08 percent of the national population.

As German Jews arrived, they scattered throughout Indiana in Bloom-ington, Vincennes, Wabash, and Lafayette. Despite being the state capital, Indianapolis did not offer Jews any opportunities until the railroad reached it, and then Jews began to arrive.[32]

Iowa had a low Jewish population of around one hundred, even af-ter the German Jews began to arrive in the United States, accounting for 0.05 percent of the state's population.[33] Most Jewish men in Iowa peddled in the state but lived in Illinois or Missouri. However, 75 percent of the Jewish-owned stores in the state had been founded by peddlers.[34]

The Shoyer brothers were the first Jews in Milwaukee, Wisconsin, and they too opened a store.[35] In fact, German Jews founded communities in Milwaukee, Madison, Slinger, La Crosse, and Appleton. Almost all these men were businessmen, and a number went into politics. By 1877, there were over 2,500 Jews in the state.[36] Wisconsin was largely a state of immigrants, with over 30 percent of Wisconsinites being foreign born in 1850. Less than half claimed English as their first language, and German was the most popular first language.[37] This common language and culture regardless of religion created a bond that resulted in acceptance of Jews as part of the German American community.[38]

Solomon Wiel was the earliest of the Second Wave of Jews in Michigan. He left Austro-Hungary and began peddling in Michigan, finally settling in Ann Arbor in 1845. Some of his extended family attempted farming when they joined him, but returned to business eventually.[39] Considering the tiny population of the state in 1850, under nine thousand,[40] the number of Jews was barely countable.

The farther west we travel, the later Jews arrived. Minnesota's first Jews were German Jewish immigrants. Maurice Mordecai Samuel was a fur trader in the 1840s. In the next decade Jews opened stores in St. Paul, and, around 1865, Jewish businesses were growing in Minneapolis.[41] Unlike other communities, the Jewish community in Minneapolis did not begin with peddlers; rather, these German Jews peddled elsewhere and arrived in the city with money to open businesses.[42]

Missouri's interior was uninteresting to Jewish immigrants until there were economic opportunities. For example, during the Civil War (in 1861) the railroad was extended to what became Sedalia, and that became the Union headquarters.[43] Sometime between then and 1864, David and Simon Levy (German immigrants) arrived there, and then their brother Moses joined them.[44] They opened branches of their store in Marshall Township[45] and the town of Nevada, once the railroad expanded there in 1870.[46] The first Jew in Springfield, Missouri, near the Arkansas and Kansas borders, was Dr. Ludwig Ullman, a German immigrant,[47] who arrived between 1861 and 1864; before this he lived farther west in Missouri in Joplin.[48] More than likely he opened his practice because the city was housing the Army of the Frontier.[49] In 1866, the railroad was given land grants to reach Springfield,[50] and in 1870 the depot was opened.[51] Springfield's population exploded, from 1,964 in 1868 to 5,555 in 1870.[52] The Jewish community exploded also, with the arrival of the Levy family and Victor Sommers around 1868,[53] and then Sommers's family and friends in the next five years.

Kansas became a state in 1861, and the town of Wichita was founded in 1863. Leopold and David Hays, German Jews, made their way to Kansas in 1864 and established a fur-trading business in Wichita. The Kohn brothers, entrepreneurs, arrived in Wichita, bought land, and opened a bank. Until almost 1880, there were less than twenty Jewish families in the city.[54] Eudora, Kansas, was a German community in which the first general store was owned by the Jew Asher Cohn, and many of the other stores were Jewish owned. In Lawrence, Kansas, there were ten Jewish-owned stores in the 1890s, the first opened by Asher and Sarah Cohn in 1854.[55]

Nebraska's Jewish history began in 1856 when the Cohns and Meyer Hellman established a store to service those traveling on the Oregon Trail. Just over a decade later a synagogue was opened in Omaha.[56]

For the most part after the German Jews were established in these growing communities, congregations were founded to provide worship and communal services. Usually, the cemetery purchase and congregation founding happened around the same time, as in Springfield, Missouri, where the *Articles of Association* for the founding of Temple Israel in 1893 included the founding of a cemetery.[57] However, in places like Lawrence, Kansas, the founding of the two did not coincide as their cemetery was founded in 1859, but their congregation began in 1869.[58] In Indianapolis, Indiana, the first congregation was organized in 1856, but the cemetery was not purchased until 1858.[59] Cleveland's first unincorporated congregation bought a cemetery plot in 1840, a year after the congregation had been worshiping together. They chartered by the end of 1841.[60] Hastings, Nebraska, had a cemetery in 1886 but no congregation until 1896.[61] It was the rare community like Wichita, Kansas, that did not charter a congregation until 1928.[62]

The Third Wave

Starting in 1880, Jews began fleeing czarist Russia in a bid to find safety from rising anti-Semitism. In the Russian Empire, Jews were restricted to where they could live and what occupations they could engage in. There was a quota on how many could enter the universities; they were taxed more heavily than their Christian neighbors; their sons were drafted by the army for thirty years of service; and, as the anti-Semitism grew, unannounced riots became sanctioned by the government. These Russian Jews contrasted with the existing American Jewish community, which was secularly educated, middle class, and acculturated. American Jews were integrated members of their local communities, having joined fraternal and charitable organizations and been elected to local government. They were fluent in English and educated. The new Jewish immigrants had almost no secular education and came from peasant backgrounds. Their knowledge of Western European culture was minimal. Thus the two communities, while from the same religious history, saw themselves and their religion quite differently. In 1880, Jews were 0.5 percent of the country's population, but by 1920 they were 3.6 percent.[63] Between 1885 and 1899, 40 percent of immigrants to the United States were Jewish, or over 342,000 Jews.[64] For example, in 1884, Cleveland had a population of 68,328,[65] and over three hundred Russian Jewish families arrived that year.[66] If these families had only four members, then they were 1.76 percent of the population. They joined the 3,500 Jews already there, thus expanding the population by 24 percent.[67] These numbers frightened the established American Jews concerned that poor, uneducated, and un-acculturated Jews could create anti-Semitism; they felt the best choice was to send them away from the established communities to the West.[68]

Most of these new immigrants desired employment in what they had done in Europe. Organizations like the Hebrew Immigrant Aid Society (HIAS) helped place these new Americans in appropriate Midwestern towns. For example, Israel Lotven, a shoemaker who left Russia and arrived in Galveston in 1912, HIAS sent to work for Julius Bookman in Springfield, Missouri.[69] The International Relief Organization, IRO, also aided immigrants, like Harry Caplan, who later requested help in having his brother join him in Cleveland.[70] These immigrants expanded the population in the Midwest.

These Eastern European Jews spurned the Reform American Judaism embraced by established Jewry. Instead, they founded Orthodox congregations. Reform Judaism, which flowered in America, espoused liberal interpretations of Jewish law and the American ideal of self-definition, while expunging what they viewed as superstition. Orthodox Judaism, at that time called Traditional Judaism, strictly followed Jewish law and adhered to Jewish communal values. The first Orthodox congregation was opened in Cleveland by 1860,[71] and one opened in Indianapolis in 1870.[72] The Orthodox congregation in Springfield, Missouri, was founded in 1918,[73] after praying together since 1912.[74] This kept the religious and social divisions between the established and newly arrived Jews alive for the next generation.

Not every town had Jews before the Third Migration. Marietta, Ohio, for example, founded in 1788, did not have its first Jews until 1891. American German Morris Luchs opened a liquor store, and Sam Sulzbacher ran a tailoring business. Morris Miller was a Russian immigrant, and he opened a junk-buying business.[75] Because of the large size of the extended families that came after these three in the next fifteen years, a synagogue was built in 1910.[76]

Minnesota never saw big numbers of Jews. The Jewish population doubled in a decade: from six thousand in 1900 to thirteen thousand in 1910.[77] They were not even 0.01 percent of the state's population of 2,076,000.[78] There were towns like Faribault that never had a Jewish population above seven families.[79] Market towns like Mankato became hubs of Judaica for the surrounding farming communities, and families would come for the Holy Days and rent rooms or stay with friends and family.[80]

Jewish Farming

Out on the edge of the Great Plains, the Jewish experience was different. A small number of Jewish immigrants moved to the New World to farm. There were those like Zalman Phillips who left Russia for the free land in North Dakota. He began with 160 acres on the Red River and would gain another 160 acres of homestead as each child was born. To support his family, he would peddle during the winter and return each spring to farm. The family left the farm because his wife did not like it; she preferred living in Fargo.[81] Others, like Harry Turnoy, specifically chose farming because for "too long had Jews been identified with trading and dealing."[82] He too went to North Dakota.

Turnoy made sure that he and his sons prayed every morning and that the family said all the appropriate prayers throughout the day.[83] There were enough Jews in the area "that on the day preceding *Yom Kippur* all the Jewish homesteaders, who were scattered over many miles, gathered their families and started on a journey to a common meeting place in order to observe the holiest day of the year."[84] Turnoy was the most Jewishly educated in the community,[85] and so he led the community in prayer.[86] Turnoy's wife kept kosher in home, made Chanukah candles, and insisted that there be a *mikvah*, ritual bath, to cleanse in after her monthly menstrual flow.[87]

Rachel Calof, also of North Dakota, opened her home to the local Jewish farmers "for all the Jewish holiday celebrations [and they] came from far and near . . . traveling for days by horse and buggy and by horseback."[88] Her husband's family, like Phillips, had been enticed by the free land.

The Jewish Agriculturists' Aid Society of America of Chicago sponsored over 140 families to go mostly to North Dakota and farm. The group worked hard at keeping the Jewish homesteaders together so that they would have cultural support and religious practice, as Jewish law requires a minimum of ten men to pray together.[89] Because almost all these homesteaders had no farming experience, a Yiddish language (Judeo-German that these homesteaders spoke) monthly, *The Jewish Farmer*, was produced to provide assistance.[90]

Jewish agricultural colonies were formed by American groups, like the Jewish Agricultural and Industrial Aid Society, and European ones, like Am Olam. There were nearly thirty such colonies in Colorado, Kansas, North Dakota, and South Dakota. Those established by Americans were done so to get poor immigrant Jews out of urban areas.[91] None of these lasted long and mostly because the leaders of the colonies were idealists and had no practical farming skills, land was not farmable, winters were harsh,[92] and colonies' sponsors did not support them once established.[93] It appears most of these failed farmers moved to urban areas and returned to capitalist ventures.[94]

Am Olam was a group formed in Europe and part of the period's socialist and Zionist movements. Their motto was: "return to agriculture, and our aim, the physical and spiritual rehabilitation of our people. . . . We shall demonstrate to the world that we are capable of manual Labor."[95] They attempted farms in Louisiana and Arkansas, which failed due to poor farming and living conditions, and so specifically chose homesteading in Dakota Territory.[96] Some communities had communal property, and others, like Cremieux, South Dakota, did not.[97] While most Jewish farmers were religious and struggled to keep Jewish laws and traditions in the plains,[98] the Am Olam communities were secular.[99] Kate Herder, one of the Arkansas Am Olam community's children, referred to the community's Passover celebration as "Easter" in her memoir.[100] This shows a dearth of Jewish religious education, formal or informal.

Conclusion

The regional division here is rather clear. The vast majority of Jews came to the Midwest as immigrants, not as Americans, and for economic prosperity. They used the skills they had as merchants to become merchants in new communities. In these towns, they started religious communities and helped each other as they had in the Old Country. For a small group, farming was a call. They tried it for a time and left because of pressure from their families. Mostly, it was the women who found the loneliness unbearable. They were used to living in communities.

Jews saw the Midwest as a place to go, a place for economic opportunity, and a safe haven where they would not be persecuted. They did not recognize the differences in regions, overtly. However, one can divide the Midwest into two distinct regions, in regard to the Jewish experience. While the Upper Midwest for most geographers includes Minnesota, Wisconsin, Michigan, North and South Dakota, and northern Ohio, Indiana, Illinois, and Iowa, for the Jews, the Upper Midwest is just the Dakotas, or the Great Plains borderlands. It was here that the Jewish experience was different than in the rest of the Midwest, if not the entire United States. Here is where the majority of immigrant Jews attempted farming; here is where socialist agricultural colonies were tried and failed. Even though throughout the region Jews arrived, peddled, and opened stores, it is in the Dakotas that the story is different. The story of the peddler Jew was not exclusive to the Midwest, nor were Jews the only peddlers, but the farmer Jew, especially the communal farmer, was highly unusual. The experience of Jews in the traditional Midwest, then, was more urban oriented and business oriented and quite distinct from the experience of Jews, typically peasants from Russia, who ventured into the Midwest-Great Plains borderlands of the Dakotas.

Notes

1   Jon K. Lauck, "Finding the Rural West," in *Bridging the Distance: Common Issues in the Rural West*, ed. David Danbom (Salt Lake City: University of Utah Press, 2015), 8–9.
2   Lauck, "Finding the Rural West," 11–12.
3   Amy Hill Shevitz, *Jewish Communities on the Ohio River: A History* (Lexington: University Press of Kentucky, 2007), 9.
4   Mark K. Bauman and Bobbie Malon, "Introduction: Directions in Southern Jewish History," *American Jewish History* 85, no. 3 (1997): 191–92.
5   Shevitz, *Jewish Communities*, 10.
6   Shevitz, *Jewish Communities*, 10.
7   Charles Thomson, *An Ordinance for the Government of the Territory of the United States North-West of the River Ohio* (July 13, 1787).
8   Max J. Kohler, "Some Jewish Factors in the Settlement of the West," *American Jewish Historical Society Journal*, no. 16 (1907): 27–29.
9   Donald I. Makovsky, *The Philipsons: The Earliest Known Jewish Settlers in St. Louis 1807–1858* (St. Louis: Judaism Sesquicentienial Committee of St. Louis, 1958), 2–3.
10 Makovsky, *Philipsons*, 8.
11 Walter Ehrlich, *Zion in the Valley: The Jewish Community of St. Louis* (Columbia: University of Missouri Press, 1997), 1:34–35.
12 James F. Baker, *Jacob Philipson: A Jewish Merchant in Missouri*, (January 29, 1987, manuscript in author's possession), p. 4.
13 Ehrlich, *Zion*, 24–25.
14 *Michigan's First Jewish Settler* (Detroit: State of Michigan Historical Marker, April 29, 1964).

[15] Judith E. Endelman, *The Jewish Community of Indianapolis: 1849 to the Present* (Bloomington: Indiana University Press, 1984), 10.

[16] Cyrus Adler, ed., "Jewish Statistics," in *The American Jewish Year Book 5660* (Philadelphia: Jewish Publication Society of America, 1899), 283.

[17] *Census for 1820* (Washington, D.C.: Gales & Seaston, 1821), 18.

[18] Hasia Diner, "Entering the Mainstream of Modern Jewish History: Peddlers and the American Jewish South," *Southern Jewish History* 8 (2005): 6.

[19] Hasia Diner, *Roads Taken: The Great Jewish Migrations to the New World and the Peddlers who Forged the Way* (New Have: Yale University Press, 2015), 14.

[20] Shevitz, *Jewish Communities*, 45.

[21] David A. Meola, "Becoming Public Jews: Jews in Baden and Hanover and Their Role in the German Press, 1815–1848" (Ph.D. diss., University of British Columbia, 2012).

[22] Joseph Jonas, letter to Isaac Lesser, December 25, 1843, reprinted as "Moving Westward," in *A Documentary History of the Jews in the United States 1654–1875*, ed. Morris U. Schappes (New York: Schocken Books, 1971), 224.

[23] "Vital Statistics: Jewish Population in the United States, Nationally," *Jewish Virtual Library*, 2015, accessed December 13, 2015, https://www.jewishvirtuallibrary.org/jewish-population-in-the-united-states-nationally

[24] Shevitz, *Jewish Communities*, 25.

[25] Shevitz, *Jewish Communities*, 26.

[26] Jonas, letter, 225.

[27] Lloyd P. Gartner, *History of the Jews of Cleveland* (Cleveland: Western Reserve Historical Society, 1987), 3–4, 7.

[28] Gartner, *History*, 10.

[29] Adler, "Jewish Statistics," 283.

[30] Adler, "Vital Statistics."

[31] *The Seventh Census of the United States* (Washington, D.C.: Robert Armstrong, 1853), viii.

[32] Endelman, *Jewish Community*, 13–14.

[33] *Seventh Census*, ix.

[34] Michael J. Bell, "'True Israelites of America': The Story of the Jews of Iowa," *Annals of Iowa* 53, no. 2 (1994): 87–88.

[35] "To Publish History of Wisconsin's Jews," *Milwaukee Sentinel*, April 24, 1921.

[36] Andrew Mulchin, "Jewish Immigrants Helped Develop Small-Town Wisconsin," *Milwaukee Journal Sentinel*, October 7, 2007.

[37] "19th-Century Immigration," *Wisconsin Historical Society*, 1996–2016, accessed November 4, 2016, http://www.wisconsinhistory.org/turningpoints/tp-018/?action-more_essay.

[38] Michael A. Meyer, "German-Jewish Identity in Nineteenth-Century America," in *The American Jewish Experience*, ed. Jonathan D. Sarna (New York: Homes & Meier, 1986), 48.

[39] Helen Aminoff, "The First Jews of Ann Arbor," *Michigan Jewish History* 23, no. 1 (1983): 4.

[40] *Seventh Census*, ix.

[41] Laura Weber, "From Exclusion to Integration: The Story of Jews in Minnesota," *MNopedia*, 2015, accessed December 15, 2015, http://www.mnopedia.org/exclusion-integration-story-jews-minnesota

42	Laura E. Weber, "'Gentiles Preferred': Minneapolis Jews and Employment 1920–1950," *Minnesota History* 52, no. 5 (Spring 1991): 167.

43	*The History of Pettis County, Missouri, including an Authentic History of Sedalia, and Other Towns and Township* (1882), 406, 410, https://archive.org/details/historyofpettisc00demu

44	"Simon Levy," *Sedalia Bazoo*, February 5, 1883; "Moses Levy Dies at Age of 81," *Leader* [Springfield, Missouri], February 20, 1928, evening ed.: 1; Moses Levy, Saxonia Records, June 14, 1864, "United States Germans to America Index, 1850–1897," accessed February 8, 2015, https://familysearch.org/ark:/61903/1:1:KDQL-5C1 (login required).

45	"Moses Levy," in *History of Saline County Missouri* (St. Louis: Missouri Historical, 1881), 759–60.

46	"Simon Levy," "History of Nevada/Vernon County," Chamber of Commerce: Nevada, MO, Vernon County, 2015, accessed February 8, 2015, http://www.nevada-mo.com/page/10354_2.

47	Ludwig Ullman, Springfield, Greene County, Missouri, United States Census, 1880, sheet 246.

48	Ludwig Ullman, Sarcoxie, Jasper County, Missouri, United States Census, 1860, page 2; Clara Ullman Wallerstein, Passport, May 2, 1922.

49	Ira Holcombe, ed., *History of Green County, Missouri* (St. Louis: Western Historical, 1883), 490.

50	John Bell Sanborn, "Congressional Grants of Land in Aid of Railways" (Ph.D. diss., University of Wisconsin, 1899), 377.

51	*Opening of the Atlantic and Pacific Railroad and Completion of South Pacific Railroad to Springfield, MO May 3, 1870* (Springfield, MO, 1870).

52	Byron Stewart, *Springfield and Green County Missouri Census Information, 1836–2010* (Springfield, MO: Missouri State University, 2011), accessed February 12, 2015, http://digitalcollections.missouristate.edu/cdm4/document/php?CISOROOT=/Census&CISOPTR=5&REC=1.

53	Star Clothing House Advertisement, *Springfield Democrat* [Missouri], April 20, 1868, 4; Trade Palace Advertisement, *Missouri Weekly Patriot* [Springfield], April 9, 1868, 2.

54	Hal K. Rothman, "Building Community: The Jews of Wichita 1860–1900," *Kansas Quarterly* 25, no. 2 (1993).

55	David M. Katzman, "The Jewish Communities in Lawrence, KS," presented to Jewish Community Women Meeting, Lawrence, KS, May 3, 2006, transcript, p. 6.

56	"Our History," Jewish Federation of Omaha, 2015, accessed December 17, 2015, http://www.jewishomaha.org/about/our-history.

57	*Articles of Association* (Springfield, MO: Temple Israel, November 4, 1893).

58	Katzman, "Jewish Communities," 5, 8.

59	Endelman, *Jewish Community*, 15–16.

60	Gartner, *History*, 30.

61	Robert E. Levinson, "Jews and Jewish Communities on the Great Plains 1820–1977," *Western States Jewish History* 35, no. 1 (2002): 40–41.

62	Rothman, "Building Community."

63	Sidney Goldstein, "Population Trends in American Jewry," *Judaism* 36, no. 2 (1987): 135.

64	Jonathan D. Sarna and Jonathan Golden, "The American Jewish Experience in the Twentieth Century: Antisemitism and Assimilation." *National Humanities Center*,

October 2000, accessed November 18, 2015, http://nationalhumanitiescenter.org/tserve/twenty/tkeyinfo/jewishexp.htm

[65] *The Cleveland Directory for the Year Ending July 1885* (Cleveland: Cleveland Directory, 1884), 11.

[66] Gartner, *History*, 105.

[67] "Generations," *Cleveland Jewish History*, accessed November 4, 2016, http://www.clevelandjewishhistory.net/gen/genmain.htm.

[68] J. Sanford Rikoon, "The Jewish Agriculturalists' Aid Society of America: Philanthropy, Ethnicity, Agriculture in the Heartland," *Agricultural History* 72, no. 1 (1988): 4, 6.

[69] Hyman Lotven, *My Life Story* (Springfield, MO: Ethnic Life Stories Project, 2001).

[70] Gartner, *History*, 122.

[71] Gartner, *History*, 163.

[72] Endelman, *Jewish Community*, 61.

[73] *Articles of Association* (Springfield, MO: Share [*sic*] Zedek, December 21, 1918).

[74] Hyman Lotven and Isadore Lotven, interview by Julie Hennigan, Springfield, MO, December 12, 1992, transcript.

[75] Amy Hill Siewers, "Judaism in the Heartland: The Jewish Community of Marietta, Ohio (1895–1940)," *Great Lakes Review* 5, no. 2 (1979): 25–26.

[76] Siewers, "Judaism in the Heartland," 27.

[77] Weber, "Gentiles," 168.

[78] *Minnesota Now, Then, When . . . An Overview of Demographic Change*, Minnesota State Demographic Center, April 201, PowerPoint, slide 8, accessed April 19, 2017, https://mn.gov/admin/assets/2015-04-06-overview-MN-demographic-changes_tcm36-74549.pdf.

[79] Linda Mack Schloff, "Overcoming Geography: Jewish Religious Life in Four Market Towns," *Minnesota History* 51 (1988): 7

[80] Schloff, "Overcoming Geography," 8.

[81] Henry Fine and Lea Fine, "North Dakota Memories," *Western States Jewish Historical Quarterly* 9, no. 4 (1977): 332.

[82] Sophie Trupin, *Dakota Diaspora: Memoirs of a Jewish Homesteader* (Lincoln: University of Nebraska Press, 1984), 15.

[83] Trupin, *Dakota Diaspora*, 92.

[84] Trupin, *Dakota Diaspora*, 93.

[85] Trupin, *Dakota Diaspora*, 96.

[86] Trupin, *Dakota Diaspora*, 94.

[87] Trupin, *Dakota Diaspora*, 55–57, 63–65.

[88] J. Sanford Rikoon, *Rachel Calof's Story: Jewish Homesteader on the Plains* (Bloomington: Indiana University Press, 1995), 85–86.

[89] Janet E. Schulte, "'Proving Up and Moving Up': Jewish Homesteading Activity in North Dakota, 1900–1920," *Great Plains Quarterly* 10 (1990): 232–33, 236.

[90] Schulte, "Proving Up," 237.

[91] Levinson, "Jews and Jewish Communities," 44.

[92] Levinson, "Jews and Jewish Communities," 45–46.

[93] Ellen Eisenberg, *Jewish Agricultural Colonies in New Jersey 1882–1920* (Syracuse: Syracuse University Press, 1995), 54.

[94] Levinson, "Jews and Jewish Communities," 45–46.

[95] Eisenberg, *Jewish Agricultural Colonies*, 25.

[96] Eisenberg, *Jewish Agricultural Colonies*, 41, 53.

[97] Violet Goering and Orlando J. Goering, "Jewish Farmers in South Dakota—the Am Olam," *South Dakota History* 12, no. 4 (Winter 1982): 237–38.

[98] Trupin, *Dakota Diaspora*; Rikoon, *Rachel*.

[99] Goering and Goering, "Jewish Farmers," 241.

[100] Kate Herder, "Memories of Yesterday," *OzarksWatch* 12, no. 1–2 (1999): 63.

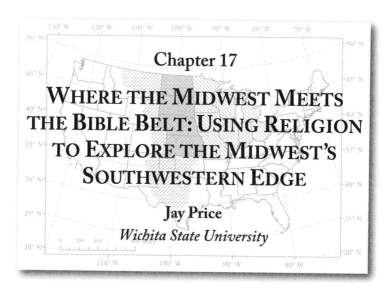

Chapter 17

WHERE THE MIDWEST MEETS THE BIBLE BELT: USING RELIGION TO EXPLORE THE MIDWEST'S SOUTHWESTERN EDGE

Jay Price

Wichita State University

D
etermining where the Midwest ends and the South begins is complicated. Southern Illinois, southern Indiana, and southern Ohio (including Cincinnati) all have aspects of Southern culture, from issues of dialect to the presence of the Ku Klux Klan and segregation. Conversely, business ties have long connected places like Louisville to Northern economic and social trends. West of the Mississippi, the border between the South and the Midwest becomes even more problematic. Missouri, ever the border state, includes the German immigrant industrial world of St. Louis, the Ozarks, the Corn Belt farms adjacent to Iowa, and the slaveholding regions south of the Missouri River. There is not even a consensus on the pronunciation of the state's name, with "Missour-ee" versus "Missour-uh" an important regional demarcation.

Beyond Missouri, the Southern/Midwestern border seems to reconstitute itself with free-state/Northern-leaning Kansas bordering Southern-leaning Missouri and Oklahoma. However, such tidy distinctions are more image than reality. From the 1820s through the 1850s, the Santa Fe Trail connected Missouri with northern Mexico. When the Kansas-Nebraska Act of 1854 established the territory of Kansas, it was initially with the assumption that Kansas would be an extension of Missouri and that Nebraska would be the continuation of Iowa. Had the proslavery Lecompton government remained in power, this western extension of the Mason-Dixon Line would have been at 40 degrees latitude (the current border of Kansas and Nebraska) or even the Platte River, given the number of boosters from what is now southern Nebraska who sought to connect their fortunes with Kansas.

The years that defined "Bleeding Kansas" saw the influx of Northern settlers, mostly from Illinois, Ohio, Indiana, and Northern states that changed the state's composition. By the time of the Wyandotte Constitutional Convention in 1859, Kansas had transformed itself from an extension of Missouri into an antislavery bastion. The Civil War, in which free-state Jayhawkers battled proslavery Bushwhackers along the border of a divided Missouri, confirmed Kansas's Northern bent. The Grand Army of the Republic was a significant political and social force while the 1870s saw the migrations of African Americans to Kansas based in large part on the state's free-state reputation. Meanwhile, Kansas positioned itself as a hub for the Northern-oriented Midwest. Geographer James Shortridge has shown that the term Midwest or Middle West began with the description of Kansas and Nebraska. The free-state legacy remained in the history books while the University of Kansas Jayhawks continued the regional tensions by facing regularly their archrival University of Missouri Tigers on the sports field. Politically, the state remained solidly Republican in politics, fielding national figures such as Alf Landon and Dwight Eisenhower, in contrast to the Democratic Party's solid presence in Missouri and in Oklahoma, at least until the 1960s.[1]

Religiously, too, Kansas related more to Northern religious traditions than Southern ones. Scholars of regional religious trends seemed to confirm this assessment. In his 1961 study of regional religious demographics, Wilbur Zelinsky marked Kansas as part of a "Midland" region that extended from the Middle Atlantic states, along the states just north of the Ohio River, through southern Iowa, almost all of Kansas, and eventually reaching the Rockies. Distinct from the Upper Middle Western region, where Lutherans and Catholics predominated, the Midland region was more the domain of Methodists. By contrast, the South, the region where Baptists defined the religious landscape, ended quite markedly at the Missouri/Oklahoma border. Sociologist Robert Wuthnow has suggested that religion in his home state of Kansas was rooted in a tendency for traditions such as Methodists and Catholics to temper the occasional expressions on the part of more radical and activist religion. Wuthnow, along with Gary Entz and others, has noted that the core of Kansas religion has been dominated by two main groups: the proverbial bodies traditionally associated with Mainline Protestantism such as Methodists, Presbyterians, and Congregationalists; and the German/Irish/immigrant-connected bodies such as the Catholics, Lutherans, and Mennonites. While not as strongly German in religion as neighboring Nebraska, Kansas's religious makeup paralleled that of the rest of the Midwest. Meanwhile, Philip Barlow and Mark Silk's work on religion in the Midwest notes that Kansas lies on the edge of the Southern Crossroads region, whereas, in the South itself, Baptists rule. In Missouri, Kansas's eastern neighbor, Southern Baptists are the largest denomination in three-quarters of all counties. In Oklahoma, Southern Baptists are predominant in virtually all counties. As complicated as the Midwest has been as a regional construct, it differed from the South in spirituality and, by extension, culture.[2]

However, like any border area, the reality was a lot more complicated and fluid than many have appreciated. The lands of northern Oklahoma and southern Kansas are so closely linked through history, demography, economics, and culture that they might better be considered a single region as much as the frontier of two different societies. Kansas had pockets of Southerners extending from Greenwood County down to the southeast. Southerners were especially evident in the mining camps of far southeastern Kansas. Nearby, communities such as Pittsburg and Baxter Springs shared important economic ties to Joplin, Springfield in Missouri, and Miami in Oklahoma. Economic ties such as the Chisholm Trail and the Atchison, Topeka, and Santa Fe Railroad also connected portions of Kansas to the South and Southwest.[3]

Oklahoma, meanwhile, has been more consistently Southern oriented, a legacy going back to the Southern origins of the Five Civilized Tribes and the Confederate leanings of many native groups in the Civil War. However, in northern sections of Oklahoma/Indian Territory, ties to Kansas were strong, and many areas functioned more akin to Northern and Midwestern areas than Southern ones. For example, the land rushes of the 1880s and 1890s involved a large number of Kansans who either migrated to Oklahoma or organized and financed the rushes. After the 1890s and 1900s, communities of ethnic groups such as the Mennonites and the Syrians developed on both sides of the Kansas/Oklahoma border with extended families caring little for whether they lived on the northern or southern sides. Similar ties bound African American communities in places like Wichita to black towns in Oklahoma such as Boley. Scholars like Tash Smith have noted that in the territorial years between 1890 and 1907, Indian Territory, with its Kansas connections, was as apt to identify with and function as part of the Midwest in contrast to the Southern leanings of Indian Territory; at statehood, the Southern elements came to prevail.[4]

This complexity showed up in religious patterns as well. For example, Joseph Parker, a founder of the Congregationalist Fairmount College (today's Wichita State University), relocated down to Oklahoma to found Kingfisher College in Enid, an institution that lasted until 1922.

In the territorial times, northern Oklahoma could resemble the Midwest in many aspects, including religion. A generation later, the Southern expressions of religion had come to dominate and started to reshape the religious landscape of southern Kansas. Northern/Midwestern bodies, from Mainline Protestants to immigrant church bodies, were shrinking in rural areas and small towns, concentrating themselves into the cities where they held on, but in the face of an expanding evangelicalism increasingly tied to Southern bodies like the Southern Baptists and Pentecostals.

The story of Baptists in the area illustrates this trend. The Baptist General Convention of the state of Oklahoma formed in 1906 with conventions representing Indian Territory and Oklahoma Territory merging and retaining dual membership in Northern and Southern Baptist Conventions until 1914, when they voted to join the SBC exclusively. Meanwhile, Kansas Baptist congregations, skeptical of the trends in Northern Protestantism, started to look to Southern traditions as a voice of their concerns.

It was in Wichita, however, where a significant Southern religious presence in Kansas became especially noticeable. Wichita long had close ties to Oklahoma, but it was the development of certain industries, first oil in the 1910s and 1920s, followed by aviation in the 1940s and 1950s, that brought waves of new residents from the upper South, from places like Oklahoma, Arkansas, and Missouri. Between 1940 and the end of World War II, Wichita's population had nearly doubled. A significant part of that growth came from the South. At the war's close, just over half of the city's population was actually born in Kansas: 8.9 percent had been born in Missouri, 8 percent in Oklahoma, 2.26 percent in Texas, and 2 percent in Arkansas. With the biggest plants of Boeing being on the south side, it was natural that the largest workers' neighborhoods extended south along the city's main east-west thoroughfare of Kellogg Avenue. Not coincidentally, this would be where many of Wichita's postwar evangelical, fundamentalist, and Pentecostal congregations developed. Wichita had become a border city straddling the North and South, and in the city proper the local Mason-Dixon Line was often Kellogg Avenue. Southern migrants from places like Oklahoma and the Ozarks established their own legacy separate from individual leaders and evangelists from official missionary efforts.[5]

By the time of Zelinsky's article on religion and regional geography, the border region of Kansas and Oklahoma was a place where Southern religion was in the ascendancy, although the implications of these trends would not become apparent until decades later. In the 1970s, this conversation about region and religion became even more complicated with the addition of yet another designation: the Bible Belt. Ever since social critic H. L. Mencken claimed credit for coining the term "Bible Belt" in the 1920s, scholars, reporters, social commentators, and the general public have struggled with whether the term was more than just an epithet and did, in fact, refer to a specific place. As geographer Charles Heatwole observed in his 1978 article on the topic, "there is virtual unanimity on the verbal definition of the Bible Belt"—namely, a region where fundamentalist and/or socially conservative Protestantism is a dominant presence; however, "the term's geographic definition is less certain." Heatwole observed that while there was general consensus about the South as the key component of the belt, the extent of the belt's western and northern boundaries were not clear.[6]

Heatwole was among the first scholars to analyze the Bible Belt as a geographical region, writing at a time when evangelical religion was first making itself known as a political force. There was little consensus, however, on whether, for example, the region's distinctive religious makeup came from fundamentalist/evangelical groups in general or the specifically Southern expression of those traditions. Heatwole linked the Bible Belt with the prevalence of a number of Southern-leaning groups, including the Southern Baptist Convention and the Lutheran Church-Missouri Synod, the Christian Church and Churches of Christ, and Church of the Nazarene. However, even here, there were noticeable gaps, especially in Southern cities where there was greater diversity of religious traditions. Moreover, parts of the upper South and Midwest may have been similar in Bible Belt theology and culture, but had populations who tended to belong to the conservative wings of national bodies rather than distinctly Southern ones.[7]

Similarly, geographer James Shortridge, in his 1976 article about religious demographics, noted that there were several regions of the country where conservative religion had a prominent presence, the Bible Belt being only one. For reasons not expressly specified, Shortridge suggested that "Jackson, Mississippi, could perhaps be called the 'buckle' of the Bible Belt, but Oklahoma City is definitely marginal, and Kansas is not in it."

Although he observed that the oil industry connected Kansas to places like Tulsa to the South, Shortridge distinguished between the Southern traditions of Oklahoma and Texas compared to those of the Great Plains and Midwest, like Kansas. In his more recent works like *The Middle West*, Shortridge has shown that religion in the Middle West has remained an important part of the regional image, but one that is more rooted in a small-town provincialism than a specifically evangelical one. Southern parts of the Midwest, such as Kansas and Missouri, had strong traditions of evangelicalism and Pentecostalism, particularly in those areas tied to the Ozarks, but, to Shortridge, these were the exceptions that proved the proverbial rule.[8]

Others, like Stephen Tweedie, aimed for a different measure, namely the presence of religious programming on television in local markets. The results showed that the West and Northeast had a general lack of conservative religious programming, and therefore, "viewed as a whole, the Bible Belt appears as a broad zone stretching from Virginia to northern Florida in the East and from the Dakotas to central Texas in the West." Within this belt were two cores, an eastern one centered on Virginia and the Carolinas and a western one that "hinges on Little Rock and Tulsa, with the secondary centers of Dallas–Ft. Worth and Wichita Falls–Lawton to the Southwest . . . and Kansas City to the north." In this analysis, fundamentalist programming—regardless of whether it was geared toward Southern Baptists, Pentecostals, or Methodists—was the determining factor of Bible Belt identity. This approach provides a useful reminder that conservative Christianity has never been a uniquely Southern or Bible Belt feature or even specifically an evangelical one. Campaigns in favor of "traditional values" in movies, or against abortion, or in favor of "traditional marriage" have been as much Catholic as evangelical in origin. In Wichita, Kansas, for example, the Summer of Mercy gained a significant part of its energy from the city's large, well-established Catholic community, complete with a number of deep pockets from influential Catholic donors.[9]

The southern reaches of the Midwest could lie within the Bible Belt designation, depending on the author. Indiana, Oklahoma, Kansas, South Dakota, and Minnesota have all been considered Bible Belt states. In a recent assessment of the region, Stanley D. Brunn and colleagues have revisited the matter by tracking the prevalence of Southern-related religious groups since the 1980s. They have found that the dominance of those religious traditions has shifted to the West, with the border of Oklahoma and Texas as the new center of a still-Southern-dominated Bible Belt.[10]

This work joins a body of recent scholarship that has shown that the connection between religion and region was not so straightforward. Looking at a particular snapshot of religious demographics, therefore, misses the truly fluid nature of American religion. Evangelical revivals were as much a legacy of the Northern part of the country as the Southern. The original "burned over district" was upstate New York. Moreover, works such as Christine Leigh Heyrman's *Southern Cross* have illustrated how the once solidly Anglican South had adapted to evangelicalism and vice versa. Mary Elizabeth Mathews has shown how the Southern connection to fundamentalism was in many ways the product of Northern-leaning journalists and writers like H. L. Mencken. Meanwhile, *Rough Country* and *Red State Religion*, Robert Wuthnow's studies of religion in Texas and Kansas, respectively, have also shown that vocal conservative religion needed to be seen in contrast to larger patterns of local practice. The Lone Star State had conservative roots, to be sure, but its more activist, political elements were more a product of the twentieth century than an inherent feature from the outset. Darren Dochuk has noted the degree to which migrants from the South established whole new communities in places like California.[11] At first, they functioned more akin to immigrant communities, bringing their religious traditions with them much as transplants from Europe attempted to recreate the festivals and practices from villages in the "old country." As the twentieth century unfolded, however, the descendants of those migrants came to transform the cultural and political landscapes of states far removed from Dixie.[12]

Recent historical scholarship has come to view religious geography less in terms of fixed areas and more as a fluid, shifting set of patterns as individuals, institutions, and places respond to historical trends and, in return, play their own influential roles. Early attempts to define the Bible Belt in the 1970s missed this dynamic process. Shortridge, Heatwole, and others were describing a region in the midst of a transformation. Shortridge's 1970s description of Kansas conservatism as different from that of the Southern-oriented Bible Belt may well have been accurate at the time of its writing. Twenty years later, the Methodist/Catholic consensus of Wuthnow's analysis was being eroded by groups whose presence in Kansas was limited and even nonexistent prior to World War II. By the end of the twentieth century, Kansas was starting to look more like its Southern neighbors. The Pew Forum's 2015 religious landscape study found that Kansas had become 31 percent evangelical Protestant, the state's largest single religious block, equivalent to that of Texas.

Percentage Evangelical/Southern Protestant (does not include
African American Protestant)[13]

	1936	2007
Kansas	5%	31%
Oklahoma	48%	47%
Arkansas	41%	46%
Missouri	28%	36%
Texas	39%	31%
Nebraska	12%	25%
Iowa	6%	28%

Meanwhile, Kansas became increasingly visible in the national media for conservative religious activity, from the 1991 Summer of Mercy to the 2005 constitutional ban on same-sex marriage, to critiques of evolution on the state school board, to the activism of the Westboro Baptist Church. Westboro's founder, Fred Phelps, was himself a transplant from Arkansas whose congregation embraced the media spotlight by picketing funerals with warnings that supporting homosexuality was causing God's wrath to fall on the United States. Initially focused on LBGT and liberal events, the Topeka-based Westboro Baptist Church turned its attention to picketing funerals of fallen soldiers in combat to draw media attention to its cause. Even conservative evangelicals faced the group's periodic protests for not being strident enough against homosexuality or disagreeing with the nuance of Westboro's strict Calvinist worldview.[14]

Drilling down further, Wichita again provides a useful case study to better understand how Kansas could be both Midwest and yet tied to the Bible Belt. By the 1960s and 1970s, evangelicalism expanded both in Wichita and in the nation as a whole as that tradition lost some of its twang and was becoming more mainstream. Evangelicalism in Wichita was changing the very nature of the city. A comparison of religious trends in Sedgwick County, where Wichita is located, with those of Tulsa and Des Moines reveals a shift to a more evangelical religious makeup.

Change in Religious Membership, Sedgwick County, 1980–2010[15]

	Percent change between 1980 and 2010	Adherents in 1980 (percentage out of total population of 367,000)	Adherents in 2010 (percentage out of total population 498,000)	Adherents in Tulsa in 2010 (percentage out of total population of 693,000)	Adherents in Des Moines in 2010 (percentage out of total population of 430,000)
Baptist: Southern	21%	24,344 (7%)	29,575 (6%)	90,187 (13%)	4,890 (1%)
Baptist: American	-50%	6,753 (2%)	3,174 (.6%)	2,027 (.2%)	1,236 (.2%)
Assembly of God	88%	3,541 (.9%)	6,685 (1%)	12,845 (2%)	9,305 (2%)
Catholic	40%	51,056 (14%)	74,600 (14%)	49,144 (7%)	82,867 (19%)
Disciples of Christ	-50%	9,252 (3%)	4,592 (.9%)	5,009 (.7%)	8,427 (2%)
Churches of Christ	129%	8,292 (2%)	19,011 (4%)	8,156 (1%)	1,858 (.4%)
LDS	327%	1,579 (.4%)	6,746 (1.3%)	7407 (1%)	3,822 (.8%)
Episcopal	-29%	3,491 (.9%)	2,465 (.5%)	4582 (.6%)	2,226 (.5%)
Evangelical Free Church	563%	341 (.09%)	2,264 (.4%)	125 (.01%)	4,620 (1%)
Lutheran: Evangelical Lutheran Church of America	-17%	3,008 (.8%)	2,488 (.5%)	2,331 (.3%)	16,540 (4%)
Lutheran: Missouri Synod	14%	6,107 (2%)	6,948 (1%)	4,163 (.6%)	7,693 (2%)
Non-denominational	32%	Counted as independent in 1990 (N/A)	16,418 (3%)	64,535 (9%)	12,575 (3%)
Presbyterian Church, USA	-29%	9,130 (2%)	6,581 (1%)	6,565 (.9%)	4,990 (1%)
United Methodist	-3%	28,613 (8%)	27,680 (6%)	64,194 (9%)	19,147 (4%)

In 1980, the religious makeup of Wichita showed a considerable evangelical presence, but the city overall was still Northern/Midwestern in orientation. American Baptists outnumbered Southern Baptists. The Disciples of Christ were more numerous than the Churches of Christ. There were more Presbyterians than Assemblies of God. By 2010, each of those pairings was reversed. By the 2000s, some 15 percent of local religious adherents were members of the Southern Baptist Convention, with 7.5 percent Christian and Churches of Christ, 4.3 percent Congregationalist, 2.7 percent Disciples of Christ, and 2.6 percent Assemblies of God.[16] By 2010, Evangelical Protestants were the largest single religious grouping in the city, at one hundred thousand, over twice the number of Mainline Protestants. That said, nearly half of residents reported no religious affiliation at all.[17]

There are other trends at work as well. Immigrants from Mexico and Latin America have been connecting Kansas and the southern reaches of the Midwest more and more to the Southwest and beyond. Already, the cities of southwestern Kansas—such as Garden City, Dodge City, and Liberal—are majority Hispanic with similar patterns in Guymon, Oklahoma, and other communities in the panhandle region of Texas and Oklahoma. In these places, Spanish is becoming the language of everyday life, soccer is rivaling football as the sport of choice, and religious trends include Spanish-language evangelicalism and Catholic devotionalism surrounding the Virgin of Guadalupe. Here regional ties are less traditional Midwest and more Southwest and northern Mexico.[18]

There are two observations that emerge from this study of religion in the Midwest's southwestern edge. First, like the Midwest, the Bible Belt is a construct with boundaries and characteristics that vary depending on who makes the analysis. Even when Bible Belt is defined in terms of Southern-oriented religious denominations, that regional designation overlaps with significant portions of the Midwest's southern boundary. From Kansas City, Missouri, to southern Indiana, Southern-oriented evangelicalism, fundamentalism, and Pentecostalism have been just as Midwestern as the rural Lutheran churches of Minnesota.

Second, if Midwestern religion is assumed to be defined by a mix of northern Mainline bodies and ethnic immigrant traditions such as Catholicism and Lutheranism, then the Midwest as a concept may itself have to adapt. Places that once contained a mix of Southern and Northern religious bodies, such as territorial Oklahoma, have become solidly Southern and evangelical. The Wichita of the 1980s and the Wichita of the 2000s belong in two different regions. Although not as evangelical as Tulsa, Wichita was moving in that direction and away from the religious demographics of a Midwestern city like Des Moines.

One way to view recent events is to see the Midwest as a shrinking area with places once part of the Midwest now shifting to being part of an expanding South or Southwest. Another approach is to think of a place like Kansas as sharing the features of two areas, a borderland that blends different regional traits. To maintain the Midwest as a valid geographical concept may, however, ultimately require rethinking what it means to be Midwestern. It may mean setting aside the stereotype of the small Lutheran country church as the iconic expression of the region and consider ways in which the megachurch or Spanish-language service may be just as valid an expression of faith in the heart of the country.

Even in a part of the world where regional boundaries seem distinct, drilling down into a matter such as religion reveals a more complicated story. Regional discussions tend to be generalizations, highlighting larger themes while acknowledging outliers. In the case of religion along Kansas's southern border, however, there is more at work than just outliers. Rather, this is a place undergoing remarkable changes. A place that had been relatively consistent for over a century is now in the midst of recent transformations that make it almost unrecognizable. As challenging as it may be to describe or assess, exploring the borders among the Midwest, the Southwest, and the South is a reminder that "where" is often really a function of "when."

Notes

1   Lauck, Jon, *The Lost Region: Toward a Revival of Midwestern History* (Iowa City: University of Iowa Press, 2013); Jonathan Earle and Diane Mutti Burke, eds., *Bleeding Kansas, Bleeding Missouri: The Long Civil War on the Border* (Lawrence: University Press of Kansas, 2013); Nicole Etcheson, *Bleeding Kansas: Contested Liberty in the Civil War Era* (Lawrence : University Press of Kansas, 2004); H. Craig Miner, *Kansas: The History of the Sunflower State* (Lawrence: University Press of Kansas, 2002); James R. Shortridge, *Peopling the Plains: Who Settled Where in Frontier Kansas* (Lawrence: University Press of Kansas, 1995); Shortridge, *The Middle West: Its Meaning in American Culture* (Lawrence: University Press of Kansas, 1989); and Shortridge, "The Heart of the Prairie: Culture Areas in the Central and Northern Great Plains," *Great Plains Quarterly* 8 (Fall 1988): 206–21; and Robert Smith Bader, *Hayseeds Moralizers & Methodists: The Twentieth-Century Image of Kansas* (Lawrence: University Press of Kansas, 1988). See also Homer Socolofsky and Huber Self, *Historical Atlas of Kansas*, 2nd ed. (Norman: University of Oklahoma Press, 1988); and Milton D. Rafferty, *Historical Atlas of Missouri* (Norman: University of Oklahoma Press, 1982). Quote from Carl Becker, "Kansas," from Frederick Jackson Turner, *Essays in American History* (New York: Henry Holt, 1910), 83–111, 87, accessed via https://archive.org/details/kansas__00beck. The pronunciation of Missouri highlights the intersection of region and dialect, illustrating the borderland nature of Missouri and neighboring Kansas. For an analysis of the topic,

see Donald M. Lance, "The Pronunciation of *Missouri*: Variation and Change in American English," published in connection with the Folklore Studies program at the University of Missouri, http://missourifolkloresociety.truman.edu/Missouri%20 Folklore%20Studies/THE%20PRONONCIATION%20OF%20MISSOURI.htm. Lance suggests that the ending of Missouri with a schwa (e.g., Missourah) may be a product of Scots-Irish immigration. However, Lance also advises caution about making blanket regional connections. The Scots-Irish Midland populations did tie Missouri to portions of the South. However, the Scots-Irish were also part of western New England. Moreover, the schwa ending pronunciation is more evident in western Missouri along the border with Kansas and less so along the Mississippi River in areas that have direct physical ties to other states that make up the South.

2   Federal Writers Project of the Works Progress Administration, *The WPA Guide to 1930s Kansas*, reprint of 1939 edition, with new introduction by James Shortridge (Lawrence: University Press of Kansas, 1988). See also Ashel, Erik, Metro Sports (Kansas City, MO), and Time Warner Cable, dirs., *Border War: Kansas Vs. Missouri*. Metro Sports/Time Warner Cable (2008). Regarding religion, see Robert Wuthnow, *Red State Religion: Faith and Politics in America's Heartland* (Princeton: Princeton University Press, 2011); Philip Barlow and Mark Silk, eds., *Religion and Public Life in the Midwest: America's Common Denominator?*, Religion by Region Series (Walnut Creek, CA: AltaMira, 2004); Paul Putz, "Toward a Bibliography of Religion in the Midwest," *Religion in American History* (blog), January 20, 2015, http://usreligion. blogspot.com/2015/01/toward-bibliography-of-religion-in.html; and Gary R. Entz, "Religion in Kansas," *Kansas History* 28 (Summer 2005): 120–45; Wilbur Zelinsky, "An Approach to the Religious Geography of the United States: Patterns of Church Membership," *Annals of the Association of American Geographers* 51 (June 1961): 139–93. Quote from Barlow and Silk, *Religion and Public Life*, 38.

3   D. W. Meinig, *The Shaping of America: A Geographical Perspective on 500 Years of History, Volume 3: Transcontinental America 1850–1915* (New Haven: Yale University Press, 1998); H. Craig Miner, *West of Wichita: Settling the High Plains of Kansas, 1865–1890* (Lawrence: University Press of Kansas 1986); W. Eugene Hollon, *The Southwest: Old and New*, Second Bison Book Printing (Lincoln: University of Nebraska Press, 1970); and Walter Prescott Webb, *The Great Plains* (Boston: Ginn, 1959).

4   Tash B. Smith, "Where the North, South, East, and West Meet: Indian Territory's Transition to Oklahoma," paper delivered at Western History Association, October 2016. See also Linda W. Reese and Patricia Loughlin, eds., *Main Street Oklahoma: Stories of Twentieth-Century America* (Norman: University of Oklahoma Press, 2013); and John W. Morris, Charles Robert Goins, and Edwin C. McReynolds, *Historical Atlas of Oklahoma* (Norman: University of Oklahoma Press 1986). See also Brett Wallach, "The Telltale Southern Plains," in *Many Wests: Place, Culture, and Regional Identity*, ed. David M. Wrobel and Michael C. Steiner (Lawrence: University Press of Kansas, 1997).

5   "Burden Church Has Fiftieth Anniversary Celebration," Kansas Southern Baptist Beams, hereafter KSBB, May–June 1947 (2,3) History of First "Baptist Church Burden, Kansas, 1885 to 2009," http://www.eccchistory.org/BurdenBaptist.htm For more context see Jay M. Price, "Dixie's Disciples: The Southern Diaspora and Religion in Wichita, Kansas," *Kansas History 40* (Winter 2017–2018): 244–61; Marjorie Stith, *Making a Difference: A Fifty-Year History of Kansas-Nebraska Southern Baptists* (Franklin, TN: Providence House Publishers, 1995); and Colin Brummitt Goodykoontz, *Home Missions on the American Frontier* (Caldwell, ID: Caxton

Printers, 1939). Craig Miner, *Wichita: The Magic City* (Wichita, KS: Wichita-Sedgwick County Historical Society, 1988); Jay M. Price, "'Peerless Princess of the Southwest': Boosterism and Regional Identity in Wichita, Kansas," *Kansas History* 38 (Summer 2015): 79–106; Bliss Isley, *Who Lives in Wichita Today and Why, in Wichita Chamber of Commerce, Wichita People* (Wichita, KS: Wichita Chamber of Commerce, 1946). See also Julie Courtwright, "Want to Build a Miracle City: War Housing in Wichita," *Kansas History* (Winter 2000): 218–39.

6   Laura Addison, "In Search of the Bible Belt: The Bible Belt: Where Is It?," *Wichita Eagle*, October 4, 1997. For context, see James N. Gregory, *The Southern Diaspora: How the Great Migrations of Black and White Southerners Transformed America* (Chapel Hill: University of North Carolina Press, 2005); Darren Dochuck, *From Bible Belt to Sunbelt: Plain-Folk Religion, Grassroots Politics, and the Rise of Evangelical Conservatism* (New York: W.W. Norton, 2001): Michelle Nickerson and Darren Dochuck, *Sunbelt Rising: The Politics of Place, Space, and Religion* (Philadelphia: University of Pennsylvania Press, 2011); Charles A. Heatwole, "The Bible Belt: A Problem in Regional Definition," *Journal of Geography* 77 (February 1978): 50.

7   Heatwole, "Bible Belt."

8   James R. Shortridge, "Patterns of Religion in the United States," *Geographical Review* 66 (October 1976): 427. See also, Shortridge's *The Middle West, Cities on the Plains: The Evolution of Urban Kansas* (Lawrence: University Press of Kansas, 2004).

9   Stephen F. Tweedie, "Viewing the Bible Belt," *Journal of Popular Culture* 11 (Spring 1978): 873. See also Dolan, "Catholics in the Midwest," https://www3.nd.edu/~jdolan/midwest.html and Gerald Nutter, *Banned in Kansas: Motion Picture Censorship, 1915–1966* (Columbia: University of Missouri Press, 2007).

10   Stanley D. Brunn, Gerald R. Webster, and J. Clark Archer, "The Bible Belt in a Changing South: Shrinking, Relocating, and Multiple Buckles," *Southeastern Geographer* 51, no. 4 (2011): 513–49.

11   Darren Dochuk, *From Bible Belt to Sunbelt: Plain-Folk Religion, Grassroots Politics, and the Rise of Evangelical Conservatism* (New York: W. W. Norton, 2012).

12   Christine Leigh Heyrman, *Southern Cross: The Beginnings of the Bible Belt* (New York: Alfred A. Knopf, 1997); Mary Elizabeth Mathews, "Building the Bible Belt: How America Came to View the South as Fundamentalist" (Ph.D. diss., University of Virginia, 2002); Joel Carpenter, *Revive Us Again: The Reawakening of American Fundamentalism* (New York: Oxford University Press, 1999); Martin Marty and R. Scott Appleby, *The Power and the Glory: The Fundamentalist Challenge to the Modern World* (Boston: Beacon Press, 1992); Robert Wuthnow, *Rough Country: How Texas Became America's Most Powerful Bible-Belt State* (Princeton: Princeton University Press, 2014); Wuthnow, *Red State Religion;* Ferenc Szasz, *Religion in the Modern American West* (Tucson: University of Arizona Press, 2000); and Szasz, "Religion in the American West: Its History and Probable Future," *Word & World* 24 (Summer 2004): 233–42.

13   This chart uses the classification of denominations as "Evangelical Protestant" as identified by the Pew Research Center's report "America's Changing Religious Landscape," 103–7. These include those of the Baptist traditions outside of the American Baptists and African American Baptists, Pentecostals, Restorationist, Holiness, and non-denominational groups as well as those from other Protestant traditions that have a more evangelical approach. Figure from 1936 includes Southern denominations that may not necessarily be evangelical, including Methodist Episcopal Church, South; the Presbyterian Church in the United States;

and the Lutheran Church-Missouri Synod. Source: Pew Forum Religious Landscape Study, accessed via http://www.pewforum.org/religious-landscape-study/state/kansas/ and ARDA Database and U.S. Bureau of Census 1936 Census of Religious Bodies.

14 Wuthnow, *Red State Religion*, 267–360; Thomas Frank, *What's the Matter with Kansas? How Conservatives Won the Heart of America* (New York: Henry Holt, 2004); Szasz, *Religion in the Modern American West*; Roger Finke and Rodney Stark, *The Churching of America, 1776–1990: Winners and Losers in Our Religious Economy* (New Brunswick, NJ: Rutgers University Press, 1992): 145–275; Wade Clark Roof and William McKinney, *American Mainline Religion: Its Changing Shape and Future*, 2nd printing (New Brunswick, NJ: Rutgers University Press, 1988); Dean M. Kelley, *Why Conservative Churches Are Growing: A Study in Sociology of Religion* (New York: Harper and Row, 1972).

15 Source: Association of Religious Data Archives, 2010 and 1980.

16 Dale E. Jones et al., *Congregations and Membership in the United States 2000* (Nashville, TN: Glenmary Research Center, 2002).

17 Cited in City-Data.com, http://www.city-data.com/city/Wichita-Kansas. html#ixzz35Owiuy8Y. Clifford Grammich, Kirk Hadaway, Richard Houseal, Dale E. Jones, Alexei Krindatch, Richie Stanley, and Richard H. Taylor, *U.S. Religion Census: Religious Congregations & Membership* (Association of Statisticians of American Religious Bodies, 2012). See also http://www.city-data.com/city/Wichita-Kansas. html#ixzz4EhwJSs9Z; and the Association of Religious Data Archives for 2010 and 1980: http://www.thearda.com/rcms2010/r/c/20/rcms2010_20173_county_name_2010.asp; and http://www.thearda.com/rcms2010/r/c/20/rcms2010_20173_county_name_1980_ON.asp.

18 Richard Longworth, *Caught in the Middle: America's Heartland in the Age of Globalism* (New York: Bloomsbury, 2008); James R. Shortridge, *Cities on the Plains: The Evolution of Urban Kansas* (Lawrence: University Press of Kansas, 2004); Marcelo Suarez-Orozco, ed., *Crossings: Mexican Immigration in Interdisciplinary Perspectives* (Cambridge, MA: Harvard University, David Rockefeller Center for Latin American Studies, 1998); Henry J. Avila, "The Mexican American Community in Garden City, Kansas, 1900–1950," *Kansas History* (Spring 1997): 22–37; and Miguel A. Carranza, "The Hispanic Presence on the Great Plains: An Introduction," *Great Plains Quarterly* 10 (Spring 1990): 67–70.

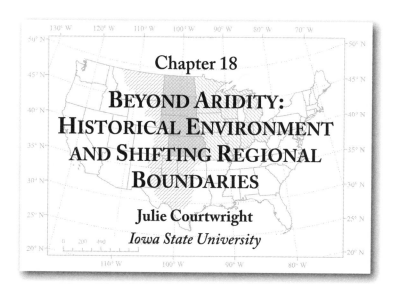

Chapter 18

BEYOND ARIDITY: HISTORICAL ENVIRONMENT AND SHIFTING REGIONAL BOUNDARIES

Julie Courtwright
Iowa State University

For most historians, water—or, more precisely, the *lack* of water—determines the eastern boundary of the Great Plains, the one shared with the Midwest and the South. Since Walter Prescott Webb's landmark study of the region in 1931, historians have used the line of semi-aridity, the point where precipitation falls below twenty inches annually (somewhere west of Wichita), to mark the shift from tallgrass to mid-grass prairie, from agricultural environment to risky agricultural environment, and from amorphous region to other amorphous region.[1] The practice is so common that, to many, it is a given, almost an absolute. Mention that Iowa might be part of the Great Plains to the wrong person at a conference, and prepare to defend yourself and your sacred honor.

Using Webb's line admittedly makes some sense, as most studies of the Great Plains have been framed in terms of agriculture, and water is indisputably critical under that land-use rubric. But defining a region by what is *not* present (at least not as much as farmers would like) is problematic. It implies that what *is* present is not worthy of consideration. Other commonly cited features of the Great Plains are the *lack* of trees, the *absence* of vertical landmarks (i.e., hills and mountains), and the *diminished* bison population. A pattern quickly emerges. In 2007, a writer for *National Geographic*, standing on a hill in Kansas, noted that what she saw amounted to a "glorious nothing."[2] Linking the word "glorious" to "nothing" made the observation more polite, but the description was ultimately more of the same. The Great Plains, a nothing place, is defined by what is elsewhere, and therefore absent, or by what used to be there, but is no longer.[3]

As prevalent as the concept of "nothingness" is, especially to those who travel I-80 at too many miles per hour in an effort to "get across" (get across *what*, exactly?) as quickly as possible, there is actually much that *is* present on the Great Plains. The phrase "glorious nothing" is a way of dismissing that which is present as unworthy of consideration. Yet the Great Plains (and the Midwest) is home to billions of grasses, flowers, insects, and other life forms. It boasts strong winds that convert into clean, sustainable, energy. It has a legacy of purposeful burning—fire used by humans as a tool to improve and manage the grasses. It has earth in which grasses, native and domesticated, grow, as well as great space, which, while frightening to some, is more than just the overwhelming absence of the above-ground vertical. Below ground, the vertical *is* present in the form of (of all things!) elusive water. Abundant (if, alarmingly, declining) water exists within the unseen but present Ogallala, which, as one of the largest aquifers in the world, stretches across portions of six states and ranges in depth from just a few feet underfoot to more than two hundred.[4] The Great Plains, a semi-arid region rather than a true desert, also enjoys water in the form of intermittently sufficient rain.[5] Historians (and others) have relied so much on aridity and agriculture to define the plains that they have missed other environmental characteristics that are equally important and *present*, but understudied and unrecognized.

Understanding and promoting current and *historical* regional environments—what is there rather than just what is not—is critical for the development of identity and should be included within discussions concerning the connections and boundaries between the Great Plains and the Midwest. Scholars of both regions must work harder to cultivate a more nuanced understanding of environmental place, both to combat the "glorious nothing" stereotype and to strengthen appreciation for what is present in the regions rather than lament what is absent. The first step is to move beyond the focus on semi-aridity (not always, but occasionally) and examine other environmental characteristics that are almost as significant, as well as *present*.

Like all good neighbors, the Midwest and the Great Plains share a good deal, and shared even more in the past. Most notably, they shared grass. The western states in today's Midwest—Illinois, Iowa, southern Minnesota, and northern Missouri—were all an undeniable part of the great ocean of grass that Euro-Americans encountered as they traveled west (British and Americans), south (French), or north (Spanish) into what was, for them, uncharted, but not uninhabited, territory. This atypical inland sea of plants stretched from Texas to Canada and from the Rocky Mountains to Illinois. Although not made of water, it nevertheless behaved much like its saline counterpart, a seemingly infinite number of individual organisms moving as one. The grassy sea extended for hundreds of miles, highlighting a great sky, long horizons, and unparalleled sunsets. It hosted wildlife, seen and unseen, and pitched and rolled with the wind, causing motion-sensitive "prairie schooner" travelers in the 1840s to get incongruously seasick in the middle of Nebraska.[6] All this grass, of course, transcended the line of semi-aridity. Species shifted, as did height, but grass itself obscured any boundary that might now exist between the Great Plains and the Midwest.

The Spanish, the first Europeans into the area, were also the first recorded sightseers to be both ignorant of and disappointed by what they *didn't see* within the grassland. Explorer Francisco Vasquez de Coronado observed that the plains was "a wilderness in which *nothing* grew, except for very small plants." (There's that word again, used in the 1540s.) Although he acknowledged that the small plants were numerous enough and nutritious enough to support "millions and millions of strange humpbacked cattle," the Spaniard remained unimpressed overall.[7]

In many ways, Coronado was just the first of many to remain oblivious to the astonishing qualities of the grassland. Later settlers may have augmented their tree-bias in the East, and even in more wooded sections of the Midwest, before traveling onto the great grassland of the plains, forerunners of those today who look at the grassland and see "nothing." They truly do not know what they are missing, however, because grass is remarkable. Although the over 140 species of grass that are native to the prairies look diminutive and modest, they are actually masters of their environment—able to flourish in the Great Plains/Midwest far more efficiently than other flora or fauna, including trees and humans.[8] The interior grassland of North America receives less rain than it might because of the Rocky Mountains. Storms that originate in the Pacific Ocean dump their moisture on the western slopes, often leaving little for the land east of the range. Rain-blocked by the Rocky Mountains, grasses flourish in wet periods, and cope admirably with dry. During drought, extensive root systems efficiently locate moisture. Proteins and sugars revert below ground, keeping the plant healthy despite a deceptive brown and bleak appearance on the surface. Grasses are built to minimize water loss and can withstand intense wind and fire better than woody plants.[9] In short, grasses emerged in the variable climate of the Great Plains for a reason. They should be celebrated rather than seen as a poor substitute for trees.

Grass, of course, grows in fertile earth, yet another shared environmental characteristic of the Great Plains and Midwest that is overshadowed by the absence of water. Coronado had no reason to worry about soil fertility, or the fact that *only* grass grew in the region. The land under all that grass was bursting with life. Again, as with all things on the prairie, this cycles back to the grass itself. Prairie root systems are so dense that they create an excess of decomposition, which is why the prairie soil is so fertile. Even sandy areas can support vegetation—native or domesticated. The difference between domesticated grasses (such as corn and wheat) and native grasses (such as Big Bluestem and Blue Grama) is the former's greater need for water and lesser ability to cope with drought.[10] The lack of water *is* an important factor. Fertile earth, however, and grass roots' contribution to fertility is also a key environmental characteristic, uniting Midwest and Great Plains, that should not be underappreciated.

Historically, grass (and earth) sheltered people in the form of sod houses. In the past (and today) it provided food for grazing animals, which then fed humans. American Indians, as well as subsequent ranchers who adopted their practices, recognized that grass grows better when the prairie is periodically burned. Therefore, they used fire to manipulate the grass and the corresponding migration of the bison, who were drawn to new green spring growth sprouting from what had been, a mere two weeks previous, blackened ashy ground.[11] Grass also indirectly provided humans with another type of energy that went beyond food—one that facilitated movement across the great space of the grassland. In the wake of the Pueblo Revolt of 1680, Spanish horses moved into the North American interior and began to eat what is essentially stored energy. When humans then traveled on horseback, they utilized that energy and acquired a more direct connection to the grass than they had before. As historian Elliott West noted in *The Contested Plains* (1998), "the crucial gift of the horse concerned not power itself but where that power came from."[12] Grass, ultimately, is the power of the prairies, and unlike aridity it unites, rather than divides, the Great Plains and the western sections of the Midwest.

Other environmental characteristics also unite the regions. Fire and wind, like the stored sunlight in grass, are both energy on a landscape. Each has a different history in the region(s), and each has a future. In human hands, fire, in partnership with climate, created the grassland.[13] Native peoples intentionally burned the grass so frequently, in fact, that they actually extended the prairie east. Fire gave grass the advantage over forest in today's Iowa and Illinois, where grass and forest mixed, but where the land was well-watered enough to allow for the easy takeover of trees without fire's regular presence. But thoughtful burning kept the trees away, gave grasses the advantage, and created good grazing for bison.[14] Fire gave American Indians a tool to manipulate the land and their prey.

In the mid-nineteenth century, however, newcomers began to settle the grasslands in large numbers. Americans brought with them new cultural traditions, new technology, and a new economy. Land-use strategy shifted to large-scale monoculture and ranching, accompanied by a corresponding shift in fire practices. A people intent on permanent, sedentary settlement—complete with frame houses, barns, fences, and acres of cash crops in the fields—had a different attitude toward burning grass than the more nomadic peoples who dominated the plains before them. Americans also settled on the high prairie—away from the semi-fire-protected stream and river valleys where American Indians had lived—and effectively put themselves directly into the path of oncoming fires. Their vulnerability to property loss, in particular, but also injury or death, caused them to view fire primarily as an enemy rather than a tool. Uncontrolled prairie fires threatened towns, homes, and farms. As a result, Euro-American settlers launched a widespread campaign to suppress fire and banish it from the landscape.[15]

They were unsuccessful in multiple ways. For one, ranchers, whose livelihoods were more directly connected to the grass, understood the value of burning and continued—much to the dismay of farmers—the fire practices they had learned from the native peoples. As the settlement period progressed, however, farmers and townspeople increasingly outnumbered ranchers and insisted that the population curtail intentional burning. The fuel load grew, in part from the suppression of fire and in part because of the decline of the bison. Domesticated grazers such as cattle were never present in sufficient numbers (even at the height of the cattle boom in 1885, the Great Plains generally was "relatively understocked") to eat down the grass. Ungrazed and unburned grass created an unprecedented fuel load on the grasslands.[16] Despite settlers' best intentions, accidents happened (as they always do with fire), and it was in the immediate post-settlement period—the time when the fire suppression campaign was the strongest—when some of the worst fires occurred. Nebraskan Robert Maxwell remembered of those days: "There was so much tall, old, grass then." Nellie Halverson, another Nebraskan, made the connection between fuel load and the reduced number of grazers. "The worst that we had to contend with the first years were [*sic*] prairie fire," she recalled of the late 1870s. "The country not being heavily grazed was covered with tall grass, and when fire started [it] was a job to put out."[17]

Prairie fire is so fundamental to the grasslands that the influence of its absence is just as keenly felt as its presence, but, unlike water, fire's truancy is entirely within human control. Thus far, rainmakers have failed to produce a reliable system for creating artificial precipitation, but the controlled application of fire is an important environmental tool that can still be used on the grassland, and it is vital that it be *present*. Without regular burning, woody plants such as juniper trees intrude onto the prairies, disrupting the ecosystem, creating an eyesore on the landscape, and sucking up scarce groundwater that would be best used for other purposes. Both above and below ground, animals, plants, and fungi depend on fire for their health. Fire also prevents the buildup of dense, matted grass. Not only is too much grass a recipe for an unplanned conflagration, the density prevents water and sunlight from reaching the earth below, and it stymies new growth. Regular, controlled burning solves these problems and maintains the grass-dominated ecosystem. Fire is so important to the region(s) that without it a grassland is unable to function as a grassland.[18]

Fire once burned across and beyond the boundary between the Great Plains and the Midwest. Like grass, it united the regions. John Cross, a child living in Iowa in the 1880s, expected a threatening prairie fire to appear at least once each year. He watched fires blaze through thick prairie grass, the wind carrying burning fragments ahead of the main line to extend the fire farther onto the prairie. They "nearly always jump[ed] over the [Des Moines] river," Cross noted, a width of between fifty and one hundred feet.[19]

Cross's memories are similar to that of Captain Eugene Ware, who described an 1865 fire farther west, set intentionally by the U.S. Army as an act of war against the plains Indians. Ware's fire burned across parts of Nebraska, Colorado, Kansas, Oklahoma, and Texas. It too was pushed by a northwest wind and jumped the Arkansas River to move onto the southern plains.[20] Two fires burning under different circumstances and in two different regions (at least as they are typically defined today), but both still prairie fire, still consuming grass, still leaping rivers. And fire is still necessary in both regions to maintain ecosystems.

Fire is important to both regions culturally, too. In Illinois, a small town boasts the name "Burnt Prairie," while "Prairie Fire" is the mascot for Knox College in Galesburg.[21] Both names indicate the historical presence of prairie fire within the Midwestern landscape. Similarly, on the

Great Plains, the Lower Brulé Indian Reservation in southcentral South Dakota is called "Burnt Thigh," named for the Brulé (or "burnt") Sioux, who themselves acquired their name from a historic prairie fire.[22] Fire is also a common theme in art and literature, and the affection that settlers had toward the beautiful fires, despite their campaign to suppress them, is evident in the historic record. A Nebraska mother, for example, wrote to her son in Massachusetts in 1887: "By the way, there is at this moment a splendid prairie fire blazing just west of us. Some of your Worester [*sic*] [Massachusetts] people never saw <u>such</u> a sight with all their privileges."[23] Through her words, the Nebraska mother took emotional ownership of her fire, a reminder that, historically, prairie fires on the Great Plains and in the Midwest were identifying features and something to be proud of, despite the perceived necessity of suppression. Modern ranchers, particularly in the Flint Hills of eastern Kansas and Oklahoma, as well as the Dakotas, still burn annually for the same reasons that their ancestors and the native peoples did—to take care of the grass and the land and, by extension, their livestock and livelihood.[24] In Iowa, little unplowed tallgrass prairie remains, but conservationists and federal wildlife refuges use prescribed fire to maintain what is left.[25]

Fire on the prairie would be far less effective and dangerous without wind to blow it across the gently rolling landscape—yet another shared environmental characteristic of the Great Plains/Midwest. Wind is a fundamental part of regional identity, a critical energy resource, and perhaps the most *felt* (whether you want to or not) of the *present* environmental characteristics. Anyone who has lived on the plains, or has even just stopped for gas out by Amarillo, knows the strength of regional wind, which is caused by a significant variance in air pressure, as well as a lack of friction, more present in other landscapes in the form of hills, mountains, trees, and other vertical topography. Wind blows from high pressure to low pressure and increases in speed if the high- and low-pressure areas are close together or differ greatly.[26] According to official sources, such as the National Oceanic and Atmospheric Administration (NOAA), the Great Plains is the windiest region in the United States, while other national organizations have named Dodge City, Kansas, with an annual average wind speed of fourteen miles per hour, the windiest American city. As one writer aptly noted, "wind is a way of life" in Dodge and across the grasslands.[27]

Visitors notice it too. In August of 2012, a blogger tracked the four most common words searched on Google when linked with individual state names. "Windy" was the number one word associated with Kansas, Montana, South Dakota, and Wyoming. It ranked number two in Oklahoma, Nebraska, and Minnesota and number three in New Mexico and North Dakota. Of the states that touch the grassland, only in Colorado, Texas, and Iowa did "windy" not make the top four. Perhaps even more significant, the term made the top four in nine out of twelve Great Plains states—core or peripheral—but nowhere else. "Windy" did not make the top four searched terms in any other state outside the region.[28] Not only is the Great Plains *actually* windy; people *perceive* it as windy. Wind therefore plays a major role in regional and state identity.

Like grass and fire, wind is not hampered by boundaries. Iowa—arguably a Midwestern, but not a Great Plains, state—is windy but is not known for its bluster compared to Oklahoma ("where the wind comes sweepin' down the plain"). Iowa is a transition zone between the Midwest and Great Plains.[29] It is also a national leader in its efforts to harness wind energy, as well as the sheer number of wind turbines within its borders. The American Wind Energy Association ranks Iowa second in the nation (behind Texas) for installed wind capacity.[30]

The Great Plains is famous for tornadoes, an enormously destructive type of wind, particularly in "tornado alley" on the southern plains. The storms are so frequent that a "tornado culture" has emerged in the region. Plains people take pride in their chutzpah in the face of tornadic threats and even, on some level, believe that, because they are experienced plainspeople, they should not take shelter in basements but ride out the threat on their front lawns, reading the weather in the clouds. Tornadoes are primarily considered a Great Plains phenomenon, and even the northern plains, less plagued than the South, has its share of storms. A devastating tornado spun through Fargo, North Dakota, on June 20, 1957, for example, and killed eight people, including five children from the same family.[31] Parts of the Midwest, too, are vulnerable to twisters. Iowa State University even adopted its team name, the Cyclones (a nineteenth-century term for tornado), after the *Chicago Tribune* reported on a game with Northwestern in 1895. "Northwestern might as well have tried to play football with an Iowa cyclone as with the Iowa team it met yesterday," the writer noted.[32]

Both the Midwest and the Great Plains are windy, now and in the past. Native peoples, used to coping with daily wind, included it in religion and lore while newcomer settlers of the mid-nineteenth century also realized the ubiquitous presence and strength of the force quite early.[33] Riding into Dakota in 1878, W. E. Lovejoy's first impression of the territory was of the wind, which, he noted, was a "fierce northwest zephyr that seemed in an awful hurry to get out of the country."[34]

Like fire, wind is energy that can be used as a tool. Settlers, who had little choice but to put up with the annoyances of the relentless blowing, quickly put it to work. Windmills dotted the landscape and told an optimistic story of adaptation to the cantankerous grassland environment. "A windmill is much needed at Lawrence," a writer remarked about the Kansas town soon after its founding. "The scarcity of water power and the abundance of wind which is always felt on the high grounds seem to render that sort of machine a necessity in Kansas." In semi-arid country, the plentiful resource (wind), not the scarce (water), milled grains.[35] From the beginning of the settlement era, windmills, in partnership with the wind, raised water from below ground, a service that, according to historian Walter Prescott Webb, "made life on the Plains possible."[36] As windmill design improved, people interested in pushing settlement west saw an even more intimate connection between the developing technology and the very foreign, large, open, and windy grassland environment. "In Kansas, these mills are to perform a great service in our future history," the *Herald of Freedom* prophesied in 1857, more than a century before power companies began constructing giant wind farms. "The country seems peculiarly adapted to their use."[37]

Using the wind's energy is one aspect of its history in the region(s), but just as important is the effect the wind had on daily lives and the emotions it inspired. Dime novel publisher Erastus Beadle, on an adventure trip to the central plains, thought the wind unsettling, and even a little sinister. He wrote a letter to his children, telling them he was truly on the "wild prairie" where "the wind blows a hurricane and shakes this frail cottonwood building, creeping in to every crevice, rattling my paper as I write."[38] In 1855, a Kansas Territory booster admitted feeling lonely as he lay in bed, listening to the sound of the wind outside his cabin, while, eight decades later, Mary Dyck of Hamilton County, in a dust bowl diary that features wind, or its rare (and therefore notable) absence in nearly every entry, ascribed her own lonely feelings not to herself but to the sound of the blow. "Wind howled today[;] it sounded very sad," she wrote in June of 1937.[39]

In addition to fear and loneliness, the unabating gales could generate anger. Ferdinand Van Ostrand, a soldier stationed in northern Dakota Territory in 1871, became so incensed that he assigned the wind its own malevolent personality. "After we left there the wind came up and blew like h---l and still does," he wrote in April. In May: "Windy as the d---l"; August: "This is the windyest [*sic*] place I have ever struck—an opinion which I formed a long time ago"; September: "the wind has blown spitefully all day"; October: "Since about 10 a.m. the wind has blown fearfully and the

dust has choked and blinded everyone. Tonight is dark and tempestuous";
March: "These infernal high winds . . . favor us with their manifold dis-
comforts. . . . A description of the weather for one day answer for all [just]
about, windy." The wind was also a practical problem for Van Ostrand
and his fellow soldiers. It interfered with river crossings and, in storms,
threatened to rip the roof off barracks. The men got so frustrated that they
renamed their fort in the wind's honor: Fort Berthold became "Fort Blow-
hard." They carved the new name on a log at the fort's edge. "We give witness to the fact that it is no misnomer," Van Ostrand concluded.[40]

The history and *presence* of wind in the Great Plains/Midwest reveals
a duality. Regional wind is a torment, a primary cause of hardship in a
difficult environment, challenged only by drought for influence and effect.
Wind blows bone-chilling, dangerous, cold one day, and the next (almost
without exaggeration) it acts as a furnace, withering crops and everything
else that draws breath. It produces destructive tornadoes as well as terrifying straight velocities capable of knocking trains off tracks or breaking
telephone polls at their base.[41] Finally, and perhaps most disturbingly, it is
almost impossible to live in the region(s) and have a good hair day.[42] And
yet (here's where the duality comes in), while wind is at best an annoy-
ance and at worst a calamity, many observers, from inside and outside the
region, both professional and layperson alike, have argued, past and present, that *controlled* wind—converted into sustainable, clean, energy—is the
region's salvation.[43]

Establishing a boundary between the Great Plains and Midwest is
tricky, if not impossible. Even just one aspect of the debate—environment—is fraught with contradictions and caveats. In discussions of this
complicated issue, historians have focused too exclusively on one factor—
semi-aridity, or the absence of water. As a result, they have disregarded
other environmental characteristics that are critical parts of the story.
Grass, earth, fire, and wind are all energies within the landscape. Like water, humans have used them all in the region(s), past and present. Unlike
water, however, these characteristics unite more than they divide the Great
Plains and the Midwest—a further complication within an already complicated boundary conversation.

Additionally, there is a distinction between current environment and
historical environment. In centuries past, applied fire, wind, earth, and
grass *all* linked Iowa, for example, with the Great Plains to the west. Today,
barely any native grasses remain within the state (although domesticated
corn flourishes), and fire has been suppressed. Only wind and earth remain
(in altered form) to connect Iowa to other sections of the tall, mixed, and

shortgrass prairies. This environmental shift, perhaps, is part of the reason that Iowa, in the last century, has, culturally, drifted away from the Great Plains and toward the Midwest.

How important is the legacy of historical environment and land-use practices versus the current incarnation of the landscape? Historians (and other scholars) must broaden their thinking about both the Great Plains and the Midwest and start asking these types of questions rather than focusing exclusively on semi-aridity, a critical, but incomplete and limiting point of study. We must focus on what is *present* in the region(s), rather than only on what is *absent*, and teach people to see beyond "nothing." We must study both the present and the past—giving attention to the current environments but also thinking about the meaning and lasting impact of historical environments. Perhaps if we better understand the commonalities of the Midwest and Great Plains, thereby expanding our points of view, we will also better identify and understand the distinction between the region(s). Determining a boundary between the Midwest and the Great Plains, after all, is not about drawing a line on a map that everyone agrees on (which will likely never happen). Rather, it is about the process of getting to know both ourselves and our neighbor a little bit better. *That* we can definitely do.

Notes

[1]   Walter Prescott Webb, *The Great Plains* (New York: Grosset & Dunlap, 1931); Craig Miner, *West of Wichita: Settling the High Plains of Kansas, 1865–1890* (Lawrence: University Press of Kansas, 1986), 7.

[2]   Verlyn Klinkenborg, "Splendor of the Grass," *National Geographic*, April 2007.

[3]   For an earlier version of this argument, see Julie Courtwright, "The Great Plains," in *The Routledge History of Rural America*, ed. Pamela Riney-Kehrberg (New York: Routledge, 2016), 70–85.

[4]   David J. Wishart, *The Last Days of the Rainbelt* (Lincoln: University of Nebraska Press, 2013), 80–81.

[5]   For an excellent introduction to the prairie/plains ecosystem, see Candace Savage, *Prairie: A Natural History* (Vancouver: Greystone Books, 2004).

[6]   Catherine Pringle, *Across the Plains in 1844* (Whitefish, MT: Kessinger Publishing, 2010), 2.

[7]   Coronado is quoted in Savage, *Prairie*, 6 (emphasis added).

[8]   See Savage, *Prairie*, 64–67; Daniel I. Axelrod, "Rise of the Grassland Biome, Central North America," *Botanical Review* 51 (April–June, 1985): 186.

[9]   Savage, *Prairie*, 51, 64–70, 96–97. The grassroots analogy is one that has been adopted by plains natives. Democratic presidential candidate (1972), U.S. senator, and South Dakota native George McGovern named his autobiography *Grassroots* (Random House, 1977).

10 Savage, *Prairie*, 92–99; Ted Steinberg, *Down to Earth: Nature's Role in American History* (New York: Oxford University Press, 2002), 61.

11 See Julie Courtwright, *Prairie Fire: A Great Plains History* (Lawrence: University Press of Kansas, 2011), 42–43.

12 Elliott West, *The Contested Plains: Indians, Goldseekers, and the Rush to Colorado* (Lawrence: University Press of Kansas, 1998), 49–51.

13 Axelrod, "Rise of the Grassland Biome."

14 The more eastern sections of the Midwest, such as Indiana and Ohio, were more forested than Illinois and Iowa. Forest generally prevailed there, but American Indian use of fire extended the expansive grassland deeper into today's Midwest than it would have via climatic influence alone.

15 See Courtwright, *Prairie Fire*; and Stephen J. Pyne, *Fire in America: A Cultural History of Wildland and Rural Fires* (Seattle: University of Washington Press, 1982).

16 Geoff Cunfer, *On the Great Plains: Agriculture and Environment* (College Station: Texas A&M Press, 2005), 48–50.

17 Dr. Robert Maxwell, interviewed March 25, 1940, by Maude Swanson, Works Progress Administration Interviews, Nebraska State Historical Society (hereafter NSHS), Lincoln, NE, Box 3, Folder 25; Mrs. Nellie Thompson Halverson, interviewed January 3–4, 1940, by Frank A. Kiolbasa, Works Progress Administration Interviews, NSHS, Lincoln, NE, Box 14, Folder 113.

18 See Courtwright, *Prairie Fire*; and Pyne, *Fire in America*; Dick Rice, interview by Frank Benede, June 2, 1973, Oklahoma Oral History Collection, Oklahoma State Historical Society, Oklahoma City, OK.

19 Mr. John Cross, interviewed April, 1939, by Frederick W. Kaul, Works Progress Administration Interviews, NSHS, Lincoln, NE, Box 1, Folder 1.

20 Eugene F. Ware, *The Indian War of 1864* (Lincoln: University of Nebraska Press, 1994), 351–57.

21 See https://www.knox.edu.

22 Glenda Riley, introduction to *Land of the Burnt Thigh: A Lively Story of Women Homesteaders on the South Dakota Frontier*, by Edith Eudora Kohl (St. Paul: Minnesota Historical Press, 1986), ix.

23 Joni L. Kinsey, *Plain Pictures: Images of the American Prairie* (Washington, D.C.: Smithsonian, 1996); and P. Jane Hafen and Diane Quantic, *A Great Plains Reader* (Lincoln: University of Nebraska Press, 2003); "Mother," Neligh, (Nebraska) to "My dear Boy," April 15, 1887 (the letter is in the author's possession; emphasis in original).

24 Jim Hoy, *Cowboys and Kansas: Stories from the Tallgrass Prairie* (Norman: University of Oklahoma Press, 1995), 113–18.

25 See the U.S. Fish and Wildlife Service, https://www.fws.gov/refuge/neal_smith/.

26 John Wheeler, "Weather Talk: Difference in Pressure Cause of Windy Great Plains," July 9, 2016, http://www.agweek.com/news/weather/4068586-weather-talk-difference-pressure-ause-windy-great-plains; Nick Walker, "Wind and Air Pressure," accessed February 22, 2018, wxdude.com.

27 National Oceanic and Atmospheric Administration, http://noaa.gov; *Hutchison* [Kansas] *News*, May 4, 1983.

28 See "Why Are Americans So . . . ," *no upside* (blog), August 7, 2012, http://blog.noupsi. de/post/28896819324/why-are-americans-so. See also Chris Cillizza, "What We Think about the 50 States — in 1 Map," *The Fix* (blog), August 16, 2012, http://

www.washingtonpost.com/blogs/the-fix/wp/2012/08/16/how-we-think-about-the-50-states-in-1-map/.

29 "Oklahoma" lyrics and music by Richard Rogers and Oscar Hammerstein II (1943). The Oklahoma legislature adopted it as the state song on May 11, 1953.

30 Leanna Garfield, "The Largest Wind Farm in U.S. History Just Got the Green Light," *Business Insider*, September 1, 2016, http://www.businessinsider.com/american-iowa-wind-farm-approval-2016-9; American Wind Energy Association, "U.S. Wind Energy State Facts," accessed December 30, 2016, http://www.awea.org/resources/statefactsheets.aspx .

31 "Fargo Tornado 6-20-57" clippings in Box #60, Coll. No. 10691, Roy P. Johnson/Louis Pfaller Collection, State Historical Society of North Dakota, Bismarck, ND. Clippings are unidentified but are likely from the *Fargo Forum* editions of June 21, 1957, and dates following.

32 "Struck by a Cyclone," *Chicago Tribune*, September 29, 1895.

33 Robert W. Righter, *Wind Energy in America: A History* (Norman: University of Oklahoma Press, 1996), 4.

34 "Early Days in Dakota Territory," W. E. Lovejoy Manuscript Collection, Pierre, SD, South Dakota State Historical Society, Box 3548B, Folder 1.

35 "News from Kansas," *Ripley Bee* [Ripley, OH], March 31, 1855; J. M. Armfield, Interview by Ida B. Landford, June 22, 1937, Indian Pioneer Collection, Volume 3, Interview ID 4541, University of Oklahoma, Western History Digital Collection, https://libraries.ou.edu/westhistory.

36 Webb, *Great Plains*, 347.

37 *Kansas Herald of Freedom*, January 3, 1857.

38 Erastus Beadle, *Ham, Eggs, and Corn Cake: A Nebraska Territory Diary* (Lincoln: University of Nebraska Press, 2001), 24.

39 *The Kansas Herald of Freedom* (Wakarusa), May 26, 1855; Pamela Riney-Kehrberg, ed., *Waiting On the Bounty: The Dust Bowl Diary of Mary Knackstedt Dyck* (Iowa City: University of Iowa Press, 1999), 71. Entry is dated June 16, 1937.

40 Ferdinand A. Van Ostrand Diary, May 7, August 28, September 22, October 4, October 11, 1871, and April 30, March 22, 1872, MSS 10007, State Historical Society of North Dakota, Bismarck, ND.

41 *The Hutchinson* (Kansas) *News*, May 7, 2014; In Andover, Kansas, sometime in the mid-1990s, I saw telephone poles broken at their base as a result of straight-line winds. It was more terrifying than any experience I have had (yet) with a tornado.

42 Trust me. I have personal experience.

43 Elliott West, "Trails and Footprints: The Past of the Future Southern Plains," in Sherry L. Smith, *The Future of the Southern Plains* (Norman: University of Oklahoma Press, 2003), 40.

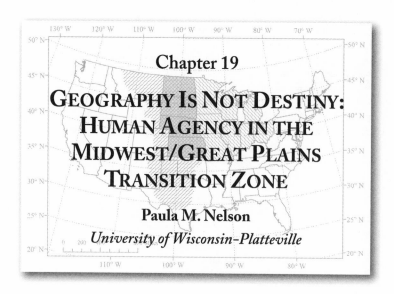

Chapter 19

GEOGRAPHY IS NOT DESTINY: HUMAN AGENCY IN THE MIDWEST/GREAT PLAINS TRANSITION ZONE

Paula M. Nelson

University of Wisconsin-Platteville

Some borders are visible and obvious, while others are created only by time and experience. The line demarcating the Great Plains from the humid, more farmable, and more livable lands in the Midwest is one of the latter. In the nineteenth century, observation and experience revealed some of the limits settlers might find on the plains. Early explorers labeled the plains "The Great American Desert," a name that map makers then applied to the vast western grasslands on their maps.[1] John Wesley Powell, explorer and naturalist, veteran of several expeditions through the American West, declared that land west of the 100th meridian was suitable for grazing but not farming. His *Report on the Arid Regions of the United States*, 1878, urged a change in federal land policy to grant homesteads of 2,500 acres rather than the typical 160 acres to better enable this use. Because cattle ranching did not bring in the population or social institutions that farming did, his plan was never enacted.[2] In the exuberance of the late nineteenth century, however, Americans believed that human agency could overcome almost any problem. An early settler who came to Sully County, Dakota Territory, in 1883, wrote, "I well remember that my early school maps represented a large tract of land . . . as 'The Great American Desert' and the greater part of the state of South Dakota was in it. Pioneers cannot

256

live and make a home in a desert. So the desert had to go and the pioneers held the fort," albeit rather precariously at times.[3]

It was not only settlers who were eager to hold the fort. Town promoters, railroad builders, land speculators, and territorial and state officials all believed they could create a new Midwest on the Great Plains. Many Americans believed that anything was possible, even changing the climate, with hard work and the right system.

Hardy Webster Campbell homesteaded near Aberdeen in southern Dakota Territory in 1879, where he devised and promoted a system of land cultivation he believed would preserve moisture and make farming profitable on dry lands. Dr. Samuel Aughey Jr., a University of Nebraska professor in the 1870s and 1880s, promoted the idea that human action could change climates. Charles Dana Wilbur coined the phrase "rain follows the plow" in 1881, which summed up several threads of popular and scientific thought on plains climate and gave the movement its battle cry. From the early 1880s until the 1930s, thousands of hopeful settlers migrated to the plains to build farms, homes, and gardens like those of the bountiful Midwest. A substantial share of them moved out when their dreams dried up and blew away.[4]

The hard times of the Dust Bowl and Depression years in the 1930s defined and institutionalized the Great Plains as a problem area. Federal government programs to ameliorate suffering and prevent it from recurring, along with the striking photos by the Farm Security Administration photographers, imprinted its distinctive problems on the public consciousness. Problem areas require distinct boundaries. Earlier maps depicting changes in soil composition, types of vegetation, or average precipitation as one headed west did not, however, demarcate a clear line defining the Great Plains, because those variables did not, of themselves, satisfactorily provide a definite line. In 1936, a congressional committee report entitled "The Future of the Great Plains" defined the problems of the region and suggested solutions, and it drew clear boundaries. Their map drew the borders of the Great Plains at the 98th meridian on the east and at the foothills of the Rocky Mountains in the west. Inside was a troubled space where residents lived in disharmony with their land.[5]

While many did fail on the plains in a series of disastrous droughts, and during the Great Depression, many adapted and survived, then prospered. Some settlers, most from Midwestern states, elsewhere in the United States, or from Europe, adapted to the conditions the region presented. Adaptation continues today. The human factor, as South Dakota agricultural extension agents called it—that difficult-to-define combination of grit, patience, ability to plan and take the long view, openness to new ideas, willingness to adopt new approaches, new technologies, new plant types, livestock breeds—made it possible to succeed on the land. Rain did not follow the plow. Geography is certainly a major factor, but it is not destiny.[6]

The agricultural transition zone in South Dakota looks more like the prairies to the east but has the geological and geographical underpinnings of the Great Plains. When glacial ice jams moved the Missouri River west from its old channel near where the James River now runs, it cut off the plateau now called the Coteau du Missouri and blocked ancient rivers that had once flowed into it. The movement of glaciers reshaped the Coteau du Missouri, just as it had done to its relative, the Coteau des Prairies, in eastern South Dakota, flattening the landscape and leaving moraines as hills and ridges. The Coteau du Missouri also includes a plateau that gradually rises nearly a thousand feet as one moves west from the James River Valley. Higher elevations mean shorter growing seasons with late frosts in spring

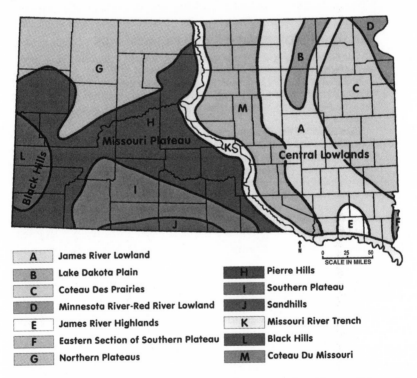

A	James River Lowland		
B	Lake Dakota Plain	H	Pierre Hills
C	Coteau Des Prairies	I	Southern Plateau
D	Minnesota River-Red River Lowland	J	Sandhills
E	James River Highlands	K	Missouri River Trench
F	Eastern Section of Southern Plateau	L	Black Hills
G	Northern Plateaus	M	Coteau Du Missouri

Herbert Schell's "agricultural transition zone" corresponds with area M on the map. The author uses the Schell term and the map term "Coteau du Missouri" interchangeably. *Map from* The Geography of South Dakota, *3rd ed., Edward P. Hogan and Erin H. Fouberg (Sioux Falls, SD: Center for Western Studies, 2001), 14.*

or early frosts in the fall. The incline is nearly imperceptible when traveled east to west. Its impact, however, must be understood for farming success.[7]

There are no major drainage systems on the Coteau du Missouri. A few creeks run into the James on the east. Others, also limited in number and size, run west into the Missouri River. The Coteau du Missouri has little running water, although small lakes fill after wet winters or rainy springs. The lakes dry up if substantial rains end. Wells are the most dependable water source for farm families. The topography of the area includes highlands like the Ree Hills, rolling prairies, and "sags," a geographical term that refers to the valleys made by old rivers, now shut off by the Missouri River's course change. Sags are mostly filled with glacial drift, the soil, gravel, rocks, and other debris glaciers deposited as they moved across the land or stagnated in place.[8] Federal surveyors—who marked the land into sections, half sections, and quarters in the 1870s and early 1880s—evaluated each section and each township in their field notes. "Rolling prairie, 2nd rate," they might write, or "land hilly, stony, 4th rate." There were plenty of "gently rolling, 1st rate" evaluations, but the surveyor summations usually noted the lack of water and timber.[9]

Historian Herbert Schell used plainly visible river valleys, from the western edge of the James River Valley on the east to the eastern edge of the Missouri River on the west, to define the borders of the agricultural transition zone. Rainfall in this region is unpredictable, making it difficult for farmers to plan from year to year.[10] The author of the 1978 Hyde County history explained the problem with precipitation. "East of the James River, fewer than one year in five" brought low rainfall and drought. Not far west of Miller, however, the risk of low precipitation and drought increased 100 percent to two out of five years.[11] There was no indication that anyone had knowledge of this increased drought risk in 1883. Until farmers moved in, weather records began, and analysis of long-term trends were undertaken, they had no way of knowing. As one early settler commented in the 1930s, "No Brookings to send them bulletins in those days."[12] (South Dakota State College in Brookings housed the Agricultural Extension Service and operated the research farms.). Huron, on the James River in Beadle County, had a national weather observation system in 1882. The transition zone stations began in 1893 in select places and much later in others. Miller began notations in 1902; Selby, in 1907; Mobridge, in 1911. More stations began record keeping as railroad lines expanded and brought towns with them.[13] By the 1930s, agricultural extension scientists wrote of the "extreme variation" of rainfall in the transition zone counties. "Between the James and the Missouri rivers, where prairie farming reluctantly gives way to plains ranching," they wrote, it was impossible to use averages for much of anything.[14] Farmers as well as agricultural scientists used averages to judge rainfall and climate, best crop choices, bushels per acre, and other production markers. Extreme variation in rainfall year to year, a delay in rain by just a few days at critical times in plant development, the blast of hot winds that reduced yields or destroyed the crop—all made farming a gamble not reflected in averages.[15]

What is the human story in the agricultural transition zone? Initial agricultural settlement began as part of the Dakota Boom after 1880. A number of factors combined to bring a settlement rush into southern Dakota Territory. The national economy, in the doldrums since the Panic of 1873, improved enough to prompt the building of railroads west across Minnesota and Iowa into Dakota Territory. Railroads brought accessibility and town/market development. Good rains and heavier winter snows helped overcome the "desert" label; several years without grasshopper depredations reassured potential residents that the pests had been an aberration. Land hunger was an ever-present drive. The resulting rush brought thousands of people in to stake their claims. By 1883, potential settlers reached the agricultural transition zone.

The Chicago, Milwaukee, and St. Paul Railroad entered southern Dakota Territory at Canton in 1879 and pushed west with vigor, platting town sites along the way. The line, generally known as the Milwaukee, reached Chamberlain, on the Missouri River, in 1880. It ended there, too, until 1906. The Great Sioux Reservation occupied western South Dakota, almost to the Black Hills, until federal land policy opened it to non-Indian settlement after 1900. The Chicago Northwestern built to Pierre in 1880, where the rails also halted. The Chicago Northwestern did not plat town sites between Huron and Pierre, opting instead for sidings, marking sites for potential towns. According to Herbert Schell, that decision caused settlement to lag in the area. The railroad wanted traffic to increase before town building, while potential residents wanted town plats and lot sales. Further north, a division of the Chicago Northwestern built a line from Ortonville, Minnesota, to a town site in Brown County they named Aberdeen. The railroad platted the site and held a sale of lots in January of 1881. The railroad arrived six months later. The line extended to Bowdle in Edmunds County in 1886, and went west from Bowdle to the Missouri River in 1900.[16]

Why did settlers come to the Coteau du Missouri? The drive to own land and achieve independence was a strong motivator for many. Some had sons whom they hoped to provide with land. The "new country" had land in large quantities, at cheaper prices. Others wanted to have a larger place in the community. Helping to build new settlements allowed participants to build their own reputations, along with their businesses, farms, and wealth. That the people in the first rush to the Coteau struggled is clear. Captain Caleb Holt Ellis, author of the 1909 *History of Faulk County*, did not hide the difficulties. Federal surveyors, he noted, "gave a most discouraging account of the whole region, 'a barren waste, scattered over with cactus,'" a comment settlers disregarded. Missouri men, looking for settlement sites in 1882, did their own assessment: Faulk County was a "beautiful, slightly rolling prairie, covered with luxuriant grasses. . . . [A] goodly land."[17] Federal surveyors did not actually survey Faulk County until 1883. The negative comments applied region wide, from earlier survey visits. The assessments of men actually on the ground meant more. Ellis, however, was very careful to note hard truths in his biographical sketches of families still in the county in 1909. Writing about a local minister, he described his faith in the country, kept "through all the dark days of Faulk County's history." Adam Sangster's story included the reminder of "the years of hail, storms, and drought with prevailing hot winds . . . [the] full share of privations." Sangster struggled on. Edward Chapman "became perfectly familiar with privation, exposure . . . trial." Chapman experienced a total loss of crops in 1888-89. Yet in 1909 he owned fine Percheron horses and "neat stock."[18]

In other counties of the region, drought and struggle also shaped experience. In 1883, Thomas Prinie came to Buffalo County as a child of six with his parents and their growing family. His family's story provides a time line of "all the dark days" that Coteau residents endured. His father was a carpenter in Cedar Rapids, Iowa, but wanted to own land and build a more secure future. They established a home near a small lake filled with wild fowl of all kinds. Abundant rains provided lush vegetation. Prairie chickens called and boomed on the prairies; songbirds danced and sang above. It was a paradise. The next year brought little moisture; the lake dried up; wells dried up. "Then our real troubles began," Thomas wrote.[19] The daily ritual of hauling water from a mile or two away consumed much of their time. Both wells dug on their claim failed to supply water. The year 1886 was also very dry. The family began to burn straw for fuel, using a straw burner that rested on the stove top. In 1887, his father returned to Cedar Rapids to do carpenter work to help support the family and was gone seven months. Crops were good in 1888 and 1889. In 1890 the family had their first complete crop failure. In 1892 they moved to an eighty-acre farm in a better location. After one good crop there, 1894 brought total crop failure again. Thomas and a sister joined an older sister in Cedar

Rapids, where they worked for wages they could send home to the family. Thomas returned to farm for one more season, 1898, while his father served as Buffalo County probate judge and also did carpentry work, "so we had considerable prosperity."The family moved to a better house, which burned in a prairie fire a few weeks later. The parents moved to a small truck farm outside Cedar Rapids in 1900, "where they prospered" and their South Dakota adventure ended. The Midwest's dependable rainfall, rich soil, and developed, well-populated, successful communities sustained them. Their small acreage in an abundant climate provided the security a much larger farm in a challenging environment had not.[20]

There were early settlers who stayed in the country for the long haul. Bert L. Hall, born on a Buffalo County claim in 1887, described the characteristics of his parents and neighbors who stayed and prospered: "determination that wind, fire and drought could not vanquish; a quiet heroism that rendered isolation and deprivation satisfying; . . . perseverance and thrift . . . a frugal conservatism which was not swept away during boom times."[21]

How did first-wave settlers apply these virtues and survive? Immigrants and children of immigrants oftentimes had demonstrated perseverance, thrift, and frugal conservatism before they arrived in South Dakota. They reapplied it here. Peter and Mary Gunderson were born in Norway but migrated to Minnesota as children. They met there and married in 1882. The Gundersons homesteaded in Brule County, where they built a one-room log cabin. Unfortunately, a tree fell on Peter while they were building the cabin. He was disabled and in pain for the rest of his life but could do most farm work. Mary gave birth to eight children; four of them died in infancy. The family lived in the one-room cabin "for many years."[22] Peter traded a horse for an outbuilding on a neighbor's farm, moved it home, and added it to the house. Mary churned butter to trade for groceries at the country store five miles away. She also knit caps and gloves from the wool of their two sheep for trade at the store, once the family's clothing needs had been met. Peter rented farm equipment from a neighbor to do field work. In 1888 they lost their herd of dairy cows, fifteen animals, when a blizzard struck suddenly and the animals froze. One calf had stayed in the barn; they rebuilt with her. The Gunderson farm was still in operation in 1986, with a grandson as owner. The 1986 plat book for Brule County farms includes the years each farm came into the families' hands. Fifty-two farms began in the 1880s, including the Gunderson farm; nineteen farms became the property of their respective families in the 1890s; thirty-two farms began or were purchased by their respective families between 1900 and 1910; the rest were later.[23]

The Matousek families of Bohemia migrated to Muscoda, Grant County, Wisconsin, in 1868, where an aunt had settled earlier. They bought farms near her and settled in. Joseph Matousek and his wife, Mary, married in 1873 and had three children in Wisconsin. Although Grant County receives thirty-five inches of rain a year, plenty to grow just about anything, the young couple was dissatisfied with their hilly, wooded land. They managed to cultivate half of it, had some land in hay, but believed their "hard labor and earnest efforts" were not rewarded. Joseph's father did not like the erosion his hilly farm suffered. The land could not support the three growing families who worked it. The entire group decided to move to Dakota Territory, after the men visited the area and saw promise there. Four families departed Wisconsin in five freight cars and one crude immigrant passenger car; one wife with children came after her house was completed. The large family was well provisioned, with twenty cattle, twelve horses, lumber for roofs, feed and seed, farm machinery, and food. They settled thirteen miles south of Kimball.[24]

One characteristic, besides careful preparation, that helped Joseph Matousek survive in his new home was his commitment to financial planning. Matousek kept a careful tally of his property and his expenses and worked to avoid long-term debt. He brought three horses, five cows, two pigs, and chickens to Dakota Territory. He built a sod stable, cutting the sod himself, and used some of the transported lumber for the roof. He bought lumber for a twelve-by-sixteen frame house and a nine-by-twelve granary, which cost him $200. Matousek also understood the processes and potential benefits in U.S. land policy. In March of 1883 he proved up on his preemption, paying $1.25 per acre for the land. Then he filed on a homestead in a nearby township as well as a forty-acre tree claim there. He moved their house to the claim, built sod additions and out buildings, and dug a fourteen-foot well to supply water. He planted a variety of crops on the forty-five cultivated acres back on the preemption. Wheat, corn, oats, flax, and food crops for the family flourished. In October of 1887, tragedy struck. Mary died of brain fever. Crops had been poor that year, the winter of 1888 was very severe. Left alone with four children aged two to ten, Joseph described his practical conclusion: "I could see no other way out than to get another wife and mother for my orphaned children." He married a twenty-six-year-old neighbor. They had five children of their own.[25]

The early years of the twentieth century were difficult, but not because of drought or harsh weather. A barn fire, hog cholera, and other disasters struck. The help of friends and neighbors, good crop years, and some debt helped them rebuild and go on. Matousek's hatred of debt led him to pay it off quickly. The family continued to build, adding a 980-foot artesian well in 1908, because the twelve wells they dug did not produce enough water. In 1909 they built a granary, hen house, fuel shed, and garage. His memoir ends in 1917, when he had four living children from his first marriage, and five from his second. In 1945, his two youngest sons still farmed the land he had homesteaded.[26]

German-Russian families also homesteaded and held on during the difficult years. Christine Kunz came to Yankton, Dakota Territory, with the earliest German-Russian settlers in 1875. Her family appears in the 1880 census; her husband was paralyzed and was not employed. He died after a long illness that exhausted their resources. She and her two children, ages five and three (the only survivors of the eight children Kunz bore), moved with a group of twenty adults and their children from the Yankton German-Russian community to Walworth and Campbell counties to homestead. Kunz brought a cow, her cookstove, flour, salt, beans, dried bread, sacks of cow chips and corn cobs for fuel, a shotgun and powder, and the Bible. The party departed Yankton in April of 1884. Kunz was thirty-four years old.

Upon arrival in southern Campbell County, Kunz had a two-room house built of mud and straw bricks. While the men of the group broke the land, Kunz and her sister dug a well. Two days of intensive, dangerous labor later, the women struck water.[27]

The next few years were difficult. The first winter brought heavy snow, which isolated them and left them living on corn meal mush with milk. The first spring brought a late frost; their grain crop froze. That fall a prairie fire burned the lands around them, but their firebreak protected them and their buildings. It also exposed the bones of numerous buffalo strewn across the prairie. Kunz gathered the bones, hauled them to Ipswich (which took two days each way), and sold the bones for $10 per ton. The flax crop in 1886 brought $37, and in 1887 brought more. Over the next decade, more German-Russian families migrated to the Sutley community and elsewhere in the two counties. A scattering of country stores grew up to serve the farm families, which reduced the time they had to spend on the road to railroad towns. In 1900 the Milwaukee road built a rail line from Bowdle to Evarts, on the Missouri River. The railroad platted three towns along the line, which brought markets and trade closer. Kunz farmed with her son, Michael, until he married in 1901. He and his wife stayed on the farm. In 1914, after twenty-nine years of the Kunz family farming that land, Michael Kunz and family moved to Java, South Dakota, where he worked as a grain buyer for thirty-two years. Christine Kunz remarried in 1903 and farmed with her new husband in Campbell County until her death in 1925.[28]

German-Russians like the Kunz family had an especially important impact on the northern counties of the Coteau. They migrated to South Dakota in large numbers after 1882 and did not leave in large numbers when hard times came. When mass migration out of the Coteau region occurred between 1890 and 1895 in response to extreme drought and national depression, the counties populated by German-Russians grew while the rest declined. Campbell, McPherson, and Walworth grew from 5 percent (McPherson) to 22.5 percent (Campbell). Campbell County was 48 percent foreign born in 1895. McPherson was 52 percent foreign born, and Walworth was 42 percent foreign born, according to that census. The counties without substantial numbers of German-Russians lost 12 to 37 percent of their population. The second settler rush into the Coteau after 1900 rebuilt the region's population across the board.[29]

The second rush across the border of the agricultural transition zone began by 1905. Many abandoned homesteads and farms were available for refiling or were for sale cheaply. Some land was more accessible with new rail lines across Walworth and Edmund counties. Land rushes to the plains west of the Missouri River advertised South Dakota across the nation. For people concerned about taking up the dry, rugged lands in the west river country, the lands in the transition zone seemed a safer bet.

Charles and Carrie Moore moved their family from Illinois to Hand County in 1908. Their story exemplifies the immense work and determination it took to survive on this land through many decades of the twentieth century. Their oldest child, daughter Dolores Moore Brady, was born in Illinois in 1905. Her memoir, *South Dakota and Me* (1989), provides a wealth of detail about ambition, determination, persistence, thrift, work ways, and farm life. Her family lived through years of rainfall and good crops as well as the decade of blowing dust and hard times on their Hand County and Hyde County farms.

Charles Moore wanted a farm of his own. As a poor man without family ties or long-time community connections, he could not afford Illinois land. The traveling butcher wagon he ran failed. South Dakota appealed to him as a place men like him might have a chance. His wife, a lifelong Illinois resident, was much less enthused. She had grown up in a particularly blessed part of the Midwest, with abundant rainfall, green grasses, productive vegetable gardens, orchards, lush field crops, trees, a comfortable home, and economic stability. Charles traveled from Illinois to South Dakota to work and to look for opportunity. After several months of hard labor, he sent money for the family to join him. "It was a hot and windy day," daughter Dolores remembered. "The little grass there was burned from the heat and drought.... Mom started to cry. She was so disappointed with our new country. There were no trees and nothing but dirt and heat." Carrie Moore never really adjusted to South Dakota life. Dolores wrote that her mother complained frequently about the dirt and dust. Years later, when the family had better housing and she realized that Charles would never go back to Illinois, she became more contented. Her actions on a visit back to Illinois, however, illustrated her longing for her previous life: "Mom got out of the buggy and walked over to a peach tree.... She picked a large, well-ripened one." She told them she had never "tasted anything so good in all my life." Carrie always reminded the family that she wanted to be buried in Illinois, not in South Dakota. She was, much earlier than anyone expected (in 1934 at fifty-five years of age, after many years of illness).[30]

The first years were difficult, but daughter Dolores "never remember[ed] being hungry."[31] They rented a farm in Hand County, where they began work with five cows and a flock of chickens. They cut and sold wild hay and had income from a cream check. After two years on the place, Moore added hogs and horses and more cows. In 1911 he broke more ground, but their crops failed. Drought and hot winds destroyed the corn. "It took courage to farm in those years, since there was so little in return for one's work," Delores recalled.[32]

In 1912 the Moore family moved to another rented farm, three miles east of Polo, still in Hand County. It was on this farm that Dolores began to help at age seven. She learned to milk and "was doing my share," an important value in this family.[33] This began a partnership with her father that lasted until his death in 1941. Carrie Moore was frail and did not enjoy or have the strength for outdoor work but maintained a spotless home and enjoyed cooking. Dolores loved being outside, loved the animals, crops, and machinery of farm life. She shared her father's goals of expansion through careful planning. That summer she dragged the fields with an improvised tool and hand-pulled sunflowers that were so large and lush the cultivator could not remove them. That fall, she learned how to mow hay.

In 1915, when she was ten, their rental farm was sold, so the family had to move. The new place was twelve miles west of Polo with a larger home, unfortunately infested with bed bugs. By this time the Moores had forty cows, plus one hundred steers they pastured for others for cash. This was an excellent year to farm. Rain was plentiful, and crops were good.

Charles Moore, with his hired man, hauled his grain to Ree Heights all winter, eighteen miles from the farm. Carrie, Dolores, and her younger brother, Mike, went to town only twice a year at that time; work on the farm kept them busy. This farm, too, was sold out from under them. A land man in Highmore found them a place in Hyde County, four miles from Holabird, with a bigger, better house only six years old, an artesian well, a cistern, and 1,280 acres to accommodate their growing herd of cattle. In 1916 they moved overland twenty-seven miles to the new place. Carrie added a larger flock of chickens, feeding as many as a thousand at a time.[34]

When this farm went up for sale in 1918, the Moore family bought it rather than move again. Charles sold the biggest, best cows to make the down payment, replenishing his herd gradually at auction sales. They also raised many hogs and kept twenty small mules, some sheep, and Carrie's chickens. Winter snows and timely rains brought good crops. Charles rented more land. The family had hired men most of the time. One year they hired six extra men just to help pick corn. After that, Charles bought one of the first machine corn pickers; it didn't work very well. He also went halves with a neighbor on a threshing machine.

The family followed certain principles in their work. Everyone worked and did their share. They saved as much money as they could. They were determined to get ahead. Charles, especially, always had new projects in mind. He raised hogs because he made double the money when he fed them the grain raised on the farm, rather than selling the grain directly, for example. Dolores mentioned consulting the *Dakota Farmer* and *Successful Farming* farm journals for answers to production problems. At one point, Charles gave Dolores sixteen acres of corn land to plant and care for. She also raised her own sheep. The profits were all hers. First and foremost, the family worked to pay for the farm. Mortgage payments and taxes were first priority.[35]

Things changed for the family in 1929. Carrie was diagnosed with advanced tuberculosis. She was sent to the Hot Springs Sanitarium in the Black Hills for care. Dolores, who had married Frank Brady in 1927, moved her family back to her parents' home to farm on shares with Charles. A neighbor woman came to live with them to help in the house. The national depression began, bringing low prices and limited markets. Drought, grasshoppers, and blowing dust destroyed crops and challenged survival. "Our country was black and barren, and in the summer there was such intense heat," Dolores wrote. "What a change from our earlier years, when rain fell and our crops were so good!" She found it hard to accept. "This took patience, and a willingness to sacrifice and live on a meager income."[36] By 1932 Charles Moore was "nearly broke." He sold some cows for $6 a head and took out a feed loan to keep other stock alive. Feed quality was poor; cows and calves continued to die. Because family resources had to go toward Carrie's medical care, there was no cash to purchase hay, as some farmers did.[37]

The South Dakota Rural Credit Board was established by legislation in 1917 to provide a lender for South Dakota farmers that would presumably grant lower interest rates and less onerous terms than banks would require—the funding for the loans being raised by the sale of bonds by the state, and the loan secured by a first mortgage on the land and improvements. Unable to make the payments on their Credit Board loans in the calamitous conditions of the early years of the Depression, Charles and Carrie lost their farm in 1932. However, the Credit Board continued to rent the farm to them since the Depression had effectively erased the market for farmland. Carrie Moore died in 1934 of tuberculosis. Charles Moore remained convinced that good times would come again and planned to buy back the farm. Unfortunately, Charles died of cancer in 1941 just as the national economy was beginning to move ahead on war fears and the demand for war supplies.

Charles Moore had paid $40,000 for the farm and owed only $5,000 on it when the Credit Board foreclosed. The Bradys bought his farm for $2,000, with $500 down, which they raised by selling calves.[38] They survived the worst of the thirties by milking cows for the cream check and for their own food, and by raising chickens for their eggs and their meat. They bought turkeys, who could survive on a grasshopper diet. The birds gorged and grew fat on the grasshoppers that plagued the region. As rains returned and grasshoppers diminished, they added sheep, more cattle, and more milk cows.

Dolores missed her father for the rest of her long life. They both loved to farm and work outdoors and with animals. His will to succeed kept him going when others gave up on the country. He finished what he started. He worked to find ways around obstacles. The two of them planned together their year's work, then assessed outcomes. They observed what progressive farmers did on their farms and adopted what worked. They were proud to be progressive farmers themselves. "We missed him in so many ways after he was gone. He . . . was our leader with his will and determination to go on, never thinking of the past failures that had crept into our live[s]." Dolores Brady admired his philosophy: "If things couldn't be done this way, we would try another way and get it done."[39] It was her philosophy, too.

In 1987 the Hyde County Centennial Committee took aerial photos of the farms in the county, then compiled the history of each farm's ownership. Dolores Brady still owned that farm in 1987; no one lived there, however.[40]

The Moore/Brady farm families were the type of people for whom the Agricultural Extension Bureau agents were writing when they researched farming problems in the widely varying agricultural regions of South Dakota. They produced bulletins full of advice to help farmers stay on the land and improve their incomes. The research farm in Highmore began in 1899. South Dakota State College in Brookings housed the economists, crop specialists, rural sociologists, and agricultural extension employees who researched and wrote about all facets of South Dakota rural economies, weather and climate, crop successes and failures, best livestock, best practices in general, home production, and home life. They drew borders of climate and geography, and showed farm families how to produce within them. One of the most interesting publications appeared in 1940. An analysis of farm reports produced by 163 farmers in the north-central wheat-producing counties throughout the decade of the 1930s, the bulletin spelled out the variability of rainfall and the difficulties of farming in the agricultural transition zone, but it also offered hope.

Some farmers made money during the 1930s. They kept more cattle and sheep, and fewer hogs and poultry, which required feed beyond the local grasses the farms could provide. Their farms were bigger but had less cultivated land. They devoted most crop land to feed crops for stock. Farmers who lost money in the 1930s planted more cash crops, especially wheat, and used the summer fallow system to conserve rainfall. It was not an effective system. The authors addressed "the human factor" in the success or failure of farms. There were farmers who could "combine the productive farm enterprises to financial advantage." As a result, these families "maintained an adequate level of living" through the worst combination of natural and economic crises in living memory. This "quality of management," though "difficult to measure," included the ability to make "rapid changes to meet economic and climate variables," and it made the difference between success and failure. The conclusion: "Even during 'hard times' farms could be successfully operated in the area."[41] In succeeding decades, new crops, new tillage programs, and better machinery and technologies in general—created and applied by those who searched for new answers to old questions—made living within difficult climatic boundaries more productive. Today fields of drought-resistant sunflowers bloom on the Coteau in the summer. Cattle graze on the hills. Milo, a feed crop, flourishes. Some farm families host pheasant hunters in the fall. The Roseland farm—founded in 1886 by Gabriel Roseland, a Norwegian immigrant, and continued by six of his eight sons after his retirement—consists of eighteen thousand total acres: twelve thousand in crops and cattle, and six thousand in a pheasant and hunters' paradise, complete with hunting lodges. The agricultural transition zone is not a land of small-scale agriculture, with farmsteads on every quarter section as people once dreamed it would be. The geographic and climatic borders here are real. Adaptation, innovation, and the human factor, however, have built successful enterprises that meet and overcome the challenges of the agricultural transition zone.[42]

Notes

1   Marytn J. Bowden, "Great American Desert," in *Encyclopedia of the Great Plains*, ed. David J. Wishart, accessed January 1, 2017, http://plainshumanities.unl.edu/encyclopedia/doc/egp.ii.032.xml.

2   Donald Worster, "Report on the Lands of the Arid Region of the United States," 1878, in Wishart, *Encyclopedia of the Great Plains*, accessed January 1, 2017, http://plainshumanities.unl.edu/encyclopedia/doc/egp.wat.024.xml.

3   Mrs. B. M. Lister and Mrs. Bessie B. Lumley, *History of Sully County*, compiled in 1939 by the Sully County Old Settlers Association (Onida, SD: Onida Watchman, 1939), 133.

4   Hardy Webster Campbell at plainshumanities.unl.edu/encyclopedia/doc/egp.ag.016. Also: *Campbell's 1907 Soil Culture Manual: A Complete Guide to Scientific Agriculture as Adapted to the Semi-arid Region*, reprint (Sydney: Wentworth Press, 2016). For rain following the plow, see "Aughey Comes to Nebraska," at unlhistory.unl.edu/exhibits/show/morrill-hall/augheyhicks/aughey; "Aughey's Scandals," at unlhistory.unl.edu/exhibits/show/morrill-hall/augheyhicks/aughey-s-scandals; and "Rainfall Follows the Plow," at plainshumanities.unl.edu/encyclopedia/doc/egp.ii.049. See also Charles Dana Wilber, *The Great Valleys and Prairies of Nebraska and the Northwest* (1881). All web links accessed on January 27, 2018.

5   Catherine J. Lavender, "Farm Security Administration," in *Encyclopedia of the Great Plains*, ed. David J. Wishart (Lincoln: University of Nebraska Press, 2004): 45; "The Future of the Great Plains," Report of the Great Plains Committee (Washington, D.C., U.S. GPO, December 1936), available online at http://babel.hathitrust.org/cgi/pt?id=umn.319510015389400;view=1up;seq=1 et seq. FSA photographers were sometimes willing to alter the scene to illustrate or emphasize their interpretation of events. Arthur Rothstein, for example, moved a steer skull around to various photo locations to convey the severity of drought. John Miller and Jon Lauck discuss the problem on South Dakota Public Radio at listen.sdpb.org/post/dakota-midday-great-depression-photo-still-sparks-debate-o. Jon K. Lauck wrote about photographer Dorothea Lange and her interpretive approach in "Dorothea Lange and the Limits of the Liberal Narrative: A Review Essay," *Heritage of the Great Plains* 45, no. 1 (Summer 2012): 4–37. Web links accessed January 27, 2018.

6   M. Meyers, *Farm Performance in North Central South Dakota, 1930–1939* (Brookings: South Dakota State University Agricultural Experiment Station), Bulletin 343,

June 1940, p. 9 (hereafter referred to as "Meyers, *Farm Performance*"); pdf version of Bulletin 343 downloaded at https://openprairie.sdstate.edu/agexperimentsta_bulletins/343/ (accessed on January 31, 2018).

7   Harry Thompson, ed., *A New South Dakota History* (Sioux Falls, SD: Center for Western Studies, 2005), 20 ("Physical Environment").

8   Thompson, *New South Dakota History*, 20–21.

9   General Land Office Land Survey Field Notes in the South Dakota Digital Archive, accessed January 31, 2018, https://sddigitalarchives.contentdm.oclc.org/cdm/landingpage/collection/p15914coll1.

10   Herbert S. Schell, *History of South Dakota*, 4th ed., with new material by John E. Miller (Pierre: South Dakota Historical Society, 2004), 11.

11   Scott Heidepriem, *Bring On the Pioneers: History of Hand County* (Pierre, SD: State Publishing, 1978), 137.

12   Lister and Lumley, *History of Sully County*, 106.

13   NOAA National Center for Environmental Information, at http://www.ncdc.noaa.gov/cdo-web/search. Brad Tennant's chapter in this volume records information from Timber Lake, South Dakota, approximately fifty miles west of the Missouri River and the agricultural transition zone. A museum exhibit there displays the precipitation amounts from 1910, the founding date, and 2014. In the 104 years of records, only thirty-one years brought precipitation of twenty inches. Brad Tennant, "West of the 100th Meridian: Where the Midwest Ends and the Great Plains Begins," fn. 29, in this volume.

14   Meyers, *Farm Performance* (see note 5 above).

15   Meyers, *Farm Performance*, 11.

16   Schell, *History of South Dakota*, 161–68, 159–61. Mark Hufstetler and Michael Bedeau, "South Dakota's Railroads: An Historic Context," for South Dakota State Historic Preservation Office (July 1998; revised December 2007), at https://history.sd.gov/preservation/docs/SDRailroad.pdf. To understand the political, social, and cultural institutions and ideals settlers brought to Dakota Territory, see Jon K. Lauck, *Prairie Republic: The Political Culture of Dakota Territory, 1879–1889* (Norman: University of Oklahoma Press, 2010).

17   Captain Caleb Holt Ellis, *History of Faulk County, South Dakota, together with Biographical Sketches of Pioneers and Prominent Citizens* (Faulkton: Record Print, 1909), 24.

18   Ellis, *History of Faulk County*: quotes appear on pages 298, 344, 363, respectively.

19   Ladies Helpers Society, comp., *History of Buffalo County, 1885–1985, Gann Valley, South Dakota* (Gann Valley, SD: Ladies Helper Society, 1985), 35. This work reprints the 1924 *History* and updates it to 1985.

20   Ladies Helpers Society, *History of Buffalo County*, 41 (quotes), 33–41 (entire story).

21   Ladies Helpers Society, *History of Buffalo County*, 25.

22   Brule County Historical Society, *Brule County History* (Pukwana, SD: Brule County Historical Society, 1977), 230–31.

23   Brule County Historical Society, *Brule County History*, 230–31. Title Atlas Company, *Pictorial Atlas Brule County, South Dakota* (Minneapolis: Title Atlas, 1986): plat book farm longevity tally, "Directory by Township," pp. 1–24, after map section of plat book; Gunderson farm, p. 1.

24   Brule County Historical Society, *Brule County History*, 313. Climate data for Lancaster, Wisconsin, the Grant County seat, indicates an annual rainfall of 35.47 inches, averaged over the 1981–2010 period. Rainfall one hundred years before may have

varied a bit. See U.S. Climate Data, https://www.usclimatedata.com/climate/
lancaster/wisconsin/united-states/uswi0384.

25 Brule County Historical Society, *Brule County History*, 315 (quote), 313–15 (story).

26 Brule County Historical Society, *Brule County History*, 313–15; 1940 *Federal Census
of Population*, Matousek family, Ancestry.com; *South Dakota State Census*, 1945,
Matousek family, Ancestry.com.

27 See 75th Jubilee Book Committee, *Pioneer Footprints: Diamond Jubilee, Java, South
Dakota, 1900–1975*. (n.p., 1975), 62; 1880 *Federal Census of Population*, William and
Christine Kunz family, Ancestry.com.

28 75th Jubilee Book Committee, *Pioneer Footprints*, 62–65; 1900, 1910, 1920 *Federal
Censuses of Population*, Christine and Michael Kunz; Ancestry.com and findagrave.
com for Odessa Cemetery, Mound City, SD, Christina Kunz Boehler, 1850–1925.

29 *Census Report of South Dakota for 1895*, facsimile ed. (Ithaca: Cornell University Library,
2016); originally published in the (Redfield, SD) *Journal Observer Press*, 1895.

30 Dolores Brady, *South Dakota and Me* (Highmore, SD: Dolores Brady, 1989), 18
(quoted matter), 10–18 (story), 26 (peach story and quote), 26–27 (visits home and
contentment).

31 Brady, *South Dakota and Me*, 18.

32 Brady, *South Dakota and Me*, 24.

33 Brady, *South Dakota and Me*, 32 (quote), 32–33 (story).

34 Brady, *South Dakota and Me*, 46–116; highlights: 29, 35, 45–46 (moves to new farms);
65 (purchases farm); 32 (Brady does her share); 60 (first corn picker bought); 91
(always new projects); 93 (Carrie's thousand chickens); 103 (interest and payments
first).

35 Brady, *South Dakota and Me*, 117.

36 Brady, *South Dakota and Me*, 119 (quote), 117–20 (story).

37 Brady, *South Dakota and Me*, 121–25; 75th Jubilee Book Committee, *Pioneer Footprints*,
72; the Jacob Bieber family bought hay and shipped it in.

38 Brady, *South Dakota and Me*, 173, 139, 173–76. For more on the Rural Credit program,
see Gilbert C. Fite, "South Dakota Rural Credit System: A Venture in State
Socialism, 1917–1941," *Agricultural History* 21, no. 4 (1947): 239–49.

39 Brady, *South Dakota and Me*, 173–74.

40 Hyde County South Dakota Centennial Committee, *Staying Power* (Pierre: Hyde
County South Dakota Centennial Committee, 1989), 402, photo of Moore/Brady
farm with ownership history.

41 Meyers, *Farm Performance*, 50.

42 Faulk County Historical Society, *History of Faulk County, South Dakota, 1910–1982*
(Faulkton and Clark, South Dakota: Moritz Publishing Company, 1982), 197. Farm/
lodge website: www.r-rpheasanthunting.com (accessed January 1, 2017).

Chapter 20

WHERE THE MIDWEST ENDS AND THE GREAT PLAINS BEGINS: A SURVEY

Michael J. Mullin
Augustana University
with Matt Fox[1]

Where a region ends and another begins is often dependent on the mental image we have constructed of the area in question. Does one think of the Great Plains as dust storms, depopulation, and farm crises? As for the Midwest, do the terms "blue collar," "rust belt," and perhaps "progressive" come to mind? Perhaps the Midwest conjures up thoughts of corn and soybeans, while the Great Plains conjures up visions of cattle ranches. Often our image of an area comes from literature. Ole Rölvaag, Willa Cather, John Steinbeck, Dan O'Brien, and Ann Daum are writers who have shaped our view of the Great Plains today.[2] Midwestern writers have done the same thing—Sinclair Lewis, Studs Terkel, Tim O'Brien, Marilynne Robinson, and Patrick Carr have each given us a distinctive image of the Midwest.[3] Whatever the source of our images, where the region in question ends and another begins can be elusive.

The quest to understand regional identity is neither new nor unique to the Midwest or Great Plains. Anyone who remembers the emergence of the "New Western Historians" in the late twentieth century understands the problems confronting scholars seeking to create, perpetuate, or defend a particular regional identity. The closing decades of the century saw a vociferous debate among historians of the American West.[4] Was the West a "place" or a "process"? This debate often pitted historians of the post-

273

World War II period against the "New Western Historians," those whose graduate training took place in the 1960s and during the immediate post-civil-rights period. The academic debates of the period were spirited and sometimes personal. In 1992, in the wake of these battles and hoping to discover how the process-versus-place debate operated "in people's minds," Walter Nugent decided to survey those who had a vested interest in the topic—academics, writers, and newspaper editors.[5] His survey raised an important question: "Do frontiers end, do regions come and go, and if so how can we tell?"[6]

Nugent reported his findings in *Montana: The Magazine of Western History*.[7] His survey aimed to reconcile the views of the adherents of the "New Western History" with those of more traditional Western historians, who were often seen as followers of Frederick Jackson Turner. While the findings of Nugent's survey are not crucial to this chapter's discussion, they provide the foundation upon which this discussion rests. Could scholars living in the states most often associated with the Great Plains and Midwest agree on the boundaries for the two regions? As Walter Nugent discovered nearly a quarter-century earlier, boundaries depend on whom you ask and where the respondents are situated.[8] Still, understanding what scholars think of the boundaries of their respective region is a step toward answering the question of where the Midwest ends and the Great Plains begins.

So what is the line of demarcation between the Midwest and Great Plains? In 1946, Earle D. Ross commented on the problems confronting the historian of the Midwest. The region, he wrote, had an "indefinitiveness [*sic*] of demarcation and designation"; there was no "regional consciousness."[9] What Ross was noting, perhaps unintentionally, was the demise of the Midwest as a field of study unto itself. As one scholar recently noted of this era, the "Midwest was fast retreating to the edges of the history profession and the popular mind."[10] Whether the Midwest's demise as a recognizable region is the result of cultural elitism or historic evolution is open to debate. But the Midwest is not the only region that is blurred in the minds of most Americans, so too is the Great Plains.

In 1958 Herbert Krause asked his colleagues, "Why can't there be a center" when it came to the study of the northern plains?[11] Krause's lament came when the cultural area theory was beginning to wane for writing Great Plains and Western history. Created by anthropologists at the turn of the twentieth century, cultural area studies reached its zenith in the interwar years of the twentieth century. It gave vibrancy to the writings of what one scholar has called "the Prairie Historians."[12] But it was not just Prairie Historians who focused on regional studies. Perhaps the most important historian within the cultural area genre was Walter Prescott Webb. A Texan by birth and inclination, Webb used the cultural area model in his 1931 work *The Great Plains*. Krause, the founder of the Center for Western Studies at Augustana University, found himself situated in both the Great Plains and the West. His lament might be a recognition that writers of the "plains" were also writing "western history."

James Malin offered a partial answer to Krause and reassurance to Ross in their quests to define the regions each man loved. Malin noted that "no two criteria determine boundaries that coincide exactly."[13] Boundaries have, it seems, ragged edges. The reason for this, as another author noted, is that too many variables enter into discussions about what constitute a region. Among a myriad of possibilities are "terrain, climate, vegetation, soils, [and] agriculture."[14] A region might be a historical creation or accident. Malin also noted that regions, like humans, can undergo transformations too. Regions can morph into some new category or become attached to an already existent identifiable area. Implicitly we know this. Today's Midwest was yesterday's "West."

One reason for Krause and Ross's lament is that writing about "place" is difficult, particularly for the interior of the nation. To paraphrase Eugen Weber, regional "history is the stepchild of our profession."[15] The Midwest is the "place between the two coasts—that place not the South—that place not the West . . . and not Appalachia."[16] Both the Great Plains and Midwest define themselves by what they are not. What complicates any study of the Great Plains and Midwest is that both regions experienced the apex of their importance on the cusp of World War I. The Midwest "reached a pinnacle of self-confidence in the 1910s."[17] The Great Plains enjoyed a different kind of self-confidence at the same time. The region doubled the number of acres under cultivation.[18] These were the years when "West River" South Dakota saw one hundred thousand settlers enter the region.[19] The future looked bright for both areas.

The interwar years, however, witnessed an attack on both regions. For the Midwest, it was an intellectual attack that challenged its claim to be a region worthy of emulation. After World War I, the Midwest was seen as a "repressive and sterile backwater."[20] Led by Carl Van Doren, the "village revolt" theory of literary history influenced how outsiders, novelists, and scholars viewed the American interior. After Van Doren's essay, people thought Midwestern literature focused on small-town life and small-town problems.[21] What did these novels have to teach cosmopolitan America? If the Midwest found itself shunted aside intellectually, the Great Plains saw itself shunted aside demographically. West River South Dakota lost almost 14 percent of its total population between 1930 and 1940, and this decade was better than the 1920s had been.[22] The region's agricultural expansion created a debt crisis that resulted in financial collapse for many. The 1920s saw the beginning of demographic exodus. Farming on the plains, it seems, "became a speculative venture."[23]

But farming on the plains has always been speculative. The Populists understood this in the 1890s, and Populism might be one way to determine a region's identity, at least in a historic sense. In the 1890s, the People's Party emerged in two distinct regions, the American South and West. In the 1890s, the American West included the states currently comprising the Great Plains.[24] The focus of the Populists was reform, specifically economic and political. The candidate most responsible for undermining the Populists was an Ohioan by birth, William McKinley. President McKinley championed the gold standard and promoted overseas colonies on the grounds they "secured markets" for American producers. Republican orthodoxy also objected to government interference in the economy. Traditional Midwestern moderation trumped Western "radicalness."[25] Populism, then, is one thing that does separate the two regions.[26]

More recently, the two regions have blurred together in the minds of many. Whether intellectually isolated or financially overextended, both regions became a "place you ought to leave."[27] Telling the story of either region, then, seemed a fight against intellectual and economic trends that emanated from outside, namely the East and West Coasts. But the difficulty Krause and Ross expressed in identifying the Great Plains and Midwest came from more than just a changing American landscape. It also came from changes in the region itself. Rural exodus and the declining importance of agriculture in the nation's gross domestic product must be balanced against the economic and demographic growth of Omaha, Sioux Falls, Des Moines, and countless other cities. One must weigh the emergence of regional business successes—such as 3M, Best Buy, or Sanford Health Systems—against the declining importance of meat producers like John Morrell or Smithfield Foods. What really chafes residents of both regions are descriptions that "the vast hinterland beyond the Alleghenies" can be summarized as being "the land of the Yahoo, the John Birch Society, and the Ku Klux Klan."[28]

That the history of these regions is the ebb and flow of people and cultural importance is not new. When the French first entered the Illinois

Valley they encountered "the transition between the two major biomes of the middle of the continent, the grasslands of the West and the woodlands of the East."[29] The region had long drawn groups such as the Illinois into it and pushed others out. Though French explorers might not know who long-time residents were and who were new arrivals, they did know they had entered a new environment. As a result, the French created "a distinct geographical entity" as they made their way down the Ohio River and up the Mississippi.[30]

This geographical identity blurred the Great Plains and Middle West. Neither Jean-Baptiste Louis Franquelin's *Carte de L'Amérique Septentrionale* (1688) nor Guillaume de l'Isle's *Carte de la Louisiane et du cours du Mississipi* (1718) suggested a difference between the Great Lakes region, or what became the modern Midwest, and the lands lying farther to the west, what became the Great Plains.[31] Both maps portrayed the drainage systems of the Ohio and Missouri Rivers as containing the same geographic features. The entire center of the continent was treeless and arid. What is important about these early cartographers, and the maps they produced, is how they set the mental image of the interior grasslands as a single entity.[32] As do all maps, the works of Franquelin and de l'Isle expressed "mental concepts and images" that French explorers had encountered a "new world."[33] Still, it would take another half-century to begin separating what became the Midwest from the plains (or prairie).

The term "Great Plains" appeared on British maps in the 1770s.[34] Despite this appellation, "maps of the plains were based almost entirely on imagination and conjecture" until well into the nineteenth century.[35] Indeed, for much of the nineteenth century, Stephen Long's description of the plains as "American Desert" defined the region for most Americans.[36] It was a place to endure, to travel through. Unlike the Ohio Valley region, what became the Great Plains was not a place to put down roots.[37] It was not until the early 1930s that the term "Great Plains" truly entered the American vocabulary with some specific connotations.

In 1931 the geographer Nevin Fenneman and the historian Walter Prescott Webb spent considerable time on "'the Great Plains Province,' a physical region of great diversity, yet sufficiently distinct from surrounding areas to merit separate identification."[38] Shortly thereafter the dust storms associated with the "Dirty Thirties" appeared. The Great Plains had emerged as distinct from the Midwest, and John Steinbeck's *The Grapes of Wrath* created its identity.[39] But what is the Great Plains' eastern border? Just how different is it, culturally, politically, socially, from the Midwest?

Do the distinctions matter? Historically, the differences between regions, or lack thereof, depended on what one used as the criteria for each region.

Complicating the Great Plains-Midwest division is the term "Middle West." This term was an effort to take Frederick Jackson Turner's idea of the frontier as a process and combine it with the cultural trappings of a particular place. As Michael Steiner once noted, "Turner had two sweeping, interrelated ideas—the frontier and the section."[40] He was interested in how communities evolved over time. This was, after all, what Turner spent a majority of his academic career doing. But the term also allowed scholars to overcome the earlier work of John Wesley Powell and Walter Prescott Webb. Both men used the criteria of twenty inches of rainfall as the boundary between the West and the Great Plains.[41] By incorporating cultural folkways and settlement patterns into the equation, the Great Plains and Midwest might be studied as entities unto themselves.

Unfortunately, the term "Middle West" of Turner's world morphed into something else in the post-World War II period. The new Middle West placed the Midwest and Great Plains (excluding Oklahoma and Texas) into a single region.[42] Geographers led this new Middle West bandwagon, and they did wonderful work. John C. Hudson and James R. Shortridge applied important theoretical frameworks for settlement patterns and cultural values and beliefs in their studies.[43] Their work forced scholars to rethink their previous assumptions about what constituted the Great Plains and Midwest. Historians such as Frederick C. Luebke also contributed to our understanding of the Middle West.[44]

Still, the researchers admitted that the Middle West's "boundaries have always been fuzzy." Its residents, however, had come to assume that the region had particular traits. For example, the "region was rural" and comprised of small towns. This image conjured up a particular set of values: honest, hard-working, and moral. The Middle West was "located between the underdeveloped West and the urbanized East," and it combined the best characteristics of Northern and Southern society. The region was egalitarian and progressive.[45] What is important here is that these images take their meaning from referencing the other areas of the country: South, North, and West. They reference what the region is not. In this case the Midwest is neither urban nor stratified.

One might ask, when it comes to the Midwest and Great Plains, do they need to be separate regions? If so, why? After all, the founders of Midwestern history were known as "prairie historians" originally, and they assumed "the history of the Middle West" warranted its own journal.[46] The recent resurgence in Midwestern studies has produced a call for reclaiming the Midwest as an important region in its own right.[47] But does this new Midwest also include the Great Plains? It seems that the Great Plains can be included in two distinct regions—the Midwest and the West. Kansas and South Dakota politicians appear in studies of "Western Populism," but nowhere is the overlap more obvious than in some recent "regional" studies focusing on place.[48]

Recent studies focused on the West and the Great Plains specifically have ascribed characteristics and geographic boundaries that overlap. Robert Dorman's *Hell of a Vision: Regionalism and the Modern American West* fits into the Prairie Historians' focus on regional identity, and the issues he identifies as "western" are the same that R. Douglas Hurt identifies for the Great Plains in his *The Big Empty: The Great Plains in the Twentieth Century*.[49] Both books depend on John Wesley Powell's 1891 map to define their areas of focus; both books have nearly identical eastern boundary edges.[50] This type of overlap is what some Midwestern scholars fear. They are afraid the Midwest is going to remain a neglected area of scholarly inquiry or, worse, disappear as a recognizable region.[51]

Any study of American regionalism begins with Frederick Jackson Turner, whose essays on sectionalism "have been probably no less influential than the frontier thesis."[52] Even his posthumously published textbook used regions to tell the history of America. Turner was reacting to the emergence of "nationalizing movement[s]." He worried that an emerging national hegemony meant "sectionalism is passing away."[53] Regional studies, therefore, from their inception as an academic enterprise, were an effort to combat the homogenizing effect "of mass culture and . . . American life."[54] These stories were not intended to denigrate the national narrative; instead, scholars hoped to give the story a nuance and depth that the macro-level narrative missed. Unfortunately, the Midwest as a region "fell off the map" when it came to "our general modes of thought, both academic and popular" in the twentieth century.[55]

If Turner gave the Midwest region importance at the national level, Walter Prescott Webb did something similar for the Great Plains. Though considered a "Western" historian, Webb was a native of the Great Plains.[56] His 1931 work, *The Great Plains*, gave the American interior its own story. Rejecting the boundaries of geographers and historians, Webb claimed the Great Plains had "three distinguishing characteristics." These were (1) "a comparatively level surface of great extent," (2) a treeless expanse, and (3) "where rainfall is insufficient for the ordinary intensive agriculture common to lands of a humid climate."[57] While admitting that these three defining characteristics were neither "coextensive [n]or conterminal" for the entire plains region, Webb argued that "the High Plains constitute the heart of what might be called the Great Plains."[58] In making this argument, Webb borrowed the anthropologist Clark Wissler's cultural area theory, though he shifted the region of importance westward from Wissler.[59]

But Webb was doing something more. He was cementing John Wesley Powell's argument about the Great Plains into the academic canon. Powell had argued that the agricultural frontier had reached its farthest limit by 1878, the eve of the great northern plains land rush. Without irrigation, Powell argued, farming would be impossible.[60] The new homestead, Powell suggested, needed to be 2,560 acres in size. Politicians in Washington, D.C., and across the plains region challenged Powell's research.[61] What Powell, Webb, and others have noted is that those living on the Great Plains have both prospered and failed as a result of either too much or too little water.[62] As Webb wrote in *The Great Frontier*, "Their methods of agriculture were those of the humid country and brought only disaster to those who followed them on the arid land." For Webb, then, the Great Plains was a place where "old ideas and institutions began to fail."[63] This was not the story of the Midwest, at the time.

For Webb, the Great Plains comprised the vast grasslands of the North American continent. Whether tallgrass or shortgrass prairie, both regions fall into the region ecologists call "plains."[64] These grasslands forced settlers to adapt to new farming techniques; unlike in the Midwest, farmers could not count on adequate rainfall to nourish their crops. Webb used aridity, then, to differentiate the "Plains proper" from the wetter East. Still he acknowledged that his "Plains proper" was "flanked on either side by marginal regions tied closely to the Plains environment."[65] Where these marginal regions ended, Webb did not say.

Webb also argued that the plains forced settlers to create new institutions to help them survive. Some of these institutions are famous (the Texas Rangers, for example); other institutions, such as water districts, were useful. Whether famous or useful, the Great Plains forced society itself to change. This differentiated the Great Plains from the Midwest. Innovation, not replication, separated the two regions.

The late twentieth and early twenty-first centuries saw another reason for separating the two regions: politics. In today's cultural wars, many people identify as "Midwesterner" or "plainsman" because they believe the region offers a particular shorthand for a set of values that sets them apart from the "left coast" or "effete east." In this new setting, geography alone will not answer the question of where one region ends and another begins; the reason for this is that the historic division between farming and ranching is disappearing. Historically, ranching defined the western plains, especially where farming required irrigation. Today, however, technology and government policy are changing the equation. From a technology standpoint, genetically modified organisms (GMOs) have allowed corn producers to extend farther west and north than previously possible. Governmental policy has helped in this push. Farmers can receive insurance for their crops, but ranchers cannot get coverage for their animals. As a result, places that were once the home of cattle operations are now generating corn and soybeans. The result is a blurring of previous divisions between the Midwest and Great Plains.

Reference materials also provide little help in separating the Midwest and Great Plains. For example, *The American Midwest: An Interpretive Encyclopedia* included the states of Kansas, Nebraska, North Dakota, and South Dakota in its twelve Midwestern states. These same states had already appeared in *The New Encyclopedia of the American West*.[66] Meanwhile, the *Atlas of the Great Plains* included the same states in its discussion of the region. No wonder there is confusion about the borders of the Midwest and Great Plains. What this confusion points to, however, is that borders are fluid and that many of the states comprising the two regions might fit into other regions too. This is why the survey conducted for this study asked respondents what other regions their area fit into.

That the borders of a region were murky did not come as a surprise.[67] Previous surveys of the two regions, all intended to discover what particular groups thought—students, professionals, and the lay public—found the same type of confusion. In one survey, fewer than half of the respondents placed Chicago in the Midwest. Respondents, it seemed, had shifted the Midwest westward.[68] Such surveys and developments tell us that defining a region is both subjective and prone to change. Perhaps environmental factors are the key to unlocking where the Midwest ends and the Great Plains begins?

Environmental factors, while useful, are also problematic. Much of the shortgrass prairie included in studies of the Great Plains often finds itself included in scholarship on the American West. With annual rainfall varying so significantly within the Great Plains, using one environmental criterion—whether it is grass type, rainfall, river drainage, or topography—can be problematic. The same problem occurs when one looks at average temperature. Still, some of the respondents to this survey used environmental factors in their determination of "region."

This blurring of borders has not prevented some scholars from studying the boundaries of the Great Plains and Midwest. Scholars such as

James Shortridge and Frederick Luebke focused on both the cultural and the physical characteristics of the Great Plains and, to a lesser degree, the Midwest. The problem they encountered was this: the "more one thinks about the Middle West, the more muddled the regional identity becomes."[69] Unlike other parts of the country, the Middle West lacks "a historical core." Its settlers came from all three Eastern cultures—Yankee, Middle Atlantic, and Southern—as well as parts of Europe.[70] Its agricultural foundations were not initially a monoculture like the South's cotton. Instead, corn, wheat, dairy production, and ranching existed side by side. The region could be understood only "in relation to other parts of the country."[71] Because of its mixed cultural and agricultural roots, the boundaries of the Great Plains, and therefore the Midwest, are fluid.

So why do people care about whether they are living in the Midwest or the Great Plains? One reason is that the stereotypes of the region give residents a sense of importance. Americans view the Midwest and Great Plains as places where inhabitants are "hard working, thrifty, [and] devoted to family values."[72] These are values to rally behind, although these are values most other regions would claim as their own too. But there is another reason to consider location: Americans' "enduring attachment to pastoral ideals."[73] This longing for what was, may be most important for understanding the two regions.

In part, the book in which this chapter resides is an attempt to separate the Middle West into two distinct regions again. The question is whether that is possible. After all, when the definitive *Atlas of the Great Plains* appeared, the editors acknowledged that no "all-purpose definition of the Great Plains" was "universally accepted."[74] At least one historian of the Midwest had said the same thing for his region years earlier.[75] Still, this author was undaunted. He decided to modify Walter Nugent's 1992 survey of Western historians and survey academics across three disciplines—history, English, and geography—to discover if they believed they could identify what separates the Midwest from the Great Plains. The author sent the survey to scholars in eleven states, most of whom found themselves located in the nebulous "Middle West." The goal of the survey was to discover if academics could tell where one region ends and another begins. Are the two regions culturally similar, or do they possess different characteristics? Does something more than geography separate the Midwest from the Great Plains?

Knowing the boundaries of either the Great Plains or Midwest is important, and not just for academics. The late twentieth century saw a number of studies appear that argued that "if a place lacks meaning to its inhabitants, it hardly can be said to exist culturally."[76] This is an important observation. At a time when the trends in restaurants, hotels, and shopping outlets tend toward national brands, a reminder that there are certain, if subtle, differences between locations is important. To quote Dorothy, they remind us that there is "no place like home." Studies focused in a particular region "define the tissue and memory of endangered local communities."[77] Whether through literature or academic studies, residents of the two regions have a "shared, spontaneous image of the region they live in," what geographers call "a vernacular region."[78] Such studies are important at least in part because they allow scholars to "apprehend the major social and geographical" realities underway in the nation.[79]

This is what some believe has happened to the Midwest as a region. Jon K. Lauck, for example, argued the Midwest "had to contend with the outright hostility of some writers and cultural critics" and what was necessary was an effort to "draw attention to the history of the Midwest."[80] But more than that, this history must "be read as part of world history."[81] This history, however, needs to tell a different tale than that of the Great Plains. In part this is because the plains emerged on the American consciousness much later. Whereas the story of the Great Plains is the history of boom and bust, the history of the Midwest is one of greatness: The [Midwest] "played a central role in American development by helping spark the American Revolution, stabilizing the young American republic, making it economically strong, giving it an agricultural heartland, and helping the North win the Civil War."[82]

History, then, might be an important line of demarcation between the Great Plains and Midwest. Certainly the economic orientations of the two regions differed. Whereas the Ohio River directed the Midwest's agricultural produce downstream, the Erie Canal, and then the railroads, oriented the Midwest toward the Atlantic Seaboard.[83] This was not the case for the northern plains. Economically, the northern plains oriented in a north-south direction. The Mandan and Hidatsa villages were tied in a vast trade network that stretched from the shores of Hudson's Bay to the Caddo villages in southern Texas.[84]

It might seem obvious that the Great Plains and Midwest are distinct regions, but what are the things that separate them? How do academic understandings of the regions differ from the average undergraduate's vision? In his article "The Vernacular Middle West," James Shortridge pointed out "that regional self-awareness should be a major factor in defining culture areas."[85] Moreover, undergraduates surveyed in Shortridge's study defined the Middle West very differently than academics did. Chicago, for example, fell outside the students' perception of the Middle West, and more than 70 percent of the respondents did not even have Illinois in the region. For American undergraduates, the Middle West consisted of portions of Iowa, South Dakota, Nebraska, Kansas, Oklahoma, and Missouri.[86]

The term "Middle West," then, is not synonymous with "Midwest." It first emerged in 1827, in reference to Tennessee. It then disappeared for a half-century, reappearing as "a product of post-Civil War expansion."[87] This time "Middle West" referenced western Kansas and Nebraska. Proponents of the term hoped to separate those two states from both the more settled (and more Mexican-influenced) Texas, the Indian Territory, and what was then called the Northwest: the Dakotas and Minnesota.[88] Eventually the appellation of "Middle West" extended eastward "to the older Northwest Territory."[89] So what does all of this mean for today's understanding of these regions? It means confusion. Let us look at just a few of the recent maps that emerged out of earlier surveys trying to identify the Midwest or Great Plains.

The first survey to explore the location of the Middle West, at least as it relates to this study, is one produced by 1,933 undergraduate students. It was taken over a few years in the early 1980s and involved students from thirty-two different states. Using the survey results, James Shortridge developed a composite map showing the states that constitute the Middle West by percentage of respondents:

70 percent included Iowa, Nebraska, Kansas, and northeastern Missouri;

50 percent included the same areas but added southern Minnesota, South Dakota, all of Missouri, northwestern Arkansas, and most of Oklahoma;

30 percent extended the Middle West to include North Dakota, all of Minnesota, Wisconsin, Illinois, western half of Indiana, Colorado, and Wyoming;

10 percent added in Michigan, Ohio, western Kentucky, all of Arkansas, Texas, New Mexico, northeastern Arizona, Utah, southeastern Idaho, and Montana.[90]

Shortridge explained that these students associated the Middle West with pastoral images. As a result, they pushed the region westward, onto the Great Plains. One reason for this is that students maintain a "persistent, universal, and overwhelmingly dominant image of the Middle West as rural America."[91] It is possible that these students represent an effort to evoke "a lost past." In doing so, they are longing for the "organic unity of simpler societies in the past" as against the "modern fragmentation" of urban society.[92] This might explain why the students ignored the "urban and industrial strength" of the Middle West.[93]

This pastoral theme is important. For one thing it "links nineteenth-century agrarian nostalgia" with "the vanishing countryside."[94] Perhaps students were acknowledging the changes occurring within their communities, changes they were just coming to terms with. Even if these students did return home, it would be different. But this theme of pastoralism defining the Midwest has some problems. For example, it excludes the people of the Great Lakes states from the Midwest: Michigan, Wisconsin, and perhaps Minnesota. For the people of these states, industrialization, mining, and timber production keep them from being "pastoral" as the students envision the term.[95] At the same time, "pastoral" is one of the images that those seeking to resurrect Midwestern history or support traditional values hold especially important. The yeoman farmer ideal—independent, frugal, and culturally traditional—stands against the liberal bias of the nation's urban areas. Whatever their reasons for drawing the Middle West as they did, what needs to be recognized is that the students have excluded states that are often assumed to be in the Midwest (Ohio and Wisconsin, for example).[96] What is also striking is how far westward the "Middle West" moved, especially when compared to Joseph Brownell's *Cultural Middle West* map of 1958.[97] The student responses do, however, explain how Joel Garreau could argue that "there is no such thing as the 'Midwest.'"[98] While most writers will not go as far as Garreau, there is little debate that the Midwest began to disappear as a distinct entity in the early 1980s. Dividing the Great Plains from the Midwest is more complicated than it appears.[99]

So if students associate the Middle West with the Great Plains, and not the Midwest, what do professional geographers do with the two regions? The *Encyclopedia of the Great Plains* offers the following composite map based on fifty different maps gathered by Sonja Rossum and Stephen Lavin, showing the range of boundaries for this region:

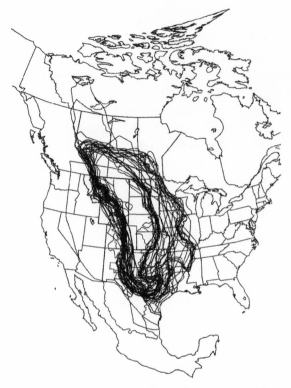

Fifty published versions of the Great Plains regional boundary. *Reproduced from the* Encyclopedia of the Great Plains, *edited by David J. Wishart by permission of the University of Nebraska Press. Copyright 2004 by the Center for Great Plains Studies.*

This map looks much more traditional than that produced by American undergraduates.[100] It clearly delineates the Great Plains from the Midwest. It also suggests that there is a consensus about where the Great Plains is located. This map also mirrors the drawing of the Great Plains that scholars did for this survey. When Walter Nugent did his survey, he found that historical imagination played an important role in people's perception of the American West.[101] That is not the case here. For the Great Plains and Midwest, historical developments and ecological realities shape the perception of where one is located.

When it comes to the Great Plains, one other problem emerged: it is not a single ecological unit. The plains is often divided into three distinct regions: northern, central, and southern. These divisions are based on history, topography, and ecology. The southern plains, for example, had slavery; the central and northern plains did not. Topographically, the western portion of the plains has a high level of relief compared to the rest of the region, with the Black Hills showing "the highest level of relief in the entire Plains region."[102] Ecologically, the Great Plains holds at least five major provinces, from forest-steppe to semi-desert.[103] Finally, there is the change from short- to long-stem grasses as one moves from east to west. Despite these ecological challenges, the Great Plains implied a specific location on the map. This is the legacy of Walter Prescott Webb's *The Great Plains*. As most people know, Webb argued that aridity was the defining characteristic of the Great Plains. The lack of rain required settlers to create new models for farming and even governance systems. This aridity helped explain the transition from tallgrass to shortgrass prairie. Webb's analysis was challenged from the very beginning by writers such as James Malin. Still, Webb gave the boundaries of the Great Plains some definition.

Before exploring the results of this survey, it is worthwhile to see where other examinations about "borders" placed the Midwest, Great Plains, and Middle West. Two particular "boundaries" will illustrate the fluid nature of the border between the Great Plains and Midwest. The regions' fluid boundaries are identified in Stephen J. Lavin et al.'s *Atlas of the Great Plains* and Richard Sisson et al.'s *The American Midwest: An Interpretive Encyclopedia*. Lavin et al. build upon the work of David Wishart's *Encyclopedia of the Great Plains* from a decade earlier. Wishart outlined the Great Plains as a region defined by its "climate, specifically climatic variation." Two other criteria defining the Great Plains were "the transitional character of the physical environment" and its "sheer distance."[104] What is important is that Wishart talked about the human landscape only after talking about the physical characteristics of the Great Plains. This does not mean humans are not important to the story of the Great Plains; the *Encyclopedia* makes it clear they are. But the decision to lead with physical geographic parameters for the region stands in stark contrast to the Midwest.

The American Midwest: An Interpretive Encyclopedia appeared shortly after Wishart's work. It begins very differently—by describing the region's people. Midwesterners are "thought of as hard-working, thrifty, devoted to family values, strong in character, comfortable with normalcy, rather sedate, and cautious about change."[105] At the same time, its residents "cannot always agree on where the region begins and ends."[106] States in *The American Midwest* "actually include parts of other regions, such as the Great Plains, within their boundaries."[107] In his introduction to the section "Images of the Midwest," James Shortridge notes that regional imagery is "necessarily idiosyncratic" and that "the Midwest is doubly difficult in this regard" because "the real estate said to be midwestern have varied considerably over the last century and a quarter."[108] In other words, the Midwest as a defined landmass, or cultural setting, is historically fluid.[109]

If encyclopedias are not a mechanism for defining the borders of the Midwest and Great Plains, perhaps literature is. Alas, the answer is no. James Fenimore Cooper was the first American writer to make the land beyond the Alleghenies subject to inquiry.[110] But his Leatherstocking series begins in upstate New York; still, the novels created "the definitive epic of the American West."[111] It is little wonder, then, that Cooper is mentioned in anthologies of Western writers.[112] Cooper is not the only author to have this experience. So too did Laura Ingalls Wilder. Wilder is another writer who blurs the boundaries of Great Plains and the West. She never lived west of the Missouri River, which is one reason why one forthcoming article on Wilder analyzes her "as a Midwestern Pioneer Girl."[113] In the essay, the author attempts to put Wilder alongside "other important Midwesterners," including Harvey Dunn and Willa Cather.[114] Fred Erisman, however, puts Wilder in the West.[115] Some of this confusion is understandable. Wilder places her stories in "the West," though they are situated on the Great Plains.[116] In this sense, she and Cather fall into the same genre. Their focus is on community and rural values, the theme of Midwestern literature.[117] We ought not be surprised, then, that *The American Midwest Encyclopedia* and *The Encyclopedia of the Great Plains* claim both Willa Cather and Ole Rölvaag as authors for their respective regions.[118] That both regions include the authors speaks highly of the artists' importance, but it also raises questions about a region's unique literary development. Both encyclopedias also make claims for understanding the regions' ethnic diversity.[119]

Recent scholarly studies do not help clarify the difference between the Midwest and Great Plains. John E. Miller's *Small-Town Dreams* can serve as an example here. Subtitled *Stories of Midwestern Boys Who Shaped America*, Miller's book focuses on seventeen important boys who grew up in the Midwest, ranging from Oscar Micheaux to Ronald Reagan. Still, what one notices is that these figures come from all over the Middle West. Sam Walton was born in Oklahoma; John Wooden was born in Indiana; Lawrence Welk hailed from North Dakota; while George Washington Carver began life as a slave in Missouri. Each of these men certainly influenced American life from art to politics to economics.[120] However, their placement in a single book on the "Midwest" suggests the region is expanding in size. Miller's work suggests that neither region has defined borders or a specific set of characteristics.

Fluidity of boundaries is not unique to the Great Plains or Midwest. Historians of the American West faced a similar problem in the early 1990s. In 1992, Walter Nugent asked his survey recipients, "Where are the boundaries for the American West?"[121] Like Ross and Krause, Nugent wanted to pigeonhole a region geographically. For the Dakotans who answered Nugent's questionnaire, the answer was "the 100th meridian."[122] However, respondents from surrounding states disagreed; they pushed the West farther east, most accepting the Missouri River as the start of the West, while some pushed the eastern edge of the "West" to the Mississippi River. This corresponded nicely with the responses of the Western Writers of America, whose members (65 percent) identified the same boundary for the West. Newspaper editors, on the other hand, did not think the West began until one got to the eastern slope of the Rocky Mountains. What is interesting about all the responses is that very few identified "the West" other than in geographical terms.[123] What all of this means is that surveys may or may not bring clarity to a particular boundary issue. What surveys can do is give one an impression of the mental map people have about the particular region in question.

Who Was Surveyed and Why

When Walter Nugent sent out his survey, he sent it to three distinct groups—writers, newspaper editors, and members of the Western History Association. For his survey, John Shortridge surveyed undergraduate students residing in the Middle West. This survey took a different approach. In part, the approach taken resulted from a lack of response on the part of Midwestern agencies contacted. They did not want their members surveyed. As a result, this survey wondered if scholars working in other fields (geography, history, and English), but often centering their work in the Midwest or Great Plains, might have different views of what constituted the regions in question.

While polling only academics might seem limiting, the question of where the Midwest ends and the Great Plains begins is one the general public really does not contemplate. They know where they live. Moreover, it is institutions of higher learning that offer students a chance to see how their lived experience fits into a larger narrative. This is done through courses and, sometimes, programs. Augustana University, for example, offers a Northern Plains Studies program for its students, and many of its honors courses focus specifically on the region. Other schools offer similar experiences to their students.

There is, however, another reason for polling the region's academics. They are more likely than other citizens to think about the region they live in as something worth considering.

Another advantage of surveying academics was to see if those teaching at smaller institutions differ from their colleagues in larger institutions in their thoughts about the region. While scholars at R-1 (research) institutions have the advantage of specialization when it comes to teaching and scholarship, scholars at smaller schools often teach a myriad of topics, giving them opportunities to explore and research topics that would not be possible at the R-1 level. Joseph Amato's *Rethinking Home: A Case for Writing Local History* is an example of this type of experience.[124]

Rather than send an identical survey to scholars in both the Midwest and the Great Plains, the author composed two versions of the survey. The first sets of questions were identical. They asked for an email address (to prevent more than one submission); if the institution offered graduate degrees and, if so, in what field(s); where the respondent's institution was located; and what academic discipline the respondent worked in. The goal here was to see if different disciplines viewed the regions differently. Do scholars in English understand their region differently from, say, historians or geographers?

Before sending the survey, an important question needed to be answered: What were the states that comprised the Midwest and those that made up the Great Plains? For this survey, the Midwest included the states of Iowa, Indiana, Illinois, Minnesota, Missouri, Ohio, and Wisconsin. The Great Plains states were Kansas, Nebraska, North Dakota, and South Dakota. Oklahoma and Texas were specifically excluded because so many works divide the southern plains experience from that of the northern plains.

The Survey Questions

The survey consisted of fourteen questions and a map opportunity. The opening questions were straightforward. Questions 1 through 5 tried to identify both the location and the type of institution where a respondent worked. For example, did the individual's institution offer graduate degrees? The idea of these questions was twofold. First, they wanted to identify if faculty working with graduate students thought of the region(s) differently from those whose schools did not have graduate programs. One hypothesis was that that faculty directing graduate students might think about regional identity differently than faculty who only teach undergraduates. Directors of graduate theses might think about regional identity in a way that undergraduate instructors do not. Second, one wondered if the field one worked in led to a different set of definitions for what constituted the Midwest or Great Plains.

The most important questions and the ones most reminiscent of Walter Nugent's earlier survey came toward the end. These questions were open ended. They asked respondents to identify the traits that defined their region or when they had left either the Midwest or the Great Plains. In his 1992 survey, Walter Nugent asked his respondents for the boundaries of the West. This new survey asked its respondents for the boundaries of either the Midwest or the Great Plains. The goal of the question was to see if scholars agreed on what the boundaries of the Great Plains and Midwest were.

The Survey Itself

The following questions comprised the survey:

Survey of Great Plains Scholars

1. Email address

2. Does your institution offer graduate degrees?
   ___ Yes
   ___ No

3. If you answered yes to graduate degrees, which degrees?
   ___ M.A.
   ___ M.A. and Ph.D.

4. In which state is your institution located?

5. Which discipline do you work in?
   ___ English
   ___ Geography
   ___ History
   ___ Other
   If other, what discipline? _____

6. Which of these organizations do you belong to?
   a. Midwestern History Association ___
   b. Midwest Writers Guild ___
   c. Midwestern Advertising Association ___
   d. Western History Association ___
   e. State Society ___
   f. If you do belong to a state society (South Dakota Historical

Society, for example), what is its name? _____
g. Add an option _____

7. What other organizations do you belong to?

8. How would you describe the boundaries of the Great Plains (on the east, west, north, and south)?
Or.
How would you describe the boundaries of the Midwest (on the east, west, north, and south)?

9. What characteristics would you ascribe to the Great Plains in general?
Or.
What characteristics set apart the Midwest, as you have defined it, from other regions of the country?

10. What characteristics set the Great Plains apart from the rest of the nation, as you have defined it?
Or:
What characteristics set the Midwest apart from the rest of the nation, as you have defined it?

11. How do you know when you have left the Great Plains?
Or:
How do you know when you have left the Midwest?

12. Can (has) your region been attached to another region? If so, when and why?

13. Do you differentiate between the Midwest and the Great Plains?

14. If the Great Plains are different from the Midwest, what criteria do you use?

15. Please draw your boundaries for the Great Plains.[125]

One notices that the first five questions are factual and designed to categorize the respondents, by type of institution, locale, and discipline.

Questions 1 through 5 dealt with email address, home institution, the institution's location, academic discipline, and whether the institution offered graduate degrees.

Thirty-one percent of the respondents (twenty-seven out of eighty-seven) worked at institutions that offered graduate degrees in the respondents' chosen fields. Eleven respondents worked in programs that offered doctorates, while another eighteen had master's programs.

Question 6 and 7 asked respondents which guilds or associations they belonged to.

Question 6 listed some specific organizations that the survey writer assumed participants might belong to. At the beginning of this survey, both the Midwest Writers Guild and the Midwestern Advertising Association were contacted about surveying their members to help with the survey. The Midwestern Advertising Association responded by saying they would send the request upward for discussion. The author never heard back. The Midwest Writers Guild responded by saying they did not want their membership list made available to potential abuses, such as advertising and other surveys.

Question 7 then provided a space for the respondent to write in other organizations that he/she belonged to. Two people belonged to the Midwestern History Association (one from Ohio and the other from South Dakota). Interestingly, these same two respondents belonged to the Western History Association; only one other respondent belonged to the WHA. No one belonged to the Midwest Writers Guild.

Question 8 asked the respondent to describe the boundaries in the four cardinal directions for either the Midwest or the Great Plains.

If one did not know that the boundaries of the two regions had become convoluted, then the responses to this question certainly made one aware. Twenty-eight of the fifty-nine Midwestern respondents (47.5 percent) extended the Midwest into the Dakotas and beyond. Most of those who pushed the western boundaries of the Midwest into the Dakotas used the Missouri River as the western border of the Midwest, although some suggested the western border went as far as Wyoming and the front-range of Colorado. For those who deemed Nebraska and Kansas as Midwestern, the western border of the region depended on rainfall. These respondents often used the 98th or 100th meridian as their cutoff line (two respondents specifically mentioned these meridians; another couple of answers were less precise— "when rain is less than 20 inches").

Respondents from the Great Plains region were more divided on where the eastern boundary of the Great Plains was. Uncertainty on the eastern border is not surprising. Ian Frazier noted how "of all the Great

Plains boundaries, the eastern one is the hardest to fix."[126] Some respondents followed political rather than geographic contours.

One interesting aspect to this question was how geographers answered it. Whereas historians and English faculty often relied on political and cultural boundaries, geographers did not. One respondent noted that the Midwest was "a giant watershed, but restricted to that part of the watershed where rain fed agriculture is possible." It would seem that here the Midwest is defined by the Ohio River drainage system, beginning in western Pennsylvania. Another defined the Midwest as containing "flat land containing rolling hills." This same person identified a region where grass and grain could be raised. As a generalization, geographers were more apt to describe the Midwest as flat, covered in either short- or long-stem grasses, and generally treeless. They also often separated the urban from rural Midwest.

One working definition of the Midwest for scholars in all three disciplines was historical in nature. The Midwest never had slavery; neither Missouri nor Kentucky found its way into the geographers' Midwest.[127] Missouri was, for the respondents, the most difficult state. In the end, most people left it off their map of the Midwest. As one respondent noted, "Parts of Missouri are exceptionally problematic." The map this respondent drew ultimately included the top third of Missouri in his/her boundaries of the Midwest. Interestingly, this region remained the most pro-Union part of Missouri during the Civil War. In defining the Midwest in this manner, the respondents clearly saw the Midwest become a region in the nineteenth century, for slaves comprised a significant portion of the region's population in the eighteenth century, as Robert Michael Morrissey's *Empire by Collaboration: Indians, Colonists, and Governments in Colonial Illinois Country* made clear.[128]

In addition to defining the Midwest by its physical characteristics, some geographers referenced the importance of Chicago to the region's economic development. Geographers are not the only ones to make this connection; historian William Cronon's *Nature's Metropolis: Chicago and the Great West* made the same connection.[129] Still, in making this connection, geographers are paying closer attention to economic influences than history and English faculty.

Question 9 asks: What characteristics set apart the Midwest, as you have defined it, from other regions of the country?

This question saw the greatest difference between Midwestern and Great Plains respondents. For Great Plains residents, what set the region apart was the land itself. Residents of the Great Plains focused almost exclusively on the terrain and/or topography of the region. Only one respondent from the region mentioned people specifically; a handful of respondents mentioned farming and ranching in their responses. Still, even with these respondents, terrain mattered the most. The most typical response concerned the region's "flat land," grasslands, and open spaces. These responses are consistent with earlier surveys. Conversely, those from the Midwest often defined their region in opposition to other areas. Typical responses include: "The Midwest for me is defined against the West"; "non-slave state"; or "former Yankee territory."

Questions 10 and 11 asked for some general characteristics for either the Midwest or the Great Plains, and how the respondent saw his/her region as different from the other.

One response that was difficult to gauge, but certainly made one smile, was "increasing number of Broncos hats and shirts."

Question 12 asked if the region in question had been attached to another region in the past.

This question assumed that both regions had, at one time, been associated with the American West. Most respondents did not answer this question. This might be because the respondent was not a scholar of the Great Plains or Midwest. As such, the respondent would not know. What was interesting, however, is that respondents from the Great Plains answered far more often than those from the Midwest: seventeen of the twenty-three respondents said the Great Plains had been attached to another region in the past.

What was interesting about the responses was that only four of those seventeen respondents attached the Great Plains to the American West. However, even these four respondents also mentioned the Great Plains being part of the Midwest, usually by "ignorant easterners who lump us with the Midwest." This association with the Midwest did bring some grumbling among the seventeen who listed an attachment to other areas. "We are often called the Midwest, which we are not," was typical. The reason for their irritability, the respondents pointed out, is how fauna and flora differed between the two regions or how the term "Midwest" is shorthand for "flyover country between the coasts."

Just over 37 percent (twenty-two of fifty-nine) of the Midwestern respondents said their region had never been attached to another area of the country before. Five respondents mentioned the Midwest as being attached to the West in the past. Most respondents, however, associated the Midwest with the Great Plains (eight); other regions mentioned were "border South" (four), West (five), and Great Lakes (three). For Midwesterners, what mattered in this answer was their location. The farther east one's location was, the less likely one was to say the West or Great Plains. Ohio respondents had the most to say about attachments to other regions. Some looked to the Atlantic Seaboard, while others attached it to the Great Lakes.

Questions 13 asked respondents to determine, via a yes/ no answer, whether they differentiated the Great Plains and Midwest as two distinct regions. If respondents did differentiate between the two regions, question 14 asked them what criteria they used.

This question revealed the lasting legacy of Prescott Webb and others, since the 100th meridian played a role in the answers provided. Every geographer responding differentiated the two regions (nine). Eighty-seven percent of the historians responding also distinguished between the two regions (thirty-four of thirty-nine). One historian said he/she differentiated between the two regions but then immediately wrote, "The Great Plains are part of the Midwest." This respondent later noted that the Midwest incorporated "all of the land east of the Missouri River to the Appalachian Mountains." This definition would place eastern North and South Dakota into the Midwest, but not Nebraska or Kansas, or the western Dakotas. In addition, 63 percent of the English department respondents differentiated the two regions (nineteen of thirty), while 60 percent of the "others" did so (three of five). This tells us that scholars do differentiate the two regions, but do they do so for the same reasons?

For many respondents, the division between tallgrass and shortgrass prairie differentiated the two regions. At least one geographer divided the prairie from the plains by shortgrass, medium-grass, and tallgrass divisions. More than half of the twenty-three respondents from the Great Plains mentioned grasslands as a means of differentiating the Great Plains from the Midwest. In addition, most Great Plains respondents mentioned aridity, or a variant thereof, in their answers. Those in the Midwest talked about the difference between farming and ranching. One respondent mentioned cowboy boots for the Great Plains, another indication of how the Great Plains often morphs into the American West. For historians, trees, or lack thereof, and topography rather than fauna played a role in what determined where one was. Those in English often mentioned some form of human presence. The most commonly mentioned human difference was the Midwest's large cities and ethnic diversity. This fits earlier surveys that found that respondents saw the Midwest as being where Northern and Southern cultural mores merged into something new. English-department respondents also mentioned how farming rather than ranching defined the two regions. But these same respondents were also more likely to mention political orientation as an area separating the Midwest from the Great Plains than their geography and history kin were. English-department respondents saw the Great Plains as more conservative and Republican (the party, not the political ideal) than the Midwest.

Great Plains respondents clearly knew when they had left the plains. To the west, mountains emerged. To the east, it became woodier or hillier. The problem for respondents was going north or south. As Walter Nugent found in 1992, most people did not think beyond the boundary of the United States. If they did think beyond the U.S. border, the Great Plains extended up to Winnipeg. For those self-identifiable Midwesterners, geography also mattered, but not through mountains. Instead, Midwesterners focused on the emerging "flatness" of the land itself.

Eighteen of the respondents did not differentiate the Great Plains and Midwest. For most of these respondents, mountains were the clearest indicator of having left the Midwest/Great Plains region. It is less clear whether the respondents were referring to the Rocky Mountains in the West or the Appalachians in the East.

Question 15 then asked respondents to draw a map of their particular region.

Below are the maps they drew:

All respondents:

In the end, eighty-two people responded to my inquiry; the response rate was a little better than a credit-card solicitation, but disappointing. However, those who responded did not disappoint. Their responses were humorous, insightful, and telling.

What you first notice is the clear delineation between the Midwest/ Great Plains and the American South and West. The Ohio River does mark a definitive boundary in the minds of the respondents. The western boundary is a little less clear, but the front range of the Rocky Mountains does mark the end of the Great Plains/Midwest for most people. At least five respondents, approximately 6 percent of the sample, included Texas. Most stopped the northern boundary at the border, but that was the result of the map representing only the United States. It would be interesting to see what would have happened if Canada had been included in the map.

At the same time, two distinct areas are noticeable. The Midwest moves down the Ohio River, crosses portions of Missouri, and continues to Kansas and Colorado. It also includes states associated with the Great Lakes: Michigan, Wisconsin, and Minnesota. Other maps tend to draw a sharp line at the eastern borders of Kansas, Nebraska, and the two Dakotas. Most respondents included Oklahoma, but not Texas, in their vision of the Great Plains.

What is also clear when looking at all the images together is that nearly a quarter of the people responding drew the cultural Midwest and Great Plains into a single entity. What is needed is a more focused examination of the maps to determine if there were discipline-specific or regional-specific responses.

English department respondents draw the regions:

English department respondents draw the Midwest (above)
English department respondents draw the Great Plains (below)

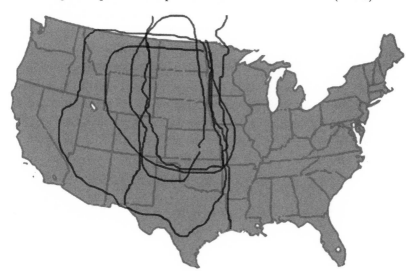

Twenty-five English department faculty who identified themselves as living in the Midwest responded to the survey, while five respondents came from the Great Plains. Clearly respondents in English departments felt the Great Plains was part of the Midwest. What is most interesting, at least to this author, is how rigid those respondents from the Great Plains drew their eastern boundary. Both groups had members who felt that Texas and Oklahoma were part of their region, but just as important, the Midwest and Plains extend west of the Rocky Mountains. English faculty were the only group to do such a thing. One reason for this decision is found in some of their answers.

It did not matter where one was located; respondents from both regions talked about Protestantism, flat topography, and a region associated with political conservatism. While most identified mountains as a sign one had left the region, the inclusion of Utah, Wyoming, and portions of New Mexico and Arizona suggested physical characteristics might be less important than the cultural elements respondents associated with the regions in question. But something else might be at work. Two of the respondents, both in English departments, mentioned how they viewed the Midwest as a "social construct." They viewed the Midwest, and its attendant image of yeoman farms and small towns, as the "ideological center of the United States."[130] If this is the case, then perhaps there is hope that the Midwest will once again enjoy a primacy in the American psyche, just as it had on the eve of World War I.[131]

Geographers draw the regions:

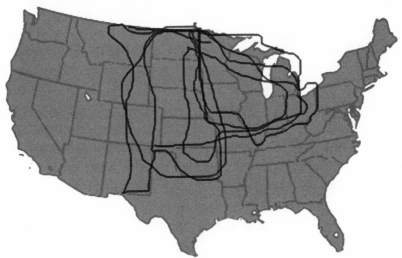

Geographers draw the Midwest

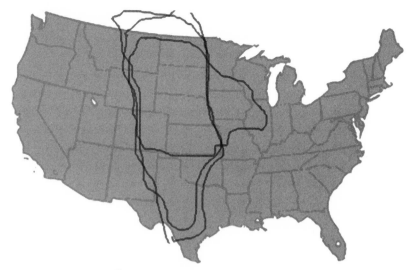

Geographers draw the Great Plains

Nine geographers responded to the survey. Three geographers were from the Great Plains, while six identified themselves as being in the Midwest. At first glance, the geographers seem the most unified in their territorial descriptions of the region; this is particularly true for the Great Plains representatives. Two of the three Great Plains geographers placed the eastern border of the plains at the eastern borders of Kansas, Nebraska, and the Dakotas. The third respondent extended the eastern border to Iowa's eastern border; he/she also placed the Prairie Coteau region of southwestern Minnesota in the Great Plains. All three respondents placed the western edge of the Great Plains along the Rocky Mountains.

Those who drew the Midwest's boundaries were less uniform in their responses. Three of the six drew boundaries that more clearly mirrored respondents of the Great Plains. That is, they said the Midwest comprised the central part of the nation, and they drew boundaries that effectively made the Midwest stretch from the western edge of Minnesota and Iowa westward to the Rocky Mountains. Its southern and northern borders went to Canada and into Oklahoma. This is a little more southward than those located on the Great Plains drew it, but not significantly different. Both groups excluded Texas from their definition of the regions under question. For those who drew a more traditional Midwest, one issue was whether Ohio was in the Midwest. Some said yes; others said no. Those who said Ohio was not part of the Midwest pointed to its manufacturing sector. Like the undergraduates of the 1980s, they understood the Midwest as pastoral.

In their written responses, geographers were more interested in topography, hydrology, and flora/fauna than the other groups were. This is not a surprise, and it is an important reminder to those working on Great Plains/Midwestern subjects to look beyond their traditional silos for new ways of looking at the regions.

Historians draw the regions:

Historians draw the Midwest (above)
Historians draw the Great Plains (below)

Thirty-nine historians responded to the survey. The images above display all their drawings superimposed on a single map. Two things become clear in the images. The first is that the Midwest has become the Middle West in the minds of respondents. Without the outlier whose map stretches from the Appalachians to the Rockies, most Midwest respondents included the twelve states that now comprise the Middle West. The second takeaway is that Great Plains respondents clearly delineate the Midwest and Great Plains regions.

Other respondents draw the regions:

Other respondents draw the Midwest (above)

Other respondents draw the Great Plains (below)

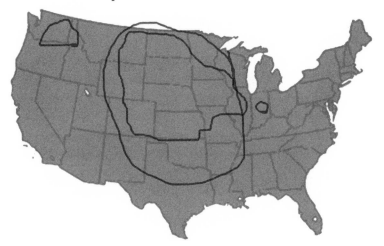

Five people who were not historians, geographers, or faculty in English departments responded to the survey. The author believes the circle in eastern Washington is a mistake, but one can still see some differences in the responses. The largest circle stretches westward to the Rocky Mountains and eastward to the eastern border of Iowa, Minnesota, and Missouri. This person thought less of historic development and more of grasslands. Another respondent also used the Rocky Mountains as his/her western boundary for the Great Plains. This person's southern edge was the Kansas-Oklahoma border (which fits much of the Great Plains scholarship) and goes northward to the Canadian border. The eastern border includes Iowa and a portion of Missouri. The third respondent's mental map of the Great Plains mirrored the definition found in *The Encyclopedia of the Great Plains*. The final two drawn boundaries clearly separate the Midwest from the Great Plains. These respondents include Missouri, and one of them includes Kentucky. Both include Wisconsin as part of the Midwest. Where the Midwestern respondents differ is in how far west the Midwest goes. One pushes the region into Iowa, while the other extends the Midwest into western Nebraska.

Conclusion

What should one take away from the varied responses of this survey? The most obvious conclusion one can draw is that respondents, like the rest of the nation, recognize that the border of the Great Plains and Midwest is not as distinct as one might like. On the other hand, respondents were more likely to mention specific characteristics that to them defined the region they were in. But there is more to take away than this.

James Shortridge began his monograph on the Middle West by reminding his readers what D. W. Meinig once wrote: "Places are created by history."[132] This survey confirms that truism. Respondents were cognizant of historical developments such as slavery. This is why some respondents specifically excluded Missouri while others mentioned the Midwest's "Yankee" roots. Others noted that the Midwest had been associated with the old Southwest in the "pre-railroad days." Great Plains respondents often mentioned aridity when it came to their region. While the number of respondents was too small for any concrete conclusions, certain truisms did emerge.

The first takeaway is the malleability of both regions. As one respondent noted, for much of American history, "the Midwest was considered the West," and the Great Plains, "particularly the Dakotas and Nebraska," was "often shuffled between the Midwest and the West." The regions under consideration are breathing entities, swelling and shrinking depending on the vision and desire of the scholar in question. Where one places a locale often depends on what one hopes to do in the study under question. Many respondents acknowledged the merging of the two regions into a single entity.

A second takeaway is how connected the regions are to other "regions." Almost no one saw either the Great Plains or the Midwest in isolation. Respondents tended to place the region(s) against others. If one identified with the Great Plains, then that reference was almost always against the West; if one were Midwestern in orientation, then the American South, the Appalachian Mountains, or the Northeast served to differentiate among regions.

Yet another takeaway is how no respondents used outmigration to define their region. Patrick Carr and Maria Kefalas identified three specific threats for rural America: "a failing farm- and factory-based economy, rising unemployment, and shrinking wages and benefits."[133] These threats are found in both the Great Plains and the Midwest.[134] Yet, despite the stereotypes of the region as a "rust belt" or a place with "no people," the persistence of other images outweighs the national image.[135] Terms like "hard work," "polite," and "warm" are what our respondents often associated with the regions in question. Perhaps the failure to mention outmigration is not surprising. After all, James Shortridge's undergraduates had envisioned the Midwest as rural, which by default means few people. Still, some respondents noted the absence of people for the Great Plains. National publications, even those trying to explore the Great Plains, often play upon the rural nature of the region, as the cover of R. Douglas Hurt's book *The Big Empty* did in 2011.[136]

What then can this survey tell us about where one region ends and another begins? The survey can tell us nothing definitive; it reminds us that borders are constructed not only by terrain but by history and intellectual affinity. Where the Midwest ends and Great Plains begins is dependent on what one wants to use as criteria: people, topography, culture, politics, or history. Walter Prescott Webb used "humidity" to define his Midwest; for this survey, a myriad of criteria were used, and many of them are beginning to wane. Corn is now grown in West River, South Dakota, and cattle are being fed in feedlots in Iowa. Government policies are driving some of these transformations, but so too is history. As the nation becomes more homogeneous, regional differences break down. Walmart, Amazon, and McDonald's are replacing regional shopping and eating patterns. One can buy Popeyes Louisiana Chicken or St. Louis-style ribs in Sioux Falls.

Although regions have unique phrases ("pop" rather than "soda," or "you betcha ya" instead of "you're welcome"), these idiomatic differences may not be enough to sustain a regional identity. Many individuals desire to belong to something more comforting than an impersonal nation-state. Benjamin Barber talked about the dilemma in his book *Jihad vs. McWorld*, and, although his book dealt with terrorism, his argument about our desire to belong to something more tangible than a large, impersonal—perhaps threatening—entity has implications for regional studies.[137] He found that globalizing tendencies undermined the notions of individual independence and personal identity.[138] As consolidation in banking or grocery shopping or other fields becomes more omnipresent and people become more transitory, whether for work, wanderlust, or something else, the desire to belong to something solid—a region, a homeland, or a past—becomes stronger. But this quest for regional identity does more than that. It also might remind Americans of their pluralistic past. Asking whether one is a Midwesterner or from the Great Plains might actually help people become "civically inclined and . . . engaged in intellectual" endeavors.[139] Where does one region end and another begin? The answer to the question often depends on what one wants to use as criteria for differentiating the regions of the United States.

Notes

1 Without the computer skills of Matt Fox, Augustana University Information Technology Services, this project would not have been possible. Matt helped organize the survey and ensured that the maps and responses would be stored and accessible. Any misinterpretation of the data is solely the responsibility of the author.

2 O. E. Rölvaag, *Giants in the Earth: A Saga of the Prairie* (New York: Harper and Row, 1964 [1927]); Willa Cather, *My Antonia* (Boston: Houghton Mifflin Company, 1918); John Steinbeck, *The Grapes of Wrath* (New York: Viking Press, 1939); Ann Daum, *The Prairie in Her Eyes* (Minneapolis: Milkweed Editions, 2001). What unites these books is the importance of land and the idea of place and people.

3 Sinclair Lewis, *Main Street: The Story of Carol Kennicott* (New York: Harcourt, Brace and Howe, 1920); Studs Terkel, *Division Street: America* (New York: Pantheon Books, 1967); Tim O'Brien, *In the Lake of the Woods* (Boston: Houghton Mifflin/Seymour Lawrence, 1994); Marilynne Robinson, *Gilead* (New York: Farrar, Straus and Giroux, 2001); Patrick J. Carr and Maria J. Kefalas, *Hollowing Out the Middle: The Rural Brain Drain and What It Means for America* (Boston: Beacon Press, 2009). These books are not nearly as optimistic as their plains counterparts are, but that is not the essential element. What these writers focus on are the underlying problems of the region, whether personal, economic, or social.

4 For a quick summary of the initial debate, see William G. Robbins, "Laying Siege to Western History: The Emergence of New Paradigms," *Reviews in American History* 19, no. 3 (September 1991): 313–31.

⁵ Walter Nugent, "Where is the American West? Report on a Survey," *Montana: The Magazine of Western History* 42, no. 3 (Summer 1992): 2–4.

⁶ Nugent, "Where is the American West?," 4.

⁷ Nugent, "Where is the American West?," 2–23.

⁸ Nugent, "Where Is the American West?," 11; James R. Shortridge, "The Vernacular Middle West, " *Annals of the Association of American Geographers* 75, no. 1 (March 1985): fig. 2, p. 50.

⁹ Earle D. Ross, "A Generation of Prairie Historiography," *Mississippi Valley Historical Review* 33, no. 3 (December 1946): 391.

¹⁰ Jon K. Lauck, *From Warm Center to Ragged Edge: The Erosion of Midwestern Literary and Historical Regionalism, 1920–1965* (Iowa City: University of Iowa Press, 2017), 2.

¹¹ Arthur R. Huseboe and William Geyer, "Herbert Krause and the Western Experience," in *Where the West Begins*, ed. Arthur R. Huseboe and William Geyer (Sioux Falls, SD: Center for Western Studies, 1978), 5.

¹² Jon K. Lauck. *The Lost Region: Toward a Revival of Midwestern History* (Iowa City: University of Iowa Press, 2013), 29.

¹³ James Malin, *History and Ecology: Studies of the Grasslands* (Lincoln: University of Nebraska Press, 1984), 220; cited in Joseph A. Amato, *Rethinking Home: A Case for Writing Local History* (Berkeley: University of California Press, 2002), 22.

¹⁴ Amato, *Rethinking Home*, 22.

¹⁵ Eugen Weber, comment on Amato, *Rethinking Home*, back cover.

¹⁶ Becky Bradway, introduction to *In the Middle of the Middle West: Literary Nonfiction from the Heartland*, ed. Becky Bradway (Bloomington: Indiana University Press, 2003), xii. Bradway's full quote is worth citing since it hints at the central problems this essay addresses: "This book is about the Midwest. The place between the two coasts—that place not the South—that place not the West (*or the Plains*)—and not Appalachia either." Emphasis added.

¹⁷ James R. Shortridge, *The Middle West: Its Meaning in American Culture* (Lawrence: University Press of Kansas, 1989), 8.

¹⁸ Ian Frazier, *Great Plains* (New York: Farrar, Straus, Giroux, 1989), 195.

¹⁹ Paula M. Nelson, *After the West Was Won: Homesteaders and Town-Builders in Western South Dakota, 1900–1917* (Iowa City: University of Iowa Press, 1986), xiv.

²⁰ Lauck, *From Warm Center to Ragged Edge*, 11–36 (quote on 11).

²¹ Carl Van Doren, "Contemporary American Novelists: the Revolt from the Village," *The Nation*, October 12, 1921, 407–12.

²² Paula M. Nelson. *The Prairie Winnows Out Its Own: The West River Country of South Dakota in the Year of Depression and Dust* (Iowa City: University of Iowa Press, 1996), 188. Nelson mentions that "the big shakeout [for people and businesses in West River South Dakota] came in the twenties not in the Great Depression a decade later" (7).

²³ Frazier, *Great Plains*, 196.

²⁴ See for example the map in Nathan Jessen, *Populism and Imperialism: Politics, Culture, and Foreign Policy in the American West, 1890–1900* (Lawrence: University Press of Kansas, 2017), 41.

²⁵ Jessen, *Populism and Imperialism*, 207. The problem with this interpretation is that many scholars see Populism as part of the Midwestern tradition too. See Jon K. Lauck, "Christopher Lasch and Prairie Populism," *Great Plains Quarterly* 32, no. 3 (Summer 2002): 183–205, esp. 191–94.

26 One respondent did identify Populism as differentiating the two regions; this respondent was also a member of the Western History Association.

27 Robert Grindy, "Desperately Seeking Blue Mound," in Bradway, *In the Middle*, 136.

28 Christopher Lasch, *The True and Only Heaven: Progress and Its Critics* (New York: W.W. Norton, 1991), 36. It needs to be understood that Lasch wrote this line to challenge the perception of who lived in America's interior; he was not suggesting he believed this caricature.

29 Robert Michael Morrissey, *Empire by Collaboration: Indians, Colonists, and Governments in Colonial Illinois Country* (Philadelphia: University of Pennsylvania Press, 2015), 12–14.

30 Ralph E. Ehrenberg, "Exploratory Mapping of the Great Plains before 1800," in *Mapping the North American Plains: Essays in the History of Cartography*, ed. Frederick C. Luebke et al. (Norman: University of Oklahoma Press, 1987), 4.

31 For Franquelin's map, see https://en.wikipedia.org/wiki/Jean-Baptiste-Louis_Franquelin#/media/File:Amerique_Septentrionale_JBF_1688.jpg; for de l'Isle's map, see http://www.libs.uga.edu/darchive/hargrett/maps/1718d4.jpg (both accessed May 31, 2017).

32 From a social theory standpoint, the maps produced gave officials a mental reference, or grid, to begin understanding the American interior. For how this works see, Robert Darton, *The Kiss of Lamourette: Reflections in Cultural History* (New York: W.W. Norton, 1990), 336.

33 Arthur H. Robinson and Barbara Bartz Petchenik, *The Nature of Maps: Essays toward Understanding Maps and Mapping* (Chicago: University of Chicago Press, 1976), 1.

34 D. W. Meinig, *The Shaping of America: A Geographical Perspective on 500 Hundred Years of History*, vol. 2, *Continental America 1800–1867* (New Haven: Yale University Press, 1993), 76.

35 John L. Allen, "Patterns of Promise: Mapping the Plains and Prairies, 1800–1860," in Luebke et al., *Mapping the North American Plains*, 41.

36 Stephen H. Long, "Country Drained By the Mississippi [River]," 1823 (map found at http://www.davidrumsey.com/maps1150.html [accessed January 21, 2018]).

37 Allen, "Patterns of Promise," 41.

38 David J. Wishart, "The Great Plains Region," in *Encyclopedia of the Great Plains*, ed. David J. Wishart (Lincoln: University of Nebraska Press, 2004), xiii.

39 Interestingly, Steinbeck's protagonists were from Oklahoma, a region many respondents separated from the plains tradition because of slavery.

40 Michael Steiner, "From Frontier to Region: Frederick Jackson Turner and the New Western History," *Pacific Historical Review* 64, no. 4 (November 1995): 480.

41 John Wesley Powell, *Report on the Lands of the Arid Region of the United States*, 2nd ed. (Washington, D.C.: U.S. Government Printing Office, 1879), 2; Walter Prescott Webb, *The Great Plains* (Waltham, MA: Ginn and Company, 1931), 17–21.

42 Oklahoma and Texas were excluded because their experiences were different from the other states. For one thing, both Oklahoma and Texas allowed slavery. Slavery is one reason why one of the respondents excluded Missouri from either the Midwest or the plains.

43 See, for example, Shortridge, "Vernacular Middle West," 48–57; Shortridge, "The Heart of the Prairie: Culture Areas in the Central and Northern Great Plains," *Great Plains Quarterly* 8, no. 4 (Fall 1988): 206–21; John C. Hudson, "North American Origins of Middlewestern Frontier Populations," *Annals of the Association of American Geographers* 78, no. 3 (September 1988): 395–413.

[44] See, for example, Frederick C. Luebke, *Ethnicity on the Great Plains* (Lincoln: University of Nebraska Press, 1980) and Luebke, Frances W. Kaye, and Gary E. Moulton (eds.), *Mapping the North American Plains: Essays in the History of Cartography* (Lincoln: University of Nebraska Press, 1987).

[45] Shortridge, "Vernacular Middle West," 48.

[46] Lauck, *Lost Region*, 31–37.

[47] Lauck, "Why the Midwest Matters," *Midwest Quarterly* 54, no. 2 (Winter 2013): 165–85, but especially 175–78.

[48] Jessen, *Populism and Imperialism*.

[49] Robert L. Dorman, *Hell of a Vision: Regionalism and the Modern American West* (Tucson: University of Arizona Press, 2012); R. Douglas Hurt, *The Big Empty: The Great Plains in the Twentieth Century* (Tucson: University of Arizona Press, 2011).

[50] Dorman, *Hell of a Vision*, 5; Hurt, *Big Empty*, xvi.

[51] Lauck, "Why the Midwest Matters," 183.

[52] Donald G. Holtgrieve, "Frederick Jackson Turner as a Regionalist," *Professional Geographer* 26, no. 2 (May 1974): 159, http://www.tandfonline.com/doi/abs/10.1111/j.0033-0124.1974.00159.x.

[53] Frederick Jackson Turner, "Is Sectionalism in America Dying Away?," *American Journal of Sociology* 13, no. 5 (March 1908): 661.

[54] Lauck, *From Warm Center to Ragged Edge*, 3.

[55] Lauck, *Lost Region*, 7.

[56] Wilbur R. Jacobs et al., *Turner, Bolton and Webb: Three Historians of the American Frontier* (Seattle: University of Washington Press, 1965), vii.

[57] Walter Prescott Webb, *The Great Plains*, 3.

[58] Webb, *Great Plains*, 4.

[59] Clark Wissler, *The American Indian*, 2nd ed. (London: Oxford University Press, 1922), 217–60, especially 218–22.

[60] Powell, to his credit, acknowledged some reasons that present-day North and South Dakota were farmed, even in 1878, without irrigation. His concern was with the land that lay west of the James River. See Powell, *Report on the Lands*, 3.

[61] Powell, *Report on the Lands*, 44. Powell was shouted down, literally, at the North Dakota Constitutional Convention when he made similar comments in 1889. When Powell was done speaking to the North Dakota Constitutional Convention, a convention attendee responded by noting that the scarcity of water meant "these plains . . . is not sufficient to make sure a good crop ever time." See Burleigh F. Spalding, "Speeches and Articles" from "Burleigh Folsom Spalding," 3 boxes, MSS 10001 A1/1/2, 128–29, North Dakota State Historical Society.

[62] Gilbert C. Fite, "The Great Plains: Promises, Problems, and Prospects," in *The Great Plains Environment and Culture*, ed. Brian W. Blouet and Frederick C. Luebke (Lincoln: University of Nebraska Press, 1979), 187.

[63] Walter Prescott Webb, *The Great Frontier* (Boston: Houghton Mifflin, 1952), 240, 241.

[64] Craig N. Spencer et al., "Forest Expansion and Soil Carbon Changes in the Loess Hills of Eastern South Dakota," *American Midland Naturalist*, 273.

[65] Webb, *The Great Plains*, 4.

[66] Howard R. Lamar, ed., *The New Encyclopedia of the American West* (New Haven: Yale University Press, 1998), 582–86, 773–76, 800–801, 1067–68.

[67] James R. Shortridge, "Changing Usage of Four American Regional Labels," *Annals of the Association of American Geographers* 77, no. 3 (September 1987): 325–26.

[68] Shortridge, "Vernacular Middle West," 49–50.

[69] Shortridge, *Middle West*, 3.
[70] See, for example, James R. Shortridge, *Peopling the Plains: Who Settled Where in Frontier Kansas* (Lawrence: University Press of Kansas, 1995), especially 1–14.
[71] Frederick C. Luebke, introduction to *The Great Plains: Environment and Culture*, by Brian W. Blouet and Frederick C. Luebke (Lincoln: University of Nebraska Press, 1979), ix–x.
[72] Richard Sisson et al., eds., *The American Midwest: An Interpretive Encyclopedia* (Bloomington: Indiana University Press, 2007), xv.
[73] Shortridge, "Vernacular Middle West," 49.
[74] Stephen J. Lavin et al., *Atlas of the Great Plains* (Lincoln: University of Nebraska Press, 2001), 1.
[75] Earle D. Ross, "A Generation of Prairie Historiography," *Mississippi Valley Historical Review* 33, no. 3 (December 1946): 391.
[76] Shortridge, "Vernacular Middle West," 48.
[77] Amato, *Rethinking Home*, 8.
[78] Wilbur Zelinsky, "North America's Vernacular Regions," *Annals of the Association of American Geographers* 70, no. 1 (March 1980): 1.
[79] Zelinsky, "North America's Vernacular Regions," 2.
[80] Lauck, *Lost Region*, 3.
[81] Lauck, *Lost Region*, 40.
[82] Lauck, *Lost Region*, 7.
[83] Meinig, *Shaping of America*, 2:320 (map).
[84] Elizabeth Fenn, *Encounters at the Heart of the World: A History of the Mandan People* (New York: Hill and Wang, 2014), 19, 80–83.
[85] Shortridge, "Vernacular Middle West," 48.
[86] Shortridge, "Vernacular Middle West," 49.
[87] James R. Shortridge, "Overview: Images of the Midwest," in Sisson et al., *American Midwest*, 57.
[88] Shortridge, *Middle West*, 16
[89] Shortridge, "Overview: Images of the Midwest," 57.
[90] Shortridge, "Vernacular Middle West," 49.
[91] Shortridge, "Vernacular Middle West," 52.
[92] Lasch, *True and Only Heaven*, 239.
[93] Shortridge, "Vernacular Middle West," 52.
[94] Lasch, *True and Only Heaven*, 85.
[95] Shortridge, *Middle West*, 11.
[96] Only 10 percent of respondents included Ohio and Wisconsin in their Middle West maps; see Shortridge, "Vernacular Middle West," 49.
[97] For this map see, Shortridge, *Middle West*, 84.
[98] Joel Garreau, *The Nine Nations of North America* (Boston: Houghton Mifflin, 1981), 5.
[99] Wilbur Zelinsky also failed to identify either the Midwest or the Great Plains as a vernacular region in his study "North America's Vernacular Regions," 1–16. He does, however, identify a Middle West, which consists of three semi-related areas: the "Middle West+Midwest+Mid-America" Fig. 2, 8.
[100] "Fifty published versions of the Great Plains regional boundary," in *Atlas of the Great Plains*, 2. This map also appears in Hurt, *Big Empty*.
[101] Nugent, "Where Is the American West?," 4.
[102] Lavin et al., *Atlas of the Great Plains*, 25.
[103] Lavin et al., *Atlas of the Great Plains*, 1–5, 31.

[104] Wishart, *Encyclopedia of the Great Plains*, xiii–xiv.

[105] Sisson et al., *American Midwest*, xv.

[106] Sisson et al., *American Midwest*, 5.

[107] Sisson et al., *American Midwest*, 5.

[108] James R. Shortridge, "Images of the Midwest," in Sisson et al., *American Midwest*, 57.

[109] This fluidity is not unique to the Midwest. Nearly 16 percent (15.9 percent) of those surveyed by Walter Nugent for his exploration of the American West's boundaries refused to identify fixed boundaries for the region. They identified the "West" as a "state of mind" or "idea." See Nugent, "Where Is the American West?," 7.

[110] Wishart , *Encyclopedia of the Great Plains*, 469.

[111] James K. Folsom, "James Fenimore Cooper," in Lamar, *New Encyclopedia of the American West*, 257.

[112] Lamar, *New Encyclopedia of the American West*, vi.

[113] John E. Miller, "Laura Ingalls Wilder as a Midwestern Pioneer Girl," in *Pioneer Girl Perspectives: Exploring Laura Ingalls Wilder*, ed. Nancy Tystad Koupal (Pierre: South Dakota Historical Society, forthcoming 2018).

[114] John E. Miller, "A Midwestern Pioneer," *Pioneer Girl Project* (blog), April 27, 2017, https://pioneergirlproject.org/page/2/.

[115] Fred Erisman, *Laura Ingalls Wilder*, Western Writers Series (Boise: Boise State University, 1994), 5–6.

[116] Perhaps no line better symbolizes the transformation of the region both Cather and Wilder talk about than Willa Cather's line from *My Ántonia*: "There seemed to be nothing to see; no fences, no creeks or trees, no hills or fields….There was nothing but land: not a country at all, but the material out of which countries are made." Cather, *My Ántonia* (New York: Barnes and Noble Classics, 2003), 11.

[117] John E. Miller, *Laura Ingalls Wilder's Little Town: Where History and Literature Meet* (Lawrence: University Press of Kansas, 1994), 17–18.

[118] Sisson et al., *American Midwest*, 474–77; Wishart, *Encyclopedia of the Great Plains*, xiv.

[119] See Sisson et al., *American Midwest*, xix; and Wishart, *Encyclopedia of the Great Plains*, xv.

[120] John E. Miller, *Small-Town Dreams: Stories of Midwestern Boys Who Shaped America* (Lawrence: University Press of Kansas, 2014).

[121] Nugent, "Where Is the American West?," 2–23.

[122] Nugent, "Where Is the American West?," 9.

[123] Nugent, "Where Is the American West?," 7. Fewer than 16 percent of the total respondents viewed the West as "a 'state of mind,' an 'idea,' 'myth,' or 'mental construct,' or something similar." Writers were far more likely to do this than editors or historians. But here, there is a caveat: the writers see the West as mythical, "and they write about and perpetuate the myth."

[124] Amato, *Rethinking Home*. Trained in European intellectual history, Amato noted, "I never expected to write a range of books on a murder, a crop scandal, an ethnic farming community, demographic decline, new immigrants, and economic and social turbulence in this region" (19).

[125] The boundaries drawn were collected at https://survey.augie.edu/admin/.

[126] Frazier, *Great Plains*, 7.

[127] One respondent did apologize to Missouri for its omission, while another specifically excluded Kentucky in his/her written response.

[128] Robert Michael Morissey, *Empire by Collaboration: Indians, Colonists, and Governments in Colonial Illinois Country* (Philadelphia: University of Pennsylvania Press, 2015), table on 147.

[129] William Cronon, *Nature's Metropolis: Chicago and the Great West* (New York: W.W. Norton, 1991), 282.

[130] Respondent from Hiram College.

[131] Lauck, *From Warm Center to Ragged Edge*, 11.

[132] Shortridge, *Middle West*, 13.

[133] Patrick J. Carr and Maria J. Kefalas, *Hollowing Out the Middle: The Rural Brain Drain and What It Means for America* (Boston: Beacon Press, 2009), 3.

[134] For an anecdotal example of these threats, at least when it comes to farming, see Ted Genoways, *This Blessed Earth: A Year in the Life of an American Farm Family* (New York: W.W. Norton, 2017).

[135] It might surprise people to learn that Iowa was the eighth-most dependent state on manufacturing in 2000 and that, between 2000 and 2003, Iowa lost more than 10 percent of its industrial base. See Carr and Kefalas, *Hollowing Out the Middle*, 10.

[136] Hurt, *Big Empty*, cover.

[137] Benjamin R. Barber, *Jihad vs. McWorld: Terrorism's Challenge to Democracy* (New York: Times Books, 1995).

[138] Wikipedia, "*Jihad vs. McWorld*," accessed February 1, 2018, https://en.wikipedia.org/wiki/Jihad_vs._McWorld.

[139] Lauck, *From Warm Center to Ragged Edge*, 101.

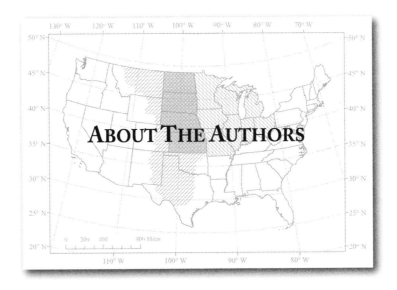

ABOUT THE AUTHORS

James Aber holds a Ph.D. in Geology from the University of Kansas and has wide-ranging experience in the Great Plains of the United States and Canada as well as international field work in northern and central Europe and South America involving glaciation, wetlands, tectonics, wind energy, and remote sensing, particularly aerial photography. Aber is a Professor Emeritus at Emporia State University in Kansas.

Susan Aber holds a Ph.D. in Library and Information Science from Emporia State University. She has traveled widely in the Great Plains of the United States and Canada with international experience across Europe and in southeastern Asia. Her specialty is in gemstones and gemology, particularly amber and pearls. Aber is the former director of the Peterson Planetarium at Emporia State University in Kansas.

Julie Courtwright is Associate Professor of History at Iowa State University, where she studies U.S. Environmental History and the history of the American West. Courtwright earned her Ph.D. at the University of Arkansas in 2007. In 2011, the University Press of Kansas published her *Prairie Fire: A Great Plains History*, which was named a Kansas Notable Book and an honor selection for the Caroline Bancroft Award in Western history. Courtwright has published articles on the World War II housing boom, Chinese immigration, and Bleeding Kansas. Her most recent, "On the Edge of the Possible: Artificial Rainmaking and the Extension of Hope on the Great Plains," won the Vernon Carstensen Memorial Award for the best article published in *Agricultural History*. Currently, Courtwright is at work on *Windswept: An Environmental and Social History of Wind on the Great Plains*. Her future research plans include histories of Great Plains water, "nothingness," tall tales, and dogs.

James E. Davis earned his A. B. (history) and M. A. (history) at Wayne State Univeristy, Detroit, and his Ph. D. (history, with a cognate in geography) at the Univeristy of Michigan. After teaching in the Dearborn, Michigan, public schools from 1963 to 1971, he taught history and geography at Illinois College starting in 1971, teaching his last class there in 2011. His major works include *Frontier America, 1800-1840: A Comparative Demographic Analysis of the Frontier Process* (Arthur H. Clark, 1977), *Dreams to Dust* (University of Nebraska Press, 1989), and *Frontier Illinois* (Indiana University Press, 1998) and a number of articles and essays, as well as reviews in *The American Historical Review, The Journal of American History*, and other journals.

Anna Thompson Hajdik is a senior lecturer in the English and Film Studies Departments at the University of Wisconsin-Whitewater where she teaches courses on visual culture, film, the Cold War, and literature of the American Midwest. She holds a Ph.D. in American Studies from the University of Texas at Austin and has published an array of essays and articles related to the subjects of Midwestern culture and identity and the role of agriculture in modern American life. With the support of the State Historical Society of Iowa, she is currently working on a book-length project examining the visual culture of the state and its broader national significance. Dr. Hajdik resides in Madison, Wisconsin.

Rachael Hanel is an assistant professor of Mass Media at Minnesota State University, Mankato. She is the author of *We'll Be the Last Ones to Let You Down: Memoir of a Gravedigger's Daughter* (University of Minnesota Press, 2013). She received a Ph.D. in Creative Writing from Bath Spa University.

Debbie A. Hanson received her B.A. from the College of Saint Scholastica in Duluth, Minnesota and her M.A. and Ph.D. in English from the University of Illinois at Urbana-Champaign. She is a professor in the English Department at Augustana University, and her special fields of interest include American literature, the literature of the Great Plains, and folklore studies. She has also been a regular presenter at the annual conference of the American Folklore Society and has had articles or reviews published in *Southern Folklore*, *Western Folklore*, and *The Journal of American Folklore*. In 2017 she received the Herbert W. Blakely Professional Award from the Dakota Conference on the Northern Plains for her paper "Lending a Feminine Touch to the B-29: Depictions of Women Workers in WWII Aircraft Industry Publications."

Maria Howe is an attorney finishing her Ph.D. at Iowa State University in the Rural, Agricultural, Technological, & Environmental History Program (RATE). Her dissertation, titled *Managing the Missouri*, is a study of twentieth-century federal water projects across the Missouri River Valley. Her advisors are Dr. Pamela Riney-Kehrberg, who serves as the RATE program coordinator, and Dr. Julie Courtwright. Prior to attending graduate school, Maria earned her Juris Doctorate from the University of Denver Sturm College of Law. She has primarily practiced water and environmental law. She is currently the Communications Director for the Midwestern History Association. Her dissertation research has been supported by fellowships and grants from the Roswell Garst Foundation, the Phi Alpha Theta National History Honors Society, the Bradley Fellows Program at the Montana State Historical Society, and the Iowa State Historical Society. In her free time, she particularly enjoys canoeing and rafting. Last fall, she had the pleasure of traveling down the last 100 miles of the Missouri River in a voyageur canoe.

Mara W. Cohen Ioannides has a degree in Jewish Studies, teaches writing and Jewish Literature at Missouri State University in Springfield, MO, and is president of the Midwest Jewish Studies Association. Dr. Ioannides has published on American Jewry with a focus on the Midwest, specifically the Ozarks.

Christopher R. Laingen is an Associate Professor of Geography at Eastern Illinois University in Charleston, Illinois. He grew up on a family farm in southern Minnesota near the town of Odin, where much of his interest in the rural landscape and regional geography began. His research focuses on changes in farming and the landscapes of the rural Midwest and Great Plains, which has been published in *Great Plains Research*, *Focus on Geography*, *The Geographical Review*, and *The Professional Geographer*. He is also the co-author (with John C. Hudson) of the book *American Farms, American Food: A Geography of Agriculture and Food Production in the United States* (Lexington Books, 2016).

Jon K. Lauck is the founding president of the Midwestern History Association, the associate editor and book editor of *Middle West Review*, and an Adjunct Professor of History and Political Science at the University of South Dakota. He is the author of *Prairie Republic: The Political Culture of Dakota Territory, 1879–1889* (University of Oklahoma Press, 2010), *Daschle vs. Thune: Anatomy of a High Plains Senate Race* (University of Oklahoma Press, 2007), *American Agriculture and the Problem of Monopoly: The Political Economy of Grain Belt Farming, 1953-1980* (University of Nebraska Press, 2000), *The Lost Region: Toward a Revival of Midwestern History* (University of Iowa Press, 2013), and *From Warm Center to Ragged Edge: The Erosion of Midwestern Literary and Historical Regionalism, 1920-1965* (University of Iowa Press, 2017), the editor of *The Midwestern Moment: The Forgotten World of Early Twentieth-Century Midwestern Regionalism, 1880-1940* (Hastings College Press, 2017), and the co-editor of *Finding a New Midwestern History* (University of Nebraska Press, 2018).

Matthew S. Luckett is the academic coordinator for the Humanities External Master's Degree program at California State University, Dominguez Hills. Dr. Luckett received his B.A. in history at Southeast Missouri State University in 2003, his M.A. in history at Marquette University in 2005, and a Ph.D. in American history at UCLA in 2014. He is currently completing a book manuscript entitled *Honor among Thieves: Horse Stealing in Western Nebraska, 1850-1890*, for the University of Nebraska Press. Although a native Midwesterner and a sixth-generation Missourian, Dr. Luckett now resides in Northern California with his wife and daughter.

Nathalie Massip is Associate Professor of American Studies at the Université Côte d'Azur. She completed her Ph.D. dissertation in 2011 on the historiography of the American West, specifically on the New Western History ("La 'Nouvelle Histoire de l'Ouest': Historiographie et Représentations"). She has recently contributed chapters to the books *Les Etats-Unis. Géographie d'une grande puissance*, ed. by Frédéric Leriche (Paris: Armand Colin, 2016), *L'Ouest et les Amériques. Entre arts et réalités*, ed. by Marie-Christine Michaud et Eliane Elmaleh (Rennes: Presses Universitaires de Rennes, 2016), and *Les Masques de la vérité dans les discours américains*, ed. by Michèle Guicharnaud-Tollis (Bordeaux: Presses Universitaires de Bordeaux, 2015). She was guest editor for two special issues of the journal *Cycnos: Les Guerres culturelles aux Etats-Unis*, 32-2, 2016, and *Frederick Law Olmsted (1822-1903) et le* park movement *américain et les années Roosevelt (1932-1945)*, 30-2, 2014.

Michael J. Mullin is Professor of History and National Endowment for the Humanities Chair of Regional Heritage at Augustana University. His work covers a variety of topics ranging from articles on American Indian history to a monograph on the South Dakota Academy of Science. More recently he has been researching South Dakota's first Senator, Richard F. Pettigrew, and his role in the anti-imperialism movement in the late 19th and early 20th century. His interest in regional boundaries and identity emerged in graduate school, where the split between Northern and Southern California produced endless debate and speculation.

Paula M. Nelson is Professor of History Emeritus at the University of Wisconsin-Platteville, where she taught for twenty-six years. She is the author of *After the West was Won: Homesteaders and Townbuilders in Western South Dakota, 1900-1917* (1986), and *The Prairie Winnows Out Its Own: The West River Country of South Dakota in the Years of Depression* and *Dust* (1996). She is the editor of *Sunshine Always: The Courtship Letters of Alice Bower and Joseph Gossage of Dakota Territory* (2006). Her research interests include the Great Plains and Upper Midwest, rural life and culture, and rural women's history.

Lance Nixon is a freelance writer in Pierre, South Dakota, where he previously edited the *Capital Journal* daily newspaper. He is also a past editor of *Montana Magazine*. He holds a master's degree in English from the University of North Dakota in Grand Forks and a master's in journalism from South Dakota State University.

David Pichaske is a Professor of English at Southwest Minnesota State University and editor-publisher of Spoon River Poetry Press. Over his fifty-year career, he has enjoyed four years of Senior Fulbright Lectureships in Poland, Latvia, and Outer Mongolia. He has published articles in places ranging from *Chaucer Review* and *Journal of Modern Literature* to the *Atlantic* monthly and the *New York Times,* and authored or edited two dozen published books including *Beowulf to Beatles: Approaches to Poetry, Chaucer's Literary Pilgrimage: Movement in the Canterbury Tales, A Generation in Motion, Writing Sense, The Jubilee Diary, Late Harvest: Rural American Writing, The Father Poems, Poland in Transition, Southwest Minnesota: The Land and the People, Rooted: Seven Midwest Writers of Place, Song of the North Country: A Midwest Framework to the Songs of Bob Dylan, The Pigeons of Buchenau* (short stories), *Crying in the Wilderness* (essays), and *Here I Stand* (a memoir).

Jay M. Price is chair of the Department of History at Wichita State University, where he also directs the Local and Community History Program and the Great Plains Studies Certificate Program. He has authored and co-authored histories of Wichita area topics with a particular interest in the intersections among place, religion, region, culture, and ethnicity. He has recently served on the boards of the Kansas Association of Historians, the Kansas Humanities Council, the Wichita Sedgwick County Historical Museum, and the University Press of Kansas.

Joseph D. Schiller is a doctoral student in the history department at the University of Oklahoma. He has published an article in the *Southwestern Historical Quarterly*, "Don't Sell Texas Short!": Amon Carter's Cultivation and Marketing of West Texas Nature." His dissertation is an environmental history of the Tri-State lead and zinc mining district at the junction of Kansas, Missouri, and Oklahoma.

Brad Tennant is Professor of History at Presentation College in Aberdeen, South Dakota. In addition to his teaching assignments, Tennant is an active researcher, writer, and presenter on a variety of state and regional topics. As a gubernatorial appointee, Dr. Tennant is serving his fourth term on the Board of Trustees of the South Dakota State Historical Society. He is also a member of several other national, state, and local historical organizations.

Harry F. Thompson is Executive Director of the Center for Western Studies at Augustana University and author of several revisionist articles about the intersection of history and literature, including a recent article on Willa Cather in *Interdisciplinary Literary Studies*. He is the editor of *A New South Dakota History*, the first comprehensive history of the state in forty years, and the author of *Voices of the Northern Plains Exhibition Catalogue*. He has published over sixty books for the Center for Western Studies.

Will Weaver grew up on a farm in northern Minnesota. A Stanford graduate, his writing has earned praise from reviewers coast to coast. *The New York Times* called *A Gravestone Made of Wheat* "... a graceful story collection, one that views America's heartland with a candid but charitable eye." Adaptations of his fiction include the award-winning feature film and musical *Sweet Land*. A recent judge for the National Book Awards, he lives on the Mississippi River east of Bemidji, Minnesota.

Gleaves Whitney has been Director of Grand Valley State University's Hauenstein Center for Presidential Studies since July 2003. He has authored or edited fifteen books. Whitney is also a senior scholar at the Center for the American Idea in Houston, Texas, the first senior fellow at the Russell Kirk Center for Cultural Renewal, a member of the college of fellows at the Dominican School of Philosophy and Theology, Berkeley, a member of the Ronald Reagan Presidential Library's Leadership Development Committee, and a scholar with the Wyoming Catholic College committee of advisors.

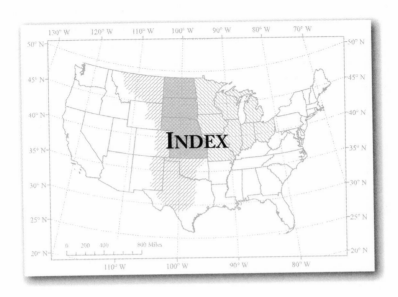

INDEX

320